GEORGE PIERCE BAKER
AND THE AMERICAN THEATRE

The Marshall Studio

Professor George Pierce Baker
February 23, 1920

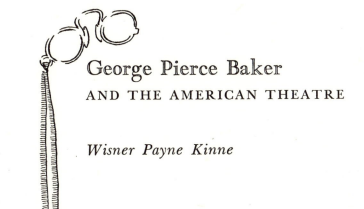

George Pierce Baker

AND THE AMERICAN THEATRE

Wisner Payne Kinne

GREENWOOD PRESS, PUBLISHERS
NEW YORK   1968

TO

HOWARD MUMFORD JONES

Contents

CONTENTS

INTRODUCTION

GEORGE PIERCE BAKER DIED NINETEEN YEARS AGO. HE was born — and this I cannot believe, because he remains so young in my memory — only ten years after Shaw. To be relentless about it, he was born in 1866, the year after Lincoln's assassination. He would have been eighty-eight, a ripe Shavian age, if he were living as I write this introduction. But there was never even a threat of the white-bearded Methuselah about him. In spite of his graying hair, he remained a contemporary in spirit, right down to 1933 when illness forced him to resign as head of Yale's Department of Drama.

Professor Baker was one of those rare individuals who must surprise themselves, as they astonish others, by refusing to stand still. He looked forward with the same ease that most people slip backward. Mr. Kinne tells us, again to my amazement, that as a high school student in Providence Mr. Baker pasted in his scrapbook the obituaries of Longfellow and Emerson, and that at Harvard he heard Matthew Arnold lecture. Notwithstanding the fact that he reached so far back to the giants of another age, was brought up on the theatre of Edwin Booth and Boucicault, and grew to champion for a while the "well-made play" as written by his friends Pinero and Henry Arthur Jones, there was something eternally young, inquiring, and enthusiastic in him which was always rushing ahead of his own generation to make him a part of the generation that he happened to be teaching.

I was a freshman at Harvard when I first heard him lecture in 1919, and it appalls me to realize that he was then about the age that I am now. Regardless of the gulf of years that separated us he never seemed old to me, nor does he to this day. He was the first person to make me realize that a calendar cannot keep those who share interests from being contemporaries. The youth of his mind and spirit must be counted among the reasons for his profound and lasting influence on our professional and amateur theatre, and hence for the writing of this book.

We are always being told, especially by those whose gifts prove the point, that there is no such thing as an indispensable man. Certainly, the relay race in all human efforts continues in spite of the runners who drop out. That this race does — and must — go on is no guarantee that without them it goes on in the same way, that its speed may not be altered, and its course changed. Even so, there are men and women whose places, though taken, cannot be filled. Indispensable in the final sense they may not be, but irreplaceable they are. In the field he made very much his own, Professor Baker was one of these.

All men are many men; Baker was many gifted men. His talents were various and contradictory. It was the incredible combination of them in one person which set him apart, made him the vital force he was, and put him in the ranks of the irreplaceable. Good directors are fairly plentiful. So are admirable scholars, diverting and instructive lecturers, excellent teachers, discerning critics, and able administrators. Professor Baker was all of these. Moreover, his was the sort of polarizing personality which inspired in people of all kinds and ages a loyalty amounting to discipleship.

Although undergraduates in his courses in the history of the drama may have thought him standoffish, those who worked closely with him in his playwriting classes or in the 47 Workshop knew better. They responded to the inner warmth of this New Englander who could be outwardly chilly. They recognized his rare gift for friendship and valued his praise the more for the Yankee thrift he showed in giving it. They were also gratefully aware that, grave as he could be and dignified as he always was, neither fatigue nor worry nor professordom could extinguish his fundamental gaiety. His blue-gray eyes were always eager to light up with laughter behind his pince-nez, and when he was amused his somewhat portly body shook with merriment.

All of us who studied with Professor Baker at Harvard or at Yale must have memories of him which are technicolor bright. I know I have. I can see and hear him in and out of class, at rehearsals, at dinner, in a conference, or making a before-the-curtain speech at Radcliffe's Agassiz Theatre, and so vividly alive is he for me that I could swear the past is the present. Although I thought I knew him well, I have learned many new and interesting things about him from Mr. Kinne's book. So, I wager, will many others who also thought they knew him well.

Shaw once expressed his debt to Archibald Henderson's "authorized biography" of him by saying that until this volume appeared he had been "the victim of a half a dozen reputations which seemed to be hopelessly insulated from one another." He thanked Henderson for having "collected" him and pulled the many Shaws together. This is what Mr. Kinne has done for the various Bakers and the task, even if simpler by far than synthesizing the many Shaws, cannot have been easy.

Every Bakerite, of course, has his own details he could add; is certain to note some names that are omitted, and to be bubbling over with favorite anecdotes which he would have included. This is inevitable in a book about a man who had so many interests, taught so many students for so many years (thirty-seven at Harvard and eight at Yale), and touched, enriched, and often changed so many lives. Nonetheless, the story is here, told at last with the thoroughness it deserves. It benefits from fresh material ferreted out with energy and affection. It is set against the changing backgrounds of the changing years, and presented so that, while all the various Bakers emerge, Professor Baker himself has been for the first time consolidated in print.

The final tribute to Mr. Baker is that, though he has gone and his like has not been found, what he dreamed of and worked for is still very much alive in community after community and at college after college. Encouragingly but ironically, in no place is it more alive than at the very Harvard which for years was officially indifferent to him.

It was always easier to admire Professor Baker than to explain the spell he cast or the contribution he made. He happened to have that talent for communication and that genius for igniting others essential to all great teachers. The paradox of his career is that he is best known as a teacher of playwriting, yet he never pretended to teach playwriting at all. His hope was to shorten the apprenticeship of those who met with him by instructing them in what, over the years, had been the common-sense essentials of dramatic technique and to show them how that technique had changed from period to period and from dramatist to dramatist.

Most of the plays his students wrote for him were bad; very bad, I am afraid. If not fantasies of a somewhat emetic sort, they either exuded that gloom in which the young rejoice or were so tough that, as Heywood Broun said, "Nowhere in the world is a woman quite so unsafe as in an English 47 play." As a rule, the good plays that Baker's more famous pupils wrote were written long after they had ceased to work with him. They were helped in writing these good plays because of the patience he showed in dealing with the bad ones they had written for him. As Sidney Howard put it, they wrote them "because he taught his students truths more valid than technique. He taught them that plays are important and hard to write; that few subjects are worthy of dramatization; that characters must be imagined beneath their words; that art is an obligation, not a Sunday suit."

Perhaps the best explanation of Professor Baker's unique service to his embryonic playwrights was given by Eugene O'Neill in the letter Mr. Kinne quotes which appeared in the *New York Times* soon after Mr. Baker's death. O'Neill did not deny that the technical points Professor Baker taught in his classes were "of inestimable value." But he added, "The most vital thing for us, as possible future artists and creators, to learn at that time (Good God! For any one to learn anywhere at any time!) was to believe in our work and to keep on believing. And to hope. He helped us to hope — and for that we owe him all the finest we have in memory of gratitude and friendship."

JOHN MASON BROWN

New York, N.Y.
July 23, 1954

xiv

GEORGE PIERCE BAKER
AND THE AMERICAN THEATRE

PROLOGUE

IN 1935, OBITUARIES FOR PROFESSOR GEORGE PIERCE Baker, affectionately known as "G.P.B.," called him the father of modern American playwrights. Since then, the caricature of him as Professor Hatcher (i.e., hatcher of playwrights) in Thomas Wolfe's *Of Time and the River* has tinged a legend with myth. By the time of the first World War, he was already a conjuror of fame to such young fellows as Edward Sheldon and Eugene O'Neill who came to write plays in his English 47 classes at Harvard.

The present university trained leadership in the American theatre owes no small part of its character to such experimenters in G.P.B.'s Harvard drama laboratory, The 47 Workshop, as playwrights Philip Barry and Sidney Howard, scenic technicians Donald Oenslager and Stanley McCandless, and dramatic critics Kenneth Macgowan and John Mason Brown. Certainly those elements of the American theatre outside our metropolitan centers are equally indebted for many of their standards to the work after 1925 of G.P.B.'s Department of Drama at Yale.

Thus Professor Baker becomes an increasingly interesting personality as the careers of his many students suggest an extraordinary influence. The question of his effect upon the work of Eugene O'Neill or Philip Barry is, unlike similar questions about Shakespeare's teachers, susceptible to something more than speculation. However, the purpose of this account of his history as an amateur of the theatre, scholar, and teacher is not to establish his specific influence upon particular individuals.

The value of his story is not what can be told of his impact upon this or that. Like countless amateurs among his contemporaries, he dreamed of a native art which should put America abreast of Europe, with, as he phrased it, "a drama of American conditions which shall have permanent value." Thus his life illuminates more than the work of his famous students; for almost fifty years, G.P.B. epitomized the lay forces at work in the evolution of twentieth-century American drama.

I   ANTECEDENTS — TOY THEATRE — THE SPIRIT OF 1876

THE STORY OF GEORGE PIERCE BAKER MAY WELL HAVE begun shortly before the Civil War, in a millinery shop next to a theatre in Providence, Rhode Island. Here pretty Lucy Cady made hats and admired the great players who passed her door—Edwin Booth, Laura Keene, William Warren, and Charlotte Cushman. Her own soprano solos in the Grace Church choir were perhaps equally admired by a promising young physician whose services were frequently sought by the theatre people. This was Dr. George Pierce Baker, a literary sort of fellow who had been a devoted student under Dr. Oliver Wendell Holmes. Certainly the Bakers were able to bring their only child, a son born April 4, 1866, a more than ordinary acquaintance with the theatre.

Whatever G.P.B.'s inheritance, the boy received from his parents the two influences which shaped his character. From Dr. Baker came the desire to emulate the writings of Longfellow, Whittier, and Emerson; with Lucy must be linked her son's share in a national mania for theatrical entertainment which left most of the adolescents of the 1880's stage-struck. However, G.P.B. knew little of his family antecedents, as he confessed years later to an English genealogist:

I am, of course, much interested by your report that a Baker family may be connected with the Elizabethan theatre, and particularly Shakespeare. Unfortunately, however, I am not an enthusiast on genealogy, and don't even know whether my branch of the huge Baker family in this country has any armorial bearings. As far as I know, my father's family came to this country from Yorkshire of

2

plain farmer stock, not long after the settlements at Plymouth and Boston . . . You will see, I think, from what I have said, that I possess no family portraits. So far as my father is concerned, I am the second generation from farmer stock.

Though father and son maintained a gardener's interest in the soil, both were afflicted by a youthful delicacy in health which determined their temperaments. A nervous dyspepsia affected both father and son and may have been the impetus to the literary ambition which both pursued, the one privately and the other publicly. Since Harvard Medical School days, Dr. Baker had idolized the witty Dr. Oliver Wendell Holmes and had taken the amiable autocrat as his model. An early page of Dr. Baker's medico-literary journal is headed by a pair of verses which catch the romantic spirit of father and son:

> Night threw her sable mantle o'er the earth
> And pinned it with a star.

During a year of illness which postponed the lad's first year of school, the Bakers gave their son a toy theatre. Some years before, there had been a vogue for them in England which has been perpetuated in Robert Louis Stevenson's recollections of his own "Penny" theatre of the 1860's. Stevenson's paper cutout characters which moved in tin grooves behind a brightly colored cardboard proscenium to imitate the theatre of Edmund Kean, Charles Kemble, and William Macready, was essentially the same as George's toy from the Providence newsdealer's shop.

With his toy, George probably did many of the plays dear to Stevenson — *Aladdin, The Red Rover, Robin Hood.* One of his playmates recalls:

I remember George's theatre very well. There was a large closet with a door which opened into the upstairs bedroom where the audience was seated. George kept his theatre things in the closet and had the toy theatre arranged on a stand in front of the closet doorway. He stood inside the closet, behind his stage, very much like a Punch and Judy operator. He spoke the lines and did everything, and we would have watched him forever.

In time, the toy theatre was succeeded by a real stage, built in an upstairs room of the handsome white mid-Victorian house. Here George began to act in costumes which his mother cleverly

3

supplied. One of the girls who was frequently in the Baker home for impromptu theatricals in the 1870's recollects:

I can see him now at about the age of ten — his features rather delicate and a certain distinctive quality about his bearing even as a child. There was something grand about George, something superior in his very precise enunciation.

He was a very neat boy — always snappy and really quite a beau. I always remember a bevy of girls at the many parties Mrs. Baker gave for her son. He was never robust, and things were arranged in the home so that he could be and was an indoor boy.

Thus the toy theatre and its juvenile drama grew to be a symbol of the boy's happiness. Even in his college days, there are inquiries for it in his letters to his father. In the last years of his life, when he was building the Yale Drama School to be a national academy of the drama, he contemplated a course in puppetry and asked one of his old Harvard students to teach it. Even after his own four sons had outgrown his old childhood toy, G.P.B. kept it in the attic at Boulder Farm, his New Hampshire summer home.

Whatever the nature of George's illness, some kind of crisis passed with the boy's tenth birthday, in 1876. All Providence was particularly aware of this centennial year; for the Corliss Machine Works was building the giant steam engine which was to power the Centennial Exhibition in Philadelphia, and Providence silversmiths were molding the "Century Vase," which celebrated Columbia's attainment of her majority. Late in August, the boy was well enough to embark with his parents on a side-wheel steamer for New York, whence they went by train to the great world fair.

Dr. Baker's diary shows that he was particularly interested that his son should see the realistic sea views and landscapes sent by Queen Victoria to the exhibition. But it was probably the pageantry of the grand show itself which most affected the boy: the flags of all nations; the panorama of peoples and cultures; the array of plants, animals, and machines; the exotic costumes of Spaniard, Russian, and Japanese. Standing with his father before the Corliss Engine, goddess of the new age of steam power, G.P.B. first saw the dramatic genius of American technology which, a half century later, he took for the theme of his own pageant, *Control*.

4

PROVIDENCE AND THE
AMERICAN THEATRE

ASTRIDE THE RAIL AND SHIP ROUTES BETWEEN NEW
York and Boston, Providence was usually an overnight stop for
actors and entertainers who moved between these centers of
American theatre business. Thus the Bakers and their fellow
townspeople saw a surprising quantity and variety of stage matters for a city of fewer than one hundred thousand. In the year
G.P.B. was born, it had the reputation of being one of the best
show towns in America. Two years later, Charles Blake's account
of the Providence stage became the first published history of an
American city stage outside of Boston and New York.

Perhaps the most important aspect of this theatrical environment in Providence was its intimate relation with even the
younger members of the community. A companion of Georgie
Baker during these years recalls:

In the summer months George and the rest of us went regularly
to the Saturday matinees at the Sans Souci Garden, not far from the
neighborhood. There was a repertory company there which did
everything. I remember "Pinafore," and later the "Mikado" and
others of the very popular Gilbert and Sullivan operas. During the
regular season we went to the Providence Opera House.

Thus it is clear that the Providence theatres, of which there
were usually three or four in operation, were an active part of
G.P.B.'s youthful environment. It was, however, the Providence
Opera House which probably gave the boy his idea of the very
nature of the theatre. His earliest memory of any stage, as he
once recalled in a reminiscing after-dinner speech, referred to this
fine old community institution: "I knew the theatre first, I think,
at the age of six. Then in early but intense recognition of the
genius of Charlotte Cushman in Meg Merrilies, I was, for the
good of the public, removed shrieking from the theatre."

It could have been but a few months after this famous theatre

5

opened its doors that the boy first walked through them to what always remained, in spite of his initial fright, the enchanted land within. And it is hardly to be believed that Dr. and Mrs. Baker were not present at the gala affair which opened the long career of the Providence Opera House.

For this theatre was, during the seventies and eighties, as nearly a civic theatre as economic and cultural conditions in America then permitted. Although primarily for professional entertainments, the Opera House was the scene of many amateur productions. Indeed, the intent of the citizens who subscribed funds for the building of this theatre was community benefit rather than private profit. Two of Georgie's schoolmates, Henry Ames Barker and Daniel Webster, Jr., made amateur careers in this local tradition which are of major importance in the history of American amateur dramatics.

On this opening night at the Opera House, which presented a revival of one of the few notable plays by American authors, Anna Cora Mowatt's *Fashion,* a prologue was spoken by the stage manager. Of the actors mentioned in this prologue's brief history of the Providence stage, the elder Booth had been dead fewer than twenty years. Charles Kean, James Hackett, and the elder John Drew were but recently dead. Edwin Forrest and Charlotte Cushman were active survivors of the relatively short American theatrical tradition. Edwin Booth was the great theatrical name of that evening and of G.P.B.'s youth.

The climate which developed G.P.B.'s dramatic ideas is reflected in these lines toward the close of the prologue:

> A truce to memories! We have come tonight
> With bursts of music and a flood of light,
> To dedicate to th' Histrionic Muse
> This splendid temple. Not alone we choose
> To garland her white limbs and crown her head
> With flowers plucked from the past, but we instead
> Would nightly on this mimic stage rehearse
> Great thoughts embalmed in purest prose and verse,
> And elevate the drama from a trade
> To what it was when Shakespeare wrote and played . . .

6

Impressed with the equipment of the new theatre, with the efficiency of the gas lighting for the stage, and imbued with a hope that American technology might unite with a native art, the author closed with an ideal which G.P.B. himself pursued:

> Then Science, Art, the Drama, linked will stand,
> The Sister Graces of the Western Land.

In spite of this wish and the dedication of the Opera House with an American play, the theatrical fare upon which the boy matured was foreign rather than native. The plays he saw were largely of three types: English comedy, such as *She Stoops to Conquer* and *Ours;* adaptations of French melodrama and comedy, such as *The Sea of Ice, The Romance of a Poor Young Man,* and *Camille;* and a few American plays about provincial characters in rural or frontier incidents. The usual routine at the Opera House was a brief farce curtain-raiser, such as *Box and Cox,* followed by the main attraction, and concluded with some entertaining afterpiece. The outstanding fact is that one went to the theatre to be amused. It was thus quite natural for G.P.B. to present on the title page of his own *Dramatic Technique* these words of Colley Cibber: "A good play is certainly the most rational and the highest Entertainment that Human Invention can produce."

III STANDARDS IN READING, ELOCUTION, AND JOURNALISM

MOWRY AND GOFF'S, THE TOWN'S LEADING PRIVATE school, was distinguished by the emphasis which its headmaster placed upon the reading of English and American literature. Here Georgie's first teacher was Mrs. Harriette M. Miller, a dynamic woman whose special subject was elocution. With her he began to acquire his mastery as a reader, concerning which Harley Granville-Barker once said, "I never heard anyone read Shakespeare so well as George Pierce Baker."

Mrs. Miller's objective was a "new style" which she described as the "suiting of *sound* to *sense,* as much as possible to insure

7

naturalness." Since the Civil War, Edwin Booth had progressed from the ranting style of his father's generation of actors to a more natural delivery. Thus the boy's training in elocution reflected the general turning away among orators and actors from mechanical theories of expression to new concepts of naturalness.

However, lest the degree of this naturalness be confused with the realism which came considerably later to the dramatic arts, it may be well to repeat a fragment of a representative playlet for children from the textbook with which she instructed George. "Honest Jacob" perhaps best represents the rhetorical and moral concepts on which the boy matured.

XLII. — Honest Jacob

Jacob, a poor laboring man. *Fritz,* his son (a small boy). *Adam,* a baker.

Scene. — The poor man's cottage. Enter *Fritz.*

Fritz. How I wish father would come home! I am so hungry! O, here he comes!

(Jacob enters, bringing a loaf of bread.)

Jacob. Here I am, little Fritz!
Fritz. I am so glad! It is so lonesome here since dear mother died! And I —
Jacob. You are very hungry? I know it, my poor boy. It wasn't so when there was plenty of work to be had. I hope these hard times will soon be over; but we must do the best we can while they last.
Fritz. O what a nice loaf you have! How good it smells!
Jacob. (*aside*). It is the last! There's no knowing when we shall have another. Here, my son (*breaks the loaf*); eat your supper at once. There's no loss without some gain; we don't have to wait for cooking when we've nothing to cook!
Fritz. O father! this isn't fair.
Jacob. What isn't fair, my son?
Fritz. You have given me the biggest piece.
Jacob. And is that anything to complain of?
Come, eat, my boy.
Fritz. But you — you have been looking for work all day; you must be so tired! and I know you have had nothing to eat.
Jacob. Ah, my Fritz! You are so good to think of me! But, really, it will do me more good to see you eat than to eat myself.

8

Fritz. But if *you* do not eat, how can you go out hunting work tomorrow? and if you find work to do, how can you do it? You must have a part of this; do break it again, father.

In its soliloquy and aside, this bit of what the boy read and acted conveys the dramatic tradition from Sheridan through Boucicault in which he grew up.

At the new Providence High School he commenced his preparation for college. He did fairly well in his first year, although some infelicity in English composition put him below the top rank which he had always held before. However, his proficiency in declamation soon acquainted him with Harry Cook, an extraordinary young man who was belatedly completing a public high school education in order to enter the ministry. Through Cook, George became a member of the Debating Society and the Duodecim Club, a literary dozen interested in art. In their last year, shortly before Harry's death, the two friends founded the Providence High School Athletic Association and the *Register,* for many years the school's weekly paper.

Harry's death may have caused George to write down the words of a visiting preacher at the Westminster Congregational Church:

He said that "Faith is the first cause of religious belief and of all religious communion." He believes in no creeds, says that we can not even formulate for ourselves a creed which written out we will keep. But that we all have faith in three things, namely — An infinite, eternal universal power, from which the spirit which was before and is after our own mortal portion comes. 2nd That there are certain things which we should do and others we should not, thus constituting Duty. 3rd Immortality. That there is an hereafter of some kind and these 3 things all believe who are called Christians.

Just a few weeks before jotting this in his scrapbook, George clipped newspaper accounts of the death of Longfellow. A few days after the sermon, he clipped the death notices for Emerson. As these flowers of New England died, he might well have considered the problem of what he believed.

George's last year of high school was thus a period of incubation for the settled principles and ambitions which took him,

9

alone among his classmates, to Harvard in 1883. As one of his own *Register* editorials of this year shows, his standards were simple: "There is a great mistake made by many in reading so much trashy fiction and so very little good, solid truth. One of the most important parts of a good education is one's reading; that is, if it be of the right kind, otherwise it is a hindrance rather than a help."

These days, his most devoted audience was his mother. Now confined to her bed, she listened to his newspaper articles, the light verse which made him much in demand at social gatherings, and the speeches which he prepared for the graduation of his class. He was just seventeen when she died.

IV   DRAMA AND REALITY

AS THE BOY GREW, IMPORTANT CHANGES CAME TO THE Providence theatres. In 1876, while he was learning elocution with Mrs. Miller, the resident stock company at the Providence Opera House disbanded and was replaced by the repertory companies from Daly's Theatre in New York and the Boston Museum; by "star shows" which toured with Maggie Mitchell, Mary Anderson, Annie Pixley, E. A. Sothern, Joseph Jefferson, and other famous personalities who had hitherto found their supporting casts in the Opera House company; and by musical and scenic extravaganzas which, with the variety or "vaudeville" entertainments, began to displace the legitimate drama. This was in addition to the visits of such highly publicized actors as Edwin Booth, Tomaso Salvini, or Sarah Bernhardt who had hitherto afforded the high points of each Opera House season. Thus the boy was able to see more great actors and to taste a wider variety of dramatic fare than would have been possible in any preceding decade.

At the same time, America was developing something of a mania for the stage. Between 1860 and 1880, along with the rise of the modern city, theatre entertainment had developed into a necessity of American city life. During these decades the number of actors in this country more than tripled while the aggregate population, reaching fifty millions, fell short of doubling itself. Accompanying this was a mushrooming of magazine and newspaper journalism which found the popular interest in the theatre a readily exploitable topic.

George's scrapbook is a testimony of the breadth of this attention to the theatre. Typical entries are the lad's clippings from Boston and Providence newspapers of reviews of the operatic work of Christine Nilsson and the acting of Edwin Booth, a magazine account of the Wagner festival at Bayreuth which includes detailed descriptions of Wagner's scenic effects, and the text of a farce, "The Pullman Car," by the editor of the *Atlantic Monthly*. Almost a full page of newsprint is devoted to the ceremonies at the Boston Museum in celebration of William Warren's golden anniversary as an actor.

During the seventies, Brander Matthews made *Appleton's Journal* and *Scribner's Monthly* outstanding for his distinguished articles on actors and acting. At the close of this decade, newspaper dramatic criticism was a recognized literary vocation practiced by such New Yorkers as William Winter and Andrew C. Wheeler, such Bostonians as Henry A. Clapp and William F. Apthorp. "Nym Crinkle" was read as avidly as any Broadway critic today.

Leading American men of letters were also interested. William Dean Howells had written "Private Theatricals" and a series of one-act plays for the *Atlantic Monthly*. Henry James was busy writing the plays which he later collected in two volumes. And Mark Twain's dramatization of *The Gilded Age* had linked his name with a popular stage success.

Yet this growth was more than an expansion of the means of amusement. There was beginning to be a response in the American theatre to the serious claims of the culture which fostered it. On the day following G.P.B.'s birth there appeared in the *Nation* an article which noted: "If anything distinguishes the epoch we live in, it is a decided tendency towards realism, or, as some call it, naturalism — a disposition to be severely true to nature. The character is stamped on all the genuine products of the time."

The writer's point, however, was that in 1866 the American theatre was not yet a genuine product of American life. It was

11

quite clearly beginning to be so by 1881, when the *Critic*, a magazine of literary and dramatic criticism from "new" points of view, was launched.

Certainly the boy was not isolated from this cultural drift. At the age of fourteen he had become a shareholder in the Providence Athenaeum, a private library replete not only with good contemporary books but elegantly furnished with paintings and statuary. His scrapbook contains items from the *Atlantic, Harper's,* the *Century,* and *Appleton's Journal. St. Nicholas,* a magazine which frequently curried the juvenile craze for home theatricals, accumulated as a bound series in the Baker library. In addition to the *Providence Journal,* his family took the *Boston Morning Journal,* a paper which carried a daily column, "Dramatic and Musical," on its front page, and a "Daily Guide to the Theatre" on its editorial page.

On October 18, 1881, George clipped from the *Providence Journal* a review of Ernesto Rossi in *Othello.* This performance in Providence came two weeks after Rossi's American debut in Boston. The boy had already clipped a Boston review of the same role and also a publicity story about the famous Italian's interpretations of Shakespeare. What, then, was the significance of these clippings about Rossi? Although George made no annotations for these scrapbook entries, he was reacting to the critical controversy raised by Rossi's style of acting. This was the question of realism in the theatre, the central issue in American drama for the next twenty-five years.

This conflict of opinion arose from the ancient antithesis of "nature" and "art." It was a question that had been argued in America between the followers of Forrest and Macready in the 1840's and 1850's, of Forrest and Booth in the 1860's and 1870's. Now, in George's experience, the partisans of the argument arrayed themselves about Ernesto Rossi and Tomaso Salvini, whose earlier success on the American stage had obviously attracted his countryman.

Since Salvini's American debut in 1873, the admirers of Edwin Forrest's romantic style had found a model in the elemental force of Salvini's "large, passionate, and fiery" Moor. In 1877, Forrest's biographer identified Salvini's style with that of Forrest. Thus, when Rossi presented a low-keyed, understated, natural conception of Othello, which was fundamentally different from the orthodoxy of Salvini's fiery grandiloquence, there were bound to be arguments.

The Boston reviewers generally favored the realism of Rossi, but recognized the popular resistance to the "new" style, as did the *Globe* critic:

In our judgment Rossi, better than any actor who has come upon the stage, has caught the spirit of the great character . . . He has made it a living reality behind the footlights . . . But the very finish of the portraiture — the sedulous care taken to avoid the slightest incongruity in aught, however great the temptation to produce an effect, may militate somewhat against the immediate popularity of such a personation.

As the critic for the *Providence Journal* saw it, "the whole effect was of a prosaic finish and the actual lowering of the dignified Othello to a good-humored soldier." Paraphrasing G. H. Lewes, whose recent *On Actors and the Art of Acting* could be had at the Providence Athenaeum, this conservative Providence reviewer delivered his final criterion: "An actor is to be estimated by his highest reach of power and not by the general quality of his versatility."

It is apparent from the following in the *New York Herald* that Rossi was often close to the effects of cinematic naturalism:

His desire to produce absolute realism, allowed Signor Rossi to enact Desdemona's murder in full view of the audience, in an almost brutish fashion, by strangling her with his hands after twisting her long hair about her neck, as he shook her violently and then dragged her about the bed and finally tossed her upon the pillows.

Such devotion to "nature" was too much for the New York audience, which preferred the "art" of Salvini's idealized rendition of this scene, and "murmurs of dissatisfaction" were orthodox comment.

Here was a foretaste of the realism which a decade later shocked American audiences when the heroine of James A. Herne's *Margaret Fleming* prepared to suckle her child. At that time, G.P.B. supported his friend's dramatic purpose for such an imitation of "nature" and admired the similar realism of Ibsen.

13

However, in 1881, the boy was familiar with the "ideal" acting which was the style of William Warren, of Edwin Booth — indeed of the whole English tradition which dominated American taste in the theatre. In his maturity, G.P.B.'s youthful enthusiasm for realism gave way to caution. Always an admirer of the intellectual styles of Booth and Bernhardt, which he imitated in his own acting, he later saw their standards of grace and diction menaced by the indiscriminate realism of the twentieth century.

If one looks back to G.P.B.'s high school days, and to his interest in Ernesto Rossi, it is apparent that two important lines of his later thinking had already begun. First was the question of the relation of Shakespeare to reality, and second was the relation of the contemporary theatre to reality. The first led him through his initial scholarship in the history of English drama. The second brought him to the central problem of an American drama for an American theatre. In the pursuit of both he affected much more than his own life and career.

v HARVARD FRESHMAN AND THE BOSTON STAGE

HARVARD LIFE WAS WRETCHEDLY LONELY, FOR THE lad was wholly without friends in Cambridge. By some error he was assigned to a single room in a small house near Memorial Hall; here he passed his first year, pitifully longing for a "chum." Toward the end of his first week he wrote in his diary: "I think my pride keeps me from making too many advances."

Now began an extraordinary correspondence with his father. Only an hour's train journey apart, father and son frequently exchanged two letters a day as they learned to accept life without Lucy Baker. In a characteristic brave show of humor, George reported the results of his examination by the college physician.

Cambridge
Oct. 3, '83

Dear Father,

I received today my book showing my physical condition. It is rather a remarkable document. I am, I find, below the general average in 18 things and above it in 7. Now some of the statements surprise me so much that I do not feel inclined to put implicit faith in them. For instance, I am, — so it states — above the average in the measurements of my wrists. Now if there was any part that I felt certain I was poor in, this was the one. However, what can have made them larger? If it was the rowing and riding, why these would still more act on the forearm which so says the pamphlet — are below. Another thing surprises me and I think will you. I am below the average in the girth of my head. I ask to be given the benefit of the doubt in this case. As I expected, I am more than usually developed about the knee and calf. I am above in the strength of my forearms, and yet they are below in the average girth. I think you will see that the matter seems a little mixed.

Yrs. affec.
George

His schedule of courses for the first term was: Greek, Latin, Classical Lectures, German, Mathematics, Physics, and Chemistry — a tacit compromise between the son's literary bent and the father's hope that the lad would turn toward the profession of medicine. Outside the curriculum, George chose a voluntary course in elocution and attended a series of evening readings in which he heard the *Frogs* of Aristophanes. This was the extent of his academic acquaintance with the drama during his freshman year.

However, he went in to Boston at least once a week for some kind of theatre entertainment. Part of his motivation is apparent in such diary notes as:

Oct. 26. Friday. In the early part of the evening felt so restless that after some debate I went to Boston and saw Gilbert's "Engaged" at the Museum. It was very silly but it made me laugh heartily, a thing which I have not done for some time.

But his real response to the theatre is indicated in his enthusiastic communication on the sixteenth of November to his father after seeing Edwin Booth in *The Fool's Revenge:*

At last I have seen acting which comes up to what I think it should be. If Booth comes to Providence and plays this part, by all means see him. I know that you prefer to go and have a good laugh but in this case, though the play is trying, yet Booth's magnificent acting pays one.

A few evenings later, he wrote in his diary:

Nov. 21. Wednesday. . . . During the afternoon I decided to see Booth as "King Lear," in the evening. I had to stand through the whole performance and my back feels as if it were broken. "Lear" surpasses as a whole, I think, Booth's Bertuccio, the fool. His rendering of the curse of Regan was magnificent. Again in the tempest scene as he lies down on the couch it is very touching. But in the mad scene, I think he is most wonderful. He manages the bunch of straws which he holds in his hand in such a way that they almost tell the story. Now they are his kingdom which he has divided between his daughters, now his bow as he draws the arrow to its head etc. His rendering of "A king, aye every inch the king" was electric, raising himself from his sad troubled posture and tone of voice, to his full commanding height while the old ringing tone almost returns. The fourth act, in which he recognizes Cordelia, was even finer than anything in "The Fool's Revenge." The tone, manner, expression, as recovering his reason he utters the words "As I am a man I do think you are my daughter" are well-nigh indescribable but never to be forgotten. The very last of this scene when he repeats "We must forget and forgive, forget and forgive" were so touching that it seemed sacrilege to break the silence with applause. The final heartbreak and death were fully up to the standard of the preceding act and filled out the rendition of "Lear" which I shall always remember and judge all others by. Throughout the tone was not as I am told Salvini's is, an awe-inspiring fearful one, but sad, oh so sad.

It is clear that George was more interested in acting than in what was acted, in the whole emotional appeal of the theatre than in the literary appeal of any particular drama. Indeed, he did not think of drama as literature; nor did his literary ambition include the writing of plays. For he had, without success, already submitted a number of poems to the *Lampoon*. As he explored and experimented with his writing, the theatre was the one bright area of his experience. Yet it seems not to have entered his prayer as he wrote in his diary on the eighth of November: "Oh if I could only write something worth while! Will it ever, ever, be or am I only a conceited boy."

Nevertheless, the criteria of effective acting and reading unconsciously colored his judgment of Matthew Arnold when the Englishman read at Harvard's Sanders Theatre that November of 1883:

16

"G.P.B.," Berlin, 1891. Sketch by Leo von Koenig

HTC

As "Sally," who greatly amused
William Dean Howells, 1885

HTC

As "Hercules III," in *A Slap in the Dark*,
Cambridge Social Dramatic Club, 1894

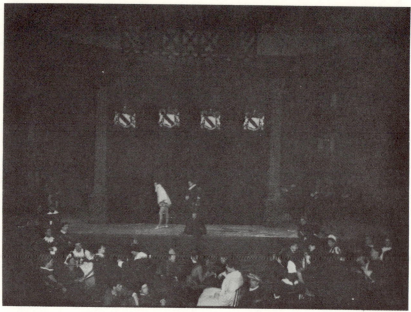

HTC

Harvard's Elizabethan Stage, 1904

HTC

Jonson's *Silent Woman* on the first Elizabethan stage in Sanders Theatre, 1895

He read several of his own poems, which, in themselves, were beautiful but under his reading lost much of their beauty. Imagine a man of somewhat the general build of Ex-Mayor Thomas Doyle, dressed in a badly fitting dress-suit, with a large head covered by thick black hair brushed neatly back and parted near the middle; with large dark eyes under rather protruding eyebrows; and aquiline nose and a large mouth with lines heavily marked on each side, which gives a rather stern expression to the face. He has the pure English pronunciation of the letter *e*, as Barkshire for Berkshire, etc.; a wretched enunciation which renders his voice, when speaking on anything but a high key, inaudible in the front balcony. I was rather sorry he did not lecture.

At the end of his freshman year George was still submitting unacceptable poetry to the *Lampoon*. Undaunted, he also sent his verses to the *Atlantic Monthly, Youth's Companion,* and *Outing*. Verse writing came easily, but prose was another matter. This he never wrote without effort.

It was the theatre, however, not books, which really aroused him. Praed and Dobson were the models for his own versification, but acting was the art which stirred his spirit. This is how Joseph Jefferson affected him:

Saturday, April 19, 1884. Got Praed and Locker's poems, *London Lyrics,* from the library today . . . After dinner went with Sandford, Campbell, and Kestner to see Jefferson as Rip Van Winkle. It is one of the finest things I have ever seen. So natural, tender, lifelike. His acting brought the tears to my eyes and equalled if it did not surpass Booth's recognition of Cordelia. Throughout, the voice was hardly raised above the conversational tone and there was no ranting. A thoroughly delightful performance.

Thus he responded to the heightened sense of reality which the theatre seems always to have given him. Earlier in the year he had seen Henry Irving and Ellen Terry in Shakespeare's *Merchant of Venice,* done with all the realistic finish for which Irving was famous, and an even more effective *Much Ado about Nothing*. The diary shows that George chiefly enjoyed the illusion of reality and was critical of Irving's acting in those places where this illusion was not produced:

Wednesday, Feb. 27, 1884. . . . In the evening went to hear Irving and Terry in "Much Ado about Nothing." It was charming.

The whole company is good and the scenery very fine. The minutest particulars are well carried out. In the revelling at Leonato's house, the maskers sang, talked, laughed, flirted, etc. In the wonderfully fine church scene each person as he or she entered bowed before the altar. The boys swinging the censers, everything was very realistic. Terry took the honors. She was bewitching. Her bows and smiles and coquetries took one's heart by storm . . . Irving is fine in his way but his mannerisms are trying; a halting gait, mouthing and mighty rolling of the eyes with a queer jerky gesture will not down but mar his acting.

Friday, February 29, 1884. . . . I had planned to study a good deal in the evening but at dinner a party was hastily arranged for Irving in the "Merchant of Venice" and I yielded foolishly and went. The scenery even surpassed that in "Much Ado about Nothing." The scene in the front of Shylock's house with the bridge at the rear of the stage over the canal and the tall buildings in the distance, in the moonlight effect, was very fine . . . Irving was better. Still his Jew seemed too intellectual a rendering.

Of Miss Terry he added with fervor, "This is acting!" For a long time he was in love with her charming Beatrice. He was also in love with the soprano Marcella Sembrich. Indeed, it is probable that he spent as much time at the Boston music concerts and at the Bijou Theatre operas as he did at the drama. However, his interest in music was more emotional and appreciative than cultivated. Of Wagner he wrote his father, April 18, 1884, noting the realism of the German in contrast with the artificiality of Italian music:

He makes nothing of trills, melodies, etc. but sings on more in the conversational way, each man doing his part to produce the desired effect. The music does wonders. The rain falls, leaves rustle. You hear drums, trumpets, flowing water, etc. The "Parsifal" music is wonderfully weird and holds your attention in spite of yourself.

Perhaps because of his attention to music and the drama he had insufficient time for trigonometry. Suddenly he was stunned by the fact that he had failed this part of his mathematics. Another disappointment was Dr. Sargent's report on his physical development for the year. On the twenty-seventh of March, he told his father:

I got my exercise book from the Gym, only to find that my development for the year has been slight indeed . . . I do not care about the prize but after working so steadily it is discouraging to find — for one thing — that your chest in repose measures exactly what it did a year ago . . . I weigh 127 lbs instead of 124 as in Nov. I stand 5 ft 7 in., a slight gain . . . I am now above the average in strength but a little below in development.

To relax the strain of the freshman year, Dr. Baker sent his son vacationing to Seal Harbor, on Mount Desert Island, Maine. Naturally gallant with the ladies, George had missed their society during the academic year. However, a resort hotel among visiting Bostonians and Cantabrigians more than supplied this deficiency. The following "rondeau" which he sent to the *Century* was a response to this tonic:

"Tennis"

She's learning tennis, when I call
She takes a lesson. I appall
 Her with vague rules, for mostly I
 Watching her think of days gone by,
Dream an Arcadian pastoral.

'Tis true she seldom hits the ball
And that she serves not well at all,
 But at each failure, ah her sigh
 Would win your heart.

Serving, I watch the light ball fall
Beyond her reach, while she withal
 To make return doth vainly try.
 She's lost the game, ah player sly.
But I, I yield me to her thrall
 She's won my heart.

Dramatic entertainments for the hotel guests sped the summer evenings. Here, too, George blossomed. These impromptu stunts gave his ingenuity full play as, in a sense, he returned to the days of his toy theatre:

Saturday, August 23, 1884. In the afternoon decided to get up a pantomime for the evening. By dint of begging from the Crowninshields got a copy of "The Brave Alonzo and the Fair Imogene." We rushed things and it went off very well indeed. Miss Jenkins was Imogene; Sullivan, the Baron — I, Alonzo.

Some of these evenings were chaperoned by a kindly maiden lady from Philadelphia, Anna Bliss, who soon encouraged George's hopes for a literary career. Under her eyes he wrote the poem which, appearing in *Life* the following November, established him at Harvard as a "writer." Her encouragement also brought together his interests in verse and the theatre. The result was his earliest extant play, *Not Sentimental,* an unpublished comedy in verse.

Aside from the practical knowledge of the theatre he had gained as a spectator and amateur actor, he seems to have had little theoretical knowledge of dramatic construction. His model was the sort of narrative in dramatic form which William Dean Howells wrote for magazine readers who occasionally adapted them to private theatricals. Yet the piece has more than a little suggestion of acting possibilities. The blank verse dialogue, though somewhat stilted at times, suits the comedy very well.

Sometime during the first week of August, George received the report of his year's work at Harvard from his father. His marks were sufficient, if maintained, to get him a *cum laude* at graduation. With a glance at his son's rather poor showing in physics and mathematics, Dr. Baker graciously abandoned his hope that George would study medicine: "I do not wish to stimulate vanity but I think it right and proper to express the entire satisfaction which I feel and to congratulate you on the good beginning you have made in your literary career."

VI   ENTER WENDELL AND IRVING

RENOUNCING THE DISCIPLINES OF MATHEMATICS AND science in his sophomore year, George began his literary studies under Adams Sherman Hill, classmate of President Eliot and Boylston Professor of Rhetoric and Oratory. In addition, George studied elocution under Henry Dixon Jones, who shortly left the Harvard faculty for the stage, and philosophy under George Herbert Palmer. He did not study with Francis James Child, Harvard's first Professor of English. Apparently the aesthetic considerations of rhetoric and oratory which might be useful to a writer interested him more than philological investigations.

Now the boyish roundness of George's face slimmed into the angularity of maturity, he wore his hair a bit longer, and the famous pince-nez glasses became a part of his countenance. He began to live in the excellent suite at No. 7 Holworthy Hall which remained his Harvard home until he graduated. These years are of a piece, unified by his writing, his growing leadership in undergraduate societies, and his study of the English drama.

The immediate influence in this second year was Hill's assistant, Barrett Wendell, an alert, blue-eyed young man of the world. In this polished kinsman of Oliver Wendell Holmes, George soon found no less an object of imitation than his father had prized in the venerable Dr. Holmes. Wendell, like his student, was also "stage-struck." His very deportment showed that he was acting a good deal of the time.

He introduced dramatic topics and theatrical personalities to the classroom, suggesting such themes as "Henry Irving, Actor and Manager." Inevitably, George wrote his first paper for Wendell on the great English actor-manager; for George had gone to every performance of Irving and Terry that fall. What teacher and pupil apparently admired was Irving's illusion of vital reality.

That Irving now supplied George's standard of realism is to be seen in his diary notation for October 6, 1884, after watching his old favorites, Mrs. Vincent and the Boston Museum company, in *The School for Scandal:* "It ranks almost on a level with Irving's presentation of Shakespeare in point of costuming, thoroughness in detail, and general good effect." When Booth played *Hamlet* in December, George preferred Irving in the role.

However, it was the vitality of Irving in the melodramatic *Lyons Mail* which won the lad's heartiest admiration:

Saturday, November 1, 1884. . . . In Dubosc his voice is perfection it seems to me. It is exactly that of a debauched drunken villain. The accusation scene, the planning of the murder, during wh. Dubosc hurried about with a half snarl on his lips like a dog waiting for a rat, the scene in the prison court yard, and the finale in the

Dubosc garret were all fine, yes, wonderful. The last scene is one of the most powerful bits of acting I have ever seen. Dubosc is drunk, tigerish, fiendish, nothing else.

Such matters obviously fixed some of his dramatic criteria, for twenty-three years later, in 1907, he told the dramatic critic of the *Boston Transcript:* "The first progressive impulse the American theatre received was when Sir Henry Irving first came to this country."

Nevertheless, the lad was not a mere idolator of Irving. Still critical of the actor's mouthing mannerisms and awkward gait, he could be severely critical in his diary entry for February 20, of such a conception as Irving's Malvolio. This he thought a "burlesque on human nature" and not "by any means the character Shakespeare wished to draw." And when, at the invitation of President Eliot and the Harvard faculty, Irving gave an address at Sanders Theatre the following spring, George wrote admiringly but objectively:

Monday, March 30, 1885. . . . Doubtless the audience was the largest ever assembled in Sanders. At last Irving appeared, looked very much as he does in the less made up parts of his repertoire except that the clear cut quality of his somewhat classic face was more apparent and so too were his shaggy eyebrows, and the iron-grey streaks in his wavy hair. His eyes too seemed more brilliant and noticeable than usual. He was introduced by Mr. Jones. Irving was rather closely confined to his notes or I should say lecture for it was evidently written out. He stood easily but I doubt if I can truthfully say always gracefully, for one of his most frequent attitudes was a sort of squaring off toward the audience in wh. he placed his hands on his hips, thus thrusting rather awkwardly back the tails of his coat.

He began by expressing his great pleasure — wh. was evidently real — in the honor conferred upon him and then proceeded to his essay, a copy of wh. I shall try to place here. The position wh. he took in regard to his auditors I must say startled me a trifle and some of the conservative Cantabrigians must I think have been even more moved than I. He spoke as if he firmly believed that in the audience of students before him were some who would enter the profession wh. he represented. The address was graceful in style and interesting, for not only was it filled with bright anecdotes and bits of mimicry, but it plainly stated Irving's reasons for his acts as manager and

22

actor. All in all, the evening increased my interest in and admiration for the man.

One significant point is thus made clear. G.P.B.'s infatuation with the theatre did not involve a desire for a career in the profession. Amateur acting was perfectly respectable and an ordinary aspect of familial entertainment in many a home like that of President Eliot. But there was indeed something shocking about doing that sort of thing for a living.

In his view of Irving there was something of the moral precision which colored the biographical studies he now began to write for Wendell on Dryden, Pope, and Sir John Suckling. Characteristically, Wendell put his finger on the difficulty. On January 13, 1885, George wrote his father: "The fifth theme, which came back yesterday, Mr. Wendell spoke favorably of, though he called me a pretty grim Puritan, for my unsympathetic viewing of the life of Suckling."

Through Professor Wendell's influence George's precise attitude toward the rather human failings of his fellow creatures grew into the broad critical sympathy with which he was able in another year to approach the novels of George Meredith. This made possible the first piece of writing to win him wide attention — his article on George Meredith in the *Harvard Monthly* for June 1887.

VII   HARVARD AND THE THEATRE

HARVARD ATTITUDES TOWARD THE THEATRE DURING the eighties were an important influence upon G.P.B. Student theatricals and musical activities, almost as old as the college, had required the completion, in 1876, of Sanders Theatre in the Harvard memorial hall already erected to commemorate her Civil War dead. In that year of centennial celebrations, the production of a Greek play seemed a not unusual way to dedicate Harvard's new theatre. However, this plan did not mature until March 1881, when the Eliot Professor of Greek announced the performance at Sanders Theatre of the *Oedipus Tyrannus* of Sophocles in the original Greek.

The name of Eliot was otherwise connected with Harvard attitudes toward the theatre; for without active support from President Eliot, there could obviously have been neither a university theatre nor plays in it. It is a bit of family history that the widower Eliot first saw his second wife when she appeared in costume on the Brattle Hall stage during a rehearsal meeting of the Cambridge Social Dramatic Club. By his own example he taught the power and beauty of effective speech; stage and platform were legitimate instruments in his educational reforms. Directly interested in the teaching of elocution, Eliot had selected his classmate, Adams Sherman Hill, to accomplish some of the original purposes of the Boylston Professorship of Rhetoric and Oratory. And he personally engaged "Harvard's Actor," George Riddle, to teach elocution under Hill.

After four years upon the professional stage, Riddle was qualified to take the lead in the Greek play and to engineer its production. During his three years on the faculty he made occasional appearances in Boston and New York theatres, where he had already played with Edwin Booth. His most famous part was as Claude Melnotte opposite Mary Anderson's Pauline in *The Lady of Lyons.*

When Riddle left Harvard for the stage after the national attention he had gained at Sanders Theatre, President Eliot appointed Henry Dixon Jones to the vacancy. One reason for Riddle's departure appears to have been the onerous duty of teaching compulsory non-credit elocution classes. Jones, however, was successful in changing elocution from its ancient function in the technical training of ministers to an elective cultural subject which counted toward an arts degree. His expressed ambition was to bring the theatre in its legitimate literary and artistic relations nearer to the influences of the university.

Thus he planned to bring such people as Henry Irving, Henry Ward Beecher, and Bronson Howard to speak at Sanders Theatre. He also wished to present a university production of *Julius Caesar.* In these things he succeeded. The result was a revival of the fervor for the stage at Harvard which had, two years before

G.P.B.'s arrival in Cambridge, brought over six thousand people to the famous Greek play. But Jones, failing in 1886 to achieve his real purpose, a chair of elocution and drama, also left Harvard for the stage.

The significance of such developments had already brought editorial comment from the *Springfield Republican:*

> Culture and liberality have made rapid progress in the last twenty years, in the last ten years, when Henry Irving, the representative English actor of the day, delivers at Harvard College an address on the art of acting; an address which presupposed . . . students wishing to adopt the stage as a profession, as others will adopt law or journalism or the ministry.

Even among Harvard alumni there was a growing awareness of new cultural values in the theatre. This was apparent when such leading Harvard clubmen as Robert Grant and Barrett Wendell played at theatricals and wrote plays. A Boston production by Richard Mansfield of Thomas Russell Sullivan's adaptation of *Dr. Jekyll and Mr. Hyde* was, as G.P.B. wrote his father, one of the events of the 1887 season: "All Boston was agog in the matter and I have never seen a finer audience than that held by the Museum on the opening night."

The conditions from which G.P.B.'s career grew were thus established during his undergraduate days, when some of the principal objectives of his own lifework were already in ferment. However, an ingrained official conservatism barred from highest academic rank both the theatre as a new vehicle of culture and the ancient subject of rhetoric. Both were involved with the applied, and therefore servile, arts.

The true state of affairs is suggested in President Eliot's belief, expressed after his retirement, that the best work of men of genius displays "the scientific quality of precision and truthfulness; and their rhetorical or oratorical work is only their second best." Here was a pattern of internal contradictions within the Harvard community which, continuing though the years, both stimulated and frustrated G.P.B.'s work in the drama. More and more, as he strove for precision and truthfulness in the American theatre, he was bound to discover that at Harvard he labored in a second-best work.

VIII   SOMETHING TO WRITE ABOUT
— HARVARD MONTHLY

THE SUMMER OF 1885 FOUND GEORGE AT MOUNT
Desert, at the Seaside House. One foggy day William Dean
Howells came into the dining hall to watch the young people
dramatize a breach of promise trial. On July 27, George wrote his
father:

> I impersonated the heart stricken Sally and had a perfect lark.
> Mr. Howells, who is here, made my fun. He came in to watch the
> trial and I supposed, lionized as he has been, that the whole thing
> would bore him and that he only came to please us. However, I wish
> you could have seen him laugh. Every point I made by gesture or
> word he took, and went off in bursts of laughter. We had a mutual
> admiration society . . . He has asked me to call when I return to
> Boston and I think I shall.

What George hoped for during his last two years of college
was to be a creator of literature, or perhaps a dignified editor.
The ideal quality of his dedication to literature is indicated in
a letter of March 27 to his father:

> Last night I ushered for the lecture by Bronson Howard, the
> playwright . . . He spoke very well, but evidently money is his
> idol. The question is not, with him, what should the audience like,
> but what do they like. The latter brings more money certainly,
> lasting fame however doesn't come in that way, I fancy.

In this spirit he wrote an essay on "Dramatic Literature in America" which attempted to show "the causes of our lack of great
writers for the stage." What he concluded is not preserved; that
it had some merit appears in the fact that Wendell read the essay
to the class.

Thus motivated, G.P.B. now wrote for Wendell a series of
themes on the predecessors of Shakespeare; there was one on the
miracle plays, one on Greene, one on Peele, and two or three on
Marlowe. Later, he wrote another series for Professor Hill: seven
themes about the boy actors at St. Paul's Cathedral, whom Hamlet
indicates rivaled Shakespeare's men, and the playwrights who

26

wrote for them. During his senior year, he began an intensive study of the life and work of John Lyly which would have been his doctoral dissertation if he had ever declared himself a candidate for the Ph.D.

However, this scholarship was not related to teaching. "Heavens, What a life!" had been his comment on learning that a friend would enter this vocation. For George, scholarship was then but the source of materials for belles-lettristic writing. In his eyes, the first great reward of his life came when he was elected editor-in-chief of the *Harvard Monthly* for 1886–87.

This magazine, a child of Wendell's enthusiasm, had been organized by Alanson Houghton and George Santayana, both largely responsible for G.P.B.'s election to the presidency of the Philosophical Club and to the editorship which he so highly prized. Possessed with the current notions of "culture" and "aesthetics" now associated with Matthew Arnold and Walter Pater, these young men thought of themselves as the center of a "New Oxford" at Harvard. This was to be achieved by advancing the study of English to a position of greater importance in the college work. In this connection, it is significant that all of G.P.B.'s college studies of the drama were pursued in courses in composition, or rhetoric.

Because G.P.B. sought a maturity of thought which could not be found in the ordinary undergraduate, his first editorial called for "a large body of advanced students, not members of professional schools, but pursuing their own researches." When it is considered that but forty-five men had received the Ph.D. at Harvard prior to this editorial, and that only a dozen had completed the degree during his undergraduate experience, it is clear that the young editor's appeal for advanced humanistic studies was somewhat in the vanguard of an educational trend.

During his editorship, which was mainly devoted to the persuasion of a number of distingushed alumni to write for the *Monthly,* G.P.B.'s contributions were few. Besides three poems, his only imaginative contribution was a brief narrative concerning an incident in the French Revolution. Written in a blunt style which may have derived from his reading of Carlyle and Dickens, the piece develops its single incident with a dramatic objectivity suggestive of the Irving melodramas G.P.B. then admired.

By the middle of October 1886, he had increased his list of subscribers from one hundred to five hundred. Of greater importance, the magazine was attracting more than a local audience. By November, fifteen hundred copies were in demand. E. C. Stedman, outstanding American man of letters of the day, wrote from New York that he considered his first issue worth the subscription price. At winter's end, Boston's leonine Phillips Brooks told George that he had put the magazine on a high literary level. The *Harvard Monthly*, no longer an undergraduate affair, was now a literary magazine of New England.

IX FARQUHAR, MEREDITH, AND A LITERARY PHILOSOPHY

IF G.P.B. DISTINGUISHED HIMSELF AS A WRITER FOR THE *Harvard Monthly*, it was because of his clear and rational essays on George Farquhar and George Meredith. Approved by the *Daily Crimson* with such comments as "well written," "straightforward," and "exceedingly vigorous," these are now of significance because they show the rough outlines of what might be called his literary philosophy. This, a sort of middle way between "realism" and "idealism," G.P.B. chose to call "non-sentimental." Although it ceased to have a name in later years, its first expression in these student essays has a direct bearing upon G.P.B's teaching of playwriting.

The article on Farquhar reveals two of G.P.B.'s basic attitudes toward dramatic technique: a desire for clearly conceived characters, and a desire that such characters be kept in constant action toward a fitting climax. After opening with a sympathetic attention to the fact that Farquhar's tragic life produced only comedies, G.P.B. observes that this comedy comes not from the minds of the characters but from their fancies. In short, the comedies lack depth of feeling and are weak in character.

He deplored Farquhar's structural unevenness and incongruity of function as regressions to the apprentice work of the

28

sixteenth century: "Farquhar does not seem to have understood the meaning of the even, steady development of a play, in which all the scenes, and all the characters do a part to produce a constant movement toward a fitting climax in the last scene."

G.P.B.'s remarks on Farquhar's attitude toward his audience are also characteristic of the philosophy which led to the 47 Workshop: "there is one function of a play which Farquhar reiterates constantly; the piece must please the audience. Hear what he says: 'The rules of English Comedy don't lie in the compass of Aristotle, or his followers, but in the Pit, Box, and Galleries.'"

With increasing clarity, G.P.B. saw that the living spirit of the theatre was the spirit of delight in amusing play. This achieved its highest value when author and audience were in harmony.

As G.P.B. brought his editorship to a close, he relinquished his chair to Bernard Berenson and began to read the work of a novelist new to many Americans. This was George Meredith, for whose novels something of a cult had grown in England during the seventies and eighties until an admiration of his work was one of the marks of an anti-Philistine. Already Boston and Cambridge knew of Meredith, for the Boston firm of Roberts Brothers had begun to publish ten of the Englishman's novels in 1885 and was about to complete its issue of the collected edition. With a plan for reviewing the series in mind, G.P.B. began to read *The Ordeal of Richard Feverel*. His enthusiasm was immediate; and he wrote his father on January 24, 1887:

I think it is a marvelously strong book, despite some very peculiar English now and then, a style that is almost school-girlish in its sentimentality at times. But beside Howells and most of the writers of today this Meredith seems like a general beside his captains. They manage successfully a handful of men, he parades before you regiments. But each man in the regiment stands out a personality. There is none of the impressionistic drawing which is so prevalent today. There must be a dozen characters introduced in the first one hundred pages, yet all are alive and different.

Four days later, George posted a special warning to his father against a certain "warmth" in this new idol. Dr. Baker was to read *Richard Feverel* "by all means, but not out loud." Certain passages might displease and, doubtless, others would shock Mrs.

Wheaton, Dr. Baker's housekeeper. "Regarded from a literary point of view," George explained hastily, "these very places are masterly."

Although G.P.B.'s review was not the first to illuminate Meredith for Americans, his statement of the impact of the novelist's work upon contemporary literary values was new. During the two decades previous, English periodicals had printed a yearly average of one critical article (exclusive of routine book notices) on Meredith. American periodicals had left Meredith alone, except for four articles during the decade before 1887 and three articles during the six months which preceded George's review. Meredith's own response to the young American's criticism indicates that he welcomed it as a new and encouraging thing.

G.P.B.'s review begins by attributing the recent interest in Meredith to the mental and moral evolution of his characters through a process comparable to that of "experiments in biology." This is distinguished from previous evolutionary fiction in that it concentrates not upon the "striking dramatic episodes in the evolution" but upon the "entire set of circumstances which made the change possible." Their interest lay in Meredith's development of the thesis that although people are what they are because of conditions of "natural disposition, of training, and of environment," men and women have god-like powers within them, to be developed "according as the men and women strive or not." G.P.B. asked if Meredith, obviously neither a "Realist" nor an "Idealist," might not be called the "Carlyle of fiction."

The significant statement in the article was G.P.B.'s anticipation of a change in literary taste:

We seem now to be at the beginning of a transition. As a character says in *Sandra Belloni*: "We are still fighting against the Puritan element in literature as elsewhere." Yet a new way seems to be opening. Last year Vernon Lee pleaded in *Baldwin* for something in fiction between French Realism and English prudery. Lately Rider Haggard has written in *The Contemporary* calling for more manliness in literature, for a more straightforward treatment of the difficulties of the world, one which will neither heighten them in color, nor lower them in tone. We have had sentimentality in literature long enough. May not this agitation bring something which will be neither strictly Realistic nor strictly Idealistic, — something non-sentimental, shall I say, — which avoiding the extravagances, will have the good points of both the old schools?

Here was the essence of the literary philosophy which tempered his own inherent Puritanism to the naturalism of the twentieth century. Hereafter he moved toward a middle way, rejecting any literary theory which could not be encompassed by the sort of common sense shown here. This is why he was able to draw out of young playwrights the genius which was truly their own without imposing upon that genius any of his own sentiment. This was the ultimate meaning of "non-sentimental."

The article, said Barrett Wendell, was good enough to appear in any magazine and certainly ought to be sent to Meredith. Soon G.P.B. had a letter from the novelist, who thus rewarded the young critic's awareness of a shift toward twentieth century values: "When at the conclusion of your article on my works, you say that a certain change in public taste, should it come about, will be to some extent due to me, you hand me the flowering wreath I covet."

x   GRADUATION — FRUSTRATION AND WANDERJAHR — ENTER CLYDE FITCH

AS THE END OF HIS COLLEGE COURSE APPROACHED, George was often in Barrett Wendell's office, where much of their talk concerned George's future. Soon an appointment in New York had been arranged for the young editor to meet Wendell's friend, Charles Scribner, Jr., who was looking for someone to edit the *Book Buyer*, a magazine of literary criticism, publishing news, and bibliographic interests. Outlining a very tentative proposal for the fall, Scribner suggested a salary of $1500. In high spirits, George celebrated his success by going to see Mrs. Edwin Booth in *Jim the Penman*, the best acting, he thought, that he had seen all winter.

A few days after his return to Cambridge, a message came from

Professor George Herbert Palmer that he might have an instructorship at a "Western University." The prospect was a professorship in three or four years. However, G.P.B. decided that the uncertain editorship was more attractive. His decision, he wrote, was largely based on his unsuitableness for teaching: "The more I have thought of teaching, the more repugnant the idea has grown." Wendell's own plays and novels showed that teaching was not the sort of life in which a writer fostered his art. In short, his preference was "for editorial and journalistic work, for a better salary, for life in the East."

At Commencement, Phi Beta Kappa was the principal distinction he wished for; and this came with eminence in English, philosophy, and history. His last act as an undergraduate was his reading of the Class Ode, in which he bespoke his own future:

> Oh, live not in visions of fancies; nor dream
>   Of achievements heroic at length;
> Act! act!

Unfortunately, the ensuing weeks were days of inaction; for he left Harvard without definite arrangements for the future. Should nothing come of the Scribner proposal, there were, of course, several alternatives. Dr. Baker wished his company on a visit to London for the celebration of the Queen's Jubilee; Miss Bliss urged him to come to Paris; and George Santayana suggested graduate study at Oxford, or perhaps Berlin.

While George waited for news from Scribner, he went on with the study of John Lyly, which was beginning to be something of a book. A letter from a college friend cheered his New York hopes with the news that his article on George Meredith was being quoted there in newspaper advertisements of Meredith's novels. In mid-August the blow fell. Mr. Scribner had decided to make other arrangements.

George's reaction was an immediate and excessive despondency. Among those who learned of this distress, a friend from the summer theatricals at the Seaside House was best prepared to help. In October, George went west to winter on this friend's New Mexico ranch. Soon the New Mexico Territory was the subject of a series of letters to the *Providence Journal*.

Although he rode daily about the ranch and among the

nearby Navajos, his notebooks show that his mind was engrossed with stories unrelated to the life about him which he hoped to write. Typical of these is his "Idea for an ugly sketch à la Maupassant" about an innocent young man and a woman of the street. By March, however, life in the saddle had restored his nerves. On his return home to make ready for the trip to London with his father, George was profoundly shocked to learn that Dr. Baker had cancer.

Sailing alone, George planned a brief stay in London, then to Italy, whence he should travel north in easy stages, returning to England some time in June. Before he left London, he bought a copy of *The Actor: or, A Treatise on the Art of Playing* in which he wrote, according to his habit: "A very scarce and interesting little volume containing facts not in any other theatrical publications."

On the second of April, he wrote his father from the Hotel Britannique in Naples: "I hope to write a letter to the Journal in a few days, on *Easter in Naples*. In it I shall try to give some vague idea of the shifting, uncertain, irrepressible thing that filled the streets here on Saturday & Sunday." Here was his first view of the living European tradition of pageantry.

There were many Americans in Paris that June; and since a number were of George's acquaintance, he was not alone in the city which he already loved. Besides Professors Palmer and Wendell, he found there Bernard Berenson and Clyde Fitch, as well as the Mosher girls from Cambridge. Mrs. Mosher, a banker's widow whose Ware Street home had been a center for Cambridge literati during George's senior year, had taken a motherly interest in George and had come to his graduation to meet Dr. Baker. Thus George was frequently at the Mosher's Rue Washington apartment with Clyde Fitch, who was writing a novel about Grace and Florence Mosher.

Before returning to London, G.P.B. visited his friend George Rice Carpenter in Berlin. Carpenter, completing two years of study in comparative literature, had made a serious study of the work of Henrik Ibsen, then living in Germany. Thus G.P.B. gained a firsthand acquaintance with the new movement in the German theatre. His earliest copies of Ibsen's work, *Gedichte von*

Henrik Ibsen and *Kaiser und Galilaer*, are inscribed: "Geo. P. Baker, Jr., Berlin, June 22, 1888."

When G.P.B. reached London in mid-July, he learned that he had been appointed an instructor at Harvard for the academic year about to begin. Toward the end of August, Carpenter arrived from Berlin, and there were introductions through him to such "Ibsenites" as Havelock Ellis and William Archer. Both Archer and Carpenter were translating Ibsen into English; but G.P.B.'s interest was not so much in these modern plays as in the old drama which Ellis was engaged in preparing as editor of the Mermaid Series of dramatic texts. It was in connection with this acquaintance that G.P.B. one day received from one of Carpenter's Ibsenite friends an invitation to drink whisky and meet Oscar Wilde, who apparently had expressed a desire to meet the young Americans.

Meanwhile, G.P.B. had sent a letter requesting an appointment with George Meredith, then on a visit in Wales. At last the reply from Meredith arrived, inviting G.P.B. to spend the second and third of September with the novelist in his small cottage at Box Hill. Such acquaintance with Wilde and Meredith was sufficiently exciting that it never lost its savor and often conveyed to G.P.B.'s conversation and lectures passing allusions which he relished no less than did his audiences. Near the end of September, G.P.B. and Clyde Fitch returned to America.

XI HARVARD INSTRUCTOR

RETURNING TO CAMBRIDGE, G.P.B. MOVED INTO 24 GRAYS Hall, across the Yard from his student quarters in Holworthy Hall. Here, in the same building as Wendell's office, snuggly settled among his growing dramatic and theatrical library, G.P.B. began the first of thirty-seven years of teaching at Harvard and Radcliffe.

It was a year of important beginnings. Another new instructor, George Lyman Kittredge, began to teach Professor Child's "Shakspere." Barrett Wendell, but recently made an assistant professor, offered for the first time a course in the drama which later became

34

G.P.B.'s. This was English 14, "The Drama, Exclusive of Shakspere, from the Miracle Plays to the Closing of the Theatres," possibly the first course of its kind given in an American university. Only the year before, James Russell Lowell, Emeritus Professor of Belles-Lettres at Harvard, had discoursed upon some of these old plays in a series of Lowell Institute Lectures in Boston.

However, G.P.B.'s principal duties were to assist Professor Hill and Assistant Professor Briggs in the freshman rhetoric classes and to help Professor Josiah Royce in the junior and senior forensic work. Since these prescribed courses were also offered at Radcliffe, the Harvard "Annex," G.P.B.'s first class each morning that fall of 1888 was with a group of young ladies at Fay House.

While he accustomed himself to his different status in the life in and about the Yard, he kept in touch with those classmates who now pursued careers in New York. On the twenty-fifth of November, Churchill Carmalt wrote G.P.B. of a reunion of old friends at Daly's Theatre to see *The Wife of Socrates* and *The Lottery of Love:*

You must see them should you have the chance . . . not so much for themselves as for Ada Rehan's acting. The fellows all asked after you and were amused as I was at Gidding's description of your tribulations with the Annex maids.

Dike tells me you have devoted your admiration of late to a pessimistic Norwegian or Scandinavian playwright. Ibsen I think the name was. Tell me about him.

As was his wont, G.P.B. soon had formed a club to talk about Ibsen and the new drama. George Rice Carpenter and Barrett Wendell were the nucleus of a company which soon included M. A. DeWolfe Howe, H. T. Parker, and William A. Leahy and called itself "The Mermaid." With G.P.B. as president, there were programs and serious papers which, in small compass, included the subject matter of G.P.B.'s intellectual history for the next dozen years. The topics and speakers for 1888–89 were:

"Henrik Ibsen," by G. R. Carpenter
 Ibsen's "Lady of the Sea," a reading by G. R. Carpenter of his own
  translation of the play
"Dumas, fils," a general discussion
 An Original Play, a reading by Barrett Wendell of his own play
"Brander Matthews," by H. T. Parker

"The Siege of Syracuse," a reading by W. A. Leahy of his own dramatic poem

"The Masque in English Drama," by M. A. DeWolfe Howe

"Is a Naturalistic School of Acting Desirable?" a general discussion

"The Present Condition of English Drama," by George Pierce Baker

"Revivals of Shakespeare's 'Winter's Tale,' " by M. A. DeWolfe Howe

During the winter of 1889–90, "The Mermaid" was augmented by George Santayana, who had just returned from Europe to commence his appointment as Instructor in Philosophy, and Jefferson B. Fletcher, a new Instructor in English. Two of G.P.B.'s senior forensics students, Norman Hapgood and Robert Herrick, also joined the group, now keenly interested in what was already called "the experimental theatre." Now an Instructor in Forensics, G.P.B. took over Josiah Royce's courses in that subject and began to develop his own course in Argumentation, a work which quickly caught the interest of President Eliot.

At "The Mermaid" Santayana and Fletcher discussed such new dramatists as Echegaray and Ostrovsky. Howe read a paper on the French Théâtre Libre. G.P.B.'s papers, however, were confined to such historical considerations as "The Child Actors of the Stuart Period" and "The Drama of Blood." Meanwhile, he occupied more and more of his leisure with the book on John Lyly. For Ibsen and the new theatre in Europe, appropriate topics at Mermaid meetings, would gather no garlands within academic walls. Yet something was happening in the Harvard environs which would, before long, turn G.P.B.'s serious study from the old drama to the new. The Annex maidens were already asking insistently about Ibsen's *Doll's House*.

In the early days of 1890, after one of George's last visits to his father's house, Dr. Baker made his will. Considering the fact that George was now twenty-four and without immediate prospect or likelihood of marriage, the old man arranged that his son should not be left alone. After providing "Auntie" Wheaton, his housekeeper, with a small annuity, Dr. Baker made George his sole heir. Thus "Auntie" went to Cambridge to keep house for George at 1 Garden Street in the autumn of 1890.

Appointed an instructor for five years, George continued in charge of the forensics work. He also assisted Wendell and Kittredge with their sophomore rhetoric and taught a new course of his own, Argumentative Composition. More to his liking was the course in the British drama which Wendell now relinquished to him. Thus he was clearly one of the "coming" young men of Cambridge when he met an attractive young lady from the Annex at Mount Desert the next summer. She was Christina Hopkinson, President Eliot's niece.

XII   ENGLISH 14

IN 1890–91, G.P.B. TAUGHT THE FIRST OF THE COURSES which became identified with his Harvard career: English 14, a study of the history of the English drama before the Puritan revolution. Developed by Barrett Wendell during G.P.B.'s senior year, the course had been offered but twice before G.P.B. began to conduct it primarily for graduate students. Until 1921, when he passed the course along to John Tucker Murray, English 14 was the one course G.P.B. taught with but minor change or interruption. From it developed his work in both the history and the technique of the drama.

It is possible to estimate some of his early teaching from notes taken in the course by William Lyon Phelps, then beginning his graduate study in English literature. Phelps, a schoolmate and friend of Clyde Fitch, soon became an intimate friend of G.P.B. Phelps's notebook, "The English Drama, Studied with Mr. Baker, 1890–91," is in the Yale University Library; for it was thence Phelps returned after taking the master's degree at Harvard.

These notes show that G.P.B.'s lectures grew from his undergraduate studies of the "old drama" and of the playwrights of the Elizabethan and Jacobean children's acting companies. More recent sources were the books in the considerable dramatic library he had collected during his travels abroad. Sometimes the young instructor was perhaps but a day or two ahead of his students in his reading; often he must have followed Barrett Wendell's suggestions rather closely. Yet three traits of G.P.B.'s teaching appear quite clearly in Phelps's notes.

These were: his sympathetic understanding of the relation between the life and the plays of each damatist; his belief that the dramas he taught were created for the stage and were to be acted rather than read; and his view that the history of the drama showed an evolution of dramatic form. In the maturity of his Harvard teaching, G.P.B.'s effectiveness with student actors and playwrights must have been determined to a large extent by these attitudes.

His first remarks upon each dramatist studied in the course were a brief exposition of the man's personality as G.P.B. assessed it. In his introduction to the plays of Robert Greene, he said: "I don't know of any life in English literature that appeals to me more than Greene's. His life is a much greater tragedy than any of his plays show."

Greene's moral degradation and repentance he regarded as biographical facts, yet G.P.B. saw the real meaning of Greene's life in his character as an artist: his "intensely pathetic feeling that in literature his life has some dignity and usefulness." Typical was G.P.B.'s contrast of Ben Jonson and Thomas Dekker, for whom he felt a "personal friendliness": "Jonson was a workman who worked from the brain out; Dekker worked from the *heart* out. Dekker is utterly different in his personality from Jonson. And this is a thing to notice in these dramatists: the strong personality in each of them. Dekker is all heart."

These lectures also show G.P.B.'s sensitivity to the psychology of the dramatist's characters. His remarks upon Marlowe's *Tamburlaine* are indicative of the insight he tried to bring to his students:

There's no regard for structure in the play — acts and scenes follow each other loosely. Marlowe doesn't seem to care anything about that. The unities are simply ignored.

But Marlowe's aim is always to bring out the central figure — his character. In every scene this is his one interest, to bring out Tamburlaine's nature. Read the play with this in your mind.

The conception of the character is great — it is consistent, perfectly clear. A perfect barbaric chieftain, reminds one of Salvini's "Othello" . . . He is superb in his strength and the faith in his own destiny reminds one of Napoleon . . . Tamburlaine trusts no gods: he always falls back on himself. This is a masterly conception of Marlowe . . . Marlowe realizes what the real foundation of the tragedy of life is. We imagine we have individuality and are masters, whereas we are really playthings of fate. Quite remarkable that Marlowe should have seen this so clearly in that time. It appears all through the play. It doesn't appear before Marlowe.

G.P.B. read each play as a script for an actor, not a text for a reader, and pointed out those things which could be appreciated only in terms of the stage. His eye caught the hints of stage "business" which are normally lost in the study. His remark on *Gammer Gurton's Needle* is characteristic: "The fun is, of course, very broad and full of filth: yet it . . . could be made very funny on the stage." Of Ben Jonson he said, "Sometimes his plays *act* well when they don't read at all."

The lecture on John Heywood, who was "first of all an actor," shows the background of dramatic technique against which G.P.B. discussed the plays:

In moments of extreme feeling, people don't make long speeches: they either say nothing or only a word. Heywood understood this perfectly.

Then notice his strong sense of the value of the *pause*, as the pause just before Frankford enters the chamber of his wife in *A Woman Killed with Kindness* . . . The suddenness of transition in character in this play is a literary, not a dramatic fault. This is a dramatic exigency. The immediate effect on the audience he gets, and that is what he is after.

He saw "audience effect" primarily in the quality of "pathos," and discussed the technical principles upon which this effect was created. In his lecture on Peele, G.P.B. appears to have spoken for the first time of the "laws of dramatic construction." However, this had reference more to the total form of the play than to any absolute principles or "laws" of a coercive nature. With the ideas of "form" and "development" he perhaps associated most of his own thought about dramatic effectiveness.

Obviously, G.P.B. meant a number of things by "form," but the word had a general reference to the end product of a kind of development in the theatre which had analogies to biological evolution. Although he does not appear to have used any explicit Darwinian terminology, he consistently voiced the idea that the history of the English drama was an evolution toward something. Typical of this line of thought are these words:

There is a natural sequence to the drama. First, in the miracle plays people are told how to live. Second, in the moralities simple pictures are given of this. In the early moralities, each character represents only one idea, one motive. The next step is to turn to real life. We then feel the complexity of life, see people struggling under various influences.

This dramatic growth produced not only an increasing technical finish, but an increasing fidelity to nature. "The significance of the interludes," he said in his October 19 lecture, "is that we are getting farther away from ethical teaching and nearer to a representation of life." He saw the dramatic growth of Greene as an approach toward this kind of truth: "In *James IV* we see a new thing. He doesn't develop his characters, but they are decidedly human, real Englishmen. They are not unreal, as is his *Orlando*. Greene is gaining as a playwright . . . in that he is coming closer to nature."

As the course proceeded toward its conclusion with the plays of Beaumont and Fletcher, G.P.B. called attention to the greater sophistication in dramatic construction. This growing finesse, which he saw marred in Jonson by wooden characters, "all puppets, pulled with a string," came to its first culmination in the plays of Middleton:

There is a decidedly different tone from what went before. We are losing spontaneity, forcible directness, as in *The Shoemaker's Holiday,* and gaining in skilful construction. Middleton is much more complex and minute. He shows an increase in power of handling characters and of moving them about in new and different situations. Middleton is much more careful in the details of his work. He knows stage-craft — how to make his plays act.

Here, in his first lectures on the drama, G.P.B. displayed the principal characteristics of his teaching of playwriting. Always he was interested in the humanity of the artist and his creation, in the truthfulness of both, and in the basic necessity of "form" to display "character" in "action." As he traced the evolution of the drama from medieval to modern times he grew increasingly interested in the anatomy of plays and in the psychology of audiences.

40

IN THE DECADE FROM 1890 TO 1900, G.P.B.'S LIFE AC-
quired the principal outlines of its maturity. During these years
he taught, studied abroad, married, continued his interest in the
drama, extended his attempts at writing, and established himself
as a scholarly member of the Harvard faculty.

At the beginning of this period he made some attempts to
leave Cambridge and corresponded with Edward Everett Hale,
Jr., concerning an appointment at Cornell University. In February and March 1891, his story, "Brother Filippo," appeared in the
New England Magazine. This told the tragedy of a young man
who gave up a life of art for a life of religion because he was forced
to do so. Unable to live without his art, the young monk died
rather than surrender his spirit to the rule of the monastic order.
In a striking way, G.P.B.'s words about Filippo applied to the
mode of life upon which he had entered at Harvard:

> Certainly this was a strange life for a brilliant, growing lad. He
> was without other companions than his manuscripts, the statues,
> and the fancies of his own brain . . . Innocent, brilliant, impression-
> able . . . It was a training to make a pedant . . . , if he had not
> been such an honest, sympathetic little fellow.

Something of this situation is suggested in a remark George
Santayana made to William Lyon Phelps a year after G.P.B.'s
death. Speaking of Oliver Alden, the hero of his novel, *The Last
Puritan,* Santayana said:

> An important element in the *tragedy* of Oliver . . . is drawn
> from the fate of a whole string of Harvard poets in the 1880's and
> 1890's . . . Now, all those friends of mine . . . of whom I was very
> fond, were visibly killed by the lack of air to breathe. People in-
> dividually were kind and appreciative to them, as they were to me;
> but the system was deadly, and they hadn't any alternative tradition
> (as I had) to fall back upon: and, of course, . . . they hadn't the
> strength of a great intellectual hero who can stand alone.

As he matured in his profession, G.P.B. sought increasingly
to stand alone. While the years passed, he built up his private

world of accomplishment whose atmosphere he could breathe freely. This, after 1912, gradually restricted itself to Massachusetts Hall, and Radcliffe's Agassiz Hall, and the dramatic activities there attendant upon his 47 Workshop. Meanwhile, he lost touch with the "system"; his intimacy with the members of the English department decreased as he gave himself without stint to the young writers and actors who fed upon his own vitality. When Massachusetts Hall and all it represented were no longer available to him in 1924, it was G.P.B.'s tragedy that he stood alone at Harvard.

The genesis of this isolation was slow. Certainly much of G.P.B.'s sense of it was the product of great fatigue; but the nature of his work, and the environment in which he did it, tended to shut him off from his contemporaries at the same time that he found the salt of life with the young men and women who shared his own devotion to the drama and to the theatre. Undoubtedly he was much influenced by Barrett Wendell's own sense of spiritual isolation at Harvard during the nineties.

The elation of escape from Cambridge appears in one of George's last letters to his father. At Wendell's invitation, he had gone to New Castle, New Hampshire, to give a talk on Shakespeare's London to some of Wendell's neighbors. G.P.B. wrote to his father, March 12, 1890:

It seems like old days when Cambridge was new and meant Longfellow and Lowell and dreamland, to be in Portsmouth again . . . Wendell has been very kind, coming down with me. Before dinner we made a call at a charming old home, to see an aunt of his; since the lecture we have called upon a Mr. Hasen, a delightful old gentleman . . . from Weimar, where he knew Goethe. He is a delightful gentleman of the old school.

The lecture was great fun. We drove out to New Castle through the mist that made the drive one of the darkest I have ever taken. We could scarcely see the road, and the toll-bridges came up out of the darkness in a startling way. Really it was very romantic to roll into New Castle through the fog, with the lights of the homes making broad yellowish lights in the mist. In the hall above the school-house about fifty men — fishermen — women and children were waiting. They listened very attentively as I told them about London in Shakespeare's time. I never had a more attentive audience . . . The excitement of speaking to this audience has quite taken me out of myself.

For a while, George thought that he would be able to write verse and prose in sufficient quantity to keep creatively alive. However, the quality of what he had time to do was disappointing. Although the New York *Independent* had called "Brother Filippo" a "story of exceptional power" which showed a subtle and dramatic appreciation of character, scarcely any other notice seems to have been taken of it. George's friend and editor of the *Atlantic Monthly*, Horace Scudder, put the matter rather kindly when he returned another story: "Greatly as I like the general theme of your sketch and the care with which parts were worked up, I could not resist the feeling that the total effect was too monochromatic, and the cause lay largely in too great elaboration, along the same line, of a single sentiment."

At the close of the 1890–91 academic year, G.P.B. applied for a leave of absence to study abroad. His plan was to complete the book on John Lyly, to gather materials for a book on Elizabethan dramatic sources, and to learn what he could about the contemporary European theatre. The first two objectives kept him in London during the summer and fall of 1891; the last took him through France, Germany, and Spain during the following winter and spring.

During this absence, he kept in touch with Harvard affairs through Barrett Wendell, who soon congratulated his young friend upon his election to Wendell's favorite Boston club, "The Tavern." A confraternal interest in belles-lettres, art, and amateur theatricals, Wendell reported, made this company of precisely the right sort, and the whole atmosphere the most delightful relief from the rather repressive environment of Cambridge.

Meanwhile, G.P.B.'s correspondence with Christina Hopkinson blossomed into romance. They met again in London in the summer of 1891, when Christina presented G.P.B. with a copy of *All's Well that Ends Well*. By 1893, the approbation of President Eliot was more than a professional or friendly matter, for the courtship ended very well that summer in a simple wedding at President Eliot's vacation home at Mount Desert.

In the following years it was primarily as a teacher of argumentation that President Eliot esteemed his new nephew. For G.P.B.'s first book, *Specimens of Argumentation* had thus distinguished him at the time of his marriage. The next year, 1894, he published his edition of Lyly's *Endymion,* a work more than sufficient to establish his reputation as a scholar. However, it was his *Principles of Argumentation* which marked G.P.B. as a valuable man to Harvard and probably won him his promotion to an assistant professorship in 1895.

The book with which he had hoped to secure fame as a dramatic scholar was *A Plot-Book of Some Elizabethan Plays,* first announced by Ginn and Company in their catalogue for 1893. This announcement explained:

> The editor aims to place in the hands of students of English Literature material which, in the main, exists only in rare and costly editions, and considerably new information as to the sources of well-known plays. The volumes are meant to be not only a convenient reference book for libraries, but also a text-book through which methods of dramatic construction may be studied, by which an insight into the minds of some Elizabethan dramatists may be gained.

Although it was so announced each year through the next six years, and although G.P.B. was at work on the manuscript as late as 1913, the book was never published.

In these years he was perhaps most popular with the Harvard law students, who found his teaching of argumentation eminently practical. This subject he defined as "the art of which Logic is the science." He was careful to tell them that "argumentation is not a thing apart, confined to the law courts, but has its important place in literary and scientific work." This emphasis upon analysis and construction undoubtedly affected his own view of the principles of dramatic writing.

As the decade came to a close, G.P.B. struggled with three mutually frustrating motives: his ambition to write; his wish to do something quite respectable in the field of literary scholarship; and his desire to teach something practical. In this conflict he found that he was again driving himself toward nervous exhaustion. President Eliot advised him:

44

It seems to me that nobody ought to work in such a way that he gets periodically exhausted, — not even once a year. If the fatigue is something which a week in the garden, or the country, or at the seaside will not repair, the work has been excessive and the mode of life is uneconomical and imprudent. The interesting question for you is, not how much work you will do in any nine months, but what you will accomplish in twenty-five years.

Barrett Wendell was also looking to G.P.B.'s future, but with perhaps more perception than "Uncle Charles," who thought the young fellow would do well to give up those activities which had nothing to do with argumentation. Wendell wrote to G.P.B., February 11, 1899:

Knowing you first as an exceptionally sympathetic pupil, and since as a constantly sympathetic colleague and friend, I can't help feeling more than common interest in those ten years to come, which must probably fix your professional reputation. I know you won't mind my writing frankly.

To this point, you have been constantly overworked and overworking. The real cause of this seems to me that you have been constantly carrying two special subjects, each by itself enough for the full energy of a scholar: argumentation and the English drama. The time is coming, I think, — if indeed it be not come, — when for your own sake you ought to stop one or the other, and force recognition as the first American authority in that which you keep.

Between the two courses, Wendell continued, he would not hesitate a moment:

As the writer of *English Composition,* I believe myself to be commonly grouped rather with elocutionists than with scholars. Kittredge's reviews, and Manly's *Specimens,* meanwhile, to say nothing of Child's *Ballads,* — have found respectful recognition not only for them but for their subject from scholars of the widest variety and range.

The goal, then, was eminence as an authority on the drama. Some time later, in a letter of March 16, 1899, Wendell showed the path to success: "You ought to give some Lowell lectures . . . on the stage conditions of the Elizabethan stage . . . I doubt whether you realize the thoroughness of your present equipment —not as compared with ideal learning, but as compared with anybody else."

IN APRIL 1891, AS G.P.B. PLANNED HIS FORTHCOMING
summer's work at the British Museum in search of facts about
John Lyly, Clyde Fitch came to Boston for rehearsals of his *Beau
Brummel* at the Globe Theatre. After an evening with the Mermaid club, to which G.P.B. had invited him, Fitch read to the
group his new one-act play, *Frederick Lemaitre,* which Felix Morris would soon open at Daly's Theatre in New York. Apparently
Fitch was then planning a similar trip to London during the summer for the rehearsals of his plays at the Court Theatre.

When G.P.B. arrived early in July, he was greeted by Fitch:

I am very glad to hear you are in London. Won't you come and
have a very "pot luck" luncheon with me on *Monday* at *two o'clock?*
I put it in this forbidding way because I am making my first essay in
the art of house keeping, & I find a "cook-house-keeper" as they are
called, is as rare as any other bona fide article or vertu!

My present one is honest, therefore the condiments prepared by
her for the daily meal(s) do not poison, and *may* nourish. They are
sometimes palatable, I confess, but never delectable, — and as I go
away in ten days I do not care to change *again!* Come any way & see
me, and see her — she's worth 2d a view, — I call her "Hedda Gabler"
for she looks like an Ibsenite!

G.P.B. had already written for advice about selling a play he
was then writing, the dramatization of a recent historical novel
about the Jacobite uprising of 1740. This was M. E. LeClerc's
Mistress Beatrice Cope, which had for its hero a dashing blade
not unlike Fitch's "Beau." Fitch advised: "You must not expect
to make good terms for your first piece, no matter how good it is;
you can offer it only for America or only for England, and stick
to it if you wish. The piece I sold Clay (Rosina Vokes' manager),
I sold him outright, all rights to him, for $300 altho 'Beau Brummel' was then in rehearsal."

So G.P.B. began his short career as a playwright of the early
nineties. It was a time when everybody seemed to be writing a
play. In the preface to the *Art of Playwriting* (1890), Professor

Alfred Hennequin of the University of Michigan wrote: "There are *thousands* of plays written every year in this country." A similar observation occurred on the seventeenth of May of the following year, when the drama reviewer of the *Boston Transcript* said in the course of his comments upon a new play which Boston's own Mary Shaw had imported from Berlin: "Those who are in a position to be informed, know that there never was so much good dramatic work being done in America as at the present. Scores of young men are writing plays from the literary point of view, and struggling to be heard."

Like these thousands, G.P.B. was impressed by the sudden fame and fortune which Clyde Fitch had achieved. Hence most of the plays he wrote were one-act comedies, which he called "comediettas" — similar to the short plays which Fitch was then writing.

Perhaps the most characteristic of G.P.B.'s comediettas was *My Nihilist,* written during his winter abroad in 1891–92. This is the story of Henry Brooks, "25, society fellow — fine — handsome — slightly sarcastic. A good amateur actor," and Madge Hatton, "19, impressionable, given to idealizing — fine ideas, but really timid and loving." After attending a lecture on Siberia by George Kennan, they meet for tea at the apartment of Bostonian Mrs. Scones. Henry, having mentioned that he is on his way to a play rehearsal, teases Madge (who is excited about "Nihilism") concerning the growing incursion of women into the man's world of ideas and action. Shortly after Henry's exit, the doorbell rings and a wildly agitated Russian enters. His mistake is clarified as the women give him tea and he tells of his nihilist activities in Siberia. Fascinated by his sinister manner, Madge is unable to leave the apartment with Mrs. Scones, who deftly escapes for help in handling the obviously mad Russian. At the nihilist's menacing approach, Madge is about to scream, when the Russian turns into Henry Brooks — disguised by his costume for *A Russian Honeymoon.* Of course, Madge falls into Henry's arms. After love has clearly triumphed over Madge's militant "feminism," there is a fast curtain.

Of similar substance was *Havana Ponies,* a comedy of errors in a parish house which results when a letter concerning a box

47

of miniature cigars intended for Parson Emery, a vicar much like
Goldsmith's Mr. Primrose, falls into the hands of the parson's
wife. She thinks the "ponies" have something to do with race
tracks and "fast" women. After considerable confusion among
the ladies of the parish, all is brought to an amicable ending and
the curtain goes down on Parson Emery lighting one of the little
cigars.

G.P.B.'s most ambitious plays were two unnamed historical
tragedies, conceived in five acts and roughly executed, but never
completed. One concerned the tragic ambition of a partisan of
Mary, Queen of Scots; the other dealt with the downfall of Charles
D'Albert sieur de Luynes, rival of Richelieu. For the story of
Luynes, G.P.B. kept a large notebook of historical research from
which he prepared a scenario for Johnston Forbes-Robertson. The
purchase of Gustave Freytag's *Die Technik des Dramas* in Brunswick, September 1891, may not have been an unrelated event; for
G.P.B. annotated the volume thoroughly.

The following spring, while he studied at Friedrich Wilhelm
University, G.P.B. acted with a group of American students and
Mark Twain's daughters before the Clemens family and a party
of American tourists. After his return from Europe, G.P.B. continued his acting and playwriting in Cambridge.

Early in 1893, G.P.B. played the part of Dennis Heron in the
Cambridge Social Dramatic Club production of Pinero's *Lady
Bountiful*. First played without marked success by Forbes-Robertson in the preceding London season, the scene in which Dennis
rocks the cradle and talks to his baby as his wife lies dying was
so touching as G.P.B. played it that an old friend wrote him: "If
it were not for a certain young lady, I should say, 'Leave all and
follow the stage.' I believe I once before gave you that advice at
Seal Harbor, and it seems to me that you have made tremendous
strides since then."

During these years G.P.B.'s acting had progressed from farce
to domestic comedy, from such roles as Littleton Lynx, a law
student, in *Larkin's Love Letters*, to Mr. Pillicoddy, in John
Madison Morton's *Poor Pillicoddy*. During his second year as a
Harvard instructor, G.P.B. played Henry Spreadbrow, in *Sweet-
hearts*, at the Barnstable Theatre; later, he was Ernest Morton, a

The TRAGEDIE *of*

HAMLET

PRINCE OF DENMARKE

By VVilliam Shake-ſpeare

As it hath been ſundrie times publikely aĉted by the right honour-
able, the Lord Chamberlaine his ſeruants

𝔗𝔥𝔢 𝔑𝔞𝔪𝔢𝔰 𝔬𝔣 𝔱𝔥𝔢 𝔄𝔠𝔱𝔬𝔯𝔰 :

CLAVDIVS, *King of Denmarke* . . . . Ian Robertſon

HAMLET, { *ſon to the late* / *nephew to the preſent* } *King,* . . . . . Forbes Robertſon

FORTINBRAS, *Prince of Norwey* . . . . VVeſt Drayton

POLONIVS, *Lord Chamberlaine* . . . . Guy Lane

HORATIO, *friend to Hamlet* . . . . Arthur Harrold

LAERTES, *ſon to Polonius* . . . . Leon Quartermaine

ROSINCRANCE, ... N. Howard

GVILDENSTERNE, } *Courtiers,* { . . . . F. Bickley

OSRICKE, ... H. Beaumont

A PRIEST . . . . Morton Bennett

MARCELLVS, } *Officers,* { . . . . J. R. Ryan

BERNARDO, ... Leonard Howe

FRANCISCO, *a ſoldier* . . . . C. Kinnaird

REYNOLDO, *ſeruant to Polonius* . . . . S. Macdonald

FIRST PLAYER . . . . James J. Ryan

SECOND PLAYER . . . . S. T. Pearce

FIRST GRAVE-DIGGER . . . . Erneſt Coſham

SECOND GRAVE-DIGGER . . . . S. Thompſon

GHOST OF HAMLET'S FATHER . . . . C. Aubrey Smith

PLAYER QVEENE . . . . Auriol Lee

GERTRVDE, { *Queene of Denmarke,* / *Mother to Hamlet,* } . . . . . . Jennie A. Euſtace

OPHELIA, *daughter to Polonius* . . . . Gertrude Elliott

Lords, Ladies, Soldiers, Sailors, Meſſengers, and other Attendants
Scene — Elſinore

HTC

The 47 Workshop Company, 1916–17: **Mary Ball**, Rachel Butler, Willodean Chatterson, Ruth Chorpenning, Mary Ellis, Ruth Fielding, Frederica Gilbert, Doris Halman, Grace Harlow, Christine Hayes, Eleanor Hinkley, Vianna Knowlton, Charlotte Read, Lucy Wright, Russell Churchill, Norman Clark, Fred Hubbard, Edward Massey, Charles Putnam, Perceval Reniers, G. Rivera, Harding Scholle, James Seymour, W. Graydon Stetson, William Willson, and Mr. and Mrs. Roger Burnham

HTC

Sir Johnston Forbes-Robertson and company, farewell performance of *Hamlet*, Sanders Theatre, 1916

young doctor in Miss E. B. Tiffany's three-act comedy, *My Lady's Jester,* at the Brattle Theatre. Known as a "quick study," G.P.B. was more than once called upon by the Cambridge Social Dramatic Club to prevent the postponement of an opening night. Certainly his election to the executive committee of this club was not unrelated to his success as Dennis Heron.

After *Lady Bountiful,* he played the good Abbé in the club's production of *Abbé Constantin* and wrote a one-act farce for the club concerning his experience in Germany. This was favorably reviewed in a Boston paper:

The private theatricals at Brattle Hall . . . for the benefit of the Girls Friendly Society of Christ church, were very successful in every respect. Mr. G. P. Baker's farce, "The Pleasures of Travel," produced for the first time, is a very amusing sketch of the embarrassments of two travellers at a small railway station in the Harz, who, with a very limited stock of German and a phrase book, are endeavoring to get themselves and their baggage, including a very large tricycle, safely ticketed and checked for Vienna . . . The farce is exceedingly clever and reflects much credit upon Mr. Baker, who was called before the curtain at the end of the piece.

At the suggestion of Clyde Fitch, G.P.B. sent this play to Rosina Vokes, whose company specialized in one-act farces suitable for vaudeville billing. Her manager replied that although they thought the little farce exceedingly amusing, it was not suitable for their work. The farce then went to Felix Morris, who also had purchased skits from Fitch. But the play was again returned, this time with a comment which may have diagnosed the principal fault of G.P.B.'s playwriting. Morris observed that, clever as the little play was, it required the intelligence of a university audience to appreciate it.

Unfortunately for G.P.B.'s hope of achieving anything like Fitch's success, most of his dramatic experience had been genuinely avocational in its origin and remained amateur in its accomplishment. Failing to sell Felix Morris an adaptation of a French farce concerning the comic affairs of a doctor's office, he tried to interest the celebrated English actress Mrs. Kendal, Tom Robertson's sister, in *The Deed's Creature,* a serious treatment of the problems of an attractive kleptomaniac married to an eminent judge. Following this failure, he revised some of his

49

earlier attempts; but he apparently ceased to write new plays after 1895. Although he never sold a play to an actor, actress, or manager, he continued to send *Mistress Beatrice Cope* to various actresses with not a little promise of success until as late as 1902. By that time, however, he was much more concerned with the plays his students were bringing to him than with his own efforts.

As G.P.B.'s writing of plays declined, so did his acting. With one exception, he did no acting during 1895, 1896, and 1897 — years when he was seeing his books on argumentation and an edition of Shakespeare's *A Midsummer Night's Dream* through the press. On January 30, 1897, he played in the first performance of *Apples of Eden,* a comedietta by one of his Radcliffe students, Beulah Marie Dix.

In the last season of the century, G.P.B.'s acting as Percinet in Rostand's *Romancers* brought the following praise from a young man of discriminating taste who had studied English 14 and was now editing *The Architectural Review:*

North Easton
Massachusetts
3d May 1900

My dear George Baker:

           I have not yet forgotten, and I want to tell you, how much I enjoyed the "Romancers." Honestly and thoroughly enjoyed, from the beginning to the end, without intermission & without any qualification. It was delightful.

The play itself seemed to me charming, and, moreover, one which was exactly adapted for non-professional use — and I don't believe that any professional company, in this country at least, could have kept, as you kept, the high spirit of the thing, — the delicate, playful mock-seriousness which was its life. Professional realism would have murdered it. To call you and Miss Sherwood "professionally" good in that play would be an insult—you were better!

Thank you, sir, for a most delightful evening.

Sincerely yours,
Winthrop Ames

Miss Sherwood is now more generally known as Josephine Hull.

Even President Eliot's opinion of George as Percinet was commendatory. One of the cousins reported that Uncle Charles, upon leaving Brattle Hall, had said in his most serious and emphatic manner, "That is good acting. George was very fine indeed."

Throughout these years, G.P.B. took an active part in the Tavern Club theatricals for which Barrett Wendell had recruited him. Returning from his 1902 sabbatical year abroad, G.P.B. was welcomed home with a request that he take the part of Robert Louis Stevenson in the club's Christmas play. Said the Taverner in charge of the play about R.L.S., "There is really no one else who could either look it or do it."

His last important piece of acting was in the play he produced for the dedicatory exercises opening the auditorium of Radcliffe's Agassiz House in 1905. This was Josephine Preston Peabody's *Marlowe,* a play he had watched through its composition with a keen interest in its characterization of Kit Marlowe. When he played this part, G.P.B.'s rendition of the Elizabethan playwright was a success with even the Boston critics. The *Advertiser's* reviewer said that G.P.B. was easily the star of the evening and considered his interpretation of the tragedy and comedy in Marlowe's personality a remarkably versatile feat. The *Journal* declared that it was "in every way an entire success." The *Transcript* reported that "Professor Baker gave a fine picture of the bold and fiery Marlowe, acting with a noticeable reserve that added to the effectiveness of the character," and called the whole performance "an unqualified success." Perhaps it was in some measure due to this success that the author wrote G.P.B. from London in June 1907, that Laurence Irving and Sir Johnston Forbes-Robertson were considering the play for the approaching season.

During these years, G.P.B.'s acting had been something more than a diversion. He had practiced it as an art which rewarded him with the satisfactions an artist desires. Such had not been his experience with writing, and playwriting had proved an even greater frustration when Thornton Ware came to him in 1893 for assistance in his own ambition to write plays. Satisfied that the writing of plays was not to be his artistic métier, G.P.B. was ready to teach what he knew about such matters.

Ware, but a few days younger than G.P.B., and so crippled

that he could not go to school as a regular student, now wished to enter Harvard. During 1894, while G.P.B. prepared Ware for Harvard, teacher and pupil jointly copyrighted a play. In 1895, Ware enrolled as a special student in G.P.B.'s English 14, along with Winthrop Ames and Edward Knoblock, who were also studying the old drama with playwriting in mind. Other members of this class were A. E. Benson, P. W. Long, J. E. Spingarn, E. E. Stoll, J. S. Tatlock, and A. H. Thorndike. The following year, Ware repeated the course, joining Jules Eckert Goodman in a further extension of the course to the purposes of playwriting.

One of G.P.B.'s earliest students of playwriting, Ware was his only collaborator in the writing of plays. The exact nature of this collaboration is not clear, but it is more than likely that Ware tinkered with G.P.B.'s unsuccessful plays. It is a matter of record that they jointly copyrighted three plays over a period of seven years: *The Mills of God*, 1894; *The Revolving Wedge*, 1896; and *Office Hours from 1 to 3*, 1901. In this time G.P.B. copyrighted but one play as solely his own. This was *Mistress Beatrice Cope*, adapted in 1891 and copyrighted, a decade after its composition, on the same day as the last of the Ware-Baker collaborations.

The Revolving Wedge, the only published play with which G.P.B.'s name is associated, was billed as "A Cambridge Thanksgiving. A Farce in One Act by Thornton M. Ware and George P. Baker" when first performed at Brattle Hall. In this performance, G.P.B. played the part of Captain Dolan of the Cambridge police, a role for which he received the following commendation and criticism:

Boston
1 Dec '95

Dear Baker

   . . . The play last night was distinctly successful — not least for your acting. There wasn't a trace of yourself in Capt. Dolan . . . The first three quarters of the play, though, is too "talky." The dialogue, which was admirably natural, was a bit prolix & too natural to be sparkling. In general, the weak point of the composition is lack of dramatic — or perhaps rather stage effect. The entrances & exits are ineffective. Slight emphasis on them as *situations* is orthodox in farce; & gives animation. In the matter of character, the work is excellent — the best being old Martin — a perfectly true type, sketched with capital restrained humor.

Sincerely yours,
Barrett Wendell

When performed as *The Revolving Wedge* in Belmont a year later, the printed programme attributed the play to Ware and did not mention Baker. Yet G.P.B.'s hand in the action and in the character of Martin, a Cantabrigian not unlike Bostonian George Apley, is clearly evident. Here, in rough outline, is the sort of domestic comedy which G.P.B. urged such later students as Eugene O'Neill and Philip Barry to find in the America immediately about them.

In later years, G.P.B. was silent about his playwriting. Since he did not act in Cambridge after 1910, except for one or two minor parts in Workshop productions, and because his later dramatic writing was confined to pageants, G.P.B.'s years as an actor and writer of plays were gradually forgotten. After his death, his own class memorial styled him — as did most of the press reports: "never a playwright, actor, or producer."

xv   A DRAMATIC LIBRARY FOR AMERICA

WHEN G.P.B. ARRIVED IN LONDON IN THE SUMMER OF 1891, one of his first points of business was to see Havelock Ellis, for whose Mermaid Series he had already begun an edition of Brome's *Antipodes*. In the course of these discussions Ellis informed him that the publisher of the series wished to retire from the praiseworthy but somewhat unprofitable enterprise. By December, G.P.B. was exploring the possibility of assuming the editorship of the series for some American publisher.

For here, in this excellent series of texts, he saw precisely the instrument for his own scholarly and editorial talents. America lacked any such native library of texts for the study of the great plays of the English language, and certainly some good but inexpensive library of plays was necessary to the university studies of the drama which were prerequisite to an educated American theatre audience. Something of what G.P.B. had in mind had also, during the summer of 1864, been attempted by James Russell Lowell and the Boston publishing firm of Little, Brown & Company; but the first volume of Lowell's editions of the Old Dramatists never matured beyond the proof sheets now in the Harvard Library. When Lowell, after some forty-four years of reading the old plays which G.P.B. now proposed to edit, read aloud sections of these works to his Lowell Institute audience in 1887, he apparently read from Dodsley's *Old Plays* and the equally British editions of Alexander Dyce. However, G.P.B.'s project of an American continuation of the Mermaid Series was not even so successful as Lowell's volume. An exploratory offer of a thousand pounds, made through the good offices of Havelock Ellis, was not enough to secure the transfer of the series to America.

Yet this failure did not diminish G.P.B.'s desire to edit an American series of the old dramas. In 1894, when his edition of Lyly's *Endymion* appeared, the commendation which that volume earned encouraged G.P.B. in the hope that other volumes might follow. Joel Spingarn told him that it might be set up as a model of its kind. Praise also came from George Lyman Kittredge, whose standards were already shaping the course of American scholarship:

> I hasten to offer my warmest congratulations on so thoroughly and scholarly a piece of work. I have learnt a great deal from it already and expect to learn a good deal more from it before I've exhausted it. Such things as this make the studies of the British Englishmen particularly pallid . . . I have only one regret — that the book, with its masterly introduction isn't in *my* series instead of in Holt's. Your command of the details of your subject is amazing.

At the same time, from Italy, Barrett Wendell was writing a letter of a somewhat different tone concerning G.P.B.'s scholarship. "I am," Wendell wrote on the twentieth of December, "overwhelmed with facts." Then he hastened to the point:

> You know me well enough, though, to understand how eagerly I long for such a type of scholarship as shall not only possess the minute accuracy which is now the fashion, but also vivify its facts with a bold constructive imagination which shall not fear to state its faith. Facts & imagination must be kept apart, of course, and not confused. But no really final work can be done without both.

Imagination you had in the old days. You have been right, perhaps, in checking it. Professionally you are certainly stronger for this work than you would have been for work of the kind which I happen to think humanly better. I heartily hope, though, that you will not end with work like this. Add to this painfully earned power the inborn power you had before; & the work which shall come will be better than either worth the doing.

Neither was G.P.B.'s publisher pleased with the Lyly volume, which sold but 188 copies in the eighteen months following its publication. To G.P.B.'s inquiry about further editions of the Elizabethan drama, the reply was the cheerless statement that the number of colleges giving courses in the minor Elizabethan drama could be counted on the fingers of one hand. Nevertheless, the publisher was interested in another sort of book, one which should deal with the history and technique of the drama. Such a volume would sell.

However, G.P.B. could not afford to do something which might not advance him toward a Harvard professorship. For he now had two sons: John Hopkinson Baker, born June 30, 1894, and Edwin Osborne Baker, born February 21, 1896. So, while he thought of an American series which should surpass Havelock Ellis' dramatic texts, G.P.B. revised and enlarged his *Principles of Argumentation,* a work in which President Eliot was interested.

If G.P.B. had never written anything else, his *Principles of Argumentation* would have made him famous. This compendium of rhetoric and logic made him something of a Petrus Ramus to the booming business culture at the turn of the century which eagerly sought such handbooks of persuasion. Indeed, it was in no small way responsible for the growth of two collegiate phenomena of the early twentieth century: "intercollegiate debating" and the "Department of Speech." Meanwhile, he saw his edition of *A Midsummer Night's Dream* through the press.

Sometime during the spring of 1900, G.P.B. was approached by the publisher D. C. Heath with the suggestion that he might be interested in organizing the dramatic volumes of a projected series of scholarly editions of literary classics, already under the direction of Edward M. Brown, of the University of Cincinnati. By midsummer the preliminary discussions of policy were nearly complete and the series had been given a name. It is more than likely that this name, "The Belles-Lettres Series," was a gesture of homage to Longfellow's successor at Harvard in the office of Professor of Belles-Lettres, James Russell Lowell.

The series, which soon appeared to be dominated by G.P.B.'s efforts, was divided into a number of sections. Brown was responsible for "English Literature from Its Beginning to the Year 1100," and G.P.B. had the general editorship of "The English Drama from Its Beginning to the Present Day." Three other sections, under the editorial supervision of Ewald Flügel, C. W. Herford, and Richard Burton, were added before 1917, when G.P.B. saw the last volume under his supervision through the press. During these years, G.P.B. played a dynamic part in the publication of twenty-three volumes — two-thirds the entire series.

In a general way, he attempted to articulate his dramatic volumes with those of Havelock Ellis. Thus it was mainly to secure the best editors for the volumes he had in mind that G.P.B. and Christina, who was expecting her third child, left Cambridge for a sabbatical year abroad in the summer of 1901. In August, they were in London when Myles Pierce was born; two years later, they named their last child, George Pierce, Jr.

By mid-October, G.P.B. thought he had persuaded Henry Arthur Jones to edit a volume. Though this arrangement fell through because of the playwright's other commitments, the acquaintance thus begun grew to a warm and lasting friendship. However, G.P.B. had better luck with Austin Dobson, who agreed to edit two plays of Oliver Goldsmith and said that his young friend's suggestions to editors were so clear that they required no explanations.

More than a few friendly suggestions now arrived from American scholars about this business. William Lyon Phelps inquired what he might do, and Henry Beers hoped to see some of the latest things in cheap shape for his dramatic courses — Bernard Shaw's comedies, a play or so of Pinero, something by Henry Arthur Jones, and a few of the older pieces, such as Gilbert's *Pygmalion and Galatea,* or Morton's *Box and Cox,* or even those brief farces which had made the opening and closing curtains of their own childhood so delightful.

Although G.P.B. made no immediate provision for the "latest things" in his series, it was from a mutual interest in the contemporary London and Parisian theatre that his new friendship with William Archer grew. When these interests took the Bakers to Paris in November 1901, Archer joined them for a couple of evenings at the theatre on his way to Rome to see Duse in D'Annunzio's new play. Archer wished to see Antoine's theatre, he wrote G.P.B., but didn't much hanker after Sudermann. Still, if G.P.B. and Christina had seen it and thought he ought to, Archer was content. Undoubtedly, there were other evenings of this sort, for G.P.B. was already excited about Antoine's experimental theatre.

Meanwhile, the editors G.P.B. brought into his project made the series a truly international undertaking. However, the speed with which the first volume of G.P.B.'s section approached publication seemed inversely proportional to the eagerness with which he awaited the event. As late as the following summer he was still in correspondence with Austin Dobson over a point which obstructed the publication of the first drama volume. As a Victorian, Dobson wished to omit from a text which would have obvious educational employment all such oaths as "By the Lord," "Lord," and "Lud"; G.P.B., as an enlightened modern, insisted upon a faithful rendition of authentic readings. To settle the matter, Dobson assumed responsibility for only the introduction and biographical and critical matter, leaving the credit for collating the text to G.P.B. Thus the title of this first volume read: *The Good Natur'd Man and She Stoops to Conquer, by Oliver Goldsmith; the Introduction and Biographical and Critical Material by Austin Dobson, LL.D. (Edinburgh); and the Text Collated by George P. Baker, A.B.*

The second volume, also published in 1903, was Felix Schellings' edition of *Eastward Hoe* and the *Alchemist*. By 1905, a half dozen similar titles had been published and G.P.B. was firmly established at home and abroad as one of the leading authorities on dramatic literature. Some time later, in congratulating G.P.B. upon another volume, Schelling wrote: "As I recollect the thoroughness and unwearing care which you bestowed upon the work which I had the pleasure of doing with you, I am filled with admiration for the high interpretation which you put upon the duties of general editor."

With characteristic enthusiasm, G.P.B. augmented the series, undeterred by Heath's anguished complaints that current sales did not justify the publication of more volumes. By the winter of 1906, the publisher told G.P.B. he was lying awake nights wondering how he could sell all the little books. Nevertheless, G.P.B. drove on toward his dream of a dramatic library for America. And it is well that he did, for such useful books made possible the widespread serious study of the drama which American club-women and members of the Drama League pursued during the decade before the first World War. Thus was the way prepared for the literate audiences and artistic plays of the twenties and thirties.

XVI   ELIZABETHAN EXPERIMENT

THROUGHOUT THE HISTORY OF THE HARVARD *Monthly*, G.P.B. kept an active interest in its affairs. Thus there was probably little surprise in the Yard at one of the magazine's December 1894 editorials on a theme with which G.P.B. was already identified. The editorial said, with a glance at G.P.B.'s Mermaid Club and at his lectures in English 14, that it might be as desirable to revive the character of the Elizabethan stage in some play of this more modern period as it was to present the character of the classic stage in the current revival of Terence's *Phormio* at Harvard's Sanders Theatre. It might even be of philological interest to see how nearly Harvardians could reproduce the Elizabethan pronunciation.

This interest in the archaeology of the Western European stage, although the latest thing among students of Elizabethan literature elsewhere, had been active at Harvard for a dozen years. In 1881, when Sanders Theatre became a classic amphitheatre and the actors pronounced their lines from *Oedipus* in Greek, a similar experiment with *Hamlet* was performed in London by the forerunners of the Elizabethan Stage Society. Four years later, G.P.B. took part in a production of *Julius Caesar* on the bare stage of

Sanders Theatre. The current production of Terence, and the *Harvard Monthly's* desire to see a revival of the plays of Thomas Heywood, Ben Jonson, or Beaumont and Fletcher, were but extensions of an established antiquarian interest in the stage.

In 1895, when G.P.B. was the only member of the Harvard English department then teaching the plays of Ben Jonson, he learned that students at the American Academy of Dramatic Arts in New York were soon to give the first revival in over a century of Jonson's *Epicoene, or the Silent Woman* and were willing to perform at Harvard. Quickly accepting the opportunity, the English department appointed G.P.B., Professor Child, and Professor Kittredge to take care of the Cambridge production. Of the purposes of this committee, G.P.B. wrote:

The committee at once took as its aim, as far as possible, to turn Sanders Theatre, on the 20th of March, into a theatre of 1609–10, the date of the first performance of "The Silent Woman." This aim subdivided into three tasks: to make the stage of Sanders Theatre into a strictly Elizabethan stage; to arrange such changes in the text as modern taste might require, and train the actors to give the comedy to the best advantage; and to drill Harvard students to represent an Elizabethan audience.

In executing the first of these tasks, the committee appears to have been entirely unaware that two years before a group of Londoners had converted the Royalty Theatre, Soho, into an imperfect imitation of the Fortune Playhouse for a performance of *Measure for Measure.* Believing that they were doing something for the first time, the Harvard committee consulted with a New York architect, but depended chiefly upon an Elizabethan drawing of the interior of the Swan theatre and upon William Henslowe's contract specifications for the Fortune. Because of the nature of Sanders Theatre, a combination of some of the features of both public and private Elizabethan theatres was unavoidable. Nevertheless, the reconstruction did provide for a pit for the "groundlings" and presented what appears to have been the first authentic Elizabethan platform stage in America. Thus began the breaking down of the proscenium stage in this country, perhaps the most revolutionary technical event in the history of the American theatre.

59

What, G.P.B. asked, was the result of all this?

In the first place, students of the drama in general and the Elizabethan drama in particular have had a chance to contrast, under proper conditions, the widely divergent methods of Shakespeare and Ben Jonson . . . Moreover, the play showed how little any but the simplest setting is needed in most plays . . . In an Elizabethan comedy the character-drawing or the situation filled the hearer's mind. A few hints as to the scene made him supply the rest . . . Were our minds not so sterile from the present abuse of scenery, our imaginations would respond as readily.

The staging of the play also provided something of a literary laboratory for testing certain ideas about the Elizabethan public theatre. One area of investigation concerned the function of the "hut" over the tiring house indicated in the Fortune plans and its possible relation to the use of "painted cloths" for scenic effects. G.P.B. summarized the committee's conclusions concerning their experiments: "They do not believe in curtains before 1616, for they could not have been possible on a stage like that of the *Swan*. How the scenes and acts were indicated, what the backing of the balcony was, just where the fops and pages sat, — all these are clearer."

The occasion was thus of more than passing importance, and G.P.B.'s part in the matter is clearly related to the history of his own ideas. Here, for the first time, he became involved in the experimental use of a theatre for the testing of dramatic ideas. Here, perhaps, was the beginning of his own laboratory use of the 47 Workshop stage.

Interest in the matter was more than local. A few years later, when William Archer was in New York to deliver a lecture on an American national theatre, he heard about the Harvard revival and asked G.P.B. for photographs of the reconstructed Elizabethan stage. Presumably these pictures were taken to England, along with the copy of G.P.B.'s account of the experiment which Archer also had requested. In any event, there appears to have been a considerable international acquaintance with Harvard's Elizabethan stage long before the work of the Elizabethan Stage Society received general attention.

Not until 1904, however, did Harvard again see so elaborate

a reconstruction of Elizabethan stage conditions. Meanwhile, the year after *The Silent Woman,* the Delta Upsilon fraternity began its remarkable series of Elizabethan revivals which continued as an annual affair until the first World War brought it to an end. Although G.P.B. had no official function in these fraternity revivals, he was frequently consulted in problems related to their production. In 1910, when James Bryant Conant was a member of the Delta Upsilon cast for *The Merry Devil of Edmonton,* the fraternity's secretary formally thanked G.P.B. for his "advice and aid" and his "estimable criticism."

One of the most successful of the Delta Upsilon revivals was a production of *Fortune by Land and Sea* at the Bijou Theatre in Boston, March 25, 1899. For this, G.P.B. gave a special lecture in Sever Hall on the play and its authors. His interest arose not only from his attention to the play in English 14 but from the fact that two of his Radcliffe students, Miss Beulah Marie Dix and Miss Pauline Wiggin, had done, as he said in this public lecture, the latest acceptable criticism of it and other works of Heywood and Rowley.

During the decade which followed the revival of Jonson's *Silent Woman,* the department of English appeared to forget its original success in a field which the Delta Upsilon fraternity preempted at home and which was soon assigned to William Poel and the Elizabethan Stage Society abroad. However, the idea of another such experiment remained fresh with G.P.B. It became a bit greener each year that he lectured to schools and colleges on "London and its Theatres in Shakespeare's Time." In various letters which he sent during 1904 to those educational organizations which he thought might care to pay his fee of fifty dollars, G.P.B. thus described his lecture on Shakespeare's theatre:

It is made from parts of two lectures I give each year in a course at Harvard College, and is illustrated with some 40–50 slides of maps, buildings, and portraits, some of them from very rare views in London collections. I aim to make very clear just the conditions under which Shakespeare produced his plays and to what extent the plays were affected by the conditions. The lecture has been stimulating to college and high school students not only in New England but also in Indiana and Illinois, where I gave it last February.

His lecture notes on "Shakespeare as a Dramatist," probably first drawn for a Radcliffe 1896–97 course, show the basic ideas concerning these conditions and Shakespeare's dramatic technique which he published in 1907 as *The Development of Shakespeare as a Dramatist*. In introducing this lecture on the master's technique, G.P.B. quoted Shakespeare's twenty-ninth sonnet, the one which refers to Shakespeare "Desiring this man's art, and that man's scope." Then G.P.B. remarked: "There is the secret — an artistic conscience . . . But he keeps flexible . . . Attains, develops, departs from technique. The greatest technician I know."

In notes for a later public lecture, "The Educational Value of Playing Shakespeare," G.P.B. expressed the importance he attached to Shakespeare's dramatic technique. "This is not merely our best poetic drama," he said, "it is, also, standard for dramatic technique, in what permanently differentiates drama."

So he worked steadily to educate his countrymen in the basic values which an American drama would have to find for its own techniques. In this work he was not limited to audiences of college and high school students, for his mail brought questions from others who, as well as he, were in a position to influence popular concern with these values. A query from the department of English at Stanford University in 1902 is perhaps typical of the assistance which academic leaders sought from him. Relayed through G.P.B.'s former student, Raymond M. Alden, the Stanford request was for information concerning points raised by the picture of the Harvard Elizabethan stage in G.P.B.'s edition of *A Midsummer Night's Dream*. More specifically, they wished light on the staging of *The Knight of the Burning Pestle* with practical historical accuracy.

Among professional literary critics, there was a similar curiosity to understand the historical bases of dramatic technique. In a note to G.P.B. on June 15, 1903, Brander Matthews wrote that a friend had an interesting paper in the first number of *Modern Philology* on the influence of the Elizabethan theatre upon the structure of Shakespeare's plays. Moreover, Matthews said, he hoped some day to know enough to tackle the subject himself. If any word characterized such thinking in these days, it was "technique."

However, G.P.B. had gone so far with his own studies in the matter that he wished to test some of his conclusions. While in England in 1901–02, he had become acquainted with the work of the Elizabethan Stage Society through William Poel's production of *Henry V* at the University of London. Shortly thereafter, G.P.B. wrote to G. L. Kittredge, the chairman of the committee which had charge of the old *Silent Woman* set, to inquire about the possibility of using it again. The following year, G.P.B. asked the English actor Forbes-Robertson if he would play *Hamlet* at Harvard on his American tour. His plan was to produce *Hamlet* on an Elizabethan stage in Sanders Theatre.

When Forbes-Robertson replied that G.P.B.'s proposal was flattering and that he should like it of all things, the idea went before the next meeting of the department of English. G.P.B. proposed that the old Elizabethan set be rebuilt to conform with the best information then available about Elizabethan theatre architecture. When the matter was clearly in his hands, G.P.B. called for professional advice upon the chairman of the department of Architecture, Professor H. Langford Warren, who had recently designed the new Baker home at 195 Brattle Street in Cambridge, along a section of what was still occasionally referred to as "Tory Row."

Professor Warren examined the contracts for the building of the Fortune and Hope theatres and investigated recent studies of the Elizabethan stage before he drew up the plans for rebuilding the old set. The result was as near an approximation of Shakespeare's theatre as conditions in 1904 permitted. Until the reproduction in the Folger Shakespeare Memorial Library of the Fortune Theatre, now widely known for the remarkable televised productions upon its stage, there was probably nothing anywhere quite like G.P.B.'s Elizabethan stage at Harvard.

That it was not merely an academic matter without effect upon the popular theatre is clear from the note America's leading actor, John Drew, sent G.P.B. on the second of April, just before what promised to be an important event. Drew, much interested in the Elizabethan *Hamlet* which G.P.B. would be directing on the Sanders stage the following week, regretted that he was committed to act at the National Theatre in Washington for those nights. However, he asked G.P.B. to send him an account of the matter, for which he wished a very great success.

This, of course, G.P.B. was glad to do, for Drew represented upon the American stage the same high standards as the English knew in Forbes-Robertson, another gentleman and scholar.

The production, according to G.P.B.'s article in the subsequent *Shakespeare Jahrbuch,* was intended to raise as many mooted points as possible; and he regarded it as distinctly another experiment. In this spirit, he explained, he had examined the texts of some two hundred Elizabethan plays in quarto and folio to answer questions twentieth-century actors asked as they trod his sixteenth-century stage. One of the practical results of the experiment was an alteration of Forbes-Robertson's handling of the Ghost scene in *Hamlet:*

The set was carefully arranged so as to show markedly the three divisions for which Elizabethan plays seem to call — "upper stage," "front stage," and "inner stage" . . . Real arras hung from the "upper stage" to the stage proper, giving through the centre and round the ends three entrances. Behind this, of course, Polonius was killed. In the upper stage, the "above" of Elizabethans, the Ghost appeared in the scene of "Hamlet" with his mother, and here the players gave "The Murder of Gonzago." When the Ghost, in mail, glided across the grey-brown background of painted cloth, in the somewhat shadowed upper stage, he seemed only a face. The first night Mr. Robertson was so startled by the effectiveness of the Ghost as nearly to miss his lines, and after the regular performance he declared that hereafter on the regular stage the Ghost in his *Hamlet* should get his ghostliness by dressing in tones which will shade into the color of the set. The effect was incomparably better than any Ghost with lime-light or electric bulb.

However, the boldest part of the whole experiment was G.P.B.'s attempt to test the various theories about the disposition of curtains upon the Elizabethan stage, a controversy which he reduced to the question: "where were the curtains hung, under the gallery or under the heavens?" His answer, derived from historical research and experimental action upon the stage itself, was that curtains must have closed the space between the pillars of the original Fortune Theatre, "under the heavens." Furthermore, he closed the space between each pillar and the rear wall with additional curtains. The effect, bound to create unfavorable criticism, was that of a highly flexible "box set," capable of many of the best accomplishments of twentieth-century stage settings, which could, by simply drawing the curtains to the pillars, immediately achieve the unlimited spatiality of the sixteenth-century platform stage.

G.P.B. believed that there was ample historical evidence to support his brilliant intuition of the technical continuity from sixteenth- to twentieth-century stage, but he defended his curtains as practical rather than historical realities:

> Their advantage, whether high or low, is that they arrange adequately for the many "curtain" scenes in the old plays, that they permit changes without the disillusionizing lugging to and fro of properties by stage-keepers, etc., necessarily employed when the curtains are supposed, as in Mr. W. J. Lawrence's article in Englische Studien, to hang where the arras did in the *Hamlet* revival.

The most important result of the experiment was not, however, the technicalities of curtain management. It was the freedom of the production from the trammels of the proscenium stage and the stifling enclosure of the box set at the same time that it achieved the dramatic values of those very devices. The simple truth with which G.P.B. closed his account of the *Hamlet* revival became one of the tenets of his 47 Workshop:

> Everything on the Elizabethan stage centered attention on the actor as the exponent of the dramatist's ideas: it focused where we dissipate; it subordinated everything to the play itself; too often we call attention first to the setting, second to the actor — and let the play take care of itself.

Without a sharp focus upon the play itself, there could be no hope for a great American play; for the American theatre gave almost exclusive attention to players and spectacle. Some startling change which should throw the limelight upon the artistic purposes of the author was needed.

Soon after this very successful experiment, the Harvard department of English, by unanimous vote, conveyed to G.P.B. its most cordial thanks for the energy, the learning, and the skill with which he had arranged the performances. His own estimate of the matter's general importance shows, when contrasted with the role of dramatics in the American university curriculum today, that an important cultural advance began with these performances at Sanders Theatre. With characteristic emphasis G.P.B. summed up:

First, Hamlet had never previously, in America, been given before a purely Academic audience. Secondly, it had never been given on a reproduction of the Elizabethan stage. Consequently, in the third place, the performance threw much light on recently much mooted questions as to the characteristics of that stage. Finally, it was the first time that an American college or university had invited an English-speaking actor to appear before it not as a lecturer but as an actor.

Thus there was more than a little irony in the request for help which came from England the following year. William Poel, who was subsequently to become famous for the very thing G.P.B. had already accomplished with Elizabethan revivals, wrote to G.P.B. as the 1905 academic year began. Sidney Lee had suggested that he write G.P.B. about an American visit to promote an English project to build an Elizabethan playhouse after the model of the Old Globe. This, Poel explained, was a matter of some difficulty in England, where he found an apathetic public and the theatrical profession against the idea.

Upon the same advice, Poel had communicated with G.P.B.'s old friend, William J. Rolfe, the Shakespearean scholar, who in turn informed G.P.B. on the twenty-ninth of September:

I have written to him that Harvard is the place, and that you are the man, to introduce his project in this country. I have referred to your work in bringing out old English plays here, and to your excellent lectures on the Elizabethan stage . . . While I am writing, let me congratulate you on your well-earned promotion at Harvard. I have wondered that it did not come long ago.

Thus 1905, the year of his second and revised edition of his *Principles of Argumentation*, saw G.P.B. elevated to a professorship largely because of the eminence this book of rhetoric and the one the year before, his *Forms of Public Address*, had gained. While his colleagues and countrymen gave him his full reward for this work, it remained for outsiders and strangers to value him for what he valued most. This irony was not to diminish with the passing years.

XVII PUBLIC LECTURES — "IS NOT THIS
THE BEGINNING OF AN EPOCH?"

BY 1899, WHEN BARRETT WENDELL SUGGESTED THAT his friend ought to give some Lowell Lectures, G.P.B. had already been talking about his hobby for ten years. One of the earliest of his addresses, "The Present Condition of the English Drama," belongs to 1889, the remarkable year of the first English production of Ibsen's *Doll's House*. During the mid-nineties he gave a talk at Smith College on Ibsen and the Ibsenites which he called, "The Descent of the New Vandals." At this time Wellesley and Radcliffe audiences heard his "The Development of Drama in the Nineteenth Century" and "The American Drama To-Day." At the turn of the century, he was already delivering his standard lecture, "The Modern Drama," to various community audiences. His objective in these lectures was, he said, "To treat the drama not merely as a literary form, but as a force in modern life, as a reflex of the thought and conduct of the time."

Knowing very well the social and individual values of seeing, acting, and writing plays, he believed all great drama to be something akin to folk art. The secret of the Elizabethan drama was that it entertained and informed: "Seeing the *entertaining*, this audience had its newspaper, its magazine, its club talk: its literature." The theatre must amuse, he said, but our idea of amusement has coarsened; our audiences need to be educated to seek in the theatre not a sedative or excitant, but an art to be respected and admired. In 1899 he told a Cambridge audience what he would soon be saying across the land: "From 1830 until 1885 or 1890 the drama was nothing but the king's jester. From this we need not believe that it can never be anything more. It must be taken in hand, remodelled and readjusted to the conditions of this and the next century."

In this transition, the new forms which were evolving must come alive from the vitals of society; any artificial separation of the drama from its national culture retarded a natural growth. The

67

most important fact in the preceding two centuries of dramatic evolution, G.P.B. believed, was the sharp distinction which had grown "between the drama, which is the acting drama, and the drama which is written by literary men." This split, he observed, had its contemporary counterpart in the struggle between the so-called "Ethical Dramatists," or followers of Dumas fils, Augier, and Ibsen, and those whom G.P.B. called "Utilitarians" — followers of Eugene Scribe who regard "merely the pleasure to be produced." Each group, in its misunderstanding of the social mass, was wrong; and G.P.B.'s advice to the playwright at the turn of the century was a catholic caution:

> Let him recognize above all that some of the instincts of this great mass of people may be truer than his own, and that in what they want and what they like beautified and sublimated by the touch of genius may lie great art. The great public is untrained; it may be dull; it may be vulgar; but it is not wholly wrong.

A literary awakening in the drama would come, he thought, not when the masses read plays but when they experienced an intellectual awakening and growth comparable to that which had occurred among the readers of novels during the nineteenth century who learned to demand truth as well as entertainment. In a general way, G.P.B.'s life work was a succession of attempts to integrate the arts of the theatre with the sound instincts of the social mass. It is important to remember that he began his work not with the playwright or the actor, but with the audience. He never had a program for playwrights; his proselytizing was always with the audience.

Thus his lectures during the 1890's made a social analysis of the state of the American theatre. Concerning this he made three points: that there was no American drama; that this condition was the fault of both playwrights and public; and that the hope for an American drama lay in the efforts of his listeners to create a demand for art as well as entertainment upon the American stage.

Of the state of the American drama he said in 1899: "There is no American drama and never has been. We are now just about where we were in the development of the novel when Sydney Smith sneered at us and compared us with the Australians."

68

What America lacked was inspiring audiences ready to insist "that drama is an art; that acting is an art." For, G.P.B. explained: "A great drama will produce great actors, but not great actors a great drama. Actors may live on the past — a drama to be vital must spring from the life of the people and be instinct with its ideas, ideals, traditions and dreams."

Here G.P.B. approached his major idea: that the best work of the theatre is art which is relevant to the life and spirit of the people. Thus he was careful to point out that the drama of Ibsen and his continental followers was not suited to America's needs, that the Shakespearean or classic mold was not the form for the great American plays of the future. These, rather, would grow from farce and melodrama, close to the hearts of the people. "All the tendencies of the last part of the nineteenth century," he said in these days, "are distinctly farce."

Sometime in 1895 G.P.B. jotted down the following notes concerning the contemporary drama and his high hope for the future of a national audience "apparently satisfied with the most inartistic productions." He asked:

Is not this the beginning of an *epoch?* Young men turning to the drama — the growing interest everywhere — the discussion of new plays. *What we need is the skilled dramatic portrayal of life from a close study of it,* plays good in characterization, in plot, in dialogue, that shall not, as at present, assume that only what is unpleasant is essentially dramatic and shall treat the unpleasant only as an incident, not as the only interest. That Pinero, Jones, and Grundy — even Wilde — are leading such a movement, I believe; that young men are standing ready to help, I believe; that today there is a better chance for a literary drama that shall treat life as it is than at any time since the Elizabethans, I begin to hope.

Four years earlier, as he sailed for Europe, he had thought of what he might bring back that should help America's "coming drama." In a notebook which he filled during the crossing, he wrote:

Why not a paper on our coming drama and how to get at it? Develop ideas of last lecture at Annex. Study Elizabethans for conditions of their theatre. Show that with them dramatists must first of all interest—that Beaumont and Fletcher and Webster were more popular than Shakespeare — that criticism was a later development and that with its spirit came liking for Shakespeare. Show from this that by painting life truthfully, realistically, interestingly he must interest. Not in moralizing plays, not in plays full of purpose, but in plays of life, in something above melodrama, yet related lies hope (See Archer) (See also Howells in this). Show that it is the honest pictures in successful plays that do this . . . Illustrate from abroad. Perhaps they can help America. Develop for Atlantic or Scribner's.

Repeatedly he scribbled his admonition to the future: "Let it be a good acting play."

In this hope, he studied the German drama during the winter of 1892 and wrote for the *Atlantic Monthly* the article which he had sketched on shipboard. His "A Glance at the Berlin Stage," though never published, should have impressed Horace Scudder with its forecast of a success in America for a new kind of play in Germany: "that play that is a study of contemporary life, that dealing especially with the bourgeoisie and working classes — to put the difference briefly, if roughly, the world of Augier rather than Octave Feuillet."

Indeed, G.P.B.'s remarks upon the future of the German drama in 1892 anticipated much of his attitude toward the American drama at the end of the century. If American equivalents could be substituted for the following German references, the sentiments would agree substantially with what G.P.B. said about the American stage in 1900.

I think anyone watching the Berlin stage to-day will feel that amid many discouragements and through many failures German Drama is coming home from imitations of the French to a close, careful study of German types and manners, from *The Maid of Orleans,* from *Tell* and *Egmont* to German history itself; that young writers are training, through their very failures, for successful work later; that actors and actresses fitted for all ordinary demands are developing for the parts that may yet be written.

In 1900, as he looked ahead into the twentieth century, G.P.B. prepared a lecture which drew the main lines of the shape of things to come. As far as America was concerned, he said in "The Drama of the Next Decade," these outlines were to be discerned in the work of Pinero and Jones:

Mr. Pinero, it seems to me — and Mr. Jones — are working towards a comedy of manners. It is these two forms — what the French call Drame, and the Comedy of manners — or even more probably a blending of the two which I believe will be the dominant dramatic writing of the near future. It meets the existing conditions perfectly and is the natural compromise between the present desires of the dramatist and the instincts of the public. For its creation complete understanding of technique is needed. For its presentation, dramatic writers of literary feeling and training are needed. It depends for its effect upon close critical study of the time, upon the possession by the dramatist of high standards of conduct and thought. In it the dramatists can paint the problems of society as much as they like, but they must not preach. They may scathe society as much as they wish, but the situations, the characters, the dialogue must be seen to be of chief importance . . . If, then, the dramatists of the present day, working toward a comedy of manners, will benefit by all the century has to teach them, they should produce a comedy that in accuracy of characterization, in nicety of phrase, in brilliancy of wit, should equal the comedy of Congreve, Wycherly, and Van Brugh. It should surpass that drama in technique and, above all, in humanity.

Anyone who hoped for a native American drama, he continued, could learn much by studying how the English audiences of 1587, apparently limited to the rant and bloodshed of Kyd's *Spanish Tragedy,* were able after 1600 to appreciate *Hamlet, Lear,* and *Othello.* The years from 1887 to 1900 in American drama might prove more than a facile parallel.

As G.P.B. considered these matters, he usually asked his audience, "What can we do to hasten the coming of this new comedy, and what to make it, when it comes, as perfect as possible?" This question, and its answer, thus grew to be the heart of his two most frequently delivered public lectures on the contemporary drama: "The Theatre as a Social Force" and "The Drama To-day." These he gave in New England, the Middle West, and as far south as Alabama before 1904, when he toured some of the southern states as the guest of Robert C. Ogden. In 1910 he gave these lectures in the summer school of the University of California; in 1912, he gave them in Texas.

After 1900, G.P.B. knew that the future of the American drama was linked with that of the American university, college, and school, that the education of the American audience was a function of the American educational community. Thus he began to ask other questions which, in time, influenced the course of both education and the drama in America:

Shall we have in the schools, in the universities stood for the best possibilities of the drama, treating it as an art? Shall we so manage that twenty-five years hence, looking back over what many of us hope may in that time develop a genuine American drama, we may claim this product as in part at least a glorious sign that here in America our colleges and universities are not the "homes of lost causes" but places in closest touch with the most vivid interests of the people at large and so guiding and developing them that always in our best products of our national life the stamps of our universities are visible?

XVIII HARVARD THEATRE COLLECTION

IN THE EARLY FALL OF 1900, NOT LONG AFTER THE death of Harvard's renowned librarian, Justin Winsor, G.P.B. learned that a valuable collection of engraved portraits of David Garrick and his contemporaries could be purchased for a few hundred dollars. Since a mutual interest in the great English actor had brought the old librarian and the young instructor together, G.P.B. thought the Garrick portraits would make a suitable memorial to Winsor, who also had indulged a secret passion for playwriting. From Winsor's impulse to collect ten folio volumes of materials for a biography of David Garrick, which led the way to G.P.B.'s 1907 edition of *Some Unpublished Correspondence of David Garrick,* G.P.B. thus took the ultimate impetus toward what is now the Harvard Theatre Collection.

To purchase this fitting commemoration of Winsor's love of the theatre, G.P.B. had begun that year to solicit subscriptions for what he called "an important dramatic collection at Harvard." One of his first letters went to Winthrop Ames, who supplied a list of possible contributors. Another such appeal went to Julian Palmer Welsh, who had also studied belles-lettres and friendship with G.P.B. The task of enlarging the correspondence and gathering the donations thus fell to Welsh and Ames during the ensuing year.

Not long before G.P.B. sailed in 1901 on his first sabbatical leave, Welsh reported the good news of a handsome gift from

Dan Griswold, a classmate of G.P.B., who possessed one of the best collections of dramatic portraiture and literature in the country. This collection, Griswold now suggested, might eventually become Harvard's. As G.P.B. embarked, he knew that at least the Garrick engravings belonged to the university.

Prior to the receipt of the Winsor memorial, November 19, 1901, the Harvard Library Accession Book entries indicate that such gifts were consigned to the Boston Public Library; after this date, it seems to have become the practice of the Harvard Library to keep donations of theatre materials. Equally clear as a point of origin for the Harvard Theatre Collection was the list of subscribers to the purchase of the Winsor memorial. For it is a curious fact that, with the exception of Robert Gould Shaw, every Harvard alumnus who contributed substantially to the growth of the Harvard Theatre Collection was first enrolled as a donor of such gifts upon the subscription list which accompanied the commemorative portraits of David Garrick.

During 1901, while G.P.B. was in England, he found that the personal library of the great theatrical bibliographer, Robert W. Lowe, might similarly be purchased. His informant in the matter was William Archer, through whom he had made the acquaintance of the Lowes some years before. Upon his return to Cambridge, G.P.B. heard from Archer that the library could be had for a thousand dollars, if haste were made.

G.P.B.'s first move was to consult Thomas Russell Sullivan, Boston's leading gentleman dramatist, who quite agreed that the chance was too good to be lost for Harvard. Alas, however, the rich and generous theatrically minded in Boston were few. Of course, there was Major Henry Lee Higginson, but he had done so much for the Boston Symphony. And Mrs. Jack Gardner was out of the question, now that she had begun her palace of art in the Fenway. Sullivan's advice was to try New York.

The most fruitful of G.P.B.'s appeals to New York went to Louis Evan Shipman, who had been a graduate student in English 14 ten years before. Shipman's reply was prompt. He subscribed one hundred dollars and promised to have a copy of G.P.B.'s letter immediately in the mail to all the actors and theatrical people whom he thought might be of use. So G.P.B.'s appeal went to

73

such eminent men in the American theatre as James K. Hackett, E. H. Sothern, and John Drew. Just a week later, Shipman telegraphed that John Drew would purchase the Lowe Collection for the Harvard Library. By the twenty-fifth of November, the collection belonged to Harvard. It was, William Archer wrote G.P.B. on that day, even a better bargain than it seemed.

In this fashion G.P.B. acquired a theatre collection of over a thousand items for Harvard University before the end of 1902. More important, he was beginning to win support for the idea that a dramatic collection was a necessary part of the library of a national university. Thus the solicitation of materials for his collection became a part of his correspondence. Typical of the relationship he developed with the original subscribers to his plan for "an important dramatic collection at Cambridge" is the following letter from one of them:

> Castle Square Theatre
> Manager's Office
> Boston
> April 18, 1905

Dear Baker,
      Regarding your note of yesterday, let me say that I shall dine with Dean Edgar Wells tomorrow, and give him the check for $500, so that it can be used at the Libbie sale, if you think best.

I do not want to impose strict conditions on the use of the money. We are quite ready to leave it to your discretion and that of Edgar. I merely suggest, however, that I shall be interested to see the money used for books which would be of actual practical assistance to Stage Managers in producing the plays, such as good prompt copies and the like . . .

I note your very neatly inserted little sentence that "this amount will come to us annually." I do not bite quite yet, but I may later.

> Yours always sincerely,
> Winthrop Ames

G.P.B.'s role in the growth of the Harvard Theatre Collection during the next decade is clear from the following memorandum he sent to William Coolidge Lane, Harvard Librarian, on November 26, 1910: "I am sending you herewith a copy of a lecture by A. W. Pinero on Stevenson. It is, as you probably know, rare. Mr. Pinero sends it because I suggested to him that he should allow it to be reprinted for reading by a larger public."

74

One of those interested in the early stages of G.P.B.'s collection was Robert Gould Shaw, '69, owner of what was reputed to be the largest and most valuable theatrical collection in the world. Moreover, Mr. Shaw had implied on various occasions that he was considering the bequest of his treasures to Harvard. Yet the years rolled by and Mr. Shaw's intentions became no more explicit than the generous feelings which he expressed to G.P.B. Meanwhile, the Boston Public Library had received an extensive dramatic collection from Allen A. Brown in December 1909, and was interested in acquiring Shaw's collection as well.

This indecisive and highly competitive state of affairs was particularly troublesome to the Director of the Harvard Library; for it was his task to provide for the housing of any such collection as Shaw's in the plans for the new Widener Library. On June 13, 1913, the Director, Professor Archibald Cary Coolidge, wrote to G.P.B. to inquire what he knew of Mr. Shaw's decision. At this time Coolidge also asked G.P.B. to exert what influence he could to secure Mr. Shaw's theatre collection for the Harvard Library.

When G.P.B. called upon Mr. Shaw, he discovered that Shaw wished suitable rooms for his collection, adequate provision for its maintenance, and the employment of a special librarian who should continue the work of collection which Mr. Shaw had so long pursued. On June 26, G.P.B. advised Coolidge:

I am quite sure that if you are willing to write Mr. Shaw . . . suggesting that you are ready to hear in detail just what he wishes, that the best step toward gaining the Collection (invaluable, I believe, to us) will be made . . .

Please push this matter as it is all wrong to have the B.P.L. get it. They have been ten years cataloging the Brown books, and this material will not begin to be used with them as it will with us. It will be a crime to miss it at Harvard.

After an interview with Shaw, Coolidge told G.P.B. that he wished to use G.P.B.'s name and Shaw's together as much as possible in order to forestall complaint about the assignment of so much space to Mr. Shaw as the collection would require. On August 5, 1913, G.P.B. wrote Coolidge:

Use my name with Mr. Shaw's as much as you like. His is a wonderful collection, not merely of programs invaluable in future writing of the history of the English stage but of priceless prints, photographs, mezzotints, and extra-illustrated books. Stress the last when you think it wise. In any case, I will stand back of the value of the collection.

However, Shaw was not satisfied with what he considered an insufficient provision of salary for the special librarian he thought necessary to the proper functioning of the collection.

Still another year of indecision, and then the matter came to some now obscure crisis. The gift had lost much of its original attraction in the protracted skirmishes about Shaw's conditions. Besides, Coolidge had grown lukewarm as he realized the enormous demands for space and the sizable demand for funds which actual possession of the collection would make upon the new library. The ideal thing, he now suggested, would be for G.P.B. to have a building of his own with Shaw's collection in it.

When it appeared that the final decision of the Library Council was to put off Mr. Shaw with some such device as delay until another building should be available, G.P.B. began to fight for the Shaw collection. He was at Boulder Farm on April 19, 1915 when he telegraphed Coolidge after hearing that the council was ready to lay down its own conditions which would have alienated Shaw. His wire read: "I protest in strongest way against treatment of Shaw. For his sake, University's, and future of my work, I count on you to do nothing until I see you."

Fortunately, Coolidge was aware of the important work his old classmate was doing with his advanced playwrights in English 47 and in that new experimental laboratory for plays, The 47 Workshop. But it is clear from an undated memorandum which Coolidge soon sent G.P.B. that G.P.B.'s fight carried the day. "You have won completely," wrote Coolidge: "Altogether this is a most satisfactory ending to an unpleasant squall. I blame myself for not having suggested that we consult the President in the beginning, though I am not sure the suggestion would have been listened to. I congratulate you on the lucky outcome of the whole thing."

With characteristic graciousness, G.P.B. concluded his part in the matter when he wrote Coolidge on the twenty-second of

August: "Let me say again how much I appreciate what you have done to bring the Shaw Collection to us. I shall now devote my attention to winning Mr. White's plays for us if possible."

In later years he told George Vinton Freedley, whom he encouraged to organize the theatre collection of the New York City Public Library: "I was the one who insisted on Harvard having a theatre collection." But by that time what he had done was forgotten; indeed, when a quasi-official history of the Harvard Theatre Collection was published in 1930, the name of George Pierce Baker was not mentioned anywhere in the account which might well have begun and ended with G.P.B.

XIX   EDUCATING THE AMERICAN AUDIENCE

UNTIL THE TURN OF THE CENTURY, G.P.B.'S EFFORTS to hasten the growth of a native American drama were exerted through the spoken word rather than through printed criticism. After his work with the Mermaid Club, which affected the limited society of the Harvard Yard, he progressed to the larger scope of the Cambridge Social Dramatic Club. Following this, he sought to influence the Greater Boston community through a group known as "The Playgoers."

Although the history of this group is now obscure, it was clearly an attempt to provide channels of dramatic study, discussion, and criticism for the improvement of the American theatre. However, like many worthy purposes, it apparently did not prosper. In the spring of 1896 the decline of the Playgoers prompted G.P.B. to ask among his elder acquaintance for advice concerning the proper function of such a group in American society.

On the first of May, Brander Matthews replied from Columbia University:

Just what the Playgoers Club can do, I don't know. They can at least help all the good shows, not merely the poetic plays, but the more unpretending dramas in which there is to be seen a real effort to catch characteristics of our life in America, (Such as Harrigan's

77

"Squatter Sovereignty," and Hoyt's "Texas Steer" with all their violence and crudity). By discussion, by analysis, by dwelling on what is truthful in these plays and also by pointing out what is less worthy, I think the Playgoers Club can help advertise the good things and can help also to create a wholesome atmosphere. Certainly it would be a pity to permit the disbanding of any body having ideals and enthusiasm.

Though the group did disband, its ideals and enthusiasm continued until, eighteen years later, President A. Lawrence Lowell of Harvard and Major Henry Lee Higginson, founder of the Boston Symphony Orchestra, organized a Boston chapter of the Drama League of America. Quite naturally, the new group chose G.P.B. for its first president.

Thus G.P.B.'s development as a public influence in dramatic matters made inevitable his writing of dramatic criticism. The surprising thing is that he apparently made no attempt to write contemporary reviews until 1898, when he began to keep a notebook of such matters. The following characteristic remarks, dated February 4, 1898, refer to Frances Hodgson Burnett's *A Lady of Quality*, which he had just seen at the Hollis Street Theatre, one of the best American theatres of the day.

In spite of the "standing room only" crowd to which Boston's own Julia Arthur was playing as the beautiful heroine, G.P.B. noted that the play was the poorest dramatic performance he had seen in a long time. The one redeeming feature was the setting. The carved oaken room of the first act, the rose garden of the second, and the view of rolling English countryside in the last act, he thought, were almost worth coming to the theatre to see. But the play! That was bad judgment, bad taste, bad work throughout. With a mechanism that creaked, the playwright had given situation and tableau precedence over truth and story action. As for Miss Arthur, he wrote:

Throughout she played on technique, not with brain and intuitive power. Now and then she seemed to me to miss the significance of her lines . . . The great scene of the murder is artificial. There is much groveling, much stage whispering, many strong glances, etc., but not one of the throaty lines, the agonized murmurs which Mrs. Fiske puts into the great murder scene in *Tess*.

78

And as for the company, he thought most of them poor. Rarely had he heard worse elocution. Sister Anne, for instance, spoke with "the hot pudding style of delivery now popular with New York girls" and was inaudible most of the time. Here, surely, was the sort of thing which the Playgoers might have attacked with gusto. Certainly it was, he concluded, "the dime novel dramatized."

Publication of G.P.B.'s dramatic criticism did not come until the season of 1901–02, which he spent in London and Paris. Then he wrote a series of articles on the drama which he sent, upon the advice of Norman Hapgood, to the *Boston Transcript*. What he wrote was obviously modeled upon the long letters which his friend and former student, H. T. Parker, had been in the habit of sending from the dramatic centres of Europe to the *Transcript* in his capacity of special correspondent. In what may well be the longest dramatic review that newspaper ever printed, G.P.B. covered the London premiere of Arthur Wing Pinero's *Iris*. Published October 12, 1901, as a letter to the *Transcript*, G.P.B.'s account told the story of Iris Bellamy, a twenty-six-year-old widow, surrounded by admirers, who cannot marry without losing the property bequeathed her by her wealthy husband. After reviewing the cast, which included Dion Boucicault the younger, G.P.B. summarized the dramatic action and commented upon the episodic breaks in the first and third acts to mark lapses of time. Although these irritated him as technical imperfections, he found the last act absorbing: "Let nobody say again — as so many have said — that Mr. Pinero cannot write a thoroughly dramatic last act. Here it is, absorbing, surprising, till the very fall of the curtain."

The maid has just shown Laurence Trenwith, the hero, into the room. After many months in British Columbia, where he has labored to make the fortune which will enable him to marry Iris, Trenwith has returned to claim his love. Unknown to him, however, Iris has lost all of her wealth and become the mistress of the villain, Maldonado. On the surface, this would not appear to be much of an advance beyond the Frances Hodgson Burnett play; nevertheless, G.P.B. found it gripping: "Iris enters from her room, all in black. 'Not mourning, only black. I could wear

79

mourning only if you ceased to love me.' Wild with joy he clasps her in his arms; but she is restless with anxiety over the coming explanation."

Slowly, by hints and then more and more directly, Iris tells Trenwith the truth, never doubting that he will in the end forgive her. But Trenwith cannot forgive.

Slowly he nerves himself, gathers up his coat and hat and passes silently out. With an agonized cry of surprise and despair Iris falls on the divan. Maldonado, who has been listening in the next room, rushes in, mad with jealousy, but triumphant at her failure to win back her lover. In his jealousy he tries to throttle her, but her cries recall him to himself, and as he realizes how near murder he has been he cries, "This ends it." She rises, horrified, inquiring. She shall go out into the night, as she came in from it. At once. Tomorrow she may send for her things. He has done with her. As she goes to her room he rings for the maid and dismisses her and her companions. Iris re-enters and silently drags herself across to the door as Maldonado jeers. Opening the door, she turns and faces you for a moment, her face drawn with numb terror and despair. Then she shuts herself out into the night. With mad laughter, Maldonado smashes whatever is within reach.

This G.P.B. found "grim," but absorbing in its presentation of the heroine's "compelling, indefinable, morally unwarrantable fascination." Yet the play's failure was one of characterization, a failure which grew out of the playwright's confusion of the functions of the novel and those of the drama:

Mr. Pinero has tried to treat in a form which can simply throw highlights on selected facts of character and carefully chosen significant acts a subject which could be convincingly treated only in the delicate dissection of the analytical novel . . . Those "episodic" curtains seem to me finger-posts signifying that the form chosen is too confined for perfectly successful treatment of the subject.

G.P.B. concluded his review by calling attention to the play's best virtue, its artistic objectivity:

There is nothing here of the method in "Frou-Frou" or "Camille," not even the attempt to win over sympathy for the leading figure which we find in details here and there of "The Second Mrs. Tanqueray." "Given this temperament which I have stated, gentlemen, placed in these conditions, behold the inevitable result!" The

HTC

Aboard the "Mayflower," Plymouth Pageant, 1921

HTC

The Pageant Stage at Plymouth

YOU AND I

To G. P. Baker
affectionately
Philip Barry

HTC

Programme Cover, by Gluyas Williams, used for
Agassiz Theatre productions of The 47 Workshop

author seems to say with the judiciality of the medical demonstrator . . . In its impartiality the play seems to me practically unrivalled in our modern English drama.

G.P.B.'s second piece of dramatic criticism was a general discussion of "The Play in London," which appeared in the *Transcript* January 4, 1902. The significant aspect of the season, he reported, was that the public did not support such "good" plays as Pinero's *Iris*. "It flocks," he said, "not to these, but to comic opera and to successes of last year, such as 'Sherlock Holmes.'" He considered an examination of this situation especially interesting, not only because Clyde Fitch's *The Sentimentalist* and Isaac Henderson's *The Last of the Dandies* were American plays before the British audience, but also because "any such analysis brings certain conclusions of significance for the American stage."

He began this analysis by describing the English audience:

There is a body of public opinion, not that of the critics or the so-called cultivated class, which certainly feels independently, unblinded by alluring billboards and press notices. I say "feels" rather than "thinks," for I believe this public jumps to its theatrical judgments rather than reaches them by reasoning. Nevertheless, I suspect that these blind judgments are determined by a quick response to certain underlying and permanent laws of human relationship and dramatic expression.

Thus the significance of the English rejection of these "good" plays was not that the British audience was unsophisticated; the plays flouted basic dramatic laws which the English theatre-goer enforced because his approach was "human, not critical, not artistic."

Now, however interesting "Iris" is as the nearest approach yet made in England to the work of the newer French school, — Brieux, DeCurel, and others — however praiseworthy as literature, it remains for this great public which judges with its heart and not its head a grim character study with few memorable dramatic situations . . . It disregards certain laws of emotional climax, of human relationship, of stageland even, which cannot be disregarded if a play is to tell its story clearly, with sustained interest and wide appeal.

The important thing in G.P.B.'s remarks is that he attributed the failures of such new plays as *Iris* to their lack of general human significance as well as to their weakness in dramatic technique.

Thus, he concluded, the English preference of *Sherlock Holmes* to *Iris* was a harbinger of valuable things to come:

No one can watch the England of today and not see that it is steadily changing. Change means action; action means dramatic situation. Change means new conditions, novelty. Why, then, will not some of these hard-working and enthusiastic playwrights give us fresh, interesting treatment of old psychological facts, old human relations in their new surroundings, that change the combinations and the emphasis, above all, with thought for the interpretation of the life the general public sees but by no means always understands.

His next article, entitled, "The Young French Dramatist, His Public as Contrasted with the American," appeared on April 9, 1902. He began by recalling an experience he had had in Paris some years before, when a rising French actor first played in one of Molière's comedies. What impressed G.P.B. then was the general knowledge of stage history among the French audience:

The audience knew the traditions of the part! When Edwin Booth and Sir Henry Irving first played Hamlet, how many people beyond the professional critics and a few amateurs of the theatre applauded either man because certain speeches, when contrasted with the renderings of other actors successful in the part, were given fresh yet convincing interpretation? Yet, just in this different attitude of the French audience lies one great advantage of the young dramatist in Paris, for the French public, as a result of some knowledge of acting as acting, can and does distinguish better than an English or American audience between a good play badly cast and a poor play saved by clever acting — judges a play more on its merits.

He attributed this difference to differences in national education. For the educated French youth, G.P.B. found, "comes to the theatre with some knowledge of the primary, the fundamental, and consequently, the permanent laws of the drama, and with a knowledge of the characteristics which distinguish it from other forms of literary expression."

Furthermore, the intellectual curiosity of the French supported a procedure of public education which G.P.B. hoped to see in America:

At the Français, at the Odéon . . . one may see from time to time, what is practically a cycle of Molière, of Corneille, of Racine, or against the background of these masterpieces . . . more recent plays

82

which have won a place for themselves in French literature . . . In Paris, too, the significant performances are not allowed to pass unemphasized, for at the Odéon a short "conference" often precedes a play, and whenever any important piece is revived, one can always find in the daily papers announcement of lectures on it. Most important of all, these chief daily papers give space freely to articles on approaching revivals, famous past productions of noted plays, and to detailed criticism of current performances.

Another educative force was that exercised by such experimental theatres as the Théâtre Antoine and the Théâtre du Grand Guignol. The work of M. Antoine at his earlier Théâtre Libre undoubtedly inspired much of what G.P.B. was about to begin for himself at Radcliffe and Harvard; however, G.P.B. saw that the original revolution of the Théâtre Libre had settled into the growing conservatism of the Théâtre Antoine. Only in such "little theatres" as the Grand Guignol could the true spirit of the amateur be kept alive. Here G.P.B. discovered something at work which he believed could be effective in America:

In this tastefully decorated room — about the size of Boston's Union Hall — an intelligent and often richly dressed audience gathers nightly to pass judgment on four to six short plays. The training which a beginner may get from this chance to write one-act plays it is hard to overestimate, for the one-act play teaches not only condensation, but also what is fundamental in dramatic work: namely, selection of material in view of special limitations, here very marked . . . Where in England or America today is there any such chance for a young playwright as the Grand Guignol offers the young French dramatist?

These educative influences upon playwright and audience, G.P.B. concluded, had made France supreme in the drama of the century just closed. The basis of this supremacy was the educated relationship of playwright and audience which made the French dramatists respond to "their country, their people, their city, even their own immediate surroundings."

In a word, just what I miss in current English drama I find in this new school in Paris — thoughtful interpretation of what seems to them amusing, alarming, suggestive, tragic, in the life about them that is new within ten years and will be past in ten years more. In Paris, then, the drama is not only an art, it is also an interpretation of French life today. A contrast of these conditions, with present dramatic conditions in America offers some interesting results.

In his third article, "The American Public and the Theatre," June 7, 1902, G.P.B. developed this contrast. He began by referring to the great increase of American interest in the theatre which had, nevertheless, "produced fewer plays of permanent value than even our English cousins." The trouble lay in neither the dramatists nor the actors of America. The "theatre-loving public itself" and its "unconsciously provincial" attitude toward the drama of London and Paris was the real villain.

This great public really wants what is clean and what represents our life, but unfortunately it puts at present little value on anything except situation and excitement in telling the story. That is, it lacks artistic standards.

As a result, the dramatist who tries to paint American life finds that he must overdo scenes of great but quiet intensity, that he must sacrifice truth to produce a momentary thrill.

To illustrate the effect of this lack of dramatic standards in the American theatre audience, G.P.B. referred to the experience of his friend James A. Herne in adapting his art to the taste of this public, which demanded such things as "the incongruous lighthouse scene in 'Shore Acres.'" Because of the pressure upon him to provide such materials in his later play, *Sag Harbor,* Herne capitulated to the popular taste. "Indeed," concluded G.P.B., "compare 'Shore Acres,' 'Griffith Davenport,' and 'Sag Harbor' and you will see just where our public is today."

In this matter he found the chief fault lay with the educated elements of the public, with those who — but for the failure of American education to provide dramatic standards — should know better than to lump together, without any sure means of differentiation, *The Gay Lord Quex, Cyrano,* and *Zaza.* "Conceive," G.P.B. said, "any person with any pretense to cultivation attempting to treat on any common basis Dvorak, Beethoven, and Sousa." When these cultivated Americans put themselves into the same relation to the drama that they had toward music, the unfavorable conditions in the American audience would disappear.

The solution to this problem G.P.B. proposed in his final

article from abroad. "A Subsidized Theatre" appeared in the *Transcript* for September 10, 1902, a few days after the Bakers returned to Cambridge. As the title suggests, G.P.B. had concluded that the instrument for establishing dramatic standards for American audiences would have to be some kind of an endowed theatre, "as free as possible from the compelling necessities attending the theatre as a mere investment."

The purpose of such a theatre would be "to teach primarily, not the actor, but the public." This was to be done by presenting plays which, for business reasons — the reasons which had governed Herne — existing companies could not produce. This meant presenting not only the rich literature of the English theatre, but the dramatic masterpieces of all time. "Must most of us," G.P.B. inquired, "know the dramatic work of Schiller and Goethe only under the most painful conditions — as school and college textbooks?" Such a procedure alone held promise of acquainting Americans generally with the new dramas of Echegaray, Tolstoi, Brieux, Hauptmann, Rostand, and Yeats. It might even draw from playwrights like Herne the plays of a truly American drama.

G.P.B.'s specific proposal was that some persons of great wealth should organize in Boston a company of stockholders to provide a theatre on the plan of the Vienna Volkstheater. This was essentially the idea which had provided Providence its Opera House during G.P.B.'s boyhood. What he visualized was an institution for the drama comparable to what Boston already enjoyed for music and art in its Symphony Orchestra and Art Museum:

It is utterly Quixotic to think of raising all at once public taste for the drama throughout the country. If instead, in some favorable places, a few persons of wealth, who genuinely care for that part of art which the drama may be and recognize its enormous potential educative and moral force, would for five years stand behind such a theatre, it would probably need thereafter only a small fraction, if any part, of their original support.

In Boston, the successful organization of the different forces making for general education is one of our chief causes for civic pride. Our famous technical schools, our colleges and universities, private initiative and generosity have given us. They have given us our Art Museum. They have given us, too, an orchestra which is not only a delight but a model . . . Is there no one who by his skill as a leader and organizer, or with munificence as ready and far-sighted as Major Higginson's, will establish such a theatre?

Behind G.P.B.'s appeal was a firm conviction that the problem was an educational one. The goal of an American drama was thus susceptible to planning and organization; native genius could well supply what the American audiences might be taught to demand. In this frame of reference he completed the only sustained venture into dramatic criticism which he ever attempted outside the lecture room and dramatic workshop. Yet these few letters to the *Boston Transcript* embraced the man's whole critique. His closing words set the theme of which all he subsequently did about the drama was but a pattern of variations:

I believe firmly that, granted all the other conditions making for an American drama . . . only widespread recognition of correct dramatic standards is needed to produce — not in one year, or five, or even, perhaps, ten, but within a generation — a drama of American conditions which shall have permanent value.

Aside from this solid faith in the generation of playwrights which would be coming to him for criticism in another dozen years, two qualities of G.P.B.'s approach to the plays of that generation are apparent in this early dramatic criticism: his sensitivity to effective theatre materials and his essential conservatism in respect to matters of taste and morality. Indeed, aside from his textbook on playwriting, *Dramatic Technique,* the body of dramatic criticism which he put into print shows that his great influence as a critic came from his personality rather than his pen.

Apparently distrustful of his abilities as a writer of dramatic criticism, G.P.B. never relied solely upon his intellectual apprehension of the values of a play. Always the final test was production, with adequate scenery, upon a stage — and with criticism an appendage to creative action. Though criticism of this sort becomes historically intangible, its immediate effectiveness in The 47 Workshop showed that whatever defects he may have had as a critic were there transformed to that paramount virtue in a counselor of playwrights: a generous encouragement of values developed by an experimental testing of intuition.

xx A DRAMATIC WORKSHOP
AT RADCLIFFE

WHEN BRONSON HOWARD ADDRESSED G.P.B. AND THE other members of the Shakspere Club in Sanders Theatre in 1886, he began with these remarks:

> I invite you to-day to step into a little dramatic workshop instead of a scientific library, and to see an humble workman in the craft trying, with repeated experiments . . . not to elucidate the laws of dramatic construction, but to obey them, exactly as an inventor . . . tries to apply the general laws of mechanics.

Two years later, while G.P.B. was in Europe, someone sent him a clipping of a letter which Howard had recently addressed to the editor of the *New York Tribune*. In calling attention to the work which Professor Alfred Hennequin was doing with the teaching of dramatic technique at the University of Michigan, Howard wrote:

> Need Columbia, Yale, Harvard and Princeton leave the University of Michigan solitary and peculiar, as it now is, in this work? . . . The only question at issue is whether the people shall see American plays and read American criticisms written by trained and skilful men, or see and read merely the experimental work which ignorance, occasionally enlightened by genius, can offer them.

This experimental approach and Bronson Howard's "workshop" may have recurred to G.P.B. when he tinkered with his own plays during the nineties and began to develop his own rationale of dramatic construction. Although the continuity of G.P.B.'s ideas about the subject was rooted in his lectures on the history of the English drama and the mechanics of argumentation, and certainly he always thought of a play as a special kind of argument, he drew equally from the contemporary discussions of playwriting which others had carried on for years. In later days, when he was interrogated about his part in the cultural movement which made the universities a force in the development of a national drama, his characteristic reply was: "When the history of this movement is written, the credit will go to Alfred Hennequin and Brander Matthews."

A change in English 14 which G.P.B. made at Radcliffe in 1895–96 was his first official step in this movement. As an experiment, he replaced his historical survey of the English drama before the Puritan revolution with a half-course entitled, "The Development of the Drama in the Nineteenth Century." Two years elapsed before he repeated this material. Then, in "The Drama from 1642 to the Present Day," he taught what became another of his standard courses — "English 39." Here, as he lectured on Pinero, Jones, Wilde, and the other late-Victorian playwrights, he was free to digress toward points that bore directly upon plays which such students as Beulah Marie Dix and Josephine Sherwood were writing and directing among the Radcliffe girls.

Although the teaching of contemporary drama thus became a part of his official duties at Radcliffe after 1897 (at Harvard after 1900), G.P.B. did not attempt to offer a course in dramatic composition until a few years later. Edward Knoblock, a mid-nineties English 14 student whose *Kismet* was later an effective vehicle for Otis Skinner, recalls in his autobiography that he and G.P.B. often talked about the addition of a course in playwriting to the Harvard curriculum. Meanwhile, he was faced with an increasing number of requests for extended technical analyses of a scene or an act of plays which students in his literature classes felt compelled to write.

To such a call for help, G.P.B. was likely to reply with an invitation to an evening appointment in the study of his half-timbered Brattle Street home. In those days at the turn of the century, there were so many such appointments to read and discuss last acts that an informal organization arose among those who met in the comfortable study. Inevitably, the group came to be known as "Baker's Dozen." And since it was, in a way, much like the fellowship of the Mermaid Club, G.P.B. welcomed this regeneration of a companionship long since lost.

Ernest Bernbaum, a member of one of the first of the Baker's Dozens, recalls that the new group met every Friday or Saturday evening from eight until ten o'clock. Then, after a supper of Mrs. Baker's spaghetti and while they assailed an Edam cheese, they talked until midnight. For the most part, it was just good talk about themselves and the theatre. They discussed foreign and domestic critical magazines, read reviews of current plays, or listened to some friend of G.P.B. who had been persuaded to talk to the group about their mutual passion. Sometimes they read their own plays, sometimes those of their guests. Between 1901 and 1913, a dozen years which were to give way to the 47 Workshop, these guests were William Archer, Henry Arthur Jones, A. E. Thomas, Edward Knoblock, H. T. Parker, Winthrop Ames, Walter Prichard Eaton, Louis Evan Shipman, Charles Klein, Clyde Fitch, and Somerset Maugham.

After two years of such evenings with the Baker's Dozen playwrights, G.P.B.'s ideas about a class in dramatic composition began to take shape. In March 1903 he spoke to his Radcliffe class in contemporary drama about a plan he had for the conclusion of the course. "In June," he said, "you are supposed to turn in a thesis on some subject connected with this period of English drama. Instead, how many of you would like to write a play?"

Out of this class of a dozen young ladies, all but one chose to write a play. The plays which showed promise were the work of an English girl who had written an article on the Castle Square Theatre stock company for the *Radcliffe Magazine;* a graduate student from Adelphi College; and Agnes Morgan, then completing her master's degree. G.P.B. called the three into his office and told them:

For a long time I have been wanting to institute a class in playwriting at Harvard and Radcliffe. I prefer to start it at Radcliffe because a class here would be sure to be smaller — I can just see the "gang" of Harvard boys that would elect such a course! — and I don't want numbers while I am feeling my way and deciding between the various techniques of conducting such a course. It will be as great an experiment for me as for the student.

It was not merely fortuitous that G.P.B. found the most favorable environment for his plan at Radcliffe. Since the early days of the "Annex," the principal social activity of these young women had been dramatic. The oldest of their clubs, the Idler, had given its first public performance in G.P.B.'s senior college year. In the fifteen years before G.P.B. began to teach playwriting at Radcliffe, acting had grown so popular with the young ladies that their "theatre" was perhaps the most absorbing part of their college life.

Although Agnes Morgan was the only one of the original trio who returned to enroll in the new course, there were ten students in the class when G.P.B. commenced the work. The official designation of the course was: "English 46. The Forms of the Drama. Practice in Dramatic Composition." Commencing the second half-year, it met Tuesday, Thursday, and Saturday at ten in the morning. From the beginning, G.P.B. and his students sat about a large round table which soon became a symbol of the course.

The work began with the writing of a one-act adaptation of a novel or a short story; after this came an original one-act play and an original three-act play. No texts were used, although G.P.B. referred his students to Hennequin's *The Art of Playwriting,* Aristotle's *Poetics,* Meredith's lecture on *The Idea of Comedy,* Freytag's *Dramatic Technique,* William T. Price's *The Technique of the Drama,* and Elizabeth Woodbridge's *The Drama: Its Law and Technique.* Obviously G.P.B. was not the first to attempt to teach dramatic technique. In his first time through this material, he tried to emphasize what he thought was fundamental. So he stressed Aristotle.

Thus the first final examination in the course devoted a half hour to questions about Aristotle's observations upon the forms of the drama as he knew it; and certainly the first descriptive title of the course suggests an Aristotelian procedure. However, G.P.B. did not really believe in such an approach. The following year he said, "If I write a textbook on this whole business, as I want to some day, I shall insist on throwing over Aristotle entirely."

The heart of the course was G.P.B.'s reading of the manuscripts, and the criticism around the table which followed. After his reading, which was essentially an imaginative recreation of the play at hand, G.P.B. tried to make everything he could understand about the author's intention crystal clear to the audience around the table. Ernest Bernbaum, a close observer of G.P.B's teaching at this time, recalls:

The secret of G.P.B.'s teaching was his simple, clear, businesslike critical approach which employed no affectation, no tricks, no special terminology or mystification but which got directly to the object of study in a determined and common sense analysis of structure and substance. He had no axe to grind. His criticism was not economic, or philosophical, or moral but was simply an attempt to see the thing as it appeared to careful scrutiny. The students liked him because he could be understood. Yet he was not easy. His delivery, although smooth and clear, was obviously the result of complete mastery of what he had at hand. The enormous diligence of his mastery would deter any student who was really lazy, for Baker expected his students to labor as assiduously as he did. The truth upon which G.P.B. based his teaching was that youth does not object to hard work so long as it knows what it is doing and understands its direction.

As another playwright of those days put it, "He went at each script as though it might contain the world's biggest gold nugget."

For two years, G.P.B. continued to experiment thus at Radcliffe. With the assistance of the Idler Club, he even saw some of his student work produced upon the tiny Fay House stage, scarcely twenty feet wide. Meanwhile, he withheld any proposal that a course in dramatic technique be added to the Harvard curriculum. But as he worked he began to believe that he was participating in some imminent and astounding discovery. He could not long withhold what was soon a conviction that in such a course at Harvard might the coming American drama flourish.

XXI COMEDY AND THE COMING AMERICAN DRAMA

WHEN, ON THE MORNING OF APRIL 2, 1904, G.P.B. walked into the upper front room of Fay House where the new Radcliffe playwriting course met, he carried in his green cloth bag the notes for his fifth lecture, "Low Comedy and Farce." This, and another stenographically recorded lecture which he delivered to the class five days later, develops what G.P.B. believed about the nature of comedy. Since these lectures show in brief compass the philosophy which may ultimately lie behind the genuine American comedy of Philip Barry and Eugene O'Neill, they offer

91

an excellent view of G.P.B. in characteristic thought and action.

As he placed the bag upon the round table and proceeded to arrange his books and papers in a neat and orderly plan, he straightened momentarily, squaring his shoulders purposefully. Although of a stockier build than Edwin Booth, he indeed resembled the great actor. After a pause which added stature and a certain histrionic tension to his medium height, he adjusted his pince-nez with a quick sweep of his hand, glanced with a thin-lipped smile at the young ladies about the table, and spoke deep-voiced in an accent almost clipped, "I should like to have the class read now very carefully George Meredith's *Essay on Comedy*."

Here he picked up the volume and passed it, with just a trace of a flourish, to the nearest young lady. His animated blue-gray eyes gentled as they rested on the essay and he said with sincerity that it was the most technical and subtle and exact of all the treatises on comedy. Then, in a manner persuasive and serious, he launched into his thesis:

Now in the first place, the ordinary definitions that are given of comedy — and I want to illustrate the difference between farce and comedy this morning — seem to me extremely unsatisfactory. The sooner, I take it, that you break free from Aristotle, the better. Aristotle's views are sound for his own particular period, but he is writing of the Greek Comedy and the Greek Tragedy, and although what he said might be true, to a certain extent, for Latin Comedy, which was based somewhat on Greek Comedy, it does not hold good for our comedy which after all is so largely in this country a development of the conditions of the drama in England, of the secular and church drama developed from the Miracle plays.

Now, when your drama has taken a totally different development because of the totally different conditions of the people, when we have what might be called vernacular comedy as distinguished from classical comedy, when all the conditions of our comedy are freer and more spontaneous than that of the classical comedy, it is absurd that we should apply the definitions and test of Aristotle to our comedy, and get any really valuable results. For instance, here is the kind of thing you will find in Professor A. W. Ward's *History of English Dramatic Literature to the Death of Queen Anne:*

As he picked up the new book, G.P.B. passed a broad practical palm over his high forehead to smooth his dark hair, parted precisely in the middle. With some sharpness he then read from Ward's book, "Comedy deals with people whose vices are of a ridiculous kind." Pausing, he repeated the definition before continuing:

It depends upon the point of view, and the point of view is selected by the dramatist. Vices might be so represented as to seem distinctly cause for tragedy. There is where the difficulty lies because, you see, here is the problem in the hands of the people of the older time. You have the distinct premise that certain subjects are fit subjects for tragedy, — that certain large, grand, extreme, intense, unusual, undue emotions are the subject for tragedy, and anything outside that range is not a subject for tragedy, but is a subject for comedy.

Here he smiled and dropped his voice slightly as he spread his arms:

Now, you cannot split things up in that fashion at the present time. In the first place, tragedy and comedy is a discovery, on the whole, of later times. Consequently, those views of life which tragedy and comedy represent, are simply a matter of where we are to place the emphasis.

Reaching for the Meredith essay, he went on:

Aristotle formulated his theories for other conditions than ours. It is of extreme value to you and me to read the old comedy writers, and see the difference between modern conditions and old conditions. Now I think this definition brings the matter out.

Then, as he briskly opened the book, G.P.B. turned slightly, putting himself a bit in profile. With his left arm thrust behind him and the book dropped well below the level of his countenance, he read with a precision of enunciation and an attention to the natural vibrance of the lines which suggested an actor reading from a script. It was not alone these young ladies who thought he looked like a Sir Henry Irving — or a Mr. Booth.

So he read the passage from Meredith's essay which begins, "Comedy presents us with the imperfections of human nature. Farce entertains us with what is monstrous." Finishing, he dropped the book to his side, thrust his left hand deeply into the coat pocket of his dark gray suit, and looked intently around the table. As if assured of their comprehension, he continued:

93

That is to say, comedy deals with those imperfections of human nature which cause laughter in those who can judge. Notice that word, because Mr. Meredith puts a great deal of force upon that. Farce is intended for those who can't judge, and who see humor only in extravagance. Now, barring that one word "judge," I think that is fundamentally and splendidly put, right straight through. For instance, any of you who have have been working with me on the matter of the Jonson comedies know perfectly well the curious methods which appear in his earlier work. Those are comedies in which you have approximations to life, but the various people are, after all, types. They all present some very marked exaggeration. There is always with Jonson the implied judgment that these people are contemptible because they are so dull or petty or vicious or weak, as the case may be. His mind acts in judgment on his people, and he has contempt for them.

With a swift gesture toward one of the books on the table, he hastened to relate past and present:

That is the attitude of the older group of dramatists. Now you can see that this is a very different attitude from the one held in that very charming — not great — but very charming comedy of Labiche: "Le Petit Oiseau," which many of you know. Or take "A Pair of Spectacles." Here is this man who is so genial and mild and sweet tempered he cannot believe anybody ever does anything he ought not to do. Of course, he is cheated, but he does not know it, and is just as happy. Then he has his sharp brother, who keeps people from cheating and is very miserable and unhappy. They change their spectacles. Then the poor old man begins to see life as his brother does. He is fantastic, if you like, but you are not for one moment made to feel anything but sympathy and affection for this kindly old man. That is what comedy at the present day does.

Removing the pince-nez, G.P.B. turned to one of the young ladies on his left and addressed her as if he were telling her something which she already knew — half in confidence, half in apology for being so obvious:

Now all comedy, it seems to me, is bound to be a variable thing. It depends so much more upon the social ideals and the social standards of the people for whom it is written than does tragedy. In tragedy, after all, we are all more or less at one. There are certain great emotions, there are certain profound sensations, which all people share, after all. We share even with the Greeks in our reverence for certain things, and our recognition of certain situations. We also, it is true, share with them the idea that certain situations are comic. But it is in comedy, largely, that you get the social standards of the time.

You cannot get any one definition of comedy that will apply to everything. There are many different kinds that are valuable and sincere and likely to be permanent, and the reason why we have had no significant drama in this country so far is that we have produced nothing distinctively characteristic of our own national life. We borrow from England, and we shall go on borrowing until we have a drama that is the result of special conditions here.

With a quick motion, he clapped the glasses to the bridge of his nose once more and looked about the table as he spoke directly to each one as if she alone bore the burden of giving America a native comedy:

If all this is correct analysis, you see you have got to get a composite definition of comedy. You can perfectly well come back to something absolute like my statement that it depends on the point of view, and that even when you are dealing with your material in order to interest, amuse, delight and please you are dealing with comedy, but when you so treat your material as to represent the dark and the grim side of life, when you wish to interest us in human suffering, in wrong and error for its own sake, you have got tragedy. You will see, of course, that in a certain way you get back to Aristotle in all this. The different types of comedy and tragedy, indeed, are all related, and the differences in them from the older types are owing to the differentiations in the life and thought of a later period.

All this, it seems to me, is really very significant, because it throws light on a good many different things we shall have to treat. It throws light on why we have no drama here. The trouble is that we are imitative. We follow others.

For a moment he raised the pile of play scripts on the table before him, then dropped them with an emphatic gesture.

We have been trying to write in the style of this or that other person, instead of doing what I asked you to do last time, namely, to find those things in the life of the years 1890–1900 which are particularly characteristic of that period, and treat those aspects of them which may be amusing, entertaining and light for your audience. Now that means a lot of thinking, and most people do not like to do that.

Now both hands thrust deeply into the pockets of the high-buttoned coat and he stepped back as he summarized his case for judge and jury:

95

It comes, you see, just to this: You think over your period first, and you find the elements of the new and the novel and the strange and the characteristic. Then you think of all these things in the light of your audience that will probably gather to see such a play, and the question is — can you treat that material for that audience so as to make it thoroughly amusing and interesting to them? Now the moment you have begun to do that, you have begun to produce the great American comedy of manners in America during the last ten years.

Moving a hand in brisk negation, he drew his long face into a slight grimace and continued:

But instead of doing that, our playwrights choose to treat those eternal subjects for comedy which have always been used. If you take a play like "Whitewashing Julia" by Mr. Jones, and all his later comedies, they all amount to the everlasting problem of how many are the amusing situations that can be got out of the lady who got herself into a somewhat complicated situation socially, and who gets herself out of it by her wits, or because she never belonged there anyhow. This sort of thing is especially characteristic of the last ten years.

Now what, on the other hand, makes Pinero's Quex interesting is that although this man is a type, he is still a differentiation within a type. He belongs to the present period, and he is surrounded with things characteristic of the present period. I am not at all sure we shall not find historians of manners fifty years hence referring to Quex in perfect seriousness as a fairly illustrative comedy of the manners and morals of our own present time.

Turning to the distinctions between comedy and farce, G.P.B. observed that farce was by no means as disreputable as it is supposed to be. "I have a strong suspicion," he said, "that the men who will have a lasting influence have written farce."

It is not very funny to produce something in which people merely fall upstairs and fall downstairs, and in which people come in and out of doors, and slam doors, and where you hide people behind furniture and elsewhere. Instead, try to see in actual, every day life a situation which is really a comedy situation, and then just underscore certain places in it, until, from being merely funny, it becomes convulsively funny. That means good farce writing, and it means a good keen eye for the humor in every day life.

Here he picked up a small paper-covered volume which he opened where a torn envelope divided the pages. The blue-gray eyes twinkled and slight dimples broke at the corners of his mouth as he glanced about the table. "I cannot make that clearer than by this very delightful scene in 'The Importance of Being Earnest.' It is the scene in which the mother summons her daughter's suitor before her, and examines him as to his qualifications as a suitor."

He began to read, and in that instant the professor in the dark gray suit metamorphosed into the British dowager, Lady Bracknell. In quick alternation, as he played the final scene of Oscar Wilde's first act, he became two young men about London, a sweet debutante, and a Cockney gentleman's gentleman. Then, as the stage disappeared and the professor stood once more before them, he smiled.

Well, now, some of these things the real mother would have said, but I doubt whether she would have said some of the other things. You see, it is only a little touching up of her questions, which makes them farcical. This whole scene is just as funny on the stage as when we read it. It is one of the most delicious bits of farce dialogue we have.

As the class hour drew to a close, G.P.B. summed up:

Now I believe that this is what I want to make clear: Farce is really a high order of literary composition. It is very largely the work of genius. It means that you can see the possibilities of the comic to such an extent that you can get from a character, a situation, or even from a dialogue, much more fun than most people would see in it, and in doing that you carry it just a little beyond the line of probability. We think of it: this is possible, but it is not probable. That is the very thing that separates it from comedy.

As he gathered together the books and papers before him, G.P.B. advised the coming generation of American playwrights: "Now don't look down on farce. If you can invent anything like as good dialogue or situation as is required in the best farces, you are to be congratulated."

On the following Thursday, G.P.B. gave his sixth lecture, "The Nature of High Comedy." Again he began with Meredith's *Essay on Comedy*, reading extensively, commenting as he went:

There you have the whole thing packed as close as Mr. Meredith packs all his critical work. When one accepts, as I personally do, all of Mr. Meredith's definitions of what makes high comedy, one almost

97

wonders if there is any opportunity for high comedy in this country at the present day. Until you can take a small portion of your public, and lead the general public out of the idea that idle and empty laughter is the most desirable of amusements, you cannot have high comedy. What you can have are plays containing a good deal of clever talk, of punning, of playing upon words, of general nonsense, and even of some farcical situations until, as Mr. Meredith says, it is only because there is such a flash of rapid dialogue, which is rather clever, combined with the general vivaciousness, and on the whole the comparative reality of the figures, to prevent your calling this whole thing a merely farcical piece of work.

Only three days before, he had celebrated his thirty-eighth birthday. As he stood in the garden of his Brattle Street home, watching another spring come on, thinking of his four growing boys, he may have framed the ideas which he now expressed to the young ladies at the round table in Fay House:

I am inclined to think that on the whole "The Princess and the Butterfly" is the best of the high comedies of the last twenty-five years. It was utter caviare to the general public, of course, but look at the situation, and you will see that it is a beautiful situation for high comedy. Here is a group of people approaching forty, and some past it. They are now no longer young. They are no longer in the situation where life is a limitless number of possibilities. You realize that one by one all the doors of opportunity are closing. You can hear them closing in rather ominous fashion. You are not going to be treated any longer as young, but as one of the worthy middle aged. There are certain things that are not expected of you from this time on. No one can approach that time of life without a certain amount of thoughtfulness, and some people it seems to depress enormously.

Now there is what seems to me high comedy. It can't succeed here because, after all, what our public demands is this: it wants in the first place situation excitement — action. It wants things to happen constantly. Now in high comedy action is not the most important thing. The delicate nuances of relationship and feeling come out more in conversation, more in dialogue, than in action, with many of the best things in high comedy. In the first place, you must have a man of literary skill to phrase all this, and then you must have your public who can feel and appreciate the value of it.

Now at the present time, the men who can see are not numerous, and the public who can understand and appreciate is very clearly nil. The result is that the chance for high comedy is small until we have very much developed the willingness of the average American to think when he is not obliged to. Until then, we shall not have any very high comedy in this country.

Then he turned to another text on the table before him.

There is another essay to which I want to call your attention. I hope to have it printed in some form. It is called "An Essay Concerning Humour in Comedy," and is in the form of a letter by Congreve. It comes only at the end of one edition of the Dramatic Works of Congreve. With the exception of this essay by George Meredith, it seems to me the most illuminating discussion we have of what is really humor in comedy.

After further reading and commentary, he moved to an emphatic point about the nature of high comedy:

It depends, above all, you see, upon a thorough grasp of human character. That is what it depends upon, and in high comedy I believe that you get at your results not through the situation, but through the characters. You see a certain number of people, and you see the difference between what each of these persons is and what he thinks he is. Now if you can represent that for your particular public, you can write high comedy. In doing that you have really hit upon the use of Congreve's definition of humor in the best sense.

As he concluded his remarks, he turned, as was his wont in such discussions, to the contemporary American scene and its relation to high comedy.

It is, it seems to me, distinctly the most difficult thing to write that there is. Yet there is your great, bustling, crowded American life of the present day. It is full of all sorts of material for the very best high comedy. Anything more deliciously amusing than many situations in American life caused by all sorts of things — caused by people who have suddenly become rich, — caused by this and that and the other things in our many-colored American life, you cannot possibly find, but how are we to present it? If we put it on the stage, we vulgarize it to the nth degree. It all consists in people's using bad grammar and in being badly dressed. That is the cheapest kind of comedy of humor. This person who speaks bad grammar, if she puts herself in the hands of a teacher of English and elocution, would get over it in a year, if she has any sense. On the other hand, there are situations in America, caused by the meeting of people of generations of cultivation and refinement, but who are not wealthy, with people who lack refinement, — these situations are of the kind that cause thoughtful laughter if, after all, they are properly treated.

Take a novel like "The Pit." I can conceive a high comedy written from "The Pit." But I imagine that as it is presented in New York, now, it is not exactly high comedy. It is more of a melodrama, probably, and I know that certain scenes in it are bound to appear which would not appear at all in a high comedy, because, in the first place, we have not enough fixed standards of American life, today, and in the second place we have very little community of standards.

His last words to the class that day were the message which he brought in succeeding years to Edward Sheldon, to George Abbott, to Eugene O'Neill, to Sidney Howard, to S. N. Behrman, and to Philip Barry. Others in the theatre heard it too, for it soon became an idea in the air, a hope in many hearts:

I believe it to be perfectly possible to take the conditions here in the Eastern states, or Middle states, or West or South, and for a person who knows the standards of these regions to write a play of conditions in the life of the present time which shall be amusing, and at the same time amuse in such a way that one finds one is thinking about the play afterward — not exactly in amusement, but thoughtfully and pleasantly.

Here, regardless of the specific influences it exerted — and who can say that *Ah, Wilderness!* or *The Philadelphia Story* might have existed without it? — is the general area of meaning within which G.P.B.'s teaching of playwriting operated. He was not particularly interested that his students write in one dramatic genre or another. However, he knew that until American playwrights believed in the validity of their own point of view, until they forsook theories and imitations and wrote about the life around them in a thoughtful and amusing way, there would be no drama that was truly American.

XXII   "THE MIND OF THE UNDER-
GRADUATE" AND PLAYWRITING

THE REASON FOR G.P.B.'S DRIFT FROM CONVENTIONAL subjects of teaching to unconventional ones, from rhetoric and literary history to playwriting, is apparent in a paper which he read during 1904 before the Schoolmaster's Association of New

York. His address, "The Mind of the Undergraduate," reprinted the following year in the *Educational Review,* is remarkable for its expression of his personal dissatisfaction with "the rank and file of the undergraduate body":

It is only by forcing, coaxing, that one can develop in these youths any interest in thinking for thinking's own sake, can make them appreciate the fact that there is a delicate pleasure in the process of thinking. I meet often the type . . . who sits in front of you with an amiably receptive expression, who smiles gently at all your neat turns of phrase, who gives you the feeling that, on the whole, your lecture is really well fitted to the needs of the class, and then comes to the desk to ask you just one question which shows his mind has not taken in one important idea from the entire hour . . . What makes this Buddhist of the West especially difficult to deal with is that he is not boorish or inconsiderate toward the instructor, but usually quite the opposite. Clad in intellectual oilskins, he is almost blithesome in his absolute imperviousness to the ideas for which he is supposed to be taking the course.

Obviously, G.P.B. was bored with the undergraduate mind. The same year, in the introduction to his *Forms of Public Address,* he wrote further words of this vein: "I have read many compositions submitted in oratorical contests. Only rarely have they even a spark of individuality, of freshness, of simple strength. Instead, they are conventional, artificial, empty, cheap." Inevitably, he was drawn to those who wished to be taught, who were keen to think and imagine. Inevitably, he was drawn to those who wished to write plays.

Shortly after the beginning of 1905, G.P.B. planned his formal proposal of a new course in the Harvard department of English. For English 39, an advanced course in the English drama from 1642 to 1900, he wished to substitute instruction in dramatic composition. On the day the department first heard the proposal, G.P.B. came late to the meeting. Professor Kittredge had already departed, but G.P.B. did not know until the next day what had happened. It was Le Baron Russell Briggs, Dean of Radcliffe College, who had presented G.P.B.'s idea of the new course and who explained to G.P.B. why the proposal had not been accepted. Unfortunately, it then seemed, Professor Kittredge was opposed to substituting such a course for an advanced course in literature.

The background of the controversy was the curricular revolution which had begun in 1869 with President Eliot's inaugural address advocating a free choice of studies for each student. In 1900, when G.P.B. had introduced the course in contemporary drama which he now wished to replace with something even more of the moment, President Eliot had told him with avuncular frankness: "Whatever new courses in the drama you may teach, George, it is for your work in argumentation that Harvard pays you." By 1905, G.P.B. was, to the view of not a few minds, dangerously near an absurd interpretation of the elective idea with a course in playwriting. In a friendly exchange of views, Professor Kittredge advised G.P.B. to have an eye to possible misconceptions as to the scope and method of the proposed course.

When, in subsequent departmental discussion, G.P.B. made it clear that the course was to be primarily for graduate students and that it would offer a kind of professional training for which he could demonstrate a growing need, the proposal was approved. Yet the serious relationship of an American drama to an American society was not thereby recognized. The point which G.P.B. won was personal; in his experience, it never became one of principle.

The new course, sightly changed in number and title from its Radcliffe predecessor, was thus described in the Harvard catalogue for 1905–06:

English Composition
For Graduates

47^2 hf. English Composition. — The Technique of the Drama. Lectures and practice. *Half-course (second half-year)*. Tu., Th., Sat. at 9. Professor Baker.

Because of G.P.B.'s impending year of lectureship at the Sorbonne, the course was not offered during 1906–07 and 1907–08. Thus the second Harvard class in playwriting did not meet until 1909.

In this year, President Eliot retired and English 47 became a full course. The new president, A. Lawrence Lowell, actively discouraged G.P.B.'s work in argumentation and debate to the point of suggesting that these courses be dropped in order that the English department might offer honors work without increasing its budget. Lowell thus secured for G.P.B. a greater opportunity to develop the playwriting course, though this was purely an accident in the general change of administrative policy. That Lowell considered G.P.B.'s ideas of education sound may be inferred from his appointment of G.P.B. to be the chairman of the committee which prepared the revised Harvard entrance requirements in 1909, a post which G.P.B. accepted only after Lowell's urging.

After 1909 and until 1921, when Professor J. T. Murray succeeded to the teaching of English 14, the courses with which G.P.B. was identified were English 14 and English 39, which covered the history of the drama from its beginnings until 1900; and English 47. After 1913, when G.P.B. began to devote his energies almost exclusively to the 47 Workshop, his teaching of the historical materials became increasingly perfunctory. Indeed, one might never have suspected the dynamic teacher of playwriting while listening to the obviously bored and sometimes mechanical rendition of the once brilliant lectures in English 14. As his historical notes yellowed, and lost their margins and corners, G.P.B. worked assiduously at making new dramatic history.

In 1915–16, English 47a, "The Technique of the Drama (Advanced Course)," was added to the Harvard catalogue. This new course was open "only to such students as have taken Course 47 with distinction." As a concession to advanced students who wished to devote all of their time to dramatic composition, the catalogue further stated that "With the assent of the instructor Course 47a may be counted for more than one course." Within ten years, G.P.B. had achieved for his course in dramatic composition some of the requisites of a department within the Harvard department of English. Not the least of these was an annual catalogue of "Courses in the Drama" which appeared regularly after 1915, and which G.P.B. prepared in order to bring to Harvard the more mature people who not only could be taught matters of technique but might also have something to say.

While G.P.B. grew less interested in the ordinary mind of the undergraduate, his professional life narrowed to a focus upon the teaching of playwriting and he began to acquire the character of a lone wolf within his own academic department. Meanwhile, his academic society narrowed to the weekly meetings of the "Shop Club," an intimate group of his colleagues and their wives which included the Fred Robinsons and the Bliss Perrys. So he lost touch with his contemporaries as he became increasingly the center of a cult of the theatre among the creative young spirits of Harvard and Radcliffe. And as these young people sought to make of the theatre an instrument of beauty in a world of business, G.P.B. moved steadily toward Barrett Wendell's ideal of a "vivifying" scholarship of "bold constructive imagination."

XXIII   ENGLISH 47

ON THE DAY ENGLISH 47 FIRST MET IN THE UPPER room in Dane Hall, ten men gathered about the round table at which G.P.B. sat. Presumably, what he had to say to them was much the same as what he had already said several times to the student playwrights at Radcliffe; yet he undoubtedly appeared in a different light at each of the round tables, and it is no small tribute to G.P.B.'s skill that he was immediately as much of a success with the young men who wished to write plays as with the young ladies.

For he was, in the eyes of these young fellows, no longer a young man himself. That spring, he marked his fortieth birthday. Nor was he a very well man; for he had suffered most of the year from a recurrence of his old "headaches." Already he was almost of an age with their fathers, in fancy if not in fact. A suggestion of the role he began to play in their young lives, and of his own comportment with them, occurs in the sobriquet they gave him among themselves — "Uncle George."

In his eyes, they were not much different from any other group of Harvard "writers" selected on the merits of their manuscripts. The graduate students were Homer E. Woodbridge, G. F. Evans, Leonard Hatch, Horace M. Kallen, and Maurice Wertheim. Of the undergraduates, three were seniors: R. G. Brown, G. E. Eversole, and Allan Davis; two were juniors, Van Wyck Brooks and Edward Brewster Sheldon. Four of the ten were professionally associated with the theatre in later years.

The real enthusiasts were Allan Davis, Leonard Hatch, Maurice Wertheim, and Edward Sheldon. Davis and Hatch had honorable careers as playwrights and directors of various theatrical activities; Wertheim became famous as a financier and played a large part in the establishment of the Theatre Guild; Sheldon was one of the first of the "university" dramatists to achieve a sustained success. Something of the general quality of the new American theatre was present in the class, yet even the broad social sympathies of Horace Kallen and Edward Sheldon might not have impressed an observer as a rippling wave of the future.

Nevertheless, an observing eye might well have marked G.P.B.'s focus of attention upon "reality" as a portent of plays to come. For one of the most persistent doctrines expounded at the round table was summarized in G.P.B.'s admonition, "Get your material from what you see about you." In this spirit, Edward Sheldon spent hours on the North End streets of Boston, sympathetically studying the labors of the Salvation Army lassies to salvage many a drifting derelict. And from these directions came the first act of a play which Sheldon showed to Minnie Maddern Fiske.

The actress, already aware that Harvard writers might provide her repertory company with new and fresh materials, had accepted an invitation of the Stylus Club to be their luncheon guest. G.P.B. was lecturing at the Sorbonne at the time; so the transactions concerning Sheldon's play about a Salvation lassie grew out of the enterprising college senior's initiative. However, he freely associated his play with what he had learned from Professor Baker; and the actress, in turn, accepted this as a recommendation. For she was on terms of friendly correspondence with G.P.B., whose advice about playscripts she had already sought for several productions at her Manhattan Theatre. It was peculiarly fitting that the first play of English 47 to receive professional production had its premiere at the Providence Opera House; for it was there that Mrs. Fiske first tried the play and found it made of the stuff of theatrical success. Thus Sheldon's initial success came while he was a Harvard student, and public acquaintance with English 47 was immediate.

When G.P.B. returned to the Yard in the fall of 1908, he found that Mrs. Fiske's continuing success with *Salvation Nell* had made the playwriting course as alluring as a gold field. That spring, twenty young men crowded the little room in Dane Hall. It is perhaps indicative of the nature of this interest in playwriting among the Harvard undergraduates at this time that of these twenty hopeful playwrights only one, David Carb, became a successful writer of plays. Each year more and more young "writers" anxiously awaited the brief note which might mean the highroad to fame: "Admitted to English 47. Please report to Upper Dane 4, the opening Friday of the term, at 3:30. How shall I return your manuscript?"

Undoubtedly, much of the impetus was the lure of an easy gamble. Some pursued a college fad. Yet the real drive among a surprising number was the hungry desire to make something of lasting beauty, which propels all artists. Much of G.P.B.'s success with English 47 must be attributed to the sensitive selection he exercised in securing for these classes those who had this desire. He knew the personal qualities he sought from his own experience with George Santayana, Bernard Berenson, and Clyde Fitch. Fortunately for his teaching, he found this creative spirit at the beginning of English 47 in Edward Sheldon. Undoubtedly his own image of the student playwright was in turn affected by Sheldon's devotion to the art of the theatre.

Yet G.P.B. was never the aesthete or artist himself to his students. Most of them who knew G.P.B.'s intimate hopes through the years knew that something of the artist drove him, too, toward some future time and place when, after retirement, he might write and direct plays. For most, however, he was not the artist but the sympathetic judge, the practical critic, the embodiment of the professional standards of the theatre. A clue to the relationship between English 47 and G.P.B.'s central point of view is suggested by one who took the course in 1911:

As I remember it, the gist of his instruction was the oft-repeated phrase: action, *action*, ACTION! It meant dramatic action, of course,

106

not entirely physical action, but he tried to teach us that every speech must advance the action somehow, not be just dialogue, no matter how character-revealing.

The final test for the artist was stage and audience.

For some members of the class, this was associated with the "well-made" plays of Scribe which G.P.B. assigned to be read. Others sought its source in one critic or another. A student of the second class in English 47 recalls G.P.B.'s practical method, suggestive of his work in argumentation: "B's chief message in playwriting was to write the well-made play, patterned after Dumas the Younger and Brieux. B. used to say that taking 47 would save the would-be playwright five or ten years of mistakes."

Another student of this class in the spring of 1908 was impressed with G.P.B.'s personal style and rhetorical mastery:

Of course, he had the advantage of a colorful and exciting subject. But he really had personality and style. He was a masterful lecturer, rather formal and untheatrical, but forceful in a well modulated way, and he had the advantage of a superb delivery — a resonant voice which he employed with great effect. When he read a scene he underplayed, had a fine sense of timing and characterization, and gave his hearers' imaginations full play.

At the round table, each found an individual meaning in what G.P.B. said and did.

The characteristic doctrine of his early lectures in English 47 may be discerned in some remarks he made in October 1910, during a course he developed to offer the theory of English 47 without the "practice in composition." This was Comparative Literature 19, The Forms of the Drama, a course which repeated the title of his original Radcliffe course in playwriting. The following notes upon these remarks show him preoccupied with his central thesis:

Drama is essentially action. Read the liturgical tropes to see what drama is. These show central action; what is done, not what is said, is of chief importance. The earliest form of drama in medieval times means story. Characterization is not the basis of drama; it is a necessity of well-developed drama, but it is not basic. Even characterizing speech is not necessary to the drama; but illustrative action is.

Drama depends on action. What is action? In the trope we have it

— a combination of speech, music, pantomime rhythmically combining to tell the story. The story is so simple in these tropes we call it episode: we have the drama in its crudest form.

Greek drama begins in dances. The chorus, music, dancing existed before the drama. The early dancing was not dramatic. As soon as the festival took on illustrative action it became dramatic.

Today a good play means one with a story to tell (not often found), done by a perfect comprehension of the people (to give us sympathy with the story) who behave as they ought to (according to their characters) in crucial situations.

The ideal play has a central story, explained in terms of consistent characterization, with a dialogue in keeping with the characters, and a charm of its own.

There can be drama without speech. The amount of talk will be cut down immensely in the future. Speech is not the essential. If the pantomime is what it should be, there are times when it is as effective — even more effective than speech. We talk too much on our stage. Facial expression, gesture, a cry and other ways of emotional expression are forgotten.

Well characterizing dialogue, with snap and go does not mean drama. It is an admirable capping stone, but it is useless without action. In the Restoration Comedy (Congreve especially) dialogue occupies about the position it ought to, historically.

Action is absolutely essential to the drama — it is its centre. Many modern plays have charm, but lack illustrative action; though they have characterizing dialogue, and have not action, it shall avail them naught.

When such a message was delivered with all of the persuasive force of which G.P.B. was capable, it mattered little whether the student really understood what "illustrative action" was. He felt confident that he knew what to do with the play he was writing, or that Professor Baker would soon make clear the nature of his difficulties.

In truth, G.P.B. was all things to his students, for there was a flexibility in his teaching which made him sensitive to the unexpressed needs of each writer. And there were all kinds of would-be writers. Occasionally, he struck some as facile or as a dilettante leading aesthetes and dilettantes who, in an earlier day, would have devoted themselves to poetry rather than to plays. Some even felt superior to what they saw as stolid, unimaginative shopkeeping of literary matters. For the sons of the families which had establishd the business culture of America were now in revolt against the society their successful fathers had made; to John Silas Reed, now enshrined with Lenin, and other young rebels who wrote plays at Harvard, G.P.B. may well have recalled the image of their fathers. There certainly was no absence of disbelief and even hostility from year to year as G.P.B. faced those gathered at his round table. Yet most of his writers idolized him, if for no other reason than that they knew he truly cared about their art and sincerely tried to help.

Through his devotion to those consecrated few like Edward Sheldon who might make a real contribution to the American drama, G.P.B. increasingly drew about him a dedicated band. At Harvard the cult centered in the "Baker's Dozen"; at Radcliffe, in the "47 Club." After 1913, the cult's epicenter was the "47 Workshop." And as the cultus looked to G.P.B. as both high priest and defender of the faith, he looked to them each year for another Sheldon.

One of the men from his third class of English 47 has expressed the feeling which grew among the successive classes:

My admiration for Baker was immediate, large, and lasting. I think that every other student in his classes felt as I did, and said so often and loudly, so that anybody could see then in Cambridge a G.P.B. cult.

And that, in a way, is a curious thing, for he was not a person who easily "gave himself" to his audience. My own relations with him were always of the friendliest, but not precisely warm — in the common sense.

Another member of this class recalls the dynamic force which made G.P.B. seem pathfinder, and even pontiff:

Professor Baker was a special spokesman for the new vitality of that period, which we might now look back on as a kind of "classic naturalism." While he preached the unconventional approach to life and the stage, he was too respectful of the safe and sane in drama to welcome many of the more radical experiments in composition or stagecraft, especially those that evaded responsibility to the audience, or those that replaced the sinews of drama by various devices that had little but novelty to recommend them.

Baker, however, was by no means a reactionary. He welcomed novelty of form and a reasonable degree of moral frankness. I once heard him laughingly deplore the hold Boston Puritanism had on him, in spite of his belief in dramatic freedom. I recall his insistence that Shaw was too contemptuous of the limitations of good dramatic technique, especially in his unrestrained bent to "talk things out." His mind was always preoccupied with that mysterious something called "dramatic effect" that exists above and beyond the printed word.

So G.P.B.'s spirit sought its own form in a procedure of teaching. Except that he gradually abandoned lectures as he evolved his workshop idea, his procedure in these early years remained consistent throughout the twenty years he taught playwriting at Harvard. Each year thus began with an attention to the recognition of what is dramatic in a theatrical sense, and to the essentials of play technique, much as they are treated in his book which grew out of his original lectures.

He especially emphasized the difference between dramatic action in the movement of a play, and what he termed action in the way of stage business. While he urged a proper notation of scenic effects, he generally deplored the tendency of young writers to spend all their efforts on elaborate descriptions of scenes and business with nothing left to put into the play itself. If he had a theme, it was Hamlet's "The play's the thing."

Very soon in the course, he set his writers to adapting stories. This he did because he believed the best way to learn what was dramatic and not merely narrative was to perform the operation of extracting the dramatic essence from pages of rambling narrative. So he gave them such stories as Stevenson's *Monsieur de Maletroit's Door* and Hardy's *Three Strangers*. These his students were to reduce to scenario form; next, they were to rewrite them as plays. Then they continued the exercise with stories of their own choosing. By the endless search through narrative fiction which this entailed, G.P.B. brought his writers to a settled persuasion that not one story in a hundred had anything usable for the stage.

In this contrite mood, they set about plays of their own invention — first one-acts, and finally a full length. Most of these he read to the class. If he liked a play, he was unsparing in his efforts to have it improved. Yet he could even be hopeful for those whose work fell far short. "Now that you have learned the technique," he would say as his students left him, "you may someday find the material and the inspiration to write a good play."

Among those who went on to a career in the theatre, his effect was varied. But for all who had even a moderate success at play-writing he accomplished two things. He taught them, as one who spoke for many has acknowledged, a sense of dramatic construction, of proportion, of hewing to the line. Above all, he made them have faith in themselves.

XXIV   IDEAS FOR A NEW THEATRE

WHEN, ON THE EVENING OF MARCH 29, 1903, CLYDE Fitch met with the Baker's Dozen, one of the topics of discussion for which G.P.B. had arranged was "A Proposed National Theatre," an idea with which he had returned from Europe the year before. Since his return, he had been engaged in negotiations to interest Major Henry Lee Higginson in providing Boston with a civic theatre comparable to the Boston Symphony. G.P.B.'s interest in an endowed theatre for Boston was but a first step toward similar theatres for the nation. In this, however, he was not occupied in a merely local enterprise. A Philadelphia group had but recently proposed to erect and endow an American Academy of Dramatic Art similar to the Comédie Française of Paris.

A few days after Fitch's visit, the editor of the *New York Tribune* published a letter from G.P B. in support of the Philadelphia project. In the American society, G.P.B. said, the position of our drama was that of the clown, or any similar entertainer. The causes of this were the lack of dramatic standards among our millions of theatre-goers and a failure on the part of the cultivated portion of the public to see that our national drama needed a home in which it should be as free as possible from the pressures of a money-making business. The purpose of all such reform, he emphasized, as he had done before and was still saying to Bostonians, was a drama of American conditions which should have permanent value.

Apparently the prospects of support from Major Higginson for a Boston civic theatre were good, at least, good enough for G.P.B.

to correspond with William Archer and Henry Arthur Jones about the matter. Archer, who had lectured in New York in 1899 on a national theatre for America, wrote G.P.B. on May 16, 1903 that he was forwarding a packet of materials relevant to G.P.B.'s theatrical scheme for Boston. In this, were the conclusions to his inquiries into the continental systems of theatrical endowment and government which he and a young actor named Granville-Barker had been gathering all winter.

As Archer mailed this packet, he must have had awaiting him in his mail a most optimistic report from Boston. For G.P.B. had already reached the point where he thought in terms of engaging a manager for the Boston civic theatre. To fill this position, he now asked Archer's assistance in securing either Dion Boucicault, the younger, or Frank Benson. Boucicault he had met through Henry Arthur Jones, and Benson's work in Shakespearean productions he had seen in London.

On the nineteenth of May, Archer advised G.P.B. that, excellent though Benson was, he would not be satisfactory to American audiences because he had too much literary intelligence. Boucicault, who might be more suited to American tastes on this score, was essentially a "long run" stage manager whose methods were wholly unadaptable to the freer methods required in a repertory theatre. Neither, he was certain, was G.P.B.'s man for Boston.

Then Archer turned to G.P.B.'s more immediate concern, the total cost of the sort of theatre he had in mind. As in so many of his enthusiasms, G.P.B.'s clear idea of a broad objective did not carry with it any distinct conception of what was involved in the expenditure of money and effort to achieve it. Fortunately, he could depend upon Archer's careful estimate that, if he were given a theatre and a reasonable initial stock of scenery and costumes, a working capital of $100,000 and a guarantee of an additional sum of the same amount would be enough to give the enterprise a fair start. It was, of course, impossible to say exactly what the theatre itself would cost, for that depended upon what one wished.

However, Archer saw that the most difficult problem, once one had a proper theatre, was to discover the right manager:

To return to the manager question — you really want two men — an artistic director and a stage director — and by the latter

112

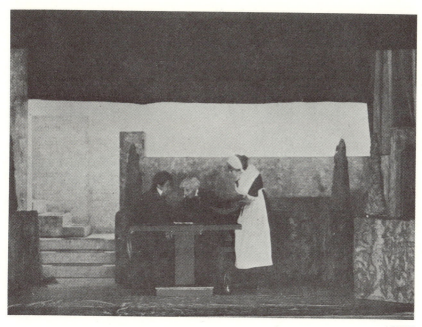

Rachel Lyman Field's *Time Will Tell*, Agassiz Theatre, 1920. Setting, Edward Ely and Rollo Wayne; Lighting, Munroe Pevear

A 1922 Harvard 47 Workshop Production, *The Mourner*, by James Mahoney. Setting, Rollo Wayne; Lighting, Stanley McCandless

With Lupe Velez and Ramon Novarro on the "Laughing Boy" set,
Metro-Goldwyn-Mayer Studios, 1933

Morris Shapiro

The Yale University Theater

I don't mean merely "stage manager" or producer. The two are to be found rolled into one in Germany & perhaps in France — not in the English speaking countries — though I believe if your theatre were started you would have a good chance of finding a heaven-born director developing himself in a few years among your Harvard men.

This idea apparently colored G.P.B.'s thinking permanently, for he pursued this division of function in the organization of the Yale University Theater. Then Archer made another suggestion:

If I were ten years younger, I would say that Granville Barker & myself were the two men you wanted. Joking apart, Barker would be the most valuable man in any such organization, though he has not as yet weight enough or experience enough to stand alone. He is a young actor (25), extremely intelligent, and thoroughly accustomed to the stage — has been on it from childhood. I doubt whether he will ever make a great actor, though he does some things admirably; but his ambition is dramatic authorship. He has written a lot of the craziest plays you can imagine — Meredith gone mad, I call them. Whether he will ever do anything as a dramatist I can't say — I think the betting is strongly the other way, his notions are so cranky. But the odd thing is that he is personally one of the sanest & one of the nicest young fellows I have ever struck, and not a bit cranky in his tastes as regards other people's work. He is a great friend & ally of Bernard Shaw's but not in the least touched with Shawism.

Nevertheless, until Major Higginson provided the theatre, talk of this nature was pleasant but not very profitable. Nor were there any immediate prospects of some other benefactor. However, as the year 1903 passed, assistance from Major Higginson came, though not in quite the manner for which G.P.B. had hoped.

The great philanthropist at last grew interested in improving the theatrical fare of Boston. After many discussions, in general terms, with G.P.B. at the Tavern Club, Major Higginson one day suggested to Lorin Deland, stage manager of the Tavern Club theatricals, that the expenses of some Boston stock company might be underwritten in order to provide fine plays at low prices. Deland, husband of novelist Margaret Deland and at one time a member of the Boston Museum company, was not only sympathetic with G.P.B.'s purposes but, as a friend of Higginson who shared the Major's interest in Harvard football, was personally better suited to promote those purposes than G.P.B. himself. When Higginson made the specific proposal that Deland should undertake the management of the Castle Square Theatre, Deland at once proposed Winthrop Ames, another interested Taverner, as a partner.

However, it seems fairly clear that Ames might never have entered upon his career of theatre management without the previous activity of G.P.B.'s hopes for an endowed repertory theatre in Boston. Ames had, to be sure, his own history of interest in the theatre since childhood; yet it is conceivable that he might have remained a member of a firm of publishers of art and architectural magazines had not G.P.B. pointed out to him what he might do for the theatre.

Since Higginson apparently did not wish to be publicly identified with the Castle Square venture, and since Deland deferred to what he called Ames's greater knowledge of the "technique of the theatre," Winthrop Ames became the principal public figure in the partnership which immediately included G.P.B. in an unofficial capacity. On May 14, 1904, Deland wrote to G.P.B.: "Things are moving along, but I am not ready quite yet to say that the thing is bound to go through, though it looks like it now." Shortly thereafter, Ames acquired the lease of the Castle Square Theatre, heir to the repertory tradition of the old Boston Museum and widely known as one of the best of the country's few remaining stock companies.

On September 17, the following notice appeared in the *New York Dramatic Mirror:* "From Boston comes a report that the Castle Square Theatre, in that city, has passed into the hands of a syndicate of wealthy citizens, whose purpose it is to make it, eventually, an endowed playhouse."

G.P.B.'s part in the project appears in the following excerpts of a letter which Ames sent him from the Tavern Club on September 30, 1904:

Thank you for your kind note about the C.S. You know how much we want your opinion and advice.

I wish you could have seen "When We Were 21." It was at least

50% better all around than "Article 47" — it really surprised me that the company did so really well with something decent to work with. Best of all, the audience liked the play very much, and we are learning the lesson of not underrating them by the frost "Michael Strogoff" is getting this week — and it deserves it.

The only actor you mention about whom I disagree with you is Miss Earle. She has tremendous energy but no flexibility whatever, and is as hard as nails, & with a voice and pronunciation that drive me to drink. I should be glad to have you see her in something else & see if your good opinion endures. I doubt it.

Macklin *is* hopeless, & goes week after next. Ditto the young comedian . . . We are trying for John Craig; but meantime leading men are not to be had at any price . . .

As to the South End Settlement people, I don't think they need worry: there are plenty of seats at the old price still left . . . There are still swarms of 25 and 35¢ seats.

An English Xmas pantomime would be interesting, but wouldn't it be dangerous? Would the actors know where they were at? let alone the audience? would a stock company succeed in such work?

Next week we play Carton's "Clean Slate" — a nice little English comedy I'm told — though I've not yet read it — it was Deland's choice. Never played in Boston before. After that "Soldiers of Fortune" then probably Pinero's "Dandy Dick" or "Sweet Lavender" (which not yet decided) followed by "When Knighthood was in Flower" — a "production" for a two-weeks run — so you see we're not feeding them such bad stuff.

As nearly as I can gather, the better *modern* plays are what the audience like best . . . It is the very devil to find those that fit all conditions — the company — contrast with predecessors — don't take too much scenery before one that does — etc etc etc.

Please suggest!

As these plans went forward in Boston, G.P.B. heard from Henry Arthur Jones: "We are making a fuss about a National Theatre — signing papers and agitating." In November, William Archer wrote: "I am at last sending you our National Theatre Blue Book — the first copy to go to America, though Brander Matthews saw it (in its earlier form) in London last summer. It may, of course, be shown to responsible persons."

Thus Winthrop Ames learned about the work of Harley Granville-Barker and William Archer. In a half dozen years, Ames assumed the directorship of the New Theatre after Barker turned down the offer because he foresaw the architectural failure which

Ames shortly found. Some dozen years after this, Archer's melo-drama, *The Green Goddess,* with George Arliss, became one of the greatest successes of Ames's producing career.

As the first year of the plan for an endowed theatre came to a close, Ames prepared to celebrate the five thousandth continuous production of plays at the Castle Square Theatre. He wrote G.P.B., May 3, 1905:

> We shall make a little fuss about it, & Julia Ward Howe is going to write a little poem & read it between the acts . . . & you *might* possibly "feel moved" to write a letter — a very brief one would do — to the Transcript, rewording something like what you said at the Woman's Education Association — that such an institution was worth while in Boston.

The letter which G.P.B. then wrote to the *Transcript* shows the historical sense with which he worked to develop a favorable environment for the coming American drama. It also served notice to the *Transcript* readers who remembered his 1902 article, "A Subsidized Theatre," that the instrument for achieving those pur-poses was at hand. He wrote, viewing the Castle Square Theatre and the preceding decade of American taste in the drama:

> During eight years marked theatrically in this country by the full development of the star system and the dominance in the best theatres of musical burlesque, this theatre has presented to the satis-faction of a large and varied public a great variety of plays. Its repertoire, ranging from frank melodrama through successes of the day to old comedy, such as "She Stoops to Conquer" and "The School for Scandal," and to Shakespeare, has given its patrons a chance to see more standard plays than any theatre without a stock company is likely to provide. The success of the theatre, with its public as loyal as was that of the Old Boston Museum, shows that there is no reason to believe that the stock company is a thing of the past. Moreover, it is to such a stock company that we must look to keep recent plays of real merit before the public, for instance, the work of Mr. Jones and Mr. Pinero . . . in a small way, this theatre has been duplicating the conditions of the palmiest period of our dramatic literature, 1590–1610. Rapidly at that time a school of dramatists lifted a fairly definite audience, week by week, from absorbed interest in the cruder and melodramatic work of the pred-ecessors of Shakespeare to delighted appreciation of his master-pieces . . . That is, just as the Symphony concerts have changed

or developed the musical taste of Boston, this theatre has developed the taste of its public.

At this time, Shakespeare's relationships as a developing craftsman with the taste of his Elizabethan public were much on G.P.B.'s mind; for he was at work on a course of Lowell Lectures concerning these matters for the winter series of 1905–06. The year following their delivery, the lectures were published as *The Development of Shakespeare as a Dramatist,* a work which Barrett Wendell was pleased to find dedicated to himself.

Imbued with thoughts of the interrelationship of audience and theatre and playwright and actor, G.P.B. urged Ames to do a cycle of Shakespeare's plays, such as had not been seen in Boston since the productions of Booth and Irving. He also wished his young friend to deal generously with the plays of Pinero and Jones. And, as Ames went forward with plans for a fine repertory of Shakespeare which was to remain in the memory of thousands of schoolchildren and sophisticates of the theatre as a standard of excellence, G.P.B. received a gloomy appraisal of the drama which threw Boston and London into sharp contrast. Henry Arthur Jones, who had but recently promised that Harvard should have his Kelmscott vellum *Chaucer* and who was preparing a lecture on the modern drama for the college, wrote G.P.B. on the twenty-ninth of October:

The English modern drama is utterly stagnant — there never was so dead a thing as our drama just now. The public has lost all interest in it. Musical comedy, childish, witless, inane, fills our theatres — there are a few absurd nondescript farces and even more absurd "romantic dramas" — of living drama or comedy not a scrap can I find on our stage this season — authors, actors, managers and public, we are all in the doldrums — all empty and brainless alike.

In contrast, G.P.B.'s world was seething with accomplishment and promise during the autumn of 1905. The Ames management of the Castle Square Theatre was in the midst of a brilliant success. G.P.B.'s approaching lectures at the Lowell Institute were the harbinger of a book which should unite his historical and technical studies of the drama; his new Harvard course in playwriting would commence with the spring term; and he looked forward to acting once more. As G.P.B. prepared himself for the role of Christopher Marlowe in Josephine Preston Peabody's play, he could feel the spirit of a new renaissance in the drama working around him. Indeed, Winthrop Ames now talked of building an ideal modern theatre in Boston.

When G.P.B. received the appointment to the Hyde Lectureship at the Sorbonne for 1907–08, Ames decided that it was an opportune moment to study the modern theatres of Europe in preparation for the endowed theatre he meant to give Boston. So he withdrew from the management of the Castle Square Theatre and planned to join G.P.B. abroad while he lectured in Paris and at the French provincial universities on the history of the English drama.

Just before G.P.B. left for Paris, he made some remarks for the benefit of the *Transcript* readers which reveal the line of thought he and Ames were following. Commenting upon the ideal size of a theatre, G.P.B. said:

Nearly all our theatres are too large for really fine acting. They are much better than they were, but there is a self-assertive style of decoration and gaudiness that distracts the true purpose of a theatre, which is its style. I have often wondered if "Candida" would have made the success it did excepting for the intimate smallness of the theatre where it was first acted. A theatre should subordinate all its salon effects to a general application of its purpose, which is focused upon the stage. There should be nothing about the auditorium to disturb one's attention there, where the one brilliant effect of the evening should be seen.

The two friends met in Paris after Ames had made a tour of sixty-four of Europe's finest theatres and opera houses, recording his observations in a carefully prepared notebook which is now in the Theatre Collection of the New York City Public Library. As the two discussed the sketches and notes of details which G.P.B. knew from previous visits of his own, the form of the "Ames Theatre" emerged. From ornamental *A's* to the mechanical details of exit lights, from exquisitely wrought salon décor to the most efficient of stage machines, Boston was to have the finest little theatre of the century.

However, the idea which had begun in Paris in 1902 and which seemed to achieve the vivid outlines of reality in Paris five years later remained but a dream when G.P.B. returned to Boston. Ames never got beyond buying the land and drawing the plans for the theatre; for in July 1908 the syndicate of New York millionaires which was building its own "New Theatre" persuaded him to become the director of that enterprise. Thus Boston, which led America with its Symphony and its Art Museum, lost the initiative to a cause that failed. But G.P.B. cherished his dream and saw it take various forms as the result of his own efforts in Boston and Cambridge before his hope of a civic theatre that "would exist to teach primarily" was realized in the University Theater at New Haven.

xxv   SHAKESPEARE'S SUPREMELY PLASTIC STAGE

IT IS ONE OF THE IRONIES OF G.P.B.'S STORY THAT THE man who denied him the achievement of a theatre at Harvard first gave him the opportunity to organize his philosophy of the drama. For A. Lawrence Lowell was not only the President of Harvard University, he was also the Trustee of the Lowell Institute. In his secondary capacity, he invited G.P.B. on December 9, 1904 to prepare a series of six lectures which G.P.B. had proposed to Barrett Wendell. This proposal concerning "The Development of Shakespeare as a Dramatic Artist" had duly been forwarded by Wendell to Lowell.

And if Trustee Lowell had not seen fit to invite these lectures, subsequently published as *The Development of Shakespeare as a Dramatist,* President Lowell might never have been confronted by the translation of this philosophy into action. For it now seems clear that English 47 and The 47 Workshop were practical extensions of the principal ideas of these lectures, delivered during the winter of 1905–06, some elements of which go back to things he had said to island fisher folk on a misty night in 1890. It is equally clear that the authority of his teaching of playwriting rested, in the beginning, upon this masterly history of the development of Shakespeare's dramatic technique and his penetrating observations upon its modern significance.

It is to be noticed that G.P.B.'s original title for these lectures presents Shakespeare as a "dramatic artist." Against the current and uncritical views that the "real Shakespeare" wrote only with an eye to the paying public, G.P.B. urged what he acknowledged to be a truism: that Shakespeare was an artist. Indeed, an underlying thesis of his presentation was that the growth of an artistic conscience in Shakespeare might well be emulated by modern dramatists. In these words he offered his image of the supreme dramatic artist:

> Shakespeare mellowed even in the powers with which he was originally endowed. He acquired powers he did not originally possess. He substituted better for poorer methods. On the other hand, Shakespeare knew better than any other dramatist of his day the real meaning of "Art for Art's sake," for time and again he moulded his material, not merely to accord with public taste of his time, or even, as was the case with Ben Jonson, so as to conform to standards drawn for the Classical drama, but so as to satisfy some inner standards drawn from his own increasing experience or from that constant beacon of the highest creative minds, the artistic conscience.

Another tenet of his philosophy set forth in these lectures was the historical relativism with which he evaluated any drama. There was, he said, a common fallacy in recent thought: "It is the idea that here are certain standards by which the plays of any period may be declared good or bad without regard for the time in which a play was written, the public for whom it was written, or the stage on which it was acted." Nevertheless, he believed he had discovered in Shakespeare's development as a dramatist some permanent properties of plays.

These great qualities of Shakespeare and the predecessors from whom he learned were not only the high points in an artistic evolution. The permanent properties of their plays came from a vital homogeneity of artist, stage, and society which became G.P.B.'s own ideal:

> They knew every peculiarity and device of the stage on which their plays would be presented; they did not write, as do playwrights to-day, for countless stages of innumerable differences in England, America, and Australia. They did not write for many companies, some of which the dramatist of to-day never sees in his plays, but for a company so well known to them that even as they wrote they

could hear the very voices of the men and lads who would play their heroes and their heroines. They did not write for a hydra-headed, sated, composite, which we call the public, but for a group of people almost as definitely known to them from repeated watching as are regular customers to the tradesmen of to-day.

When revived today, these Elizabethan plays show a remarkable acting quality which merely means that they were so skillfully devised to fit their public that they acquired permanent dramatic appeal.

Of further import to G.P.B.'s philosophy was his belief that Shakespeare wrote for an audience which read very little and for whom the theatre performed the functions of most of the modern media of communication. Indeed, said G.P.B., the Elizabethan went to see and hear a play in a mood which was delightfully childlike. Thus Shakespeare found the greater part of his audience had but a single critical standard: "Does it interest me?"

With a caveat that much of what his own "reading" audience found of delight in Walter Pater and George Meredith might, a century thence, strike latter day readers as arrant fustian, G.P.B. recited to his Lowell Institute listeners a passage from Thomas Kyd's *Spanish Tragedy* which still delighted those who heard it begin:

> O eyes! no eyes, but fountains fraught with tears;
> O life! no life, but lively form of death:

This passage, G.P.B. allowed, was fantastically mannered if read without sympathetic imagination and emotion; for here was an example of the Elizabethan dramatist's awareness that on the stage it is emotion, more than thought, which hits home to the audience. What, he asked, did the Elizabethan spectator need more than the poses, expression, gestures, and tone of the actor's voice to understand that this was the anguish of an aged father at the death of his son? What matter the mannered phrase, if Hieronimo's agonized "O eyes!" still carried its original emotional appeal? This alone explained why the leap of the heroine of melodrama was more moving for today's audiences than the sobbing departure of Iris from the rooms of Maldonado.

Sketching the evolution of the Elizabethan stage, he showed the extraordinary advantages which that stage afforded actor, playwright, and scenic artist. Dramatists, he explained, did not then consider their stage to be a rigid, fixed mechanism such as the twentieth century knew as its inheritance from the nineteenth. Instead, they worked with what he called a "supremely plastic" instrument which could be "planned for whatever they desired" as one scene melted swiftly into others. This emphasis which G.P.B. gave to the mobility and plasticity of the Elizabethan stage can be seen in its proper perspective if one recalls that it preceded by almost a decade the motion picture art of David Wark Griffith. Certainly it was a part of the growing understanding which finally broke the twentieth-century drama from its picture-frame stage and gave it the movement and adaptability that have made possible the popular renaissance of Shakespearean production since the second World War.

In developing this idea of the plasticity of the Elizabethan stage, G.P.B. returned to his old thesis, gained from experiment since 1895 with Elizabethan revivals, concerning the multiplicity and variability of curtains which permitted a practically unlimited arrangement of space upon the Elizabethan stage. For he saw there what he now wished to see in his own time — a stage amenable to the creative imaginations which employed it.

The practical effect of such a view was to explain two things which the reading of Shakespeare as "literature" rather than seeing it as "theatre" had long obscured. The succession of scenes in Shakespeare's plays now appeared as a solid bar of action nearly like the effect of a motion picture; no longer did editorial divisions of acts and scenes or the immobility of the proscenium stage break the continuity. Furthermore, it could now be seen that Shakespeare's effects of contrast and juxtaposition in successive scenes were a subtle and important part of his art.

Germane to this insight was his interest in the technical equivalents of Elizabethan mobility and plasticity which the new century might find in lighting and special stage devices. From such insight has come the character of such mid-century Shakespearean productions as those of Margaret Webster and Laurence Olivier and the extraordinary recent success of Shakespeare on film. Because of such teaching, the twentieth-century drama achieved a technical and artistic freedom which is now taken for granted.

Yet if scholars found insufficient support for some of G.P.B.'s views of the Elizabethan stage, the ideas which he was already elaborating in his Lowell Lectures were really directed at the playwrights, directors, designers, and audience which was the American theatre. It was to these that he said the words which later concluded his scholarly second chapter of *The Development of Shakespeare as a Dramatist:*

> Though the stage of Shakespeare was different from our own . . . the actors, thrust out into the midst of the audience as they were, could get a quicker response than can our own, who are always framed in like a picture. In a word, the conditions of the Shakespearian stage were intimate to an extent we scarcely realize and permitted a detail not possible in our larger theatres. Above all, everything in the performance tended to make the play the thing: no lavish scenery drew off the attention, properties were usually employed only to the extent the play demanded; there were no "stars," and both actor and hearer must give themselves up to the author, the one to interpret, the other to understand, if the play was to produce its full effect. Is it not evident that, for the dramatist, conditions were far better than to-day, indeed, well-nigh perfect.

XXVI   "AMATEUR DE TOUT CE QUI TOUCHE AU THÉÂTRE"

ON NOVEMBER 4, 1907, THE TEMPS OF PARIS PRINTED its story about the new James Hazen Hyde lecturer at the Sorbonne. Just arrived, he had been interviewed immediately; for considerable interest attached to the exchange of professors at the University of Paris with ones at Harvard. Barrett Wendell, George Santayana, and Archibald Cary Coolidge had preceded this "littérateur qui passione le théâtre." Obviously charmed by the visitor, the reporter introduced G.P.B. to Paris as an "amateur de tout ce qui touche au théâtre."

Discussing what the story called his "veritable et curieuse école d'art dramatique," G.P.B. disclosed some very good news he had just received. Two of the plays recently written in his playwriting course had been purchased for production that winter by the leading American actors, E. H. Sothern and Julia Marlowe. Then, with "une bonne grâce parfaite," he confided that in coming to Paris he had realized something very close to his heart: an opportunity to study the contemporary French theatre.

In early December, G.P.B. gave the first of the lectures which he repeated in the spring at the universities of Aix, Lyons, Marseilles, Nancy, and Bordeaux. His Sorbonne course, "le Développement de la tragédie et de la comédie anglaises de 1590 à 1800," was at once a success. Christina sent the good news home:

Everyone seems pleased with Geo's *method* of delivery, finding his enunciation clear and distinct & his delivery emotional and varied. The solidity and structure of the lectures also strikes the professors — the man who teaches Eng. Lit. at the Sorbonne, Mr. Legouis, thanked Geo. after the first lecture, for distinctly new ideas   also his assistant the same. The audience, last Tuesday was larger than ever before . . . Tonight G. goes to a dress rehearsal of a new play of Bernhardt's.

So the days and evenings passed pleasantly, and always there were interesting and appreciative people. Something of this environment appears in further lines of Christina's letters home:

George was taken, by Morton Fullerton to call on Mrs. Wharton (of the House of Mirth) & she at once called on me . . . She invited us to lunch while I was in Switzerland. Geo. went. He enjoys her work and likes her. She is eager to know the *Révue de Paris* people; so we have asked Mr. & Mrs. Wharton to tea at 5 tomorrow. M. & Mme. Bérard are coming, M. Auber, who writes for the *Révue,* and M. Gaullis, one of the prominent newspaper men here.
     . . . We had Mrs. Wharton & Winthrop Ames here to dinner last Sat.

On June 6, 1908, as the Bakers collected luggage and children aboard ship, the *Harvard Crimson* announced to Cambridge that Professor Baker was sailing for home. G.P.B. returned to a world not only considerably different but somewhat changed. For one thing, the plans for Ames's endowed theatre had been indefinitely postponed. Also, G.P.B. contrasted the attention and genuine interest in his work which he had met in France with what he found on the same cultural levels at home. What seemed to count most in America was the kind of success which had just come to Edward Sheldon's *Salvation Nell.* As G.P.B. prepared to resume his teaching, he made an important decision.

He could see that the success of his work in teaching dramatic technique, which the French thought well worth while for its own sake, hung on the sheer chance of some manager or actor liking a student manuscript. Obviously the time had arrived when he must devise some apparatus for insuring a repetition of Edward Sheldon's success. Somehow, the forces of actor, playwright, audience, and theatre must be brought into a working relationship at Harvard which should prepare finished drama for the American stage. G.P.B. decided to find the necessary liaison between English 47 and what could be described only by the vulgar phrase, "Broadway success."

Fortunately for this decision, one of the changes which had occurred during his absence was directly related to this problem. In early March, Ned Sheldon and some of the Baker's Dozen had met with other undergraduates at the Harvard Union to form the Harvard Dramatic Club. The *Crimson* for March 13 explained their purpose:

It is the plan to devote at least half the year to the production of plays written by the undergraduates themselves. It is needless to dilate upon the splendid chance this offers to those interested in dramatic composition. It is hoped that Professor Baker's course in "The Technique of the Drama," to be given next year, will supply a large share of this material.

Three principles distinguished this group from the other Harvard and Radcliffe societies concerned with theatricals: the club was to confine its productions to original plays; it proposed to use men and women in its casts; and it determined to employ a professional director for each production. For their "Graduate Committee" of advisers, the men chose H. T. Parker, *Transcript* dramatic critic; Winthrop Ames; and G.P.B. Here, apparently, was a group amenable to G.P.B.'s ideas and possibly plucky enough to put them through.

The first play produced by the Harvard Dramatic Club was Allan Davis' *The Promised Land,* a tragedy concerning the Zionist movement, written for English 47. A report on the club and its play in the February 1909 issue of *The Burr McIntosh Monthly* presented pictures and a summary of the plot:

In brief, the story concerns itself with an attempt on the part of a Jewish diplomat of European birth to gain Palestine as a home for his people during their bitter persecution in Russia. He is hampered by lack of funds owing to the rich and selfish members of his own race refusing to subscribe to the project. Unable to gain Palestine, which his followers have grown to regard as the promised land, he turns his attention to accessible territory in Africa, where he hopes to start a colony as a temporary halting place until they are able to secure Palestine. Blinded by bigotry and ignorance, his followers refuse to accept any substitute for Palestine and turn against him in the hour of triumph.

Mr. Wilfred North, stage manager for Minnie Maddern Fiske, directed the production and achieved a professional finish which was generally remarked.

The following spring, the club produced a bill of one-act plays, all products of G.P.B.'s course, which were equally successful. Moreover, the club productions already showed the kind of discipline associated with professionals. In this group, the Idler Club of Radcliffe, and his courses in dramatic composition, G.P.B. began to discern the elements of an effective apparatus for developing marketable plays. Only a proper theatre was lacking.

To supply this want, he determined to appeal to the Harvard alumni for assistance by means of his editorial position on the *Harvard Graduates' Magazine*. The growing contributions of Harvard men to the American theatre merely emphasized this lack at Harvard, where the H.D.C. shows already demonstrated the economic feasibility of a university theatre. While in France, G.P.B. had delivered lectures on the Harvard and Radcliffe dramatists whose work he knew intimately. To these discussions of Percy MacKaye, Edward Knoblock, and William Vaughn Moody, he added his estimate of the work of Allen Davis and Edward Sheldon to make his plea for alumni support. This appeared as "A Group of Harvard Dramatists" in the June 1909 issue of the *Harvard Graduates' Magazine*.

To G.P.B.'s suggestion that Harvard should supply the leadership and the standards of the coming American drama by assuming the cultural responsibility which must sooner or later devolve upon American universities, Percy MacKaye replied, June 20:

At so vital an era of promise & growing achievement in our country's drama, it is a rare joy to me, as a worker, to have your fellowship and to feel your friendly critical hand in mine. I thank you from my heart. And you have set forth the situation so admirably in your article: it is an excellent work of education for the academic readers of the Graduates' Magazine in that respect and will open their eyes, I believe, by the specific suggestion it gives of a greatly important field of "liberal education."

To support his thesis that the universities had an obligation to foster new playwrights, G.P.B. now tried to guide the H.D.C. away from its exclusive concern with undergraduate writing. With plays of MacKaye, Knoblock, Owen Davis, Josephine Preston Peabody, and Moody in mind, he was pleased to see the group choose Percy MacKaye's *The Scarecrow* for its 1909 fall production. Thereafter the club sought far outside the Yard for plays which promised box office success.

While the H.D.C. rehearsed MacKaye's play, G.P.B. watched for professional reactions to his growing apparatus. For the first month's repertory of the New Theatre, Winthrop Ames had already selected plays by Knoblock and Sheldon. There was every good sign of a practical relationship now between the H.D.C. and the New Theatre, with Ames as the principal liaison. Here, plainly to be seen, was proof of Harvard's incumbent leadership in the American drama; for the New Theatre bid fair to be the great national theatre and academy of future dramatic standards. However, there was no official response at Harvard to these challenging opportunities. Except for G.P.B. and the small group around him, few at Harvard seemed to hear this call to greatness.

Thus the discouraging opening night of the New Theatre brought more than an immediate distress at the apparent failure of Ames's directorship. In a mood of depression G.P.B. wrote to Henry Arthur Jones, who replied on the last day of November:

I hope you will not give way to depression, but will keep on grinding away. I think it is quite possible that you may not see any great results during your lifetime, but I am sure your work will be recognized hereafter, and when I say hereafter, I do not mean in another and better world, but in this very world where you are living. What a help to me you would have been when I was beginning to write plays!

Coincident with these words of reassurance from Jones, came rumors that some wealthy New York theatre manager had offered to endow a theatre at Harvard. As friends sent G.P.B. newspaper clippings about an amazing offer from the manager of the Hudson Theatre, G.P.B. went ahead with his plan to present one of Moody's plays in Cambridge. If, it seemed reasonable to conjecture, the work of William Vaughn Moody could be shown at Sanders Theatre, the disparity between what Harvard was doing to foster the drama and what she could do might be emphasized.

On December 22, 1909, with the approval of the department of English, G.P.B. requested the advice of Henry Miller, who was then rehearsing Moody's *The Faith Healer* for its New York opening. On the same day, he wrote to the manager of the Hudson Theatre to inquire what prompted the repeated newspaper reports that he wished to endow a university theatre.

XXVII   THE NEW THEATRE AND HOPES FOR A HARVARD THEATRE

FOR THE LAST WEEK OF APRIL 1907, G.P.B. AND CHRIStina had as their house guest William Archer, who was returning to London from a recent visit to New York concerning the directorship of the already much discussed "New Theatre." This was a project very like the idea of a civic repertory theatre which G.P.B. had been promoting in Boston for nearly half a dozen years and which Winthrop Ames appeared ready to realize. Undoubtedly, Archer would have preferred an association with G.P.B. in the theatre which Ames planned to build and operate along the line of his successful management of the Castle Square Theatre. For Ames had already secured the land and wished only time to study the best European theatre practices before settling the design of an ideal theatre for Boston. However, it was the wealthy New Yorkers who were ready to engage a director, and it was in somewhat of a competitive spirit that G.P.B. and Ames regarded the Englishman's visit.

It may well be that Archer's association with the New York plans hastened those of Ames, for certainly the sketches and notes which Ames showed G.P.B. in Paris that fall indicate an advanced organization of decision concerning the design of a superb small theatre. And when, the following spring, G.P.B. heard from London that Archer and Harley Granville-Barker were going to New York for further talks about the directorship, the prospect of a friendly rivalry for theatrical excellence between Ames and Archer in America must have eased his departure from a most pleasant year in France.

It was thus something of a reversal of events for G.P.B. to learn upon his return that Ames had been named the director of the New Theatre. Not only was Ames to do for New York what he had intended to do for Boston, but he was pursuing a course contrary to their mutual conclusions from firsthand study of the finest European theatres.

Instead of an intimate theatre, designed especially for the most effective production of plays, Ames began that July to supervise the construction of one of the largest theatres of the day. Indeed, the insistence of the New Theatre founders upon a mammoth stage and auditorium, more suitable for opera than for drama, appears to have prompted Archer and Granville-Barker to reject the plan. It is thus a mark of G.P.B.'s loyalty and characteristic of his willingness to test even the least auspicious ideas of his students that he supported his friend's decision and remained throughout Ames's directorship a staunch supporter of the New Theatre.

After the disappointing opening on November 6, 1909, at which G.P.B. sat upon the stage with J. P. Morgan, Governor Hughes, Senator Root, and the founders, G.P.B. sent two of the souvenir booklets to Henry Arthur Jones. Ames's production of *Antony and Cleopatra* seemed to lack the verve of his Castle Square Shakespeare, and G.P.B. was disturbed at the poor acoustics and a general unwieldiness of the theatre attributable to the conflicting purposes of music and drama it served. On the thirtieth of the month, Jones replied: "Apparently the start has not been a very auspicious one, but it is, of course, an enormous experiment and could not be expected to work quite smoothly at the beginning. You must keep on banging away at it."

The opinion of the London *Times* dramatic critic, Arthur Bingham Walkley, which H. T. Parker printed on his page of the *Transcript,* shows the foreboding with which many of G.P.B.'s acquaintance viewed this opening. To be rightly understood, said the Englishman, the New Theatre had to be seen as part of a great intellectual movement, conspicuous in America but at its maximum energy in New York:

Is the stately New Theatre, with its marble walls and hangings of crimson and gold, to be the home of a new American drama, or, if not that, at least a really active force in the life of this great city? Or is it to be like so many others, a monument to a "fine purpose" frustrated and abandoned?

For his opening repertory, Ames chose (besides the Shakespeare and John Galsworthy's *Strife*) two plays by former students of G.P.B. These were Edward Knoblock's *The Cottage in the Air* and Edward Sheldon's *The Nigger*. In February, he added Hermann Hagedorn's *The Witch,* an adaptation of a Scandinavian play to the conditions of the Salem witchcraft trials. Though this predecessor of Arthur Miller's *The Crucible* was perhaps more like Sardou than Salem, Ames tried with such choices to stimulate the production of good new American plays. Of course, G.P.B. was delighted.

However, it was perfectly clear that Ames would have to find every season at least half a dozen plays as good as or better than Sheldon's *The Nigger*. For the native plays showed up pitifully against Shakespeare and Galsworthy, and there evidently was not a ready supply of American plays even so good as Sheldon's. It would take time, G.P.B. said — five years, ten years, perhaps a generation — but he was sure the New Theatre would hasten the day.

Not everyone was so pleased or so patient. In mid-December, Henry B. Harris, manager of New York's Hudson Theatre, asked: "Of what good is the endowment of a theatre if no good plays can be furnished it?" At the same time he announced to the American press that he was ready to be the first of ten men to give twenty-five thousand dollars toward establishing a chair of dramatic writing in an American university.

For several weeks, Harris' offer continued to appear in the national press. When subsequent variants mentioned Harvard and G.P.B. as recipients of such largesse, G.P.B. wrote to Mr. Harris on the twenty-second of December:

I have received newspaper clippings to the effect that you have generously offered $25,000 on the condition that nine other persons will contribute a like amount toward the founding and the maintenance of the work in Harvard College in playwriting. May I ask if this is correct? If so, I should like to see you as soon as possible in order that I may set about interesting the other nine givers.

We do need badly just about the sum you named, for unless a chair in the subject is endowed here, I much fear that in case anything happens to me the work might be run in very different fashion. What will make the work of permanent value will be an endowed chair under carefully specified conditions.

I should hope that such a sum as you name might provide not only the endowed chair, but a building containing a small, but perfectly equipped theatre, some rooms for conferences and lectures, and a small library of plays, dramatic prints, models of historical stages, and current publications of the drama in different languages.

If the reported offer is not a mere newspaper rumor, I should be glad if I might talk with you during the Christmas recess, which begins tomorrow, and lasts until Jan. 3. I think I might be able to raise an appreciable part of this sum during a proposed visit to New York at the end of next week.

Two days later, Percy MacKaye sent G.P.B. the following warning:

Mr. H. — the manager — is, I think, only half serious in his published announcement (seeing an "ad" in it); but he would, I think, readily be persuaded to be enthusiastic. However, I am very anxious that you should not be inveigled into supplying a managerial "ad," & the desideratum of a Harvard theatre put into a wrong light . . .

But the warning came too late. Harris' publicity man had already released the story and G.P.B.'s letter to the national press services.

Whatever questionable construction this publicity device placed upon the question of a theatre for Harvard, the time for action was at hand. On Christmas day, a striking story appeared in the *Boston Advertiser:*

STUDENT THEATRE AT YALE UNIVERSITY

Yale is to have a fully equipped theatre for use by student players and professional companies invited to appear before the university. The sum at hand is $8500, and it is planned to devote part of the receipts from annual tours of the Yale glee, banjo, and mandolin clubs to the fund.

Preliminary plans are for a structure seating 1400 people, with completely equipped stage, club, and library rooms for the dramatic association, musical clubs, and the Yale orchestra. Here the two productions of English plays each year and those of French, Spanish, and German will be given.

It has been suggested that Yale name its theatre after William Dunlap, New York's famous early dramatist and manager and founder of the new Yale academy of design.

Thus the genuine educational need for a theatre at Harvard was publicized under conditions which were bound to be repugnant to serious and conservative natures. Not only was the matter associated with all the possible vulgarities of "show business," but it was immediately thrust into the category of a questionable rivalry with Yale. To his chagrin, G.P.B. now discovered that Mr. Harris attached impossible conditions to his gift, with the consequence that an independent search for endowment was necessary to avoid a miserable fiasco.

In haste, G.P.B. presented his plan for raising the necessary funds to President Lowell. After consulting with the members of the Harvard Corporation, Lowell replied, on January 18, 1910:

I brought up the question of your raising money for a professorship and theatre before the Corporation yesterday. They were glad to accept the professorship, but very reluctant about the theatre. In fact, they were disinclined to consider the theatre at all unless it could be used for other purposes, including music.

Here was the same frustrating conception of a theatre as that which the founders of the New Theatre had maintained.

Nevertheless, the possibility of an endowed chair was not merely a minor good. In the hope that all would yet be well, G.P.B. addressed the following appeal to James Hazen Hyde on the nineteenth of February. Similar letters went to all persons of wealth who might be favorably disposed, and the most was made of the now extensive advertisement of Mr. Harris' offer. G.P.B. wrote:

I hope I can interest you in a proposal to endow at Harvard the work which I have been doing in the history and the technique of the drama. This has grown from a statement recently of H. B. Harris's, the theatrical manager of New York, that he would give $25,000 as the first subscription toward a fund of $250,000 to endow a professorship here and build a building to be devoted to the courses in the drama. The Corporation, while most cordial to the Professorship, feels that the building is not at the moment so much needed as are some other schemes for which they are already begging, and has therefore asked me to raise at present only the amount needed to endow the Professorship. While I believe the building to be more imperatively needed than the Corporation realize, I readily acquiesce with their wish for the Professorship as the first step, and the building will very shortly be seen to be imperative. The sum needed for the Professorship is $100,000 to $120,000. Winthrop Ames and Mrs. David Kimball have practically doubled the offer of Mr. Harris. Ames is most hearty in his support of the work, telling me to come back later if the full amount does not come in readily. He bade me, in interesting you, tell you of his thoroughgoing support of the plan.

As G.P.B.'s hopes for a university theatre at Harvard brightened, Winthrop Ames saw his own hopes for the New Theatre grow dim. On the occasion of the first anniversary of the great marble halls and the hangings of crimson and gold, Ames invited G.P.B. to give one of the dinner addresses. Already the huge theatre was a failure as G.P.B., in his now almost illegibly hurried hand, jotted the following notes for his speech:

I was glad to accede to Ames's request because, as most of you know, from the first I have sympathized heartily with your ideals. I am grateful for what in their beginnings you have already accomplished; I trust that the remaining difficulties may be solved. Your reward, of your success, is clear enough — & we who have believed in you will not find it hard to justify you to the youth who watch you: but should you fail — the movement cannot fail for sooner or later — & sooner rather than later — somewhere in this country the drama will have a home where permanently it can give to the best advantage the best of the past & experiment with what seems promising of the offering of the present.

That the New Theatre may be this home has been & still is my hope.

After G.P.B. had addressed the assembled millionaires and had returned to Cambridge, a note of thanks which Ames wrote on the twenty-eighth came in the mail:

It was very good of you to come on to make that speech at the Founders' dinner, and it really made a very wide-spread impression. I had a talk with some of the "Commercial Managers" later — people like Klaw and Erlanger — and they were extremely complimentary and said it did not sound like a "Professor's" speech and was extremely good common sense. Henry B. Harris also spoke of you in most complimentary terms, and said that his offer of money toward the foundation was still open, although the others somewhat chaffed him about it.

"Good common sense" was the character which G.P.B. cultivated in the theatre. There the aesthetic sensitivity of his youth seemed to give way to a kind of Yankee shrewdness. This, however, was not so deep as it seemed; for underneath was the lover of woodland and flowers, of horses and hunting dogs. Hence the quality which always impressed the theatre professionals, in one who was frankly an amateur, was his extraordinary "feel" for what was theatrically right.

Some of this Yankee character undoubtedly came from his long habitual summer residence in northern New England. Before his departure for the Sorbonne lectures, he chose from the New Hampshire land looking up to Chocorua mountain a stony piece on which to build the idyllic retreat whose name, "Boulder Farm," united practical and impractical. It was thus characteristic of this inner man that he had proceeded for some time with his endowment program before he saw the incongruity of seeking funds for a nonexistent professorship.

To aid him in this solicitation, the Harvard Corporation made him Professor of Dramatic Literature. At the news of this elevation, Brander Matthews sent his humorous compliments, May 28, 1910:

Let me hasten to welcome you to the seat in the chair which I, alone in all the world, have occupied now for ten years and more.

Hereafter I shall be able to suggest to all the writers of plays (sent to me to read from the uttermost corners of the globe) that you are the one who ought to read and to criticize encouragingly.

As a matter of fact I think you should have demanded the chair in dramatic literature years ago. And I hope that you will sit in it for as many years as you like.

So it was that, almost two years after the initial offer of Henry B. Harris, sufficient pledges of money accumulated for G.P.B. to assume that the Corporation would soon announce the endowment of both chair and theatre. On November 16, 1911, H. T. Parker wrote to G.P.B.:

I hear — how accurately I cannot judge — that you are on the point of announcing the completion of the fund for a building to house a theatre, the theatrical library and your own department at Harvard.

I take it that with the announcement will go some statement of the purpose to which the building will be put and maybe some word about it on its architectural side. I can hardly believe that plans and all that have yet been drawn.

Plans there were, for Professor Langford Warren of the Harvard Department of Architecture had prepared drawings for a conversion of Dane Hall to such purposes. This would have placed the Harvard Theatre in the vicinity of Memorial Hall, upon the site now occupied by the Littauer Building. Later, a site which Harvard subsequently deeded to the City of Cambridge for its Central Fire Department was also considered. However, 1911 wore into 1912 with no such announcement published. This was, ostensibly, held in abeyance until the completion of President Lowell's main construction program — a "group of dormitories and dining halls" which he had proposed in his inaugural address. Meanwhile, assured of his hope, G.P.B. was content to wait.

XXVIII   IDEAS FOR A CIVIC THEATRE

AT THE CLOSE OF 1909, AS G.P.B. BEGAN HIS PERSONAL solicitation of funds for a theatre at Harvard, he was involved in a scheme for a "civic theatre" in Cambridge. Percy MacKaye, then lecturing on the social need for what later became known as the "Little Theatre Movement," wrote to him on the last day of the year: "I've been thinking a great deal about what you said regarding the project for a theatre in Cambridge, & I sincerely hope you will keep that in abeyance until the much more important matter of the Harvard Theatre is put through."

Earlier in the year, G.P.B. had lectured publicly on what he entitled "The Theatre in Civic Life," and for the next two years he spoke repeatedly from New England to the Middle West on "The Civic Theatre." However, because MacKaye published his lectures on these matters in 1909 and 1912, and because G.P.B. did not publish his, the mutual association of these friends in the general ferment of theatrical reform is not now remembered. Curious, thus, is a 1925 British royal commission report upon the relation of the drama to adult education which stated that the success of the Little Theatre Movement in America was to be attributed mainly to the work of Professor Baker at Harvard.

Perhaps typical of G.P.B.'s part in the beginning of this movement was his talk, in 1910, to the people of Manchester, New Hampshire, on "The Civic Theatre." Only the notes which he sketched on the stationery of a local hotel survive, but they indicate the main lines of his thinking. In his first three of five points, he sketched the contemporary conditions in the American theatre which had killed or retarded an earlier progress toward a national drama. The reasons were obvious: cheap vaudeville and picture shows — the rising cost of the gallery ticket at such good theatres as the Castle Square in Boston. The answer lay in some American adaptation of the European city theatres.

Turning to the schemes abroad which he knew intimately — the Schiller Theatre in Berlin; the Liverpool Theatre, with 1400 subscribers; Miss Horniman's theatre in Manchester, England — he told them how this might be done. He told them about the Volksbühne movement in German and outlined the financial and managerial arrangements of the German civic theatres. Then he sketched the workings of the only American municipal theatre — the one which belonged to the town of Northampton, Massachusetts.

His enthusiasm is apparent in the notes:

You can have this here: (a) a group of guarantors on building & $30,000–40,000 more, (b) many subscribers at $100 a share — 1000 for instance, but better still (c) the people as a whole — .50 to come in, then .25–.50 for seats. Make it *democratic*. Above all, suit all tastes. Don't be highbrow: the people must have their chance. (The highbrow should have his special experimental theatre.) *Make this the entertainment of the masses by the masses.*

Concluding his talk, he addressed the practical question of how to begin such a program:

Why not a civic pageant to draw the people together? Find an occasion. Put Manchester & its manufactures & past life into the pageant. Bring all walks of life together. Then in common desire for dramatic expression find your scheme. A simple building — anything at first — not a New Theatre — a good company — a varied bill — low prices — a wise manager. Then, *in time,* see if the city will not build & lease a fine building — the House of Thalia!

Another lecture which he began to give in 1909, "The Square of the Social Forces," called the attention of his audiences to the evolution of their civic institutions. First the church. Then the school and its adjuncts, the library and the museum. Then the press. Only the theatre was lacking in this framework which had evolved from the New England Puritan community. Only the theatre was needed to complete what G.P.B. submitted was the broad base of an educated society.

Yet another public lecture from these years, "The Theatre in Civic Life," states the ideal of a community theatre which he had already proposed for Cambridge:

What we need in each city & indeed in each town of 10,000 people is a *standard* theatre, with a good company, not for the most possible performances, but enough to meet demands of public without killing actors or art. Largely these theatres should depend on their effective playing rather than novelty in plays; these should be places at which to see time-honored, established pieces done to the best advantage — Symphonic playing . . . Let us think of a theatre seating 1,000–1,500 — Sanders Theatre — quietly decorated — comfortable but not luxurious. Such exist in great numbers in Germany.

He apparently had in mind a composite of the virtues of the Elizabethan playhouse, the Providence Opera House, and the modern community theatres of Professor Max Littmann of Munich. During the academic year of 1910–11, G.P.B. outlined his ideas for the sort of theatre he had hoped Winthrop Ames would build in Boston. By early June 1911, Warren had prepared architectural plans for a theatre, modeled upon Professor Littmann's Prinz-Regenten Theater, but adapted to the needs of a university community such as Cambridge.

This theatre would have provided an attractive auditorium seating a few more than a thousand persons, two lecture rooms suited to G.P.B.'s Harvard and Radcliffe classes in English 47, and shop and stage facilities to meet the purposes of a community theatre. Unfortunately, it was soon apparent to G.P.B. that such plans were too expensive, and it seemed unlikely that town and gown would coöperate to fund the $250,000 or $350,000 necessary.

Although these plans of 1910–11 were not realized, they involved G.P.B. in the grass roots rebellion against the commercial theatre which soon spread community footlights across America. However, the improvised nature of this activity as far as G.P.B. was concerned appeared when he gave Warren's drawings to Percy MacKaye to show to George M. Cohan, whom MacKaye almost persuaded to endow a university theatre at Harvard during these very months. Such help from "Mr. Broadway" stuck on the conflicts of interest between those at Harvard who desired a music auditorium and those who wished a theatre. When an architectural compromise was suggested to serve both these purposes, G.P.B. demurred.

Through these years G.P.B. learned to see the vital elements in both Broadway and the revolt against it which would shape the future of the American theatre. So he concluded that the American society needed perhaps several kinds of theatre. Two, he thought, were now functionally necessary: one a theatre of entertainment for the masses who wished simply to be amused, the other a theatre of art and experiment for those with cultivated tastes. For it was obvious even in Cambridge that one theatre could not serve every demand of town and gown. Indeed, the rock upon which the New Theatre was then foundering was the attempt to be both an art theatre and the theatre of the masses. It is at least a partial measure of G.P.B.'s character and influence that he was never doctrinaire about either.

XXIX   PAGEANTS AND THEATRES

FOR AMERICA

AS THE CENTURY OPENED, G.P.B. WAS ALREADY BREAKing away from his work in argumentation and dramatic literature, toward a direct creation of the materials of the theatre. This was not quite the turning point which Barrett Wendell had urged G.P.B. to take, though a real opportunity to advance along this avenue did not occur until the beginning of 1910. At this time, the widow of Edward MacDowell communicated to G.P.B. her plan to present a pageant the following August at "Deep Woods," near Peterborough, New Hampshire, where the composer had written much of his music about America. Could he, she asked, dramatize the themes of her husband's music?

Later, listening to her play the piano scores for "Indian Idyll" and "1620," the idea came to him that he could tell the history of the little town which MacDowell loved through the man's music. With hearty enthusiasm, he undertook to produce the whole pageant. Here was a chance to illustrate in contemporary terms a truth from his historical studies which he had taught now for many years: the unity of the arts of drama, music, and the dance.

So he called Chalmers Clifton, who had written the music for the Harvard Dramatic Club production of Percy MacKaye's *The Scarecrow,* and asked Clifton to play some of the MacDowell music. As G.P.B. listened to Clifton at the piano, the details of the pageant took shape; together they set aside one composition after another until they had the material for sixteen musically derived episodes.

For the lyrics, G.P.B. called upon another former student, Herman Hagedorn, now one of his youngest colleagues in the English department. Throughout, G.P.B. later recalled, MacDowell's spirit dominated their work:

Poetic, dreamy, suggestive, it forbade pure realism in most of the pageant; suggestion, as in the music, must replace that. This fact and the stage, a space about 150 feet square levelled on a hillside among great pines, forbade as obtrusive any stage settings. The Elizabethan appeal to the imagination was tried, and successfully. Moreover, under this influence, my search in Peterborough history became not merely to find the dramatic and pictorial, but that which could be fused with the moods of the MacDowell music and expressed by it. The brief musical scenes, in most cases unusually brief for dramatic action because limited by the length of the MacDowell compositions, called for some scheme to bind them together more than the fact that they were all expressed in MacDowell music. Moreover, the length of these musical scenes made it inartistic that the intercalated purely dramatic scenes should be of much greater length. It became necessary to say one's say in the most condensed way. These complicated demands made my writing of the pageant — the selection of the music, of the episodes to be presented, the composition of the prose portions — perhaps the most delightful dramatic task I have ever faced. To balance fact and fancy, the serious and even the tragic with the amusing, to determine the proportions to be given, because of the nearness of our stage to the audience, to the spoken word, singing, dancing, pantomime, all this was absorbing because at every turn so different from the conditions of the regular stage.

He called his pageant, "The House of Dreams."

It is significant of his frame of mind that he now styled himself "Pageant Master." For he not only thereby assumed an ancient and honorable title, but he also asserted his command of the means to a revolutionary development in American culture. The programme note with which G.P.B. introduced the first production of his pageant shows the ambitious end for which he hoped to employ his new device:

In two ways the Peterborough Memorial Pageant is experimental. Believing that pageantry stimulates local pride in past achievement, strengthens community spirit, and reveals unexpected artistic resources, those responsible for this pageant wish it to help in demonstrating that for artistic and pleasurable results pageantry need not be confined to great centres, need not necessitate vast expense, but is perfectly possible for small communities. The Peterborough Pageant aims to prove, also, that movement, color, pantomime, and music should count more in pageantry than the spoken word.

While G.P.B. directed the farm hands and textile workers of Peterborough in their community pageant, he emphasized that "suggestion rather than realism" should be their cue. In contrast with this method was the huge pageant of progress which Boston was then preparing, a realistic recital of its history, "Cave Life to City Life." Other kinds of recent pageantry were Maude Adams' "Joan of Arc," in the Harvard Stadium the summer before; and Percy MacKaye's Gloucester Pageant; but these were plays set in the framework of pageantry, and thus subservient to the current realism of the drama. What G.P.B. was trying to do at Peterborough was something new in the history of pageantry. "Thus far in the United States, the pageant has not gone much beyond the historical and episodic representation of the past," he said in "Pageantry," his article for the November 1910 issue of *New Boston*. "Even yet," he concluded, "it is dramatically indeterminate." What he really sought was a new dramatic form.

Toward the end of 1910, he received an invitation from the secretary of the Oregon Conservation Commission to submit whatever ideas he might have for a pageant which could be presented at the approaching centennial celebration in Astoria. On the tenth of December, G.P.B. replied, inquiring about the possibility of using for the pageant site a park about two miles beyond Portland, where the river curves near at hand. Because of the importance of the Columbia River in the history of the area, he believed it necessary to use a river in any pageant such as he had in mind. "It makes no difference," he added, "that it is the Willamette River, instead of the Columbia, for kindled imagination will make the change for the audience." Nature would be his backdrop, the river and nearby mountains his properties. In its cast of two thousand, the pageant should touch all the kinds of people and all the diversified interests of the state.

Clearly this was an extension of the Peterborough Pageant to a second or third power, yet the basic factors of the one were to be those of the other. Explaining that he could not at the moment submit a scenario for the pageant, G.P.B. detailed the four main divisions he had in mind:

I. Nature and the Wilderness. This by music and dance and drama would suggest the receding of the glaciers and the formation of the rivers and mountains. This through the orchestra and two or three hundred dancers. On this would follow three or four of the Indian myths and legends, such as that in regard to the creation of the Indians, and perhaps that of the Island of Death and the Bridge of the Gods. Throughout this section the music accompanying part of it, and the brief overture, in part, would use themes taken from the music of the Indian tribes indigenous to the region. I hope to find for this section an Indian legend accounting for the troubled waters at the mouth of the Columbia, so that through this myth I may connect with the second.

His second division concerned the "discovery of the Columbia River and the coming of the New Races." Here, by dramatic action, he wished to show the spell that hung over the river, making the Spanish, Russian, and English sailors miss the entrance to the river but allowing the Yankee skipper of the *Columbia* to navigate the treacherous waters. To conclude this section, G.P.B. continued:

I particularly want to use a park-like space near the river, in order that in this section the audience may see a duplicate of the Columbia swing into sight, and may watch recreated for them the landing of Gray and his men. And that section, when the mysterious spell that has hung over the mouth of the river has been broken by the Yankee skipper, should end in a great chorus of triumph from several hundred voices, probably of hidden figures, chorusing thankfullness that the first step in the winning of the Pacific slope has been made.

The third and fourth sections, developed on a similar scale, detailed "The Era of Discovery" and "The Era of Industrial Development." For the conclusion, G.P.B. wrote:

I want to have the whole pageant close in a hymn of praise, for a thousand or more voices, with all the performers before the audience. This hymn, written of course for the occasion, while emphasizing the patriotism of the past, should be a great triumphal Song of Oregon, which at the same time becomes a hymn of American patriotism in the broadest sense of the word.

This grand spectacle of nature, man, music, song, dance, and story was a new dramatic form which was unrealizable in 1910 only because sound and color had not yet come to the motion pictures and because movie cameras had not yet been employed for such outdoor panoramic effects. Not only was it characteristic of G.P.B. that his vision was at least a quarter of a century ahead of Hollywood, but he had posted his sketch of the pageant less than forty-eight hours after receiving his inquiry from Portland.

Perhaps fortunately for the pocketbooks of many Oregonians, the pageant never enhanced the banks of the Willamette. A decade later, however, parts of it were woven into the pageant which commemorated the tercentenary of the landing of the Pilgrims at Plymouth. With astounding new lighting effects, G.P.B. brought the *Mayflower* into Plymouth harbor and achieved the great hymn of America which he had first imagined in his vision of the landing of the *Columbia*.

A little more than a week after posting his scenario sketch of the Oregon pageant, G.P.B. received a letter from Mrs. MacDowell, who had just returned from a lecture tour of the western states. She wrote, December 18, 1910: "In every place I have spoken, several have asked me about you, and there is a large movement on foot, all through the West in regard to this subject of Pageantry."

Sometime later, in reply to an inquiry for his services as "Master of the Pageant," G.P.B. expressed the hope he held for this newly evolving revival of an old dramatic form:

Pageantry in this country is in so formative a state that unless it is carefully managed it will soon degenerate and lose its opportunity. I believe if properly conducted, we may make of the Pageant something as significant of our day as the Masque was for the days of Elizabeth.

As he now turned from history and criticism to creative work, the path along which he had come was appropriately marked by a friend. In this year of new directions for G.P.B., Walter Prichard Eaton dedicated his 1910 volume of dramatic criticism, *At the New Theatre and Others*:

To
George Pierce Baker
Professor of Dramatic Literature in
Harvard University

Founder in that Institution of a Pioneer Course
for the Study of Dramatic Composition

Keen and Catholic Critic

Inspiring Leader in the Movement for a Better
Appreciation among Educated Men of the
Art of the Practical Theatre

xxx   PRIZE PLAYS

SOMETIME AFTER WINTHROP AMES LEFT THE MANAGER'S office of the Castle Square Theatre, the managerial control of this theatre passed to John Craig, an intelligent, cultivated actor who seemed to have taken John Drew as his model. Associated with him in this control was a former student in G.P.B.'s forensics classes, Horace Baxter Stanton. To learn some things which his legal training had not included, Stanton began in the spring of 1909 to attend English 47 unofficially. On June 3, at the close of the term,

Stanton wrote G.P.B. that he had been much interested in the work of the class and would be glad to do what he could to obtain a production for plays likely to prove successful. Thus, although 1909 passed without a Castle Square production of an English 47 play, G.P.B. found himself once more in friendly communication with the management of the Castle Square Theatre.

Another friend in the local theatres at this time was Forest Izard, a recent Harvard graduate who had become the assistant manager of the Bijou Theatre, an intimate little house already famous as the home of Keith-Albee vaudeville but now generally known as a "high-brow picture show" which also presented one-act plays. To Izard probably belongs the distinction of producing the first play directly negotiated from the round table in Dane Hall. For in the spring of 1910 the Bijou presented Frederick Chamberlin's *The Connecticut Peach.* That G.P.B. regarded the occasion highly is suggested by the fact that when he was already deeply involved in the preparation of the Peterborough Pageant he took Chalmers Clifton and Gluyas Williams to see a Bijou matinee of the Chamberlin play.

While Izard and Craig were beginning to be interested in producing English 47 plays, attention was widely drawn to a prize won by a poetess and playwright whose name was locally associated with G.P.B.'s work. In March 1910, Josephine Preston Peabody won the Stratford-on-Avon Prize. Competing in an international playwriting contest sponsored by Frank Benson, her five-act drama, *The Piper,* took all honors. This event, coming at the time of Izard's Bijou Theatre production of *The Connecticut Peach,* apparently provided the necessary connection between the plays of English 47 and the commercial theatre. For the idea of a prize play competition to put his student plays upon a Boston stage now occurred to G.P.B. By a fortunate chance, Horace Stanton and John Craig were thinking the same idea.

Saturday, April 30, 1910, was "Harvard Night" in Boston at the Shubert Theatre for Winthrop Ames's touring New Theatre production of Ned Sheldon's *The Nigger.* Naturally, much attention in the newspaper publicity for the event was directed to Sheldon's association with English 47. Four days later, the John

Craig Prize Play Competition, the first of its kind in America, was announced.

The terms of the competition had been established in correspondence between Stanton, Craig, and G.P.B. during the preceding month; but these remained essentially the conditions which Craig presented in his letter of March 28 to G.P.B. In this he said:

> I talked the matter of the prize play over with Mr. Stanton, and we evolved something new and a little different from my original idea, or yours as put in your letter.
>
> . . . I will offer for this, the coming season, a prize of five hundred dollars ($500.00) for the best play in prose in three to five acts, written by an undergraduate, a student in the graduate school, or a graduate of not more than one year of Harvard or Radcliffe College, and produce that play chosen as the best for one week in this theatre, during that season. Of this five hundred dollars, I will pay two hundred fifty dollars to the successful author, and two hundred fifty dollars for the purchase of books to develop the Harvard Collection on the History of the English Drama.

Thus John Craig would continue what John Drew had begun with his gift of the Robert Lowe library, and would himself begin something that had not yet been done.

To this G.P.B. had assented gladly, but with a few cautious questions about Craig's proviso that a one-quarter interest in the prize-winning play be assigned to him. For G.P.B. saw this project in relation to his own university theatre, which then seemed an imminent reality, and he had carefully explained the nature of the proposed competition to President Lowell, who also thought that an unlimited assignment of such a right to Craig might later cause trouble. It was perhaps such ready interest and counsel from Lowell, together with other marks of the President's esteem, that assured G.P.B. of the immediate prospect of Harvard's own theatre.

During that summer and fall, the judges of the John Craig Prize Play Competition — Craig, Stanton, and G.P.B. — read manuscripts. Each of these, by a proviso which G.P.B. added to the rules, represented work begun in English 47. It was not enough that each contestant be one of his students; to forestall any difficulty from materials which had not developed under his supervision, G.P.B. specified that the complete history of each prize-winning manuscript should be a matter of his own knowledge.

On January 14, 1911, the winning play was announced in the *Crimson*. The judges had selected Florence Lincoln's *The End of the Bridge,* a convincing demonstration that sound professional training was to be had in English 47. Soon an outstanding success at the Castle Square Theatre, the play repeated its Bostonian achievement wherever John Craig took it on tour. After it had played two weeks at the Blackstone Theatre in Chicago, Henry Miller added it to his repertory in San Francisco. From coast to coast, it became an additional proof of the magic touch of the Harvard professor of playwriting.

Thus the first of the Craig Prize Plays advanced the theatrical prosperity of John Craig. The second enjoyed no particular distinction. However, the third won a national reputation for Mary Young, the wife of John Craig. With John Barrymore she played for twenty weeks at William Brady's Thirty-ninth Street Theatre in Fred Ballard's *Believe Me, Xantippe!*

Already actors, actresses, producers and the various entrepreneurs of Broadway success had begun to seek out the playwrights of English 47. The quality of their product, perhaps, was not quite so important as the novelty and seeming magic of it. For here was something as new and fresh in the theatre as once had seemed the work of university men Robert Greene and Christopher Marlowe among hackneyed professionals of another day. Moreover, there was the inveterate desire of entertainers to exploit the name if not the substance of success. As a result of the publicity which the New Theatre had given Sheldon, Knoblock, and Hagedorn as Harvard playwrights, something of a craze for more of the same appeared at the opening of the 1911–12 season in New York.

At that time, Holbrook Blinn was playing in Sheldon's *The Boss,* and William Brady was ready to produce his new play, *Romance.* Ned was also writing a play for Dorothy Donnelly. Furthermore, Otis Skinner was preparing to open in Knoblock's *Kismet,* already a London success. And there were several English 47 writers, besides David Carb, whose plays were under option to Brady and other managers. Certainly many a hardened professional looked toward Cambridge this season with the same bright-eyed hope that had brought George Abbott to the magical round table that fall. As Abbott now recalls this atmosphere, "Everyone knew that Sheldon had been Baker's pupil. It seemed like the open sesame."

XXXI   "THE THEATRE OF BEAUTY"

IN THE SPRING OF 1911, AS G.P.B. PREPARED A BRIEF article on "Practical Academic Drama" for the *New York Dramatic Mirror,* he received a note written in the editorial rooms of the *Boston Evening Transcript.* From "H.T.P.," this was ostensibly concerned with the annual dinner of the Harvard Dramatic Club, in which Parker maintained a genuine interest as a dramatic critic and as a human being. Ned Sheldon, who had succeeded Winthrop Ames on the Graduate Committee, could not be present — but G.P.B. was to be toastmaster, and H.T.P. the principal speaker.

Parker's note got to its real issue when he said that he would like to suggest to the assembled youth that dramatic criticism offered them a rich and widening opportunity; that it was just as much worth while as what they loved to call "creative" work; and that in the next generation it would count for more in America than it then seemed to. Here Parker touched upon a critical point which his intimacy as an old student of G.P.B. permitted him to develop in later years. This was his growing awareness of G.P.B.'s technical preocccupation, of his concern with standards of technique and with values apparently more related to the form of drama than to its content.

In a way, H.T.P. was unfair. For G.P.B. could, honestly, concern himself only with the means of expressing ideas and emotions on the stage. His studied avoidance of any critical dogmatism about the content of his student plays, aside from guarded pronouncements upon the maturity or immaturity of certain lines of thought, derived from his natural liberality of mind and ingrained Victorian electicism as well as from a clear understanding of his own function as a teacher. This did not include the function

147

of the critic as H.T.P. practiced it, asserting always a unified personality and a characteristic taste and point of view necessary to his job of evaluating and judging. On the contrary, G.P.B. cultivated a variable point of view, a diverse personality, and an eclectic taste so that he might draw out individual thought and emotion in his writers rather than impose it upon them. As he later wrote in the introduction to his *Dramatic Technique*:

> The teacher who is not widely eclectic in his tastes will at best produce writers with an easily recognizable stamp. In all creative courses the problem is not, "What can we make these students take from us, the teachers?" but, "Which of these students has any creative power that is individual? Just what is it? How may it be given its quickest and fullest development? Complete freedom of choice in subject and complete freedom in treatment so that the individuality of the artist may have its best expression are indispensable to the development of great art.

It was, hence, a meaningful ritual at G.P.B.'s round table that the function of criticism fell to the disciples.

Nevertheless, G.P.B. recognized the valid elements of H.T.P.'s friendly remonstrance and sent to him through the years those people in English 47 who were not so likely to prove creative of art as of criticism. It is perhaps proof of the rightness of G.P.B.'s teaching as well as the excellence of H.T.P.'s criticism that English 47 produced no school of critics but a variety of individuals — such as Kenneth Macgowan, Robert Benchley, Heywood Broun, Hiram Moderwell, and John Mason Brown — to deepen and broaden dramatic criticism in America.

Moreover, he was interested in the various philosophies of art which motivated contemporary movements in the theatre. Since the Peterborough Pageant, he had been practically involved in considerations of the unity of the arts and had watched the work of William Butler Yeats with particular attention. Indeed, at the beginning of 1911 he had given a series of six lectures on "Movements in Contemporary Drama," of which one lecture explained "The Drama of a People: The Irish Theatre." Yet G.P.B. had remained outside all these specific persuasions, no more doctrinally committed than he had been as a student editor to the aestheticism of his predecessors on the *Harvard Monthly*. It is perhaps significant of the character of his mind that, although sympathetic to Unitarianism, he was not in his maturity a communicant of any church.

Yet there was in G.P.B. a strong urge to ally himself with the thought of others, a concomitant of the energy with which he espoused new ideas or fought for unorthodox ones — such as the George Junior Republic, or colleges for the mountain people, or the simple and natural right of a grown man to dance through the New Hampshire countryside. In his role of champion, he was often pitifully alone on points where he desired the greatest company. Certainly his intellectual eclecticism did not always fit him so comfortably as his conservative clothes nor grace him as did his genteel manners and his quiet gallantry.

And if there was any time in his life when he would have welcomed a message to tell, it was in the year following the success of the first Craig Prize Play. What he should have liked that fall of 1911, as he prepared once more to meet his writers, would have been to sail on the *Kronprinzessin Cecilie* to study the new movement abroad in the theatres of Europe already forming under the banners of Appia, Reinhardt, and Gordon Craig. For Ames, countering the failure of the monstrous New Theatre, was off to learn what he could for the gem of a Little Theatre he had started to build in New York. On the twenty-first of September, Ames wrote G.P.B. from aboard ship: "Please come on early in the winter & see my 'little' theatre a-building. It's going to be a little Pullman car of a place — & most attractive I hope."

Though G.P.B. could not yet study the new movement at its sources, some of its creed and one of its prophets had come to America as Ames sailed. While G.P.B. read manuscripts at Boulder Farm for the second Craig Prize Play, Boston received the Irish Players from Dublin. With them were William Butler Yeats and Lady Gregory. To G.P.B. came at once a letter from H. T. Parker's new assistant:

18 Sept. 1911

Dear Mr. Baker —
May I suggest that Wm. B. Yeats would be a very good man to use as a speaker at the H.D.C.'s first meeting in the union? He should prove a good drawing card.

149

I presume that you'll soon be back in Cambridge convoking the Dozen. I hope you enjoyed a more restful summer than last.

Sincerely,

Kenneth Macgowan

Yeats spoke before the Harvard Dramatic Club on October 5, 1911. His topic, "The Theatre of Beauty," presented the basic ideas of his own work in the Abbey Theatre and, in broad outline, the central thesis of what he called the "New Movement" in the European theatre:

The ordinary theatre makes absolutely no use of its greatest opportunities for scenic effect, that is, through lights and shadows. In the usual out-of-doors scene the light is cut up by drops so that it is impossible to get a natural effect. The present stage is constructed in the wrong way to allow natural outdoor scenes.

This G.P.B. knew perfectly well from the contrast of the outdoor theatre at Peterborough with the stage at the Castle Square. As he talked with Yeats that day about the innovations which Gordon Craig had devised for the Abbey Theatre, G.P.B. probably came nearer to a state of conversion than he had ever before. Concerned with what he wished to see develop in American pageantry and with the ideal theatre which he hoped soon to build at Harvard, G.P.B. caught the spark of Yeats's zeal for the theatre of beauty.

Something of the enthusiasm with which G.P.B. reacted to this appears in an incident which occurred a few days later. Having learned that Yeats and Lady Gregory expected some trouble from South Boston's Irish patriots if the company presented J. M. Synge's *The Playboy of the Western World*, G.P.B. called upon the H.D.C. men for action. His plan was to go to the Plymouth Theatre on October 16, the opening night of the play, and constitute both a claque and a cordon of special police. On this night, G.P.B. placed his lieutenants about the theatre so that they could signal to him the places occupied by trouble-makers. Then he took his seat in the orchestra where he could observe the whole theatre.

As the curtain went up and the play began, there was a palpable restlessness in the audience. Then the first hissing commenced. According to plan, G.P.B. received the signal which directed his eye to the offender. Motioning his men to remain seated, G.P.B. strode to the hissing critic before the theatre was yet aware of the sound. White with anger, G.P.B. lifted the culprit by his collar and carried him, dangling at arm's length, from the theatre. As the audience became aware of what was happening, the Harvard cheers in support of G.P.B. brought applause from the crowd for the play. After that night, there was no trouble in Boston for *The Playboy*.

Others who were impressed by the Irish Players were Horace Stanton, Lorin Deland, and Joseph Lindon Smith, a fellow member with G.P.B. of the Tavern Club. Indeed, a ferment of ideas about Yeats's "Theatre of Beauty" was working in Boston, and particularly among the friends of Mrs. Lyman W. Gale. With the assistance of Stanton, Deland, Smith, and William C. Willson, Mrs. Gale planned to remodel an old Lime Street stable to make a tiny theatre which should bring a measure of the revolutionary "New Movement" to Boston. Designed to seat but 129 persons, the theatre was appropriately named the "Toy Theatre."

G.P.B.'s relationship to the venture is indicated by a report which Willson, who acted as stage manager, sent him on the sixteenth of December concerning one of the early meetings of the group. A certain embarrassment had arisen because Amy Lowell, the sister of Harvard's president, and chairman of the Toy Theatre's Play Committee, had exercised a bit of poetic license in assuming not only the criticism of plays to be chosen but an unlimited authority to direct and manage their production. In this situation, G.P.B. was called upon for suggestions with the assurance that his advice was final.

Not the least colorful event of that season in Boston was the St. Catherine's wheel which ignited when Amy Lowell learned that her function had been resricted to those critical duties proper to her present chairmanship. Amid letters to Boston editors and an exchange of retorts, Miss Lowell departed from Mrs. Gale's theatre of beauty. Certainly the whole affair could not have been calculated to impress President Lowell with the attractiveness of "theatre" personalities.

Yeats's visit had, however, another and more direct effect upon the career of G.P.B. On February 24, 1912, Baker wrote his friend

William Chauncey Langdon, master of the "Pageant of Thetford," in whose work the Russell Sage Foundation was interested, to ask if he thought the foundation would grant money for a study of the new forms of the drama in Europe. Langdon replied that he did not think so.

A month later, on the twenty-sixth, G.P.B. wrote to Robert Underwood Johnson, editor of the *Century*, whom he had known at the MacDowell Colony:

I am going to Europe in July for six months and I expect to spend my time watching the newer plays and the newer methods of staging. I mean also to study if I can the outdoor plays on Lake Geneva and very probably the German Errinnerungsspiele . . . I should like to know before long whether there will be any opportunity for such work in the Century because my itinerary will depend a good deal on whether I am to write up at once any of the material that I gather. As next year the Manchester Players of Miss Horniman will be coming to this country somewhat as the Irish Players came this year I should think that an interesting article on their history and their work might be prepared. I expect to watch their work rather closely for I know Miss Horniman. The Experimental Theatre at Glasgow has developed something of a school of new writers and it is quite conceivable that an interesting paper might be put together about that theatre. Now that our public is so deeply interested in the Irish Players would an article on the Ulster Literary Society with its headquarters at Belfast, with Purcell, and Rutherford Mayne as their chief playwrights, be of interest? I have thought quite seriously of going to Stockholm to watch Strindberg's plays as given by people trained by him and, if possible, to meet him. I shall be watching in Germany, at Hamburg, Dusseldorf, Berlin and Munich, the newer methods of staging which are already beginning to have their effect here. Something interesting, I think, might be done in this field. I am not yet quite sure, but I think I shall go to see the work at the theatre in Moscow where the ideas of Gordon Craig, which Yeats is now using, have been tried out. You see there is varied material here of vital interest to those deeply interested in the stage and the drama in this country. I should think that with proper illustration almost any one of these subjects might be made attractive to the general reader.

Johnson, although personally interested, decided that the subject matter which G.P.B. outlined was of insufficient general interest to *Century* readers to warrant a commission for such articles.

While G.P.B. prepared for this trip, a call came from a citizens committee which proposed to operate the Northampton Academy of Music as a civic theatre. They wished G.P.B. to nominate someone for the position of director. Conferring with Winthrop Ames, now returned to New York, and Henry Miller, G.P.B. nominated Bertram Harrison and Jessie Bonstelle to manage America's first municipally operated repertory company and was happy to hear of their employment.

On the seventeenth of July, a few weeks before G.P.B. sailed, Ames asked him to keep an eye open for any new plays for the Little Theatre, which had recently opened with Galsworthy's *The Pigeon*. Wrote Ames:

> I have never met Reinhardt, but I am delighted to give you a letter to Ordynski, who is one of his assistant stage directors, and he of course can put you in touch with Reinhardt.
>
> Your tour is so much more interesting than anything I have ever made theatrically that I feel enormously jealous. The only thing that I have to recommend is the work at the Lessing Theatre in Berlin. This is less tricky and novel than Reinhardt's, but it seems to me that I have seen the finest *acting* there of anywhere. I never got to Moscow.

At this time, G.P.B. told a reporter for the *Boston Post* the purpose of his trip. In a story which H.T.P. should have written had he not then been in Berlin reviewing the music and drama for his *Transcript* readers, G.P.B. said:

> I believe that the municipal theatre will become as much of an institution in America as it is today in Germany, although, of course, the nature of the American playhouse must of necessity widely differ from the European town theatre . . . It is principally to inform myself about the town playhouses of Europe and their management that I am going abroad this summer.

He could not very well have said so, but he was also going in search of ideas for a university theatre at Harvard. As he boarded ship that July, he was thinking of a theatre of Beauty as well as the theatre of Broadway.

AT TIMES G.P.B. BECAME IMPATIENT THAT THE PRE-
ponderant interest in what he cared so much about was feminine.
Of this he was aware, for most of his audience as he spoke here
and there around the country about the American theatre and
its drama was the American clubwoman, housewife, and mother.
In April 1912, writing to the director of a new theatre stock company which the citizens of Pittsfield, Massachusetts had organized,
he inquired pointedly how many of the stockholders were women.

Indeed, it was with no little uneasiness that he announced the
second winner of the Craig Prize Play Contest. Like the first, it
was one of his Radcliffe writers. It was true that his important
students on Broadway thus far had been Jules Eckert Goodman,
Louis Evan Shipman, Edward Knoblock, and Edward Sheldon,
but there seemed no way of insuring that men of their caliber
would come to English 47. When he began his campaign for
funds in January 1910, the endowment which he needed for a
university theatre seemed to hang upon further Harvard successes on Broadway. But his most promising writers were women.

One of these Radcliffe playwrights, remarking his search for
another Sheldon, said that she felt his success should not be meas-
ured by such rapid-fire work as Sheldon's. For, if the average
young playwright was to have his work pushed on the stage before
he had a chance to think long and hard and to acquire more
knowledge than was natural to a beginner, the loudest successes
would later turn out the saddest failures. Those, however, who
had been equipped with the power to work happily toward the
highest ideals might write plays that would last forever. To secure
such results, she suggested that the MacDowell Club of New York
might be willing to provide a fellowship in playwriting at Harvard.

Thus began a new idea in American higher education, for
within a fortnight G.P.B. was in correspondence with the Mac-
Dowell Club's secretary concerning the provisions of a gift which
should make the writing of plays as academically respectable as

was research in history. G.P.B. wrote on the eighteenth of February to Mrs. Ben Ali Haggin: "The fellowship is to be for a student in dramatic composition, not in the history of the drama, though very naturally he may supplement his work in composition by historical courses. That is, we must avoid any chance of giving rise to a query whether research rather than creation is to be rewarded here."

On February 23, 1910, the President and Fellows of Harvard College voted to accept the MacDowell Fellowship in Dramatic Composition. One of the consequences of this gift, made possible by New York clubwomen, appeared at the 1911 commencement. Along with certain young men who received the A.M. for advanced studies in literature, such as Thomas Stearns Eliot, the master's degree also went to Charlton Andrews, the first MacDowell Fellow. Among those who became masters of arts that day was John Frederick Ballard, the first candidate for that degree to offer original plays as his qualifying accomplishment. These were *Believe Me, Xantippe!* two other three-act plays, and *Good News,* a one-act tragedy. Thus Harvard granted what G.P.B. liked to refer to as "the first advanced degree for creative writing." When *Believe Me, Xantippe!* subsequently became the third Craig Prize Play and ran for almost six months on Broadway with John Barrymore, it appeared that a persistent feminine support of English 47 had produced the masculine results for which John Craig and G.P.B. had hoped.

Henceforth, while G.P.B. taught at Harvard, dramatic composition was a full-time subject of graduate study in the Yard. This new status made possible the later attendance of Eugene O'Neill and Thomas Wolfe in English 47. By a wry academic irony, O'Neill, admitted as a special student, could not receive the A.M. for his playwriting. Wolfe, now famous for his novels, received the A.M. for graduate work which was largely devoted to the writing of plays. By 1919, after the publication of *Dramatic Technique,* G.P.B. viewed with "some alarm" the "recent mushroom growth" of courses in playwriting across the country. "I gravely doubt," he then said, "the advisability of such courses for undergraduates."

Another effect of the strong feminine support for English 47 came in the spring of 1910. At this time his Radcliffe class in playwriting petitioned him to give them a second year of instruction. The petition came as a letter from Florence J. Lewis, who wrote, on the second of March: "You know, I can see, dimly, a second year wherein the students might co-operate with a theatre — either the Bijou or Castle Square and mount, rehearse and produce their plays until Cambridge gives them a theatre of their own."

Although the petition was not then granted, G.P.B. began to think of such an arrangement for the experimentation and tinkering which the "47" plays required. In the spring of 1912, as he contemplated his tour of European experimental theatres, he began to speak publicly of an idea he had first raised ten years earlier in his *Transcript* article on the young French dramatists, who could "try out" their plays at such theatres as the Grand Guignol.

Now a contributing editor of *The Drama,* the magazine sponsored by the Drama League of America, he was asked to speak to a Drama League group in Pittsburgh about the problems of the "young American dramatist." On this occasion G.P.B. said that the young playwriter in this country

has no place to "try out" his plays except with amateurs, or on the professional stage. People go to the first, not to see acting, but to see their friends act. It means no chance for many plays, for when presented on the professional stage, many with one or two acts good, are rejected by a critical, unsympathetic audience; whereas, if given in an independent "trying out" theatre they could easily be reconstructed. At present, all that can be done for such plays is some juggling on the part of the manager to the despair of the unfortunate playwright, and a total rehashing of the production until little of the original remains.

A trying-out place is sadly needed in this country . . . The experimental theatres in this country today are Winthrop Ames' small theatre in New York and the Toy Theatre, of Boston. Both of these are pure experiments, but both are doing good work.

At this point, the first two winners of the Craig Prize and Mrs. Lilian Shuman Dreyfus, president of the Radcliffe 47 Club, came to G.P.B. with a rough plan and some money for an experimental theatre. Mrs. Dreyfus, a friend of Lady Gregory and a participant in the Toy Theatre activities, had first mentioned her idea for a laboratory theatre for English 47 to Miss McFadden. Before G.P.B. left Cambridge in July, the main characteristics of what later became "The 47 Workshop" had been worked out.

One of G.P.B.'s last instructions before sailing was a request that Miss McFadden write a full explanation of the scheme to Timothy Spelman, president of the Harvard Dramatic Club. This she did in a letter from Chocorua, August 19, 1912:

The plan is to establish an informal organization of the 47 people in and around Cambridge, for a twofold purpose: first, to bring plays written in Eng. 47 to the test of actual production at an early stage in their development thus giving to the author at the time when he most needs it, the inspiration and instruction of seeing his work tried out; and second, to experiment whenever the nature of the play permits, with some of the new methods of staging, scene-painting and lighting now in use in the Continental theatres.

Let me hasten to add that it is no part of this plan to compete with the Harvard Dramatic Club. The status of the 47 Experimental Theatre has been fixed by Mr. Baker as "a feeder to the Harvard Club, not a competitor." Thus a play showing a distinct dramatic value, on being tried out in the Experimental Theatre, will be worked over and made as good as possible and then offered to the Harvard Dramatic Club or the professional theatres. The audience before whom the Experimental Theatre will present its plays will be invited, (no tickets sold) and will be strictly limited to people whose interest in the theatre is technical.

In language which might well have been G.P.B. speaking for himself, the letter continued, sketching with uncanny prescience the rest of G.P.B.'s career:

The second purpose, that of experimenting in new methods of staging — has evolved itself as a sort of side issue from the original plan, but it is a phase of the subject which interests us keenly. Personally, I should like nothing better than a chance to try out, and to see others try out some of the new methods of staging suggested by Gordon Craig, Reinhardt, and the Irish Players. The matter of stage lighting seems to present many fascinating problems and I hope that we may be able to find in the engineering course at Harvard some man or men who would like to experiment in a small way with the lighting problems presented by our plays; that we will

157

find among those studying art or architecture a few who would like to try their hands at the designing of costumes and scenery, and others who will work at the actual work of staging.

When the plan was presented to the Radcliffe 47 Club, the members promptly pledged five hundred dollars and voted to back the scheme to the limit. As news of the project came to G.P.B. in his ensuing months abroad, he may well have understood why the revolution in the theatre which he had come to England and Ireland to study was so largely the work of Lady Augusta Gregory and Miss Annie Horniman.

XXXIII ENGLISH AND IRISH EXPERIMENT

G.P.B.'S THOUGHTS AS HE CROSSED TO LIVERPOOL ARE not a matter of record, as are many of his feelings and ideas during the remainder of his tour. Yet it is unlikely that his thoughts neglected the auditorium of Agassiz House, where the experimental work for English 47 would have to be done. He knew the stage and its limitations intimately from his own acting upon it. The basic problem was that of giving a cramped and inflexibly arranged stage the illusion of spaciousness and variety. The simple answer was to vary the perspective by mechanical devices and lighting. As G.P.B. toured the theatres of England, Ireland, and the continent during the next six months, his point of view was largely controlled by this question and these answers.

On the first of August 1912, he landed and went as quickly as he could to Manchester, where he wished to see Miss Annie Horniman and her company at the Gaiety Theatre. Not only was he on terms of friendly acquaintance with Miss Horniman, but he had met her director, Lewis Casson, when Casson spoke to the American Drama Society of Boston the year before on "Steps toward a Civic Theatre." As the president of the Drama League of Boston, a rival organization, G.P.B. had not, of course, been one of Mr. Casson's hosts in Boston. Nevertheless, one of G.P.B.'s principal reasons for coming to Manchester was to discover the secret of Casson's eminently successful directing of Miss Horniman's company.

158

Of his journey to the Gaiety, he wrote in the first of a series of notebooks which record the events of his tour:

On the way, reading the morning paper, I found that Miss Horniman's chief company is at Cyril Maude's The Playhouse in London . . . playing Houghton's *Hindle Wakes* (*Wakes* are a festival, a holiday beginning the Monday after the Sunday nearest the 4th of Sept.) . . . When I sent in my card by a courteous doorkeeper at the stage entrance, word at first came that Mr. Lewis Casson was rehearsing & could not see me unless on very important business. I had learned that Miss Horniman was in London at her apartment there. I held my ground, saying that I had come from the States to see the company & its workings. Almost at once Mr. Casson appeared, a bit flustered and apologetic for not having recognized me at once from my card. At first he seemed loath to let me watch a rehearsal on the ground that it was not allowed & might flurry the second company of younger people — then rehearsing. But as I urged a bit, he yielded, saying, "Well, if you stand back a bit, they need not know you from the workmen, who are all about." Hardly knowing whether to be amused or angry at the man who in Cambridge had asked me to come to rehearsals when I should be in England, I followed him as he scurried through a rabbit warren of a building passage.

As he followed Mr. Casson about the theatre, G.P.B. compared it with what he knew in Cambridge, for the stage of the Gaiety presented some of the conditions of the Brattle Hall and Agassiz House stages:

I am told Miss Horniman when she bought the Gaiety from a syndicate, which then controlled 3 Manchester theatres, practically made over all except the outside framework. Unfortunately, she could not press out the rear wall of the stage for it hugs an alley. Consequently, the stage is not deep — 30–35 ft. for a guess — about the size of Brattle Hall stage as it is usually set. However, space in the wings is very crowded. All the conditions much remind me of the conditions at Brattle Hall before it was made over behind the curtain . . . Later I heard from Miss Horniman that her tiny office space of the past was being so enlarged that anyone talking with her could sit down . . . I state all this that it may be clear that her good results come not from complete creature comforts.

Perhaps he suspected that adversity might bring success to the crowded Agassiz stage. Certainly much of what he saw during the next few weeks was encouraging, for many of the theatres were even smaller than Boston's Bijou. After watching Mr. Casson conduct the rehearsal, G.P.B. concluded:

> In an hour of watching I could not see any different method in his work. He corrected movements, intonation, pronunciation — usually quietly from his chair, but occasionally getting up to show how something should be done. To my great surprise he soon sent his wife over to speak to me . . . I was surprised that he was willing to have talking in the wings. From the watching I got no idea at all of any special method or of the special power that in the *Hindle Wakes* company turns out so even a performance. But with the exception of Mrs. Casson . . . the people were young and crude — very like good amateurs. So I decided to go on at once to London.

It is a curious thing that G.P.B. associated the company's success with its prices, which he noted as "about like those at the Castle Square: best seats, 3 to 5 shillings; gallery, 1." "Beauty in the house," he observed, "special safety, special comfort, none of these counts in the success. It is prices far above all." Later, when he talked with his friend Professor C. H. Herford, of the University of Manchester, he learned that the Gaiety was not often crowded but enjoyed a steady business. G.P.B.'s final remark on the Gaiety was, "It is educating its own public."

When he arrived in London that night, there was no time to waste before curtain time. Quickly he chose the Granville-Barker production of G. B. Shaw's recent comedy, *Fanny's First Play*, at Lena Ashwell's Kingsway Theatre. Afterwards, he wrote:

> It is Shaw at his best & his most exasperating. That is, he interests you in problems of conduct for seemingly real people & then, at a moment's notice, turns the whole thing into a banter that he may turn on you at the end in the dialogue of the critics & tell you that he has briefly re-presented the regular group of melodrama. For instance, the incident by which the butler turns out to be the younger brother of a duke is pure extravagance crudely introduced into a play that has gripped your emotions time and again. If only Shaw would take his art seriously and himself not so seriously, he might do great things.

In a comment characteristic not only of his historical perspective but of his view of Shaw, G.P.B. approached a question which seems amusing now:

Clever as the play was, however, it was so local in mood & hits that I doubt if it will go well in the States. I could not help thinking of Ben Jonson's part in the *War of the Theatres* as I watched Shaw writing as if London & its interest in him were the world itself. *How can these plays, brilliant as they are,* but so much *of the hour,* survive even 20 yrs?

On his second night in London, G.P.B. went to see Miss Horniman's production of *Hindle Wakes* and took a five-shilling balcony seat. "Quite good enough," he thought; "I was foolish to pay 7/1 last night." Of this play he wrote:

The play is the best I have seen in years — as fine & sure in technique as Pinero at his best after years of practice — and this is, I think, Houghton's second play. Moreover, it is absolutely of the new spirit. On an initial situation the characters act & react, & the ensuing complications form out of the individuality of the characters in their reactions even as suspense comes because you do not know just what a character will do, not from suspense in the Scribian sense . . . I wrote Houghton in my enthusiasm.

To G.P.B.'s kindly gesture, Houghton replied with a grace which further ingratiated his excellence:

Marine Hotel
Criccieth
August 7, 1912

My dear Sir

      It is indeed good of you to express so kindly your opinion of *Hindle Wakes.* It is, of course, with the utmost pleasure that I read the letter of a man who is a master of his subject, as you are. Had you criticized me adversely I should have listened to you with respect; for your generous praise I cannot sufficiently thank you.

Hindle Wakes is to be acted in America by Brady — I think first in Chicago. Also the *Younger Generation,* though when & where I do not know. I hope to come over & see the productions if it is at all possible.

Your hope that I may write some good plays is one that I echo. I fear however that I shall probably be forced to consider the public & the managers more than I have done in *Hindle Wakes.*

Yours very truly
Stanley Houghton

Subsequently they lunched together in London and began a warm friendship. Before he left England, G.P.B. wrote again of his young friend:

He has come to stay. I think him a better and subtler technician than Masefield, & just because he is first the dramatist, second the preacher & theorist & untroubled by experience with paltry rules, theatrically ahead of both Masefield & Galsworthy. But with these three, English drama need have no fear!

A year later, in the haunting way it had of coming to those who caught G.P.B.'s affections, death came to Stanley Houghton. Mark Reed, a student in G.P.B.'s class in contemporary drama at the time, thus remembers the effect of the news upon G.P.B.:

He came into English 39 and told us Stanley Houghton had just died; then he went on to evaluate the man's work and what a loss it meant to the theatre to have this fresh original genius cut off in its prime. The hour took on the aspects of a memorial service. It was very personal. The living theatre had suffered, and we were a part of it.

The rest of G.P.B.'s London theatre-going can be summed up in the word "vaudeville," for he wished to see the one-act plays which were done only at theatres like the Coliseum and the Hippodrome. His third evening he spent at the Coliseum, where the Irish Players were doing Synge's *Shadow of the Glen*. This he thought Synge's "least clear" and "most intimate" play. With perhaps a glance at the New Theatre, he noted that the Irish Players were "swamped in the vast space that holds thousands."

Among the people from the Abbey Theatre he met Fred O'Donovan and his "delicately pretty young wife," who took him in hand and helped plan his visits to the Irish experimental theatres in Belfast and Dublin. When G.P.B. returned to his hotel, he set down his thoughts about a ballet on the evening's program:

The Russian ballet, with Kosloff, was glorious in color. He is a beautiful creature to watch as so many of these Russian dancers are. Watching them one realizes that the human body can be very beautiful — but how rare such beauty is . . . I think the scenery never saw Russia, but was faked up in London from photographs of Bakst's work. It was crude & garish even on the big stage. But the costuming interested me greatly, for in the use of the polka dot & in the daring combinations of color, as well as much of the movement, I was steadily reminded of *Sumurun*. Evidently Rhinehardt [sic] has been taking a note out of the Russian's experiences. I wonder if we shall find that through Bakst, Craig & others Russia is now really controlling our new stage coloring and setting?

And the emotional color of Albert Chevalier's cockney singing stirred him too: "What a genius he is. When he sang *My Old Dutch* there was a breathless silence & hardened theatre-goer that I am, my eyes dimmed even as I was half angry that such art should fool me. That is something that I could hear him do again and again."

The next day he met Henry Arthur Jones's children and went with them to the Hippodrome matinee to see Ethel Irving in their father's farce, *Dolly's Little Bills,* a piece which had been cut from three acts to a vaudeville one-act. "Somehow," G.P.B. noted, "it seemed a bit forced and more interesting than funny." Then, at the request of young Oliver Jones, G.P.B. took the family to see *Find the Woman.* Of this he wrote:

If ever a play proved that out of its own country, a play runs danger of being misinterpreted, this does. Not one person really got the American types Klein drew . . . Miss Vanbrugh does not understand our girl of the public schools . . . who is a copy of her superiors & may adapt herself to almost anything.

Sentiment took him to see the American actress, Fay Davis, whom he had seen play Iris Bellamy in Pinero's *Iris* ten years before. Her play, *Ann,* a new one at the Criterion, he thought "slight & not very well played." But Miss Davis was still "charming."

On the tenth of August, he returned to Manchester to watch some more work at the Gaiety. The next day he left for Stratford-on-Avon, convinced that Miss Horniman's organization displayed no excellence that was not available to him in Boston. Winthrop Ames had assembled as good a company at the Castle Square, and John Craig's was perhaps potentially as good.

In Stratford, he enrolled at the "Shakespeare Summer Season," where F. R. Benson was presenting not only a festival of Shakespeare's plays but also a variety of lectures on subjects allied with the drama. Most of G.P.B.'s attention, however, was absorbed by Cecil Sharp's "School of Folk Song and Dance," which drew him daily through his week at Stratford. In Sharp's school he took lessons in "Morris Dancing," "Sword Dancing," and "Country Dancing." Between times, he saw Benson's productions of *Henry the Fifth, Antony and Cleopatra,* and *Othello.* On the sixteenth of

August, he saw the school give a grand demonstration of folk song and dancing. Here began G.P.B.'s ardent devotion to English country dancing, which he transplanted most appropriately to the New Hampshire countryside about Boulder Farm.

Returning to Manchester, he journeyed in a few days to Belfast, where he made a brief survey of the work of the Ulster Players. On August 26, he arrived in Dublin at the Russell Hotel, whither he had been directed by the O'Donovans. However, because of the crowding of "Horse Show Week," he was assigned to a bed in the smoking room. Fortunately, his interest in Dublin was not in his creature comforts. He wrote:

> At once to Abbey. Found seat reserved, but behind pillar so that everything was bisected. A cosy theatre in size, 562 people. Only one gallery of old type, supported on pillars. This was originally — or before it became Abbey Theatre, Mechanics Association, with entrance through what is now Pit entrance from Abbey St. Main entrance now was then Morgue — river Liffey is just at hand.

What interested him immediately was the proscenium and the stage. Here was something he might use for the Agassiz auditorium. With more enthusiasm than art he drew several sketches of what caught his fancy. Then he wrote:

> Proscenium is curious because of the way in which the front comes down a solid mass. It seems that in accordance with the ideas of Craig this part can be lowered or raised, even as the sides can be pushed in & out. This permits small or large settings — an admirable idea — But it might be more artistically done were the part lowered painted skilfully on the side toward the audience. (Don't forget free curtain needed in any theatre.)

With some pains he drew a sketch of the proscenium and marked it "adapt." This was one of the things to which Yeats had referred when he was in Cambridge. Upon questioning Lennox Robinson about another device, G.P.B. learned that it was an invention of Gordon Craig and was called a "screen" or a "model." Essentially a variation of the Victorian dressing screen, it could be manipulated into many planes and masses which, illuminated in different ways, gave infinite variety in a little room. Such devices might solve the problems of the Agassiz House stage, particularly if one could get imaginative lighting too.

Eager to learn if similar equipment could be obtained for his own purposes, G.P.B. wrote to Craig, who was then in London organizing money and materials for his new school of the theatre which he proposed to build in Florence. Craig replied: "We must talk about the model when we meet but I think it would be better to wait until we have got our school and can come over to America and demonstrate with you . . . I am only in London because of my school which is shaping very well. In fact I have half the money for it."

On his second night in Dublin he went to see Lennox Robinson's *Patriots* and Lady Gregory's *Workhouse Ward*. Having noted the "closeness of relation of pit to actors," he wrote of these plays:

A perfect program. *Patriots* is well characterized, beautifully played, a moving, simple play of great promise for R's future. It lifts him out of the experimental stage, for though the first act is mainly exposition by talk it is so in character & creates so much suspense that one does not mind. Curtain on Act I somehow not quite right, but probably more from lack of just the right emphasis in the acting than in text.

On the last day of August he left for Coole Park, Galway, the home of Lady Gregory, whither he had been invited for the week end. After almost a day's journey in bad weather, he arrived at the Gort railway station, where he was met by Lady Gregory's coachman. With an attention to descriptive details which was reminiscent of his juvenile literary sketches, G.P.B. recorded the event:

He looked odd in his buckskins & cockaded top hat driving the jaunting car. A somewhat old looking & ratty-tailed nag drew it, but willingly enough. Out through rain that was at times hard we jaunted, through the market place & by scores of cabins, many of them roofless & falling into ruins. (I could not make out whether this marks decay or a turning to a different type of house.) A mile, perhaps, out of town, after going through a country not unlike parts of lower N. H., or better of Maine, we turned in at a gate guarded by a lodge. Then up a driveway a mile . . . A glimpse of a large Georgian mansion square-fronted to the world . . . designed by Sir Wm's father or grandfather late in the 18th or early 19th century . . . Just inside the door Lady G. was waiting for me with most hospitable greetings and Yeats just behind her.

Because of the storm, the three were alone for the greater part of two days — "Free," G.P.B. noted happily, "to talk & talk again of our common interest." As they chatted before a fire in the library, G.P.B.'s eyes took in the autographed pictures of the distinguished men who had been there. "Women," he observed, "are mainly conspicuous by their absence; it is a house for & of men." In a bookcase he noticed "most of the volumes as yet published by the Irish authors who are the movement of which the Abbey is a part." Yeats, who had just written an introduction to some poems of Rabindranath Tagore, was eager to read what he had written as well as some of the poems. All this G.P.B. found "frank & simple" but "curiously unreal" until they talked again of Yeats's own dramatic work and of the Irish Players:

Of what didn't we talk — of the uselessness of the Chicago Drama League to the Irish Players & the temerity of the national president of the Drama League . . . She did not dare send out notices to her members asking them to attend *The Playboy,* tho' she knew the Boston League had backed it. On the other hand, Lady G. had kept quiet about all this out of gratitude for what the B. League had done. This debt both she & Yeats acknowledged again & again in the most cordial terms. "We reaped as an audience in Boston what you had 20 yrs. been preparing for us," Lady G. said laughingly.

The following day, which was a Sunday, G.P.B. wrote a long letter to Miss McFadden:

Coole Park
Cork
Co. Galway
Sept. 1, 1912

Dear Miss McFadden: —

What better place than this from which to write you of *The Workshop,* for that is what it seems to me we could call our experiment! "Experimental Theatre" seems to me too grand. First of all, let us begin just as quietly, almost as secretly as we can. The whole scheme *must* be kept out of the papers. Any announcement of it will mean statement & counterstatement — that we are in opposition to the H.D.C., the Toy Theatre, etc: that we are about "to create a new drama" "to recreate the American stage" etc. etc. Therefore, I have been annoyed to learn from K. MacGowan [*sic*] that he wants information for the press as to "this new experimental theatre at Radcliffe." I am writing him that there is nothing to publish and that nothing but a part, so to speak, of class-room work is afoot.

First principle: Keep out of the papers.

Second principle: Make it so difficult to see these performances that little by little people clamor to get in. But we don't want outside people until we are sure we have something to offer. Take just the opposite course from the *Toy Theatre.* If this is to start right, it must be merely the workshop where I try out before my old & present students the better & best things produced. At first I should confine it rigidly to students & a few trusted friends of the cause, such as Dean Briggs, Miss Coes, etc. *Keep out* the professional critic such as Parker and MacGowan, not because they are unfavorable or will be, but because you don't want the whole matter talked of before it is in good working order. I feel *very* strongly about this.

Third principle: In no way must this plan interfere with, but rather supplement the *Craig Prize,* the H.D.C. competitions, the *Bijou* and other such contests. Therefore, a playwright, if his or her play seems ready for any of these competitions should be urged to compete. If his or her play fails in these, then we can take it up. The great outside public must always be the court of last resort. Our special audience should prepare, sustain, encourage the man or woman till accomplishment making for success with these prize contests is attained.

Therefore, I believe that whatever you do before I return should be done very quietly "just to see how certain plays for one reason or another not yet ready for the prize competition look when acted." Keep as quiet as you can, holding information just to the group working up the matter until you are ready to issue your invitation to the performance. Even then, perhaps, issue it not for a scheme, but apparently for this play alone? Try the experiment, get your breath, have the committee take account of losses and gains, & then decide whether by a second play to get things more into shape for me before I return . . .

As I write — a soft Irish rain silts down outside. At the other end of the table in this high room lined with books, Mr. Yeats is answering his mail . . . In the next room Lady Gregory has been playing with her grandson who in his jersey suit of Irish green looks like a gnome. I go on toward Belfast & the Ulster Players tomorrow. Already my fardel is full of packages, for on every hand I pick up enriching and stimulating things.

It is a great pleasure to feel that in my absence Mrs. Baker has such good friends about her.

Sincerely yours,
Geo. P. Baker.

THROUGH THE FIRST THREE WEEKS OF SEPTEMBER, G.P.B. visited experimental theatres in Belfast, Liverpool, and Birmingham. Those in Scotland, he noted in his journal, were closed temporarily: "No answer to my letters." When he again reached London, he had arranged an appointment to meet Gordon Craig.

As G.P.B. sometimes recalled in later years, their engagement was for lunch at a club in Piccadilly. Craig, the younger man, was not only late but he made an appearance which seemed a studied attempt to overawe the American professor. For the Englishman wore an old and ragged shepherd's coat, as if to set unkempt simplicity against impeccable propriety. Although G.P.B. chose to be amused and carried the matter in the friendliest fashion, Craig's bizarre behavior may have prejudiced G.P.B.'s attitude toward some aspects of the "new movement" in the theatre, of which Craig was no tongue-tied prophet. Before G.P.B. left London, however, he had other and more hospitable entertainment from Gordon Craig.

On the twenty-second of September, G.P.B. saw the Granville-Barker production of *The Winter's Tale* at the Savoy Theatre. The *Times, Globe,* and *Standard* reviews which he clipped from the next day's papers were agreed that the production was "startling." The *Times* reviewer, who called it "Post-Impressionist Shakespeare," thought it quite Bohemian: "The costumes are after Beardsley and still more after Bakst; the busbies and caftans and deep-skirted tunics of the courtiers come from the Russian Ballet, and the bizarre smocks and fal-lals of the merry-makers at the sheep-shearing come from the Chelsea Arts Club Ball."

The *Standard* wondered if this was "an attempt to conform in some halting measure to the ideals of Mr. Gordon Craig." That G.P.B. may have been in doubt of his own opinion is suggested by his failure to record it. Perhaps Craig's shepherd's coat came a bit too freshly to mind.

168

Real congeniality, however, came with his old friend Henry Arthur Jones, who gave G.P.B. a jolly time looking up various great ones of the London stage, and calling upon Miss Horniman one evening at her flat for supper. On the second of October, G.P.B. wrote again to Miss McFadden:

I have been crowded trying to finish before leaving here, an edition of *Hamlet* for Professor Neilson. Now I am waiting for dinner just before leaving for Rotterdam.

I think perhaps the best play for you is Merrill's college woman play.

Thus he chose the first 47 Workshop production, *Lina Amuses Herself,* by William Fenimore Merrill, Harvard's MacDowell Fellow in Dramatic Composition.

From Amsterdam on the following day he wrote a long letter to Miss McFadden concerning matters which suggest the influence of Gordon Craig upon the early days of the Workshop:

Here is Mr. Ames' good letter which I forgot to send with my last . . .

Will you see that the librarian — whose name I completely forget and so I cannot write to her — of the Radcliffe library orders at once a book announced for publication, *Towards a New Theatre,* by Edward Gordon Craig, 40 designs for stage scenes . . .

Yes, Robert Jones is the man to help you. He goes in for the bizarre and is better in costume or at least more experienced there, but he should be of use to you.

I don't know whether Sam Hume — I think that is his name — Craig's pupil is coming or not. From what Craig and his wife let slip, I think he might be difficult; but try to find out whether he is in Cambridge & have him looked up.

Then G.P.B. proceeded to arrange the details of the Workshop's opening night with a gusto that was to characterize his management of succeeding first nights:

Were I to be present, I should be as forth-putting as any actor-manager & insist on the first night on making a curtain speech before the performance, laying down the rules of the game.

Now, shall we ask any persons present other than 47 people to submit their comments? Shall we accept any comments orally, not in writing? All written comments must be signed with full name as guarantees of good faith.

169

If possible, get the authorities to allow you to have the audience walk about in the large room across the hall between the acts, or at least in one entr'acte — so that discussion & comment may be rife. If you have but one chance, put it probably before the last act. Shut out as steadily as you can all the amateurish rushing up at the end to say, "My dear," "Old Man," "you were wonderful. Don't see how you do it, etc." On the other hand, see that your audience treats the actors as actors, appreciating, not coldly sitting from curtain to curtain undemonstrative, but at right moments applauding good work. Above all, at curtains & particularly at the end, if the actors have done well, see they get their full share of applause. Be rigid as to curtain calls, however, that bring the dead to life, etc.

For an evening of short plays which would give him his first chance to direct the Workshop company, G.P.B. tentatively suggested Josephine Preston Peabody's *Fortune and Men's Eyes.* "In that," he wrote, "I should be willing to act myself, for I have always wanted to do it & I think she might be glad to have me." A play which he might have seen in 1902 and which he now saw in Amsterdam reminded him of the revolution in dramatic technique since his own last public performance, nearly a decade ago, in Miss Peabody's *Marlowe.* Rather nervously he observed: "The German play is curiously out of date. Like so many German plays particularly of its time it is talky, slow in exposition: but for three acts it does not go badly, even today. But in the fourth! How times have changed!"

After ten days in the Low Countries, he departed for Germany, where he expected to join his nephew, Samuel A. Eliot, Jr., in a tour of the German theatres. In Duisburg he saw the new municipal theatre, the best he had yet seen, and wrote in his journal: "Think of theatre in Harvard Square with view from corner of Quincy Street." A few nights later, he was in Brunswick, where he attended a production of *Hamlet.* This he noted without enthusiasm was "in modern fashion." Then, with perhaps more than a slight glance at Granville-Barker's production of *The Winter's Tale,* he set forth the main question which he saw in such treatments of Shakespeare:

Question whether Shakespeare, except in hands of genius like Craig, if then, gains or loses. This is a great setting for imaginative work dealing with unrealities. Maeterlinck, Yeats, etc., but not, I fear, Shakespeare. Certainly the settings at the Boston Opera for Pelleas were better in the sense that they illumined & expanded — were fitting. My only doubt comes from Craig's models. Can he do it? Russia must show.

Soon he was sharing young Sam Eliot's enthusiasm for the costumes and scenic effects which the "new movement" was producing in Germany, but with a certain guarded reserve. Now he wrote "neu inszenierung" instead of "in modern fashion" and sought the secrets of the new effects in the mechanical and electrical contrivances of the German stage. At each municipal theatre they visited, G.P.B. took notes upon the stage machinery: the "drehbühne," or revolving stage; the "wagenbühne," or wagon stage; the "schiebebühne," or sliding stage; and the various kinds of "horizont," or cyclorama.

It was fortunate for G.P.B. that he had Sam's youthful impetus and eager knowledge to assist him at many points of transition from the theatre of the past, for the many inadequacies of that tradition were now increasingly apparent. On October 24, they arrived in Berlin, where an evening at G.P.B.'s once beloved Lessing Theater gave the measure of the change. Returning to their hotel from Ibsen's *Die Frau vom Meere,* G.P.B. wrote: "After 21 yrs. to the Lessing and dingy enough it looked. In 1891 — built for O. Blumenthal in 1888 — it seemed fine. Now, in the light of the new buildings seen, it is cramped . . . and badly needs redecorating. A sense of dust on everything in the auditorium."

Almost intuitively, he now felt the need of simplicity in what had been a standard of excellence. His shifting values show in his further remarks:

The staging of the play good — that is, it was evidently painted from facts of Norwegian nature — in its fiords and mountain gorges. Well acted . . . but sometimes the setting seemed over-elaborate for the necessities of the play. Indeed, Ibsen himself seems to have lugged in much. And why so long a play — why not all of it in 3 acts instead of 5? . . . All this left me with an odd feeling that Ibsen saw & sympathized . . . but lacked the scientific training to understand perfectly what he had to express.

Perhaps the new standard was to be found in the Moscow Art

Theatre production of Gordon Craig's *Hamlet,* which G.P.B. now planned to see with Sam.

More immediate plans were involved in such memoranda as: "Linnebach, Adolph. Schauspielhaus — Dresden. This is the one which has the schiebebühne with elevators." Scheduled were interviews with the secretary of the Neue Freie Volksbühne, with the director of the Schiller Theater, with the secretary of the Berliner Allgemeine Elektrizitäts Gesellschaft to see this company's display of the new Fortuny lighting system and a portable "kuppel horizont" which folded like a buggy top.

However, his central concern is indicated in the circular letter he sent to the municipal theatres of Barmen, Hildesheim, Duisburg, Kiel, Lübeck, Halle, and Hagen. Of the items of information he sought, the first characterizes his motives:

Can pictures of exterior and interior, showing proscenium, and prints of ground plans for interior, such as are posted in corridors be had? I want particularly to study seating arrangements and division of space back of stage, for dressing rooms, scenery, etc., indeed how all the space in the building is used.

Although primarily concerned with building and operating costs, he also inquired: "Is the stage equipped with Rundhorizont, Drehbühne or Schiebebühne, or any special system of lighting such as the Fortuny?"

Thus G.P.B. learned the practical impact of the "new" ideas before he was fully conversant with the doctrines of Craig and Appia. It is significant that his copies of their books which he obtained at this time are unmarked, with some pages uncut. Since he was attracted by those things which appeared to offer practical solutions to his own problems and to those of the American municipal theatre, very little of his interest in the current revolt in the theatre could be doctrinaire. A year later, when Sheldon Cheney sent a presentation copy of *The New Movement in the Theatre,* G.P.B. wrote in the margin opposite an exposition of Craig's desire to subordinate all to visual effects: "Is this the way? Let us keep our reason."

While he admired the rational procedures of Max Reinhardt at the Deutsches Theater, G.P.B. was characteristically investigating the arrangements between the University of Berlin and the

Opernhaus and Schauspielhaus to provide reserved seats at reduced prices to university students. A performance of Offenbach's
Orpheus was interesting because its curtains "covered with notes
that come down all about Eurydice as she yields to the charm of
the music" might be a useful idea for a Hasty Pudding Club
show. A certain part which he observed under Reinhardt's direction was possibly "For Miss Anglin or Miss Donnely or Mrs.
Fiske." And he was forever jotting such connections with the
theatre he knew as *"Die Zarin* is for Leslie Carter." But his most
characteristic response to the totality of this new life in Europe
was this query in his notebook: "Why not in 1915, at San Francisco, models of stages — theatrical exhibition with specimen
players?"

The aesthetic principles of Appia and Craig and Littmann
and Linnebach were thus perceived in terms of the problems of
the stage at Agassiz House. At the Deutsches Opernhaus, which
was said to have the largest and most modernly equipped stage
in Europe, he observed a false proscenium in the Craig manner
which had a "cheap effect" because he found the "cloth not too
smoothly laid on." With his mind's eye on the Agassiz proscenium, he wrote: "We need the contracting and expanding arch."
At the Kunstler Theater in Munich he concluded: *"Lighting,*
then, principal thing here. Find out just how these lightings are
gained."

His most effective schooling in such matters came at Reinhardt's Deutsches Theater, under the tutelage of Baron von Gersdorff, one of Reinhardt's principal assistants. Of his introduction
to this instruction, G.P.B. wrote:

Thursday. Nov. 5. By request to call on Baron von Gersdorff, one
of the dramaturgs of the Deutsches Theater. He speaks English
perfectly . . . Taken through room after room to his about half the
size of my study. Not a jammed workshop but a pleasant study with
a few drawings or models about. Certainly, I may see pictures. He will
have his people in the theatre show me what they have within a few
days.

Through the Baron he met Reinhardt, Ernst Stern — Reinhardt's
chief designer — and Hans Bohm, the young photographer for
the Deutsches Theater who helped G.P.B. make a collection of

lantern slides of the scenic designs of Appia, Craig, and Stern.

Reinhardt's methods of production, which appear to have affected G.P.B.'s own procedure, were observed and noted:

When R. plans a production he explains what he wishes to do and then leaves details to his special workmen in scenery, costuming, lighting, etc. Originally he called in well-known artists to design sets, etc., but now the artist of the theater wishes to do all this. If at any time he goes, the old method will be used till a new artist of the theater again insists on doing all . . . At rehearsals a drama-turg watches & his word as to cuts is of main importance. Later on Reinhardt may veto, but apparently doesn't . . . As to the Dreh-bühne, he has a model made and studies that with the proper assistants till the problems are solved. (Could an old model be had, I might, for my classes — or could I have one duplicated & at what expense?)

Von Gersdorff, aware of G.P.B.'s fascination by the model of the revolving stage, conducted him on a tour of the Deutsches Theater's "drehbühne," which was set for the current production of the first part of Shakespeare's *Henry IV*. G.P.B.'s account of the event, however, shows that he was really more interested in the lighting employed with the revolving stage:

Came in at stage left. We pushed back some curtains. Stooped & over in the padding of the Heath road that wound up semi-circu-larly. We had come in under the "solid sky," the "horizont-wirkung," which ran around the circular stage . . . Solidly made of plaster cement, this was wire on steel rods. Through this cement wall, like sutures in a hand that has been wounded and has healed, tiers of plaster beneath which are electric wires so that as the current is shut off & put on stars twinkle . . . It ran high up out of sight from the front. On this lights of the spots are focussed. I think even rods with lights are laid down where needed along its base, or as desired. It takes its color & changing colors from the lights. As my guide said, supporting what all along I have said, "The lighting is the great secret of all this modern setting."

Close inspection showed that the whole stage was amazingly small and the revolving stage set so close to the plaster "sky" as to seriously limit work on the scenes not in use. The usable space, G.P.B. estimated, was "not much larger with this great wall than the stage of Brattle Hall." Von Gersdorff apologized for the noise of the heavy revolving machinery and explained it as the result of compromises unnecessary in a new installation. Enthusiastic about the effectiveness of the revolving stage in *Henry IV*, both parts of which he had seen already, G.P.B. concluded rather cautiously from his direct experience:

Study at home the revolving stage at New Theatre. Has Ames one at Little, & what does he think of it? Mr. Glasenapp seemed to think it is giving way to slide stages — as at Deutsches Opernhaus. It must be much labor to fit all needed into this small space. It seems to me, fundamentally, nearly as artificial as old method, though quicker.

After a month in Germany, by far the bulk of G.P.B.'s daily commentary was concerned with the literary techniques of the plays and the dramatic art of the actors. A typical notation concerns Strindberg's *Totentanz:*

The most perfect acting I have seen — as good as any production. The piece a horror with not a single sympathetic figure — yet absolutely mastery in chosen characters.

Query: Does Strindberg ever get outside himself — draw anything except himself & his drink superinduced moods & the people he sees in them? Is there, then, here real & lasting greatness?

The limitations of his visual imagination are suggested by the comparative rarity of his attention to visual effects for their own sake, though he frequently notes such curosities as the following observed at the opening of the Deutsches Opernhaus: "Go again & investigate what are the electric lights in closets at corner of 1st Balcony, with man in charge." Also apparent is a growing personal preference for what might be termed the plastic effects of stage lighting rather than the linear effects of stage decoration.

Whether his desire to see the Moscow production of Craig's *Hamlet* had now cooled, or whether the rapid approach of the second semester at Harvard contributed to his change of plans, a brief bout of influenza put an end to such thoughts. On the fifth of December, G.P.B. saw Adolph Linnebach's production of *Everyman* in Dresden and pronounced a judgment which indicates his wariness lest the new power of the scenic designer should usurp or suppress the intention of the playwright. After watching the old morality play which he knew so well and had taught for so many years presented in terms quite other than historical, he wrote:

Compared with Poel's *Everyman* this lost vigor and universality and power of the original . . .

Moral: When you revive a play great in its day, trust it and try to give it as nearly as possible as it was given. Had it not had something great & gripping in it, it could not have lived as it did. Try to get at that & present it. Don't make over. Represent as accurately as possible or write for today & don't tamper.

His final conclusion concerning Linnebach's work shows the trend of his own taste: "Lighting here again the important point."

On December 14, G.P.B. was in Munich for an interview with the famous theatre architect, Max Littmann. Much of their initial talk centered upon the new stage mechanisms, many of which Littmann had first devised but which he now treated rather conservatively. G.P.B. summarized:

At Stuttgart — Drehbühne given up or rather not installed, because noisy and because settings for it can in many cases be used only on it & in a house where the repertory must change constantly this means too great expense . . . Side schiebebühne, particularly with schieb-hinter bühne make, he says, the ideal system.

Before long, their conversation was directed by G.P.B.'s question about the best plan for a municipal theatre for the ordinary New England community. Littmann quickly produced plans, models, and estimates. From these he concluded that it would be very difficult for G.P.B. to build a theatre seating a thousand to two thousand people for less than two hundred thousand dollars. Of Littmann, G.P.B. wrote:

The most striking thing about the man is that he is the first architect I have seen who is as much interested in, as fully equipped about, what is behind the curtain as in front of it. When we get that in the U. S. we shall have the right kind of work . . . Evidently would like to come to America and speak.

Following his interview with this "wizard of the stage," G.P.B. spent an afternoon in which he was entranced by the magic of the Munich Marionette Theater. If one is to judge from the extent of his commentary, of greater length than what he wrote about

Steel, by Harold Igo, Yale University Theater. Setting, Monroe Burbank;
Lighting, Clarence Johnson

American Wing, by Talbot Jennings, Yale University Theater. Setting
and Lighting, Mildred Sutherland and Monroe Burbank

Pueblo, by Covington Littleton, Yale University Theater. Setting,
Donald Oenslager; Lighting, Stanley McCandless

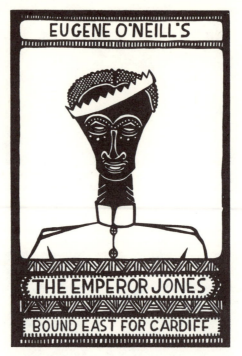

Yale University Theater Programme Cover,
by Donald Oenslager

Yale University Theater Programme Signet,
by Monroe Burbank

Max Littmann or anything else in Germany, the hours he spent at this children's theatre delighted him more than anything else he had yet seen. It was, he wrote:

A toy theatre indeed! A little building one story high & perhaps covering in ground space ⅔ of the Boulder Farm house . . . Above entrance door some verses . . . enter in the right mood, not as grown-ups but as children . . .

The proscenium is itself small — the curtain space perhaps 2½ to 3 times that of an ordinary toy theatre . . . Up goes the curtain, revealing the old fashioned box or wing set. The figures are perhaps 10 inches high, not more. Sitting as I did in the second row I saw very clearly the many strings controlling the figures. They are carefully and cleverly dressed and with a skill that does not fear to exaggerate ear rings or scarf pins, knowing that if in scale they will not be seen, and if significant when seen will be forgiven if a little out of proportion.

. . . Extraordinary is the only word for it. They moved in and out of rooms, they danced, they jumped on tables, they gesticulated with a real semblance of truth — especially Kasperl . . . The dance of Kasperl and the pigs was really funny. There was real climax when the father discovered the Princess giving the disguised Prince the 100 kisses in order to get the wonderful musical machine which set all dancing — and how well she fainted in the last act!

Why shouldn't we have this sort of thing in one of our poorer quarters, particularly at a Settlement House?

As he prepared to leave for Paris, G.P.B. set down a rather sharp view of the German stage:

The way these German actors drop out of their parts is a scandal. No wonder some companies make a reputation, where there is discipline, pride in the history of the house, feeling for the art as art. If ahead in stage mechanism and experiment, if leading in plays, still this country is, in average of ability in acting — not in diction — behind not only France, but England and the United States.

In Paris for but a few days, he was shocked to discover what had happened to the theatre of André Antoine: "Poetry, philosophy, real beauty, bigness, all gone in cheap, spectacular musical appeal to the senses. Ye Gods & this is Antoine! I am told it is hard to fill the big Odeon — 2000 odd — except with musical material or something that permits it."

As he returned to America, G.P.B.'s judgment of what he had seen and learned put the work of Max Reinhardt distinctly in the forefront. A review of Reinhardt's *Henry IV* which G.P.B. wrote for H. T. Parker shows the frame of mind with which he approached his own direction of the Workshop. In this, his only published account of his study of the "New Movement" in the theatre, G.P.B. said:

> No other producer whose work I have watched has caught so closely as Reinhardt the alert Elizabethan sense that the mere use of a few characteristic details or changes in them will kindle imagination to supply the rest of the required scene . . .
>
> There has been much talk lately, and some of it has reached America, that Reinhardt is not really a great manager, but is, rather, the trainer of supernumeraries and crowds — the somewhat spectacular producer seen at his best in "The Miracle" and "Sumurun." After "Henry IV" I do not believe this. He is a great producer in the best sense of the word. Here, as in "Sumurun," I had the delight of feeling the unity of artistic effect, the perfect composing of details, which is present only when a master mind is managing.

XXXV "THE NEW MOVEMENT"

AND THE WORKSHOP

AS IF TO WELCOME G.P.B. HOME, THE *Harvard Advocate* for January 24, 1913 published an editorial appeal for alumni support of a theatre at Harvard:

> The New Theatre has died a natural death. Where shall the new educational theatre arise? Where, if not at Harvard University, where Professor Baker's labors have placed the drama ahead of its position in any university in the world? The necessary funds have been collected for a Harvard Music Building. Why not a Harvard Theatre?

A few days before this, on his return to Cambridge, he had found waiting a letter from Winthrop Ames; this pointed up the main problem which confronted G.P.B. in making the Workshop a vital advance over ordinary collegiate dramatics. Not only had he to overcome the old socially motivated "amateurism" which never devoted itself wholly to excellence, but he must replace its confused pursuit of commercial values with the ends of art.

Ames had, a few weeks previously, joined H. T. Parker in viewing an H.D.C. production of an English 47 play which the boys hoped to take to New York. On the sixth of January, Ames wrote from his Little Theatre:

It was planned to invite the New York Critics to see the play, and — alas! — I know these kind gentlemen. With their animus against anything "academic" or "educational," they would have been only too certain to have taken the view that the play represented, and was presented as, an exhibition of the work of your course. And, honestly, it did not seem to me wise or fair that this play should be so viewed. For one thing: the play is directly of the "professional" type — made with an eye to box office . . . I felt that it would be much more advisable that the Harvard Dramatic Club should make its first venture into New York with a play of a more different sort: say of the type of MacKaye's "Scarecrow," rather than something like the ordinary run of plays produced by commercial managers.

This suggests the transition in standards with which the Workshop and G.P.B. were to be occupied. As G.P.B. tried to give his playwrights experience in the realities of the theatre for which they must write, he sought also to convey to them the total art of the theatre he had so recently observed abroad. From the first, he encouraged the Workshop people to devise their own scenery and lighting for each play in terms of the playwright's purpose; but he also tried to open the eyes of his writers to the new ideas of mass, color, light, and shadow which he now knew to be as substantial stuff as plot.

Thus there were practical as well as artistic forces in the American theatre which G.P.B. wished to unite in the Workshop. By a strange coincidence, the main forces of growth in the American theatre during the next dozen years were to be seen in plays by three of G.P.B.'s former students which occupied Boston playhouses during the week of his return from Europe. These were: *Milestones,* by Arnold Bennett and Edward Knoblock, at the Tremont Theatre; *Believe Me, Xantippe!* by John Frederick Ballard, at the Castle Square; and *The High Road,* by Edward Sheldon, at the Hollis St. Theatre. The same week, on the eve of G.P.B.'s return, January 23 and 24, the 47 Workshop presented its first play.

In the Knoblock collaboration, produced by Klaw and Erlanger, was the hard-headed, money-making force which would exploit vaudeville, motion pictures, or drama of a literary quality so long as profit promised. In the Sheldon play, produced by Minnie Maddern Fiske and her Manhattan Theatre company, for which Barrett Clark was stage manager, was the mixture of artistic idealism and business acumen which later characterized the Theatre Guild. In the John Craig production of the Ballard play was a clever presentation of new material by a manager and a company representative of the best traditions of the repertory theatre in America. And in the Workshop production was the tributary stream of artistic experiment which would cut a new channel within the main current of the American theatre.

At this time, G.P.B. wished to see the best of American materials and execution, as lately exemplified in Belasco's *The Return of Peter Grimm,* given more solidity of structure, more literary value, more beauty, and more harmony by means of a closer translation of the author's purposes into design, color, and light and by the ultimate interpretation of those purposes through the actor's art. It was a conservative rather than a revolutionary objective he expressed in his favorite phrase, "The play's the thing."

It was thus an additional coincidence that a true revolutionary of the theatre, one of Gordon Craig's students, was on hand to assist in the first Workshop production. Samuel J. Hume, at Harvard to complete his education after nearly three years of study in London and Florence, was perhaps the dominant personality of the first Workshop play. Quite free to dominate the group as actor, designer, and director during G.P.B.'s absence, Hume was surprised to find that G.P.B.'s acquaintance with the new theories of stagecraft was but so recently acquired as his lantern slides of the designs of Ernst Stern, Adolph Appia, and Gordon Craig. Enrolling in English 47, Hume was disappointed to find his new teacher essentially a critic of the written play with little real feeling for the pictorial or decorative revolution in the theatre to which the disciples of Craig were committed. As G.P.B. assumed the direction of the second Workshop production, it is significant that he secured the assistance of Livingston Platt to direct the setting and the lighting of the Workshop plays.

The majority of the Workshop personnel was, as Irving Pichel recalls, unacquainted with the revolution which Hume represented. To be sure, some had seen Winthrop Ames's importation

180

of the Reinhardt production of *Sumûrun* the preceding winter. Others had studied the notably "new" sets of Joseph Urban for the Boston Opera Company and Livingston Platt's more native scenery for the Toy Theatre. For others, the current Delta Upsilon production of *The Comedy of Errors* in the manner of Craig's recent Moscow Art Theatre *Hamlet* was the first "modern scenery" they had observed. Otherwise, most were habituated to the painted wings and backdrops in perspective, the flooding illumination, and the stereotyped costumes which were the stock in trade of the hacks who set the stage for the contemporary American theatre. Few had ever seen a cyclorama, and for most, G.P.B.'s lantern slides were their first view of what was soon to be known as the "new stagecraft."

Out of deference to the Workshop audience, who knew even less of these matters, G.P.B. held the first Workshop productions to a conservative employment of the ideas with which he had returned. However, once the Workshop was established, he encouraged a more radical response of the experimental spirit. Toward the end of October 1913, the Workshop presented the wordless fantasy which Sam Hume had written for English 47. Staged by the author, the scenery was executed by Gardner Hale, who had prepared the sets for the Craig-inspired Delta Upsilon *Comedy of Errors,* perhaps the first American production of its kind.

Hume's pantomime, somewhat in the manner of *Sumûrun*, was a sufficiently important event for H. T. Parker to request permission to see it. Since the performance was not public, he wrote nothing about it for the *Transcript;* but this markedly decorative use of the stage may have prompted his question the following week, in his column for the fourth of November: "With all allowance for youth in these university playwrights, are they not more concerned, so far as their work discloses them, with effects in the theatre and the making of them than with the observation of life, study of character, the play of the imagination over action."

After this production, G.P.B. took the stand which characterized his later teaching. He now said that the theatre must advance as a whole, design along with other elements of production, but that the advance must be balanced and ultimately subordinate to the playwright. It was this position, misinterpreted sometimes as a hostility to the decorative renaissance for which Robert Edmond Jones worked, that marked G.P.B.'s central influence upon the American drama. By 1921, G.P.B.'s requests for assistance led his friend Professor Arthur Pope to give a course in scenic design in the Harvard Department of Fine Arts.

In the spring of 1914, however, Sam Hume withdrew from the Workshop after differences with G.P.B. which seemed at the time to reflect an opposing polarity of views toward the theatre arts. Having begun to organize his historic First American Exhibition of Stagecraft, Hume subsequently took his exhibit from Cambridge and lectured upon the "New Movement" about the country. A half dozen years later, a young architectural student saw Hume's stagecraft models in St. Louis and decided to investigate the problems of stage lighting which they posed. Thus the original decorative impulse which had operated in the beginning of the Workshop returned to its closing years at Harvard as a dominant emphasis upon lighting through the personality of Stanley R. McCandless.

The conservative employment of the new stagecraft which G.P.B. desired was to be seen in the 1914 production of Elizabeth's McFadden's *Why the Chimes Rang,* later one of the most widely used plays in the repertory of American "little theatres":

> The first and last acts show the interior of a peasant's home with brown walls, the red flame from fire and candle gleam lending the only touches of bright color. This scene darkened and dissolved into a cathedral set, which had a great window in center background of . . . stained glass through which light streamed on a high altar beneath it, gules of gorgeous color falling on it in a pattern. The crowd of worshipers in the cathedral were in brilliant mediaeval dress, cardinal red, vivid blue, and orange predominating. The change from shadow to this brilliant scene was most effective.

In this instance, G.P.B.'s taste seems not greatly advanced from the values it had found, years before, in the church scene in Irving's *Much Ado about Nothing.*

With the third Workshop production, Miss Eleanor Coburn's *Molly Make-Believe,* G.P.B. distributed among the members a little brochure. Summarizing the principles he had laid down in his letters to Miss McFadden, he indicated the general lines along which he wished to see the Workshop develop. At this time he also outlined the points he wished treated in the criticisms which members of the audience had to write as a condition of their attendance at each performance.

When one of the first of these leaflets, not intended for the public, came to H. T. Parker, he wrote G.P.B. on the tenth of April:

That circular is sure to fall into many hands. Some of those hands may turn it over to a newspaper and you will wake up some morning and find the Workshop half described and half conjectured in popular journalistic vein. Moreover, the performances of *Molly Make-Believe* are likely to make it much more widely known and generally interesting than it has been. For example, I heard talk of the play and the shop in managerial offices in New York last Sunday.

H.T.P. suggested an official account in the *Transcript*. This, he said, Kenneth Macgowan would be glad to write.

Thus the Workshop ceased to be a careful secret and the public became acquainted with the attractive little programme signet by Gluyas Williams which symoblized the group. With four masked Pierrots, Williams caught both the spirit of the enterprise and the meaning of its endeavor; for these appealing figures suggested not only the serious and comic materials of the Workshop, but the ideal and practical association within its theatre of actor, author, audience, and scenic artist.

Something of this spirit was also active in the town of Pittsfield, Massachusetts, where a community theatre was being organized. Word came to G.P.B. from the theatre's director:

I don't think anything of the kind has ever occurred before and I do wish you could come up some night this week for it is quite thrilling — to find *the people* want a company here and are working shoulder to shoulder to get it. It would mean a great deal if you could find time to write us a letter that could be read at one of the nightly meetings this week.

A word from you would mean so much and make the people feel that they are a part of a big movement that can be and should be possible in every town and city in the country.

183

In addition to encouraging this grass roots movement, G.P.B. now worked at a new missionary message: the need for mechanical improvement in American scenic design and stage presentation. In June 1913, some of his opinions upon this matter were repeated in the *New York Tribune*. Calling attention to the fact that "Germany is far ahead of us in successful stage devices," he said: "We must insist that our stages shall be just as plastic as the German. The revolving stage, the suffusing lighting which gives the effect of distance, the elevator stage and the simple background of curtains for Shakespearian plays, all must come."

During the summer of 1913, one of the things G.P.B. wrote in his woodland study at Boulder Farm was the rough draft of an article for the *Alumni Bulletin* which he entitled "A Proposed Building for the Work at Harvard in Dramatic Technique." Its opening paragraph, which did not appear in the published article, shows the spirit of his now ruling passion:

It is above all as a workshop, a laboratory, that the building is needed for the work in the history and technique of the drama. As early as possible in their study, students of dramatic technique should be able to learn thoroughly all the details of a well-equipped modern stage, in order that they may not so write as to necessitate immediate changes when the play is favorably considered by actor or manager because of its value as writing. To ward off and correct such slips resulting from lack of intimate knowledge with the stage, is a large part of my work. This effort is largely wasted because students must take my word for their ineffectiveness; did they understand the equipment of a regular stage well, such errors by them would become impossible. At present, I am, so far as Harvard is concerned, a chemist working without proper vials or retorts, yet held responsible for perfect experimentation.

While these plans went forward, G.P.B. asked the firm of C. H. Blackall, leading theatre architects, to prepare publishable drawings of his ideas for a university theatre. Meanwhile, he bade farewell to scholarly publication with what is probably his best piece of critical writing, an essay on "Dramatic Technique in Marlowe," which appeared in the fourth volume of a series of studies by members of the English Association. Although his edition of *Hamlet* and his "General Introduction" for the drama section of President Eliot's Lectures on the Five-Foot Shelf of Books were also published in 1914, they had been written the preceding year. The dramatic section of the Belles-Lettres Series now moribund, he published nothing other than his *Centenary Pageant of Allegheny College, 1815–1915* until 1918, when his editions of *Plays of the Harvard Dramatic Club* and *Plays of the 47 Workshop* appeared. Through these years, his writing was concerned almost entirely with the manuscript of his *Dramatic Technique,* which he agreed in 1913 to write for Houghton Mifflin.

Through the second season of the Workshop, G.P.B. withheld his article appealing to the alumni for funds for a theatre as he began a private appeal to those who had responded to his previous requests for help. John Drew, recently in Boston with Laura Hope Crews and Mary Boland in *The Tyranny of Tears,* wrote from Chicago, where he was preparing to join with Ethel Barrymore in a New York production of *A Scrap of Paper:* "Of course I am at your command in the matter." And support came from Ned Sheldon, whose *Romance,* starring Doris Keane, was running toward its second year as one of the most popular plays of all time. With a committee of such notable sponsors, G.P.B. released his article for a May 1914 issue of the *Alumni Bulletin,* just before the usual generous assembly for commencement.

Thus the alumni learned of the theatre which G.P.B. proposed as a worthy addition to the Yard. In his text for the architectural drawing, he explained:

The Georgian building of brick is two stories high in front of the stage, five stories high behind it. The auditorium seats between 400 and 500 on the floor and some 300 in the one gallery. When not needed the latter can be shut off by curtains. The stage space is large because, though it can be used only with the usual equipment of the American stage, it is also provided with all the most recent Continental devices for expeditious shifting of scenery and effective lighting. Yet the proscenium opening is of moderate size and everything is arranged for productions, under ordinary circumstances, on the scale customary in "intimate theatres."

This, the second of G.P.B.'s theatre plans to appear in blueprint, was a modification of the ideas which Professor Warren had drawn in 1911. Smaller in its auditorium by almost three hundred seats, the stage of this theatre for Harvard University was much enlarged as a result of G.P.B.'s 1912 tour. Neither an intimate theatre for the very few, such as Winthrop Ames's Little Theatre in New York or Max Reinhardt's Kammerspiele in Berlin, nor quite so large as Reinhardt's Deutsches Theater, it was still in the Littmann tradition which had begun with the Prinz-Regenten.

Moreover, it carried not only the sound principles of this tradition, but it presented a compendium of the best of recent German stage design. On either side of the proscenium opening G.P.B. had provided ample space for the maneuvering of sliding stages and experimentation with *wagenbühne* and *schiebebühne*. But the most striking thing about G.P.B.'s new stage plan was its provision for a revolving stage area such as Reinhardt had in the Deutsches Theater.

Since Winthrop Ames had already installed two of the existing three American revolving stages in his own theatres during the past two years, G.P.B. was not exactly an innovator in the American theatre in this respect. Yet his plan surely represented a desire to employ the device which Ames had hitherto left practically unused in his productions. Had this theatre been built at Harvard, there undoubtedly would have occurred some interesting employment of stage devices which are still relatively unknown in the American theatre; and the revolving stage might not have remained the commercially impractical thing that it is today.

Unfortunately, G.P.B.'s desire to experiment with the striking possibilities of the *drehbühne* and other such devices, however it may have appealed to those of the alumni who were interested in the theatre, did not persuade President Lowell. Indeed, if he lacked an antipathy for such theatre projects, it could but have been created by the expansiveness of G.P.B.'s plan. Whatever the causes for Lowell's rejection of it, G.P.B. later wrote upon his copy of the *Harvard Alumni Bulletin* for May 13, 1914: "This contains the injudicious plan which disturbed President Lowell and delayed the chances for a theatre because the plan was too elaborate."

On the day that G.P.B.'s "Proposed Building for the Drama" was published, President Lowell sent G.P.B. a letter which, in effect, barred him from further pursuit of funds for his theatre and nullified the efforts of such a committee as that of John Drew.

That these labors might not be included in the "best interests" of the University had not occurred to G.P.B. Certainly he never entertained the slightest doubt about the legitimacy of his efforts to produce a new American drama within the broad function of a national university. That the President, having agreed to his efforts to procure the endowment of his professorship, might not permit him to seek the thing which would complete his teaching was something he had not anticipated. Hurt, and profoundly disturbed, he turned to the 47 Workshop.

XXXVI   "PROPOSED DRAMATIC EXHIBIT"

IN THE EARLY DAYS OF 1914, AS G.P.B. WORKED ON HIS idea for a university theatre, there came to him news of a proposed "Pan-Pacific Exhibition" in San Francisco. The approaching inauguration of the Panama Canal, with existing transcontinental railways and projected transcontinental telephone service, marked the end of frontier America and the growing continental unity of the United States. To a number of gentlemen of San Francisco it seemed an auspicious time for an exposition of American culture. Indeed, G.P.B. had been involved in plans for a world's fair in Boston in 1915, a project which had just been relinquished in favor of a Panama exhibition on the Pacific Coast. With such reports came an invitation for G.P.B. to provide a sketch for a pageant for the San Francisco fair.

In reply, he sent west a plan which he had been considering for some years and which he had already worked out in some detail for the "Boston–1915" exposition just abandoned. The document which went to San Francisco is characteristic, both in scope and tone, of the modest proposals which G.P.B. pounded out from time to time on his Oliver typewriter. He had acquired the machine just before the turn of the century, but had reserved its use for matters of record; for his quick and scrawling longhand, though it sometimes defeated his own divination of its meaning, was eminently more suited to the swiftness of his thought. If he purchased the machine in order to make his playscripts more salable, it was matters such as his "Proposed Dramatic Exhibit" which were now preserved in the bright blue typescript of the old Oliver.

This proposal, though perhaps less germane to San Francisco than to Boston, sought to organize the materials demonstrative of the continental stature of the American theatre. Summarizing G.P.B.'s view of the drama and the theatre at the very time when Eugene O'Neill was preparing to study playwriting with him, it is a curious document. So far as he knew, nothing like his plan to employ the drama as a cultural exhibit had ever been attempted. As a matter of fact, a dramatic exhibit had been part of the plan for the Philadelphia Exhibition of 1876, but the details suggested in the original catalogue of this fair had never been realized. At least, no one had seen them in relation to such an artistic and educative exposition of the development now outlined by G.P.B.

Hoping to show the development of the play in England, the United States, and the continental countries, he had a broad plan:

A list of plays would be selected so that, in a brief space of time, any one interested might see performances of a Greek tragedy, a Roman comedy, and the Italian *comedia del' arte,* and one or two Spanish types (all these in translation, of course), the English miracle play (for instance, Everyman), plays of Shakespeare and some of his contemporaries, a Restoration comedy or two (Perhaps Etheredge, Congreve, or Farquhar; perhaps Gay's Beggar's Opera); Sheridan and Goldsmith; Tom Robertson's Caste; and then in larger number plays of Pinero, Jones, Wilde, Shaw, the new Irish group; Galsworthy, Masefield, and Houghton. In addition, some American plays should be given, probably a famous one of the Revolutionary period; another of the first half of the nineteenth century, and then selected plays of the last fifty years (for instance, Bronson Howard, Clyde Fitch, etc.) to illustrate our own dramatic growth.

The desideratum would be, he said, "good performances of a list of plays short enough to permit anyone to get a conspectus of the drama internationally in a fortnight's attendance at the theatre."

This plan was to be carried out in two ways. There could be formed a stock company large enough to put on different plays afternoon and evening. Or special companies could be invited to give performances suited to their particular excellence. He did not think it would be difficult to induce some of our American companies, the Irish players of Dublin, the Manchester players under Miss Horniman, a Max Reinhardt company, or Granville-Barker's company to arrange for a 1915 itinerary which would place them in San Francisco at a desired time. Whatever the organization of productions, there would need to be some expository apparatus of lectures, exhibits, and the right kind of brief introductions, such as the "classical matinees" at the Odéon in Paris had used for years.

So far as possible, the stage for each play would be set like the stage of its own time. In any case, models and pictures of those stages would be close at hand for examination. This would also be appropriate to the newest types of theatres here and abroad, the work of such distinguished theatrical architects as Seeling of Berlin and Littmann of Munich. Thus Americans would learn about the revolving stage, the side stage, and the elevator stage — the contracting and expanding proscenium arch — the revolutionary Fortuny system of lighting — the cupola horizon's simulation of natural light from the sun. Here, too, should they learn the revolutionary work of Gordon Craig, Leon Bakst, and Max Reinhardt. "I should hope," he suggested, "to induce two at least of these men to be present at the exhibition or to take some definite part in it." The effect of such a procedure upon the American stage in the next ten years, he firmly believed, "might easily be similar to the effect upon our arts of the Philadelphia Exhibition of 1876, — stimulating to the point of transformation."

However unrealistic it may have been to expect that even a modest number of those who would come to the Panama Exhibition might enjoy a fortnight of such activity, it was a magnificent idea which gains brilliance as one relates it to the "streamlined Shakespeare" in a thatched Globe Theatre which was the dramatic excellence of a later "Century of Progress." As G.P.B. concluded his prospectus, the splendid vision which now illuminated all he did shone in his final words:

Looking over this outline I seem to have emphasized the foreign theatre a little at the expense of the American. This is not because I do not want in every way to recognize in the Exhibition all the

American theatre has been and is doing; but because in several respects, particularly in mechanical devices, newer theories of staging and richly developed drama, the older countries are naturally ahead of us. I should want this Exhibition, while showing fully what the United States has done, by pointing to much that we might adopt or adapt, to lead to rich and varied development for our drama and the theatre in the next twenty years.

Apparently a tentative agreement to present some of the features of this plan was concluded. For G.P.B. was engaged in working out the details of an exhibit which would produce a revenue of three hundred thousand dollars during the summer of 1915 when the assassination at Sarajevo brought an end to this activity. So the bright blue typescript went into G.P.B.'s files along with other proposals which might have been executed, as G.P.B. so persuasively said, "with little difficulty" — if not without considerable expense.

Thus, when in the spring of 1916 Major Henry Lee Higginson inquired of G.P.B. if he might recommend someone to write a pageant for the Plymouth Tercentenary Celebration, the proposals for the Pan-Pacific Exhibition were exhumed. Before long, the Major's Tercentenary Commission received G.P.B.'s "brief outline" for a pageant and a film play of the landing of the Pilgrims. As America's entry into the war drew near, both proposals went into one of the old-fashioned box letter files which G.P.B. added to the shelf of correspondence he had saved since the mid-nineties.

Like many of the ideas with which these dossiers grew, these sketches were but the beginning of something. Five years later, G.P.B. produced the great pageant at Plymouth. However, nothing quite like his "Proposed Dramatic Exhibit" has yet appeared — unless it is the Ford Foundation's television program, "Omnibus," directed by Alistair Cooke, one of G.P.B.'s students during his last years at the Yale Drama School.

BEAUTY VS. BROADWAY —
ENTER EUGENE O'NEILL

THE LAST TEN YEARS OF G.P.B.'S CAREER AT HARVARD
had the unity of a third act. With growing exclusiveness he dedicated himself to the Workshop, its people, and its work as these
coalesced in a pragmatic school of the theatre arts. Unlike Gordon
Craig's school in Florence, this one in Cambridge had no program to advance, no personal theories of the drama to expound.
It merely sought the development of original artists. From the
various enterprises of this informal school, which is not to be
confused with G.P.B.'s courses and which had no official relationship with Harvard, came new skills and standards for the American theatre.

In the decade from 1914 to 1924, many artistic talents of various origin associated themselves with the Workshop to provide
for many a young playwright the opportunities which one of them
has thus acknowledged:

> Simple and unprofessional as some of the productions there were,
> I absorbed a great deal of knowledge about the spoken word — and,
> I think, gained a sense of structure. Only when I lost this contact
> did I realize how much more I could have learned about acting and
> lighting, scenic design and direction — and their potential contribu-
> tion to any play.

Among G.P.B.'s Harvard colleagues who helped directly and
sent their own good men were H. Langford Warren, Professor of
Architecture, and Arthur Pope, Professor of Fine Arts. From them
came Rollo Wayne, Donald Oenslager, and Stanley McCandless.
From the Massachusetts Institute of Technology came Munroe
Pevear, an architect experimenting with light and pure color.
Typical of the Harvard undergraduates who brought talents in
music or the graphic arts were Chalmers Clifton and Gluyas
Williams. By no means was everyone in the Workshop a play-
wright.

However, there had been from the beginning a nuclear group
of would-be playwrights, the "Baker's Dozen," which had rather

dominated the scene. Thus there was always a somewhat autonomous literary cadre from which G.P.B. drew his chief lieutenants, but the life of the Workshop was its individuals. Obviously, when people like Sam Hume or Alexander Dean or Munroe Pevear participated in a Workshop production, their contributions were individual. As a consequence, after 1924, this tradition of independence and leadership provided G.P.B. with such people as Stanley McCandless, Philip Barber, Donald Oenslager, and Boyd Smith for the staff of his Drama Department at Yale.

Surrounding this corps of leaders was the society of artists, authors, critics, and devoted amateurs — not necessarily Harvard and Radcliffe alumni and alumnae — which sustained G.P.B.'s work with their intelligence, energy, and money. In accord with G.P.B.'s philosophy, it too developed its own organizational character and leadership from the beginning in such people as Edward Goodnow, Agnes Crimmins, and Alice Howard Spaulding. And beyond these circles were the only official educational realities in this congeries of forces, the Harvard and Radcliffe classes in English 47.

Indubitably these forces were impelled by a great popular intuition that entertainment would shortly rank among the nation's major industries and that riches befitting royalty awaited the inventors of pleasure for the masses. It is thus almost impossible to define the specific influences of this school which grew about G.P.B. Certainly there were forces operative there which were independent of him; yet it was he who remained always the element of continuity and the focus of loyalty. It was he who, more than all else, meant opportunity and encouragement for young hearts. For the truth and the gleam which G.P.B. brought to all who would be led was the amateur's love of creation and the professional's love of art which, now and then, produce masterpieces. Thus G.P.B. concluded his book for playwrights: "Whoever aims to write plays chiefly or wholly because he would like fame or money . . . in fact he who writes plays for any other reason than that he cannot be happy except in writing plays, better give over such writing."

By the summer of 1914, then, G.P.B. was the recipient of many requests for instruction from people in all walks of life and with varying educational backgrounds. One letter which came that July was distinguished from those which sought the way to the big bonanza of Broadway. Its author, who clearly could not be happy except in writing plays, wrote:

> July 16, 1914
> 325 Pequot Ave.
> New London, Conn.

Dear Sir: —

Mr. Clayton Hamilton, the dramatic critic, to whom I have frequently mentioned my ambition of becoming a playwright, has given me permission to use his name, and advised me to write to you personally regarding the possibility of my entrance, as a special student, into your several dramatic courses at Harvard University.

Let me explain my exact position. I am twenty-five years old. My university training consists of one year (Freshman) at Princeton University, Class of 1910, where I started to take a Litt. B. course. All my life I have been closely connected with the dramatic profession. My father is James O'Neill, the actor, of whom you may perhaps have heard; so, although I have never been on the stage myself, and my direct connection with the theatre is confined to a half-season as assistant-manager with Viola Allen in "The White Sister," nevertheless I can claim whatever knowledge there may be gained from a close connection with members of the profession.

Less than a year ago I seriously determined to become a dramatist and since that time I have written one long play — four acts — and seven one-act plays. Five of the latter are shortly to be published in book form by The Gorham Press of Boston. None of my plays have as yet been submitted to any manager for production but, of course, I intend to try and obtain a hearing for them the latter part of this summer.

Although I have read all the modern plays I could lay my hands on, and many books on the subject of the Drama, I realize how inadequate such a hap-hazard, undirected mode of study must necessarily be. With my present training I might hope to become a mediocre journey-man playwright. It is just because I do not wish to be one, because I want to be an artist or nothing, that I am writing to you.

Will the Harvard regulations regarding special students permit my taking your courses — and whatever supplementary ones you would be kind enough to suggest as likely to help me? And if so, may I have your permission to enter your course?

One word more about myself: If varied experience be a help to the prospective dramatist I may justly claim that asset for I have worked my way around the world as a seaman on merchant vessels and held various positions in different foreign countries.

Hoping you may look favorably upon this earnest desire of mine to become your student, I remain

Sincerely your's [*sic*]
Eugene G. O'Neill

What recollections of *The Count of Monte Cristo* and the Providence Opera House may have thronged G.P.B.'s memory at the name of James O'Neill can only be conjectured. The fact is that he accepted the old actor's son as a candidate for English 47 upon the provision that he submit some of his dramatic writing. Two weeks later, on the twenty-ninth and from the same address, the young man wrote again:

Dear Sir: —

I am sending under separate cover two one-act plays, completed a short time ago, from which you will be able to form a judgment as to my suitability for taking your course.

As for my standing at Princeton, I am hardly proud of it. I went there with the idea of getting through with the smallest possible amount of work, and I succeeded in paying so little attention to the laws regarding attendance, etc. that I was "flunked out" at the end of the Freshman year for over-cutting.

I do not think it would be fair to judge me by my Princeton record. I was eighteen then, but now I am fast approaching twenty-six, and the Princeton Freshman and I have very little in common.

In accordance with your suggestion, I will write to Mr. Hart [Secretary of the Faculty of Arts and Sciences] as soon as I hear whether my plays fulfil your requirements or not. I don't suppose it would be any use writing to him until I could tell him that you were willing to accept me.

Thanking you for your consideration and again hoping that I may become your student, I remain

Sincerely your's
Eugene G. O'Neill

In due time, O'Neill entered upon his special studies in English 47 for the fall of 1914. During the first half of the year he wrote for his classroom adaptation a one-act play which he called, *The Dear Doctor*. His long play for the course was *The Personal Equation*, in four acts. Much of what G.P.B. gave the class was "old stuff" to O'Neill; and when the young man showed the professor what he considered his best work, G.P.B. told him quite frankly that *Bound East for Cardiff* was not a play. However, G.P.B. thought O'Neill's short story adaptation good enough for vaudeville and urged O'Neill to try to sell it. Unfortunately, these plans came to nought when O'Neill discovered that his source had been pirated from an already successful vaudeville skit.

Later, O'Neill said, "The plays I wrote for him were rotten," and dismissed the things he wrote that fall and winter as "Nothing of importance." However, in spite of his impatience with this apprenticeship and his peripheral relations with the Workshop, he was fond of the professor and got from him the one thing he needed most — encouragement.

Lee Simonson, a classmate of Ned Sheldon, recalls the relationship between G.P.B. and other young men of talent which was both a prelude to G.P.B.'s influence upon O'Neill and an illuminator of it:

> The immense influence that Baker had on so many generations of students was not due primarily to his taste or to his particular opinions as to what was good play-writing and what was not, for much of which some of us had scant respect, but to the sense of our effective importance which he instilled in us. We were living intelligences who could affect actual issues before they were irrevocably decided one way or another. We mattered.

One of the men who sat at the round table with Eugene O'Neill recalls the personal qualities which G.P.B. brought to those meetings of English 47:

> His love of the theatre was completely selfless, and this was undoubtedly a big factor in his hold upon all of us both in the classroom and the Workshop. No other profession generates egotists like the stage. But Professor Baker or his career never came between the theatre and his students. He gave us the theatre clear-cut, unclouded by personal bias or vanity . . .
>
> Professor Baker also possessed to an incredible degree the ability to make us would-be playwrights feel we were good, that our work was already important. Just how he did this is hard to say. Certainly not through praise. Perhaps his absorption in all things theatrical came to his aid. Even very bad work could be important to him; analyzing its defects brought out the principles that made work good. Of course,

too, he was a man of great courtesy, tact, and friendliness. From watching men in class after class, he must have quickly realized that morale is perhaps the most important weapon in the playwright's arsenal. Discouraged men don't write good plays.

It was this simple encouragement of the artist's own genius that was G.P.B.'s great gift. Yet this was not a matter of sentiment but a matter of settled principle; he truly believed that his function was to the end "that the individuality of the artist may have its best expression." It was this intelligent encouragement that O'Neill remembered with deep appreciation, after G.P.B.'s death, as a "profound influence" upon the "birth of modern American drama."

In this respect, it is a striking contrast that the Craig Prize Play for the year O'Neill was at Harvard was more nearly in the tradition of the theatre of James O'Neill than in that of the coming American drama. This was Cleves Kinkead's *Common Clay*, a strong play about the "double standard," which soon established itself as a Broadway hit, starring Jane Cowl, after its initial eighteen weeks at the Castle Square. Certainly this was effective theatre, liberally spiced with sex, but it was clearly the grasp of a clever artisan and not the reach of an artist.

Its production at the Castle Square brought an article from a member of the Workshop, Lottie Chase Ham, which created a considerable controversy when H. T. Parker printed it in the *Transcript*. In her criticism of the Craig Prize Plays, which she entitled "Questioning Harvard Drama," Miss Ham asked:

What are they worth, judged as the creative work from a course in playwriting at Harvard College under one of the most inspiriting and devoted instructors in the college? I do not hesitate to say that they have been worth nothing. They have not contributed one iota of value to the theatre of today. In all of them is not one original thought or expression . . . I do not wish to be precious in my judgment . . . I merely wish to inquire as to whether Harvard College is in the main teaching a lucrative profession, or whether it is trying to inculcate some of the first principles of dramatic creation?

H.T.P. may have intended only to promote a lively discussion, for he immediately invited Walter Prichard Eaton to write a reply. Nevertheless, Miss Ham's criticism was very close to the line H.T.P. had taken in criticizing the Henry Miller production of

Moody's *The Faith Healer* in Sanders Theatre. Of course, the faithful followers of the Workshop resented what they took to be a direct attack and the fight was on. Soon Miss Ham wrote to G.P.B. protesting that her remarks were not an attack upon him, as they had been widely interpreted. Moreover, she submitted her Workshop membership card for him to accept or reject. To this G.P.B. replied:

The 47 Workshop
February 17, 1915

Dear Miss Ham: —

     I am glad to have your recent letter. You are, of course, like every other member of the 47 Workshop audience, entirely free to say what you think of the work offered there or the products of English 47 or 47a offered elsewhere. I see no reason why you should return your ticket, for if attending the Workshop, even when its products displease you, interests you, you should certainly be in its audience.

     It is pleasant to know that you had no intention of attacking me personally, though I think you must not be surprised if many people, both former students of English 47 and outsiders, gathered from the general tenor of your article that it was an attack, at least by implication. After reading your article carefully, my disappointment was to find that during the year that you attended the course you had apparently so little understood my attitude on the vital and fundamental matters. If I could not make them clear to you in the meetings you attended, I doubt if it would be possible for me to make them clear to you now. You seem not to understand what I teach my students as to their relation to the public, the relation of plot to characterization, or the relation of naturalism to other kinds of dramatic writing . . . By what I teach, I am absolutely ready to stand. By what I am often said to teach, I am by no means willing to stand and do not see why I should. Mr. Eaton has put the whole matter admirably, so why not let the subject drop?

Yours sincerely,
George P. Baker

What O'Neill then thought of the question is not a matter of record. It is quite possible that he might have agreed with Miss Ham's criticism of a play that was, essentially, no more modern or American than *The Count of Monte Cristo*. But certainly G.P.B.'s teaching was not lost upon O'Neill when he said:

The man who grows from a technique which permits him to write a good play because it accords with historical practice to the technique which makes possible for him a play which no one else could have written, must work under the scrutiny of three great Masters: Constant Practice, Exacting Scrutiny of Work, and, above all, Time. Only when he has stood the tests of these Masters is he the matured artist.

Kinkead, it is to be observed, wrote no more plays; O'Neill now awaits only the test of Time. For both, G.P.B. was a masterful teacher.

XXXVIII   WAR AND TRANSITION

THE SEASON OF 1914–15, EUGENE O'NEILL'S YEAR IN English 47, was marked by signs of major change in the American theatre. The influence of motion picture techniques upon those of the legitimate stage appeared for the first time in the use a new playwright, Elmer Rice, made of the "flash back" scene in relating the testimony of witnesses in *On Trial*. New standards in artistic production appeared in the repertory which Harley Granville-Barker and his Savoy Theatre company, sponsored by the Stage Society, brought to Wallack's Theatre before that famous old home of English drama was torn down. And the insurgent force, now known as the Little Theatre Movement, came to Broadway with the founding of the Washington Square Players. These were but portents of the evolution in the American theatre, culminating in O'Neill's own plays, for which G.P.B. had worked.

While the Washington Square Players were rehearsing their first one-act play, Granville-Barker gave an exciting production of Anatole France's *The Man Who Married a Dumb Wife,* which introduced Robert Edmond Jones as an American designer of first importance. Few people had been able to see Jones's scenic arrangements for the initial Washington Square production, Lord Dunsany's *Glittering Gate,* but thereafter the scenic renaissance on Broadway was as assured as the use of the flash back. Though the English company also brought the first American productions of *Androcles and the Lion* and *The Doctor's Dilemma,* it was not

198

Shaw but Granville-Barker's production of *A Midsummer Night's Dream* that took G.P.B. to New York.

Not only was he interested in Norman Wilkinson's designs for scenery and costumes, but he wished especially now to see Cecil Sharp's dances; for he had missed this production at the Savoy in 1912. Moreover, there was some controversy concerning Granville-Barker's direction of the play, and the New York critics had found fault with the too rapid pace with which the English actors delivered their lines. After a hurried trip which did not permit a meeting with his friends in the company, G.P.B. conveyed his pleasure at the performance in a brief note to which Granville-Barker replied:

> Wallack's
> Broadway & 30th Street
> New York
> February 19, 1915

My dear Baker:

Your letter made me most happy. It almost goes without saying that I would sooner please you over a Shakespearean production than anybody else in this country. But I wish you would pull me to pieces a bit . . . Don't do anything publicly unless the spirit moves you, but *do* write and tell me whether you find it unintelligible gibberish or not. If so, I will take the blame, for I forced that pace and method, and they did their best, so it isn't fair to abuse them.

The next time you are in New York please do miss the train and let us see you. Also — I want to do a Greek play in the Harvard Stadium in May or June. There!

> Very sincerely yours,
> H. G. Barker

On May 18 and 19, Granville-Barker presented *Iphigenia in Tauris* and *The Trojan Women* at the Harvard Stadium. The second of these was already associated with the work of Maurice Browne's Little Theatre of Chicago, for Browne's company had gained a national reputation with its "modern" production of the Greek play from coast to coast earlier in the season. On May 27, after audiences at the Harvard Stadium had made the Granville-Barker program an artistic if not a financial success, the Englishman wrote G.P.B. as he sailed for home: "It ought, of course, to have been better."

It was in reference to such independent growth outside the commercial theatre that Gordon Craig wrote G.P.B. from his school at the Arena Goldoni some time during Eugene O'Neill's year at Harvard: "The movement in America. How do you think it is going — I note many a good man or woman contributing to the advance, & one or two over conceited."

During 1915 two "little theatre" groups of later importance to O'Neill were formed: the Provincetown Players, who began to give plays on Cape Cod that summer, and the Neighborhood Players, a New York settlement theatre not unlike that of the Hull House Players in Chicago. On the production staff for the Neighborhood Playhouse was Agnes Morgan, and somewhere in almost every one of the burgeoning little theatres was to be found some other former member of English 47.

At the end of the 1914–15 academic year, G.P.B. urged Eugene O'Neill to return for a second year of work in the longer plays, which G.P.B. felt he could not yet manage properly. However, O'Neill had plans which would take him to Greenwich Village rather than to Cambridge. By the time O'Neill left Cambridge, G.P.B. was acquainted with the work of some of his former students among the Washington Square Players. Since the first of the year, they had been producing the plays of Percy Mackaye, John Silas Reed, and such quondam English 47 writers as Lewis Beach and Edward Massey. Meanwhile — except for contact through some of the Washington Square people who were also involved in the Provincetown Players, and through Colin Ford, a "47" classmate with whom O'Neill collaborated in writing a play that year — O'Neill and G.P.B. lost touch.

Europe was now at war, and the men in the Workshop were fewer. Among those who left English 47 in 1916 were Samuel N. Behrman and Sidney Coe Howard. Percival Reniers, who had assisted G.P.B. with "The Pageant of Hollis Hall" and "The Centenary Pageant of Allegheny College," remained for a graduate year in English 47a and assisted in assembling some of the material for G.P.B.'s book on "Dramatic Technique" before he, too, went to France.

In these days, one of the most difficult tasks G.P.B. had was that of keeping the Workshop financially solvent. At the beginning of 1916, he wrote to Thornton Ware's sister:

The 47 Workshop
January 26, 1916

Dear Miss Ware: —

An idea has occurred to me which I want, in accordance with your kind suggestion, to submit to you. I should like to have some of the performances of the Workshop named annually after someone who has helped the cause here or loved the drama deeply. The production of a new play of three to five acts costs in the Workshop something over $300. I think it may safely be said that $350 defrays all expenses of one of our productions, which means two or more nights, but usually two. Our last production last season has brought Mrs. Chorpenning the Craig Prize. One of our productions this year is likely, I think, to see a professional theatre before long. Now why not the "Thornton Ware" performances? . . . They would be in a sense dramatic scholarships to be assigned each year to the authors of plays we deem specially worth production.

. . . When I came back from abroad three years ago, I fully expected to have him associated with me in this work in some way, so sure was I of the keenness of his interest, and I really cannot be content till he is in some way associated with it.

I am going into the country to rest tomorrow morning, and shall not be back probably, before Tuesday night, so take your time to think the matter over. I shall be in town for two or three days after next Tuesday, and then I shall go to New York for some days.

Sincerely yours,
Geo. P. Baker.

Thus G.P.B. remembered students and friends whom death had taken from the scene with memorial Workshop performances. After the Thornton Ware performance, there were other funds for memorials to Lilian Shuman Dreyfus, Paul Mariett, Jack Wendell, Edward MacDowell, and William Vaughn Moody. In this characteristic way, G.P.B. turned sentiment into solvency for the Workshop.

However, the continuing stability of the Workshop through the war years came from Radcliffe and its uninterrupted supply of students as well as from the unflagging zeal of such loyal workers as Miss Alice H. Spaulding, a high school teacher of dramatics and playwriting. Thus, by the time the war really began to empty the Yard, G.P.B. had established the ᵣₒₙₒp on a self-supporting basis.

Among the casualities of the war was the Craig Prize, for the last was awarded in 1917 to Kenneth Andrews' *The Year of the Tiger*. Amid these cruel times, the deep pine woods that rolled from Mount Chocorua to the rambling house and gardens of Boulder Farm were an inviting refuge. Perhaps G.P.B.'s interest in English country dancing there during these years was an idyllic escape. Certainly it was something new to America.

Beginning in 1913, Cecil Sharp and Claud Wright, a young fellow from Sharp's English Folk Dance Society, helped G.P.B. with this hobby. During the summer of 1914, G.P.B. sponsored a Folk Dance School at the Chocorua Theatre; the next year, Mrs. James J. Storrow of Boston joined in organizing the American Branch of the English Folk Dance Society, of which G.P.B. was the first president. For twenty years, country dancing grew to become a national craze as G.P.B. and his friends continued these attractive dances in the outdoor theatre at Boulder Farm.

In the spring of 1917, two days after G.P.B.'s fifty-first birthday, the United States declared war on Germany. Too old to serve in the armed forces, he watched his oldest sons, John and Edwin, prepare to do their part — John, two years out of Harvard, and Edwin, about to take his degree *cum laude*. There was something of a farewell to youth that summer at Boulder Farm as G.P.B. watched his two younger sons, Myles and George, playing in the natural amphitheatre where the land sloped away from the front of the house toward the great stone wall and the road. At this time, Hermann Hagedorn, his own family now tragically divided by the war, was staying with the Bakers. In a mood nostalgic, G.P.B. and these young people rehearsed a masque which Hagedorn had written. For this, G.P.B. danced and played the part of Pan, Spirit of the Woods.

There was also in these years a major transition within G.P.B.'s own way of life, for the horse which he had kept since his marriage was now succeeded by an automobile. Since boyhood, he had loved riding. In Cambridge, he had ridden regularly with Dean Briggs, but the increasing pace of his career had now outdistanced his use of saddle and carriage. Though dogs continued a part of his home affections, the horse now went with the days of his youth.

In the dusk of another evening that summer, G.P.B. bade farewell to the green of his outdoor theatre as the Ragged Man in Lady Gregory's *The Rising of the Moon.* For with the summer's mobilization, he had been appointed chief of the Department of Scenarios in the United States Bureau of Public Information. Here he had the responsibility of selecting and preparing scenarios for public information movies. Through 1917–18 he did this job and kept his eye on the Workshop, which was busy entertaining troops in New England encampments.

During 1917, G.P.B. began to edit for publication some of the Workshop plays which had at least a modest literary quality. However, these were intended not primarily for a reading audience but to supply materials suitable for the fifty-odd "little theatres" then successfully operating in the United States. The first collection, published by Brentano's in 1918 as *Plays of the 47 Workshop,* was published simultaneously with a second collection G.P.B. also edited, *Plays of the Harvard Dramatic Club.* Other volumes in both series soon followed.

Because the Workshop was now widely imitated within the Little Theatre Movement — in the Theatre Workshop of New York, The Playshop in Chicago, The Vassar Workshop, and in such groups as the Morningside Players, for which Elmer Rice was writing — G.P.B. prefaced the first of these volumes with a history of the Workshop and the principles upon which he had built its reputation. The real significance of all this activity outside the regular theatre, G.P.B. explained, was the opportunity it gave to new playwrights:

It will not hurt any ambitious young playwright to try his hand at every one of the activities connected with such an organization as The 47 Workshop, though it is not easy to make him understand this. If he has shifted scenery, he will make few, if any, unnecessary demands for elaborate and heavily constructed pieces. When he has had his part in the handling of stage properties, he will not call for them to an unnecessary extent, nor will he clutter his stage with what is artistically undesirable. When he has assisted in lighting, he will be less likely to ask the light man to provide the atmosphere and the subtler gradations of feeling which it is his business to provide by his text. Studying rehearsals, he will better understand the value of the spoken word, and will come to see why it is not wise, as a rule, merely to sketch in his characters . . . Indeed, he will learn a hundred and one details as to the absolute essentiality of writing with actors in mind rather than for a reading public.

In the summer of 1918, G.P.B. spent several days observing the little theatre on the Provincetown wharf where the Provincetown Players were doing O'Neill's *Bound East for Cardiff*. Quite by chance, teacher and student met and renewed their friendship over the piece which G.P.B. had not considered a play when O'Neill wrote it for an assignment in English 47. The following October, G.P.B. saw the one-act bill of the Washington Square Players which included O'Neill's *In the Zone*, but he again lost track of "Gene" except for what he heard from John D. Williams, an early member of the Baker's Dozen and now business manager for Charles Frohman. Williams was interested in O'Neill, he told G.P.B., particularly in a new play of his called *Beyond the Horizon*.

In these days, G.P.B. watched with great interest the efforts of some of his old students in the Washington Square Players — particularly Theresa Helburn, Lee Simonson, and Maurice Wertheim — to form the Theatre Guild. With them in mind, apparently, he wrote:

We need badly to develop in this country a group of men and women as nearly corresponding as our conditions will permit to the *intendants* and *régisseurs* of the continental theatres — men and women managing theatres because from their youth they have loved and studied the theatre and the drama; people of cultivation, determined, while they kept the public thoroughly entertained and amused, to give it as much of the best in the past and the present of the drama as their public can be induced to accept. These are the conditions which most speedily will give us American drama able in the number and quality of its plays to hold its own with the drama of older nations.

Shortly before he resigned from his war job, G.P.B. heard once more from Eugene O'Neill:

West Point Pleasant, N. J.
May 9, 1919

My dear Professor Baker:

Not once but a dozen times since our chance meeting in Provincetown two years ago have I determined to write to you, but each time I hesitated, reflecting: Better wait until you have something real to relate. Not that the possession of any grand achievement emboldens me at present writing; but at least the burden of a yowl at Fate gives me ballast.

I have been hoping all during the past theatrical season to be able to give you the date and all other data of a forthcoming production of my long play, "Beyond the Horizon," which has been under contract to John D. Williams since last spring. It is a play of two brothers, and Williams was sure he would produce it with the Barrymores in the cast — a fair hope, that! — as soon as "Redemption" petered out, as the consensus of wide opinion decreed it must. "Redemption," however, refused to peter. And now comes "The Jest" — a very mocking irony of a title, it seems to me — which promises to beat all records for endurance.

That, in brief, is my plaint; and who can gainsay its justice when he sees this native-son steam-rollered by that foreign invasion? True, Williams has renewed the contract and promises a production before next December, and is still full of hope that in the end his devout wish will be consummated. Ah, yes — in the end! But my system has absorbed so much hope in the past six months that I am now immune. I turn a callous, cauliflower ear to all managerial fair promises. I have ceded my winter home in Spain for a permanent residence in Missouri.

Since you last saw me I have completed three long plays. The first, finished a year ago, was immediately taken by Williams — with the resultant blighted dreams recorded above. The second, "Chris. Christopherson," is now awaiting the verdicts of both Hopkins and Belasco. I really have every confidence that, in spite of the fact that it is far removed in nature and treatment from the usual run of acceptable plays, it will eventually find a producer. The third play, ["The Straw"] the last act of which I have just finished rewriting, is still untyped. It is the best of them in my opinion, but on account of its subject matter, I anticipate a long period of waiting — unless the Theatre Guild like it enough to face the music.

I wish you could read these three plays. They would interest you I feel sure, because they are sincere and because they demand a freshness of treatment and a widened scope for the playwright's subject material. Will you let me send one or more of them to you sometime this summer? I know you are at your busiest just now. In truth, it has been the conviction that you have no season that isn't busy that has prevented my sending them to you as they were finished.

I hope you escaped seeing the production of my one-act plays by the Washington Square Players and Greenwich Village Theatre a year ago this season. You would have acquired a false opinion from these productions of the worth of the plays as written, I am sure. And as for "In the Zone" as mutilated by the vaudeville folk — it ran for over thirty weeks until peace and the Flu intervened — I had better turn the page. Well, a vaudeville audience never reads an author's name, anyway.

Under separate cover I am sending you a copy of the book of my one-act plays just published. All of the seven have been produced in New York, most of them originally by the Provincetown Players. I wish very much for you to have this book as a small token of my remembrance of all I owe to my year under your guidance. Let me only hope that these plays will justify that year in your eyes. I realize I must have seemed woefully lacking in gratitude because, seemingly, I have never had the decency to write — and I know the interest you take in the work of your former students. But I'm really not as bad as that. In all honesty, I have waited more out of small-boy ambition than anything else. I was confident that the night would come when I could approach you with that digesting-canary grin, and, pointing to the fiery writing on the wall of some New York theatre, chortle triumphantly: "Look, Teacher! See what I done!"

Very sincerely yours,
Eugene G. O'Neill

P.S. I hope you will pardon the typewriting; but I realized that this letter is long, and my handwriting is small, and your time is short.

In June 1919, the college year over and Commencement past, G.P.B. collected the reviews of *Dramatic Technique* which he had clipped through the end of winter and the spring to paste them in a scrapbook. Other chores, such as the answering of correspondence from former students who now wished to send him their students, occupied him as he prepared for the summer's move to Boulder Farm. One of these letters was from Fred Koch, who now taught playwriting at the University of North Carolina and wrote to ask about the possibility of graduate assistance at Harvard for some of his own Chapel Hill playwrights.

At this time G.P.B. heard again from O'Neill, who wrote on June 8:

A word of explanation as to why I failed to come back for your second year. I wanted to. It was none of my choice. I just didn't have the money, couldn't get it, and had to take a job as a New York dramatic critic on a new theatrical magazine which never got beyond the promotion stage, although I was religiously paid a small salary for doing nothing for three months or so. But please do not believe for an instant that my failure to report was caused by any doubt as to your helping me further. I was too well aware of the faults in my work to harbor any such erroneous idea of my own self-sufficiency. My one year helped me tremendously — in more ways, perhaps, then you can imagine, — and I was not blind to the fact that without the short-cut of your advice I would have learned (if I have learned!) by a laborious process of elimination. Oh, indeed I wanted to come back!

G.P.B. was at Boulder Farm, cultivating his roses, when another letter, dated June 30, came from "Gene":

It's a great joy to me to hear that you liked the title play ["The Moon of the Caribbees"] of my book so well. That has always been my pet play of all my one-acters but, with few exceptions, all the votes I've received on it have been dissenting — "It isn't a play," etc.

I'll await your verdict on the long play ["Beyond the Horizon] with the keenest interest. As a great favor, will you let me have the script back as soon as you are through with it? I don't mean by this that I want to hurry you up in reading it. I wouldn't for the world have you feel that, or have you even glance at it until you feel in the humor. But this is the only script I have and when it isn't used I like to have it by me in case anything should crop up from Williams in regard to its scheduled production.

To this, O'Neill added a warm postscript which should have been for G.P.B. an increasing comfort with the passing years: "Thank you so much for your willingness to have helped in enabling me to take that second year. I'm darned sorry I didn't speak up — but I'm just as grateful to you as if I had."

IN THE FALL OF 1919, THE WAR OVER, THERE WAS A
spirited group of writers at G.P.B.'s round table. Outstanding
were Frederick L. Day, Harding Scholle, Alan Reynolds Thompson, Philip Barry, and an astonishing undergraduate by the name
of Kenneth Romaver-Ron Raisbeck. As romantic and mysterious
as his name, he had deftly assumed the secretarial duties which
Perceval Reniers left when he went to war. In his third year at
Harvard, whither he had come from some obscure origin that
often seemed northern England though it was in fact American
Middle West, he was brilliantly completing his degree with an
amazing promise that clearly impressed G.P.B. For the lad wrote
with a flair which G.P.B. had sought since his own undergraduate
days.

Indeed, Raisbeck seemed almost an aesthetic throwback to
those days. In direct contrast with the social awareness and realism of which Ned Sheldon and Eugene O'Neill were typical,
Raisbeck was *fin de siècle*. Some of his attitudes must have reminded his older professors of Berenson and Santayana. His wit
often smacked of Oscar Wilde, and his air of an artist menaced
by a Philistine society echoed the Oxford Pre-Raphaelites. Furthermore, he spoke with an astonishing sort of Oxonian diction
that, being neither a successful copy nor an obvious fraud, produced a distinctive speech which was, like Barrett Wendell's, an
invention of his own.

Indefatigable at the labors of bringing the *Dramatic Technique* to publication, Raisbeck remained G.P.B.'s chief lieutenant
until the summer of 1922. But if it was Raisbeck who made himself indispensable to G.P.B. in the busy details of these postwar
years, it was in Phil Barry that G.P.B. found his most promising
playwright since Ned Sheldon. This engaging young man from

To Professor George P. Baker —

With the hope that these plays may prove to him that at least some of his constructive advice and criticism of 1914-15 stuck midway between my ears.

Eugene G. O'Neill.

Eugene O'Neill's inscription for a volume including *The Moon of the Caribbees, Bound East for Cardiff*, and *The Long Voyage Home*

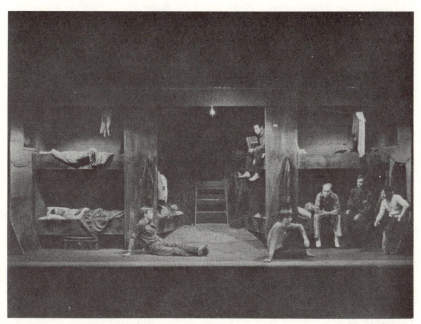

Morris Shapiro

Bound East for Cardiff, by Eugene O'Neill, Yale University Theater. Directed by Alexander Dean and Constance Welch. Setting, Robert Scott; Lighting, Stanley McCandless

Morris Shapiro

King's Coat, by Frederick Kleibacker, Yale University Theater. Setting, Donald Oenslager; Lighting, Stanley McCandless; Costumes, Frank Bevan

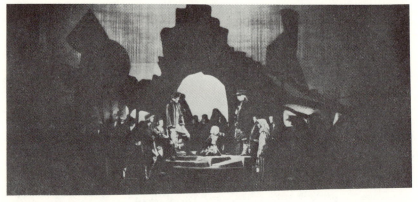

Morris Shapiro

Brand, by Henrik Ibsen, Yale University Theater. Setting, Donald Oenslager; Lighting, Stanley McCandless

Morris Shapiro

The Winter's Tale, by William Shakespeare, Yale University Theater. Setting, Donald Oenslager; Lighting, Stanley McCandless; Costumes, Frank Bevan

upstate New York had just taken his degree at Yale, where he had been Billy Phelps's student. It was Phelps who had sent him on for graduate work in English 47. Barry's healthy, pink-cheeked Philistinism — in sharp antithesis with Raisbeck's Bohemianism — merely emphasized G.P.B.'s broad interest in potentially effective playwrights.

Meanwhile, arrangements were under way for the opening of Eugene O'Neill's *Beyond the Horizon* at the Morosco Theatre, owned by Oliver Morosco, who had revived the Harvard Prize Play Contest with a new prize for $1000. For this contest, Winthrop Ames joined G.P.B. and Morosco in reading manuscripts and in choosing Rachel Barton Butler's *Mama's Affair* as the 1919–20 winner. Because of O'Neill's première, the winning play opened in Ames's Little Theatre rather than at the Morosco on the twentieth of January 1920.

Three days after O'Neill's opening, the Workshop presented Raisbeck's *Torches,* a baroque creation, strikingly staged and costumed, with original music. But if O'Neill's horizon was on the twentieth century, Raisbeck's was on the fifteenth, on Borgia intrigue, and on the loves of an incomparably lovely Gismonda. At the same time, Barry was trying to dramatize the high comedy he saw in the American scene and in the revolt of his generation against that of his father.

In these days G.P.B. completed an edition of modern American plays for Will David Howe, a former English 14 student, now a partner with Harcourt and Brace in a new publishing firm. It was Ned Sheldon's greatest success, *Romance,* which G.P.B. chose for this book, along with David Belasco's *The Return of Peter Grimm,* Augustus Thomas' *As a Man Thinks,* Louis Anspacher's *The Unchastened Woman,* and Edward Massey's *Plots and Playwrights.* Massey's play, written in the class in which O'Neill had failed to distinguish himself, had first been produced by the Workshop, and then, in 1917, by the Washington Square Players.

G.P.B.'s introduction to *Modern American Plays,* published shortly after O'Neill's success at the Morosco, took notice of the change which had come in the American audiences of the past twenty years:

209

A public which heartily welcomes *Beyond the Horizon* is not the old public. It seems now as if there really were in New York an audience large enough to make successful any kind of drama worthy attention. With that newer public created out of the War, with the probable greater effectiveness of the dramatists who have been writing successfully for us, with the promise shown by the newer writers, this is no time for pessimism . . . surely we have the right to hope that the next decade will give us an American drama which, in its mirroring of American life, will be more varied in form, even richer in content.

While the success of O'Neill's play grew, G.P.B. paused often in his own busy career to inquire kindly for the welfare of his students or to send an old friend greetings. It was Barrett Wendell whom he remembered upon his last birthday and who replied on St. Valentine's day: "Your good words make a happy Valentine. No end of thanks for them, and of gladness for the friendship which has kept unchanged." Nor was there any flagging in the personal attention he gave to such communications as the following from one of the Cambridge ladies who so loyally supported the Workshop:

I remember several years ago proposing John Marquand as a member of the 47 Workshop. Nothing was done about it, as I remember, as he shortly afterwards went to the war. Now he is here with me for the winter, and is most anxious to again become a member. He is intensely interested in the drama, and is trying his hand at writing plays himself.

But in spite of incessant demands upon his time (he had promised Will Howe another volume of American plays), G.P.B. now began to negotiate a contract for the pageant of the Plymouth Tercentennial Celebration. In the first week of February 1920, he wrote to the secretary of the Governor's commission for the celebration: "It is my hope to make the pageant a really significant contribution to the drama and to history and something particularly noteworthy in American pageantry."

At this time he sent the commission copies of the pageants he had already written. "No one of these pageants," he wrote, "is on as ample scale as the one of which we are thinking." For a cost of one hundred thousand dollars he proposed to give a pageant which should "combine some of the dramatic values of the Al-

legheny pageant with the musical quality of the Peterborough."
A week later he had a contract, at five thousand dollars, to prepare
the book of the pageant by the first day of 1921. For a like sum he
was to prepare a moving picture scenario and arrange for the production of a motion picture of the pageant.

Immediately he planned a trip abroad in order to give his
materials the freshness which he hoped would come from firsthand
experience. This he explained to the commission with perhaps an
unconscious forecast of the difficulties ahead:

I have strong belief in regard to pageantry that it is not the mere
rewriting of certain historical scenes but that every pageant should
have its own particular core of meaning and carry its own particular
message and that I think the spoken word is of as great importance in
its place as processions or group movement. I believe that all the Fine
Arts should collaborate in any pageant presentation of some definite
message contained in the historical material. The usual difficulty is to
find the message or the best message. In the case of the Plymouth
pageant the message is so obvious that the difficulty is to give it freshness of appearance.

Some of the difficulty arose because he must deal with history
so well known that literal accuracy seemed inescapable and imaginative coloring unthinkable. Not only were the gray tones of
the Puritans a pall upon his imagination, but the bare truths of
the Plymouth adventure were hard, grim, and dramatically unsympathetic. There were further difficulties in fitting his creation
to an amphitheatre yet to be built upon land yet to be made in
Plymouth harbor. And the great task lay in shaping everything
to a tolerance of but a few minutes within two hours of playing
time. Speed, he knew, could be all.

Obtaining a leave of absence for the spring term, he set out
at the beginning of March 1920, with Kenneth Raisbeck as his
secretary, for England. As he had done some thirty years before,
he journeyed by way of Italy. From Taormina, Sicily, he wrote
to Edward P. Goodnow, in whose hands he had left much Workshop responsibility:

Here winter and the drama are far enough away. The gardens
here riot and there seems to be no season for this or that flower as
with us. The last bolt fell on me today when I spied lilacs blowing side
by side with roses, geraniums, stock, and close to palm & orange trees.

I felt as with Alice in Wonderland, for to me lilacs have meant the early spring in New England when my roses have hardly sprouted and when my palms & orange trees — but words fail me!

Once again in London, there were pleasant evenings with Archer, Jones, Granville-Barker, Edward Knoblock, and other old acquaintance before he began to retrace the steps of the Pilgrims. So days and weeks of that spring and summer wound through village registers and down the byways of official records as G.P.B. strolled about the parish where William Brewster was baptized, or along the river Idle to its junction with the Trent, where a small bark once awaited in darkness.

In mid-July, upon the invitation of Sir Sidney Lee, G.P.B. described his work at Harvard to the Conference of American and British Professors of English in the Shakespeare Memorial Theatre at Stratford. At this time, he was in correspondence with T. P. Robinson — in charge of Workshop production during G.P.B.'s absence — concerning a plan proposed by the Cambridge Dramatic Club whereby the Workshop should produce their plays in return for control of Brattle Hall as a permanent Workshop theatre. There was obvious attraction in the suggestion, though G.P.B. considered the Agassiz Theatre generally superior to what he would have at Brattle Hall. However, he decided against such a move on the principle that it would take the Workshop out of the academic world and into an equivocal semiprofessional one.

On the twenty-second of the month, he wrote Robinson:

My belief is then, that we should stay at Agassiz House this coming year, making meantime every effort to get the building we need.

The *Times* is to have an article shortly on the Workshop. My talk at the Conference of English and American Professors has stirred up some interest at the Universities. A request of members of the Drama League here to the Minister of Education to have courses in the drama given at the Universities roused considerable newspaper and periodical comment. The new publication, *The Mercury,* editorially somewhat slurred American methods of teaching play writing. Granville Barker came to the rescue in a letter, and promises more later.

For a short time, he was ill in London. Then he resumed his research for the pageant.

What he sought as he looked and read and photographed was

not history. He desired no mere procession of historical scenes but a dramatic production that brought to life the spirit with which the Pilgrim Fathers had come to America. There was, however, in his quest the meticulous concern for details which is the mind-set of the scholar. Increasingly, his regard for history inhibited the bold manipulation of fact which made Shakespeare's drama superior history. Before leaving Holland to return to England where he hoped to begin writing his pageant, he wrote to Arthur Lord, a member of the Tercentenary Commission:

> It may seem that many of the matters which I have been treating are of small importance, especially for a Pageant, but the sum total means that I see the Pilgrims, both as a group and as individuals, with a clearness which would not have been possible, had I not visited the places connected with them and considered all the evidence.

Toward the end of September, he saw the New England coast once more. Home again, he was still unpacking notes, pictures, maps, and an unfinished manuscript when Christina came to the study to say that a young man wished to see him about admission to English 47. She said he was a tall, odd-looking fellow and very shy, painfully shy. Very well, then, though the dozen for the coming year had been selected some months ago, G.P.B. would see him.

Suddenly, with long strides, there was a giant in the room. It was an awkward tousled giant, whose trouser cuffs rode high on his anklebones and whose coat sleeves were too short. In a low voice, he said that he had studied playwriting with Professor Koch at Chapel Hill and that his name was Thomas Clayton Wolfe.

XL   WORKSHOP CRISIS

FOR TEN MONTHS AFTER HIS RETURN FROM ENGLAND and Holland, G.P.B. had little time for the young giant from Chapel Hill or for the other writers in English 47. To be sure, the class met as usual in Lower Massachusetts Hall; but most of G.P.B.'s students that year probably saw as much of Kenneth Raisbeck as they did of their professor. Until the pageant rehearsals began in June, G.P.B.'s principal interest was in bringing the

Plymouth venture to a successful fruition. Another event, scheduled for early spring, monopolized what little time the pageant did not consume. This was the Workshop's projected "road show" tour of Cleveland, Buffalo, and New York. As an indirect contribution to the publicity for these events, G.P.B. wrote an account of the Workshop for the February 1921 issue of the *Century Magazine*.

Over the years, the organization already generally associated with his name had developed a character of its own. Three large folio volumes which constitute the archives of the 47 Workshop show that the history of the group is not the same thing as G.P.B.'s leadership of it. Always a coöperative enterprise, it had evolved as an association of actors, scenic artists, critics, authors, production personnel, and intelligent audience. This association grew not only around G.P.B. but around the individuals of marked talents in these supporting groups.

Of course, G.P.B. continued to be the dominant figure in the Workshop and the source of its continuity. The influence of his personal tastes appears in such Workshop productions as the *Revesby Sword Play* and *Eyvind of the Hills,* the first a revival of a medieval mumming play and the second a modern piece by the Icelandic playwright, Jóhan Sigurjónsson. In these, chosen because they gave imaginative opportunities in scenic and costume design not afforded by the preponderant realism of the English 47 plays, G.P.B. exercised the historical interest, fondness for folk dances, and regard for native dramatic materials which he had already displayed in the Peterborough Pageant. However, there was developing in the group a corps of artists whose ideas affected G.P.B.'s own work. Without such Workshop personalities as Munroe Pevear, Donald Oenslager, and Stanley McCandless — who had no connection with English 47 — the proliferating ideas of G.P.B. would have lacked agents for their accomplishment and inventors for their perfection.

Since the departure of Sam Hume and Livingston Platt, there had been a continuing coterie of such technical assistants as T. P. Robinson, H. C. Forbes, and Lucy Conant, whose competence is attested by the following comment on their production of *Eyvind of the Hills:*

The play brings a new note into the English-speaking theater, a note that has something akin to Synge in the poetry of its naturalism, and something akin to Wagner in the huge scale of its simplified plot . . . The 47 Workshop has performed a public art service in producing this novel work in English.

To attract new designers, the Workshop announced in 1919 a design competition open to any Radcliffe or Harvard student. This contest brought forward Rollo Wayne, whose winning sets for *Time Will Tell* and *The Mystery of the King's Birth* were the first of a series of distinguished productions which gave the Workshop a marked artistic character. At this time, the Workshop required its designers to make color sketches, scale models with costumed wax figures, and architectural plans for their setting and lighting.

By 1921, the Workshop artistic and producing force was made up of a remarkable group of talented people: Henry Hunt Clark, Munroe Pevear, T. P. Robinson, James Seymour, Rollo Wayne, Donald Oenslager, Eleanor Eustis, and Stanley McCandless. At this time, Professor Arthur Pope and other members of the Harvard division of Fine Arts began to offer instruction in the theory and practice of stage design with the coöperation of the Workshop. The following year, this luxury of talent was combined in the designs of Wayne, Oenslager, McCandless, and Miss Eustis for a production of Gertrude Thurber's *Pastora,* lighted by Munroe Pevear. Now began to appear on Workshop programmes in regular association the names of Oenslager, McCandless, and Philip Barber — three whose ideas affected the construction of the Yale University Theater and the organization of the Yale Drama School.

Long since, Donald Oenslager recalls the character of the forces working in the Workshop through those vital years:

On fresh rebel signposts one read the directions of the theatre's future course — the revival of the masked actor, the übermarionette, the theatre theatrical, the fusion of the living elements of the theatre, constructivism, expressionism, neo-realism. These and a hundred more were catch phrases and labels of theories of sincere and genuine artists whose common aim was the liberation of the theatre from the manacles of realism. Whether their individual theories proved successful or not, is of no importance. As a group they succeeded in bringing about a selective and arbitrary illusion in stage setting by overstating or understating the appearance of nature's sequences. Not one manifesto or collective experiment was projected that did not stress and exhibit the importance of the function of light in the new theatre.

If the details of Workshop history thus lead away from the personality of G.P.B. and are not the legitimate concern of his biography, what is important is his conception of the organization which by 1920 was affecting him as much as he affected it. The simple experimental apparatus which it had first been for him is clearly set forth in his 1912 correspondence with Elizabeth McFadden. Undoubtedly it became many things for him in the twelve years of its existence, not the least of which was an arena for his own genius. However, the complex significance of the Workshop to G.P.B. during his last years at Harvard is to be seen in his *Century* article, "The 47 Workshop."

He begins with an attractive picture of historical Massachusetts Hall, at the official entrance of Harvard College, where the Workshop has its home. Entering a low double door, one finds himself in a rectangular room created by the removal of all interior walls and partitions. In this rough space, thirty feet by one hundred and fifty, as jumbled as an attic and as comfortable as a stable, the Workshop lives. After passing under a medieval archway and between property marble pillars, one confronts a welter of things: tree-trunks, staircases which lead nowhere, fireplaces, Russian pots, and New England teakettles. Stacked against the walls, surrounding all, is flat after flat of scenery.

At the lower end of the room, drops and gauzes rest on brackets. An ungainly wooden structure just in front of these drops, which looks like a medieval battering ram, is a staging of different levels for scene-painters. Not even the middle of the room offers wholly free space. The ceiling rafters, put into place long before the days of iron girders, require the support of two iron pillars. From these, broad white lines run slantwise to piles of scenery at the back of the room. On these lines wooden chairs have been so placed as to suggest a room with doors and windows. The space thus inclosed, twenty feet at the front by twelve feet deep, represents the stage in Agassiz House.

This suggestion of a stage, with its improbable limitations upon scenery and movement, is both challenge and catalyst; for from its impossible problems in stagecraft and the crib-like confinement it imposes upon actors comes the peculiar excellence these artists achieve. Immediately in front of this imaginary stage is a small dark table; in front of it, a gilded high-backed bench. From this bench and across this small table come G.P.B.'s directions to those rehearsing. Once properties of Sir Johnston Forbes-Robertson, this bench and table are souvenirs of his farewell performance of *Hamlet* at Sanders Theatre.

Here, at the center of this life of coöperative make-believe, G.P.B.'s image of the Workshop took its origin. Or perhaps the image grew from old memories of his toy theatre, and of children playing happily upon the stage his parents had made for him. Certainly the freedom which he had there enjoyed became a part of his idea of the Workshop:

At the earlier meetings there is no attempt to force any set of movements or any definite interpretation of character on the actors. The basal idea in all branches of the Workshop is to discover what special ability, if any, each person has, and to help him to develop it.

A first rehearsal with all the actors moving as they liked, exploring their freedom, obviously brought a deep and abiding pleasure to G.P.B. And when the main positions had been thus freely arrived at, he often suggested — as does a parent to his children — some element of added grace or beauty. After a successful passage by the actors, there usually came from him at his table the questions which encouraged and reassured: "Now do you feel easy, and is this what you wish to do?"

Enveloping this freedom, however, was the discipline which makes play successful and secure. For G.P.B. set for himself and the company a high ideal:

Discipline must lie back of all good rehearsing, but not the immediate, unquestioning obedience of militarism. The producer works mainly through persons, not groups or masses. To work, not in spite of, but with, the individual, there lies the difficulty, the everlasting problem, and the inspiration of producing. Moreover, putting on a play is not, properly, to find a field for the exhibition of the producer's fads, a very common fault among amateurs, and certainly not unknown among professionals. Students of producing must be made to understand that a play is not its scenery; its lighting; its theories of movement, gesture, voice-handling; its schemes of color: but recorded emotional states which will fail of their proper effect if they are not

217

made to produce in any audience the emotional response desired by the author. This they must do with whatever aid settings, lighting, or other accessories may give, but not as secondary to them or despite them. The producer's art is interpretation by all these aids not.of his own individuality read into the play, but of the author's purpose divined by close study of the piece and, better still, by sympathetic consultation.

Yet he never saw himself as a docile conductor of another man's music. The Workshop, he often said, was not the place to further personal idiosyncrasies or to foster fads, however clearly the intent of the author. Neither was it the place for systematizing theatre practices, for conserving and venerating what had always been done. With a sense of the fire and dash which lay always beneath the surface of his own direction, he said of the Workshop: "Its very breath of life should be rebellious experimentation."

So the Workshop was for G.P.B. a romantic thing, however much he gave the impression of mature detachment and pragmatic wisdom as he sat upon the gilded bench from which Hamlet had often soliloquized. "Rehearsals," he said, "the world over are pretty much alike, dull enough after a few minutes, unless the watcher is specially interested." His special interest as he watched a major Workshop production through its routine of rehearsing three or four hours every day for three weeks was not only in the romance of creation but in the exciting possibility of creating something which might yet be applauded by all America.

However, the immediate applause he sought was the intelligent criticism he would receive in writing from each of the two hundred who came on a Workshop opening night to the Agassiz Theatre. Out of some four hundred seats, only a few more than two hundred gave a complete view of the stage, which had been designed as a lecture platform. Narrower at the back than at the front and inflexibly limited by steel-girded walls, it could not have been less representative of real stage conditions. With no space off stage to accommodate scene-changing, all changes involved movement back and forth through halls and doorways between the stage and a nearby room. Yet G.P.B.'s enthusiasm and love of the theatre made an unfailing romance of every Workshop curtain time.

This moment had grown, in the course of a dozen years, to be a ritual. For G.P.B. it must have been one of the most vivid aspects of the Workshop:

It is eight o'clock. The director comes to a place just in front of the stage, and for a few minutes reports to the audience, as to a large committee, on the developments in the Workshop since the last production and on any matters of special interest concerning the play to be performed. As he retires, a few late-comers enter. Chimes sound, and the house is darkened.

Yet, as the seasons passed and the Workshop augmented its excellence, the limitations which had spurred imagination became galling irritations. Bitterness and frustration stained the image as G.P.B. contemplated the work he might do with adequate equipment. During his last years at Harvard, G.P.B. no longer stifled the rancor provoked by the iron-girded ceiling which hugged the top of the curtains, or by the unalterable doors, down stage, too close to the proscenium. Some of this he expressed in his *Century* article:

the director has frequently been blamed for his critical and uncomplimentary attitude toward a stage which seems to many who have not examined it to do whatever is needed. Is it not clear, however, that a stage which does not provide representative or even adequate lighting conditions, where all scenery must be specially designed, constructed, and painted for it, where all scene-shifting is far more complicated and time-consuming than it would be on the stages of high schools or club buildings, where stage positions cannot be freely handled, but become largely a question of avoiding the furniture, is not a just place on which to ask any one to train people either as playwrights or producers? How to meet the problems of production on a normally equipped stage should be the question, not the performance of acrobatic feats in adjustment not likely to be called for anywhere else in the country.

Unfortunately, no one had asked G.P.B. to do what he was trying to do for the Amercian theatre. Most of the work he now did was extracurricular. True enough, the Workshop was the logical extension of the purposes of English 47; but no official request had ever come for him to give such a course, much less project the course into a professional school of the theatre. So the bitterness grew and was shared in the Workshop, until G.P.B. must often have felt like a partisan leader fighting in the mountains of his homeland, without equipment and isolated from forces which he knows must triumph.

Tragically, then, the Workshop came to mean less of what it was as he thought increasingly of what it might be. The Workshop, created from nothing, was now overmastered by the image of the theatre which should, in its perfection of equipment, inevitably destroy the Workshop. Yet it was for the life of the Workshop that G.P.B. pleaded to his *Century* readers:

> Cramped, overcrowded, bursting with energy which all this youth, working coöperatively, insures, the Workshop pleads for an adequately equipped building of its own. Without this it cannot do properly the work which it is called on to do; without it there can be no development of instruction for which there is a steady, insistent demand from people so competent that their needs should be met — needs in play-producing, lighting, and stage design.

Here was his call, loud and clear, for a Harvard School of the Drama, albeit an appeal somewhat over the head of President Lowell. Almost desperately, now, G.P.B. hoped that his plea would win response from those who might see the Workshop on tour with Philip Barry's play. Surely the Plymouth Pageant, produced by Workshop alumni, would convince its national audience.

XLI   PLYMOUTH PAGEANT

THROUGH THE AUTUMN OF 1920, G.P.B. STRUGGLED TO complete his book for the pageant. During the early winter, in his Lowell Lectures on the Pilgrim leaders, he spoke with more than common sympathy of William Brewster: "That man must naturally have been in his youth singularly sweet natured and right minded. That was his charm . . . It is a man who all through his life can hold to an ideal at any cost." For in Brewster he had found the spirit he sought for his pageant and the dramatic sympathy he so desperately needed.

However, a great whirl of materials kept him altering and changing and transposing. A tangle of details grew like burrs between the lines and crowded the margins of his scenario. Toward the end of January 1921, already late with his pageant book, he wrote Perceval Reniers that he was bringing the text into approximately final shape. A few days later, he entered the following notation in his script: "Axe helves of different stages of completion — tools for working on them for 10 men." Until the final rehearsal, he was preoccupied with such minutiae of reality, and with countless changes.

Indeed, there were important changes during the five years that the pageant grew in his mind. Not only was there the radical shift from his original plan of a daytime pageant which he outlined in the spring of 1916 at Major Higginson's request; until the last of the pageant's dozen performances, no two were exactly alike. But the most profound change came when he saw that his outdoor pageant must be presented at night if its most dramatic effects were to be achieved. Only the curtain of darkness and the mobility of artificial lighting could provide the pace which the script required.

Instead of the ponderous movement and tedious delay hitherto unavoidable in outdoor pageantry, he sought a fluidity of motion and a continuity of effect which even the contemporary theatres had not yet attained. So G.P.B. moved from a conventional to a revolutionary conception of pageant production. What he envisioned was a pageant of light.

Whatever its precise history, this idea appears to have developed from his desire for a pageant which should be inherently dramatic rather than spectacular. Furthermore, his concern with lighting had been clearly a part of his interest in establishing the Workshop. Since William Butler Yeats's lecture on the subject, he had been keenly interested in the effects of artificial light in the theatre. And before his 1912 tour of the German theatres he had made the acquaintance of a young architect, Munroe R. Pevear, whose lighting effects for the Toy Theatre had marked him as a genius. From its beginning, the Workshop productions had depended upon Pevear's ingenuity and art.

The process of translating the pageant script into reality probably began one day early in the spring of 1921 when G.P.B. and Munroe Peavear stood at the crest of Cole's Hill in Plymouth and looked out over the raw earth and yellow sand which were being leveled to make a stage between the foot of the hill and the water's edge. They looked across the harbor to Clark's Island, where the Pilgrims spent their first night ashore, and to the Gurnet, where centuries earlier Thorvald the Norseman had slain and been slain. To their right, as their eyes fell once more upon the caravan of dump carts, they saw the Town Brook. Nearby Leyden Street, along which had fronted the first Pilgrim dwellings, would soon be an aisle to the now forming stage.

Almost as sharp and clear as in an amphitheatre, the voices of the workmen and the ring of horseshoes on gravel came to the crest where G.P.B. stood. This character of the spot he had known at the beginning of his writing, and because of it had written more speeches into his pageant than was usually possible. Even the great rock off there to his left would have a voice. As a unifying device, the "Voice of the Rock" showed the persistence of the Pilgrim spirit throughout American history. Music and poetry also provided transitions and continuity; but the central problem, G.P.B. knew, was not to be solved by auditory means. As the pageant script now stood, only speed could bind together its many and diverse elements. Speed depended upon proper lighting; on effective lighting hung success.

What was obviously required was a tower atop Cole's Hill to mount spotlights and other paraphernalia, much as one mounted such things on the balcony of any theatre. But the execution of lighting arrangements, Pevear's job, was not so simple. In the first place, at the distance of one hundred and fifty feet through which light from any tower on the hill would be projected to the front of the stage, no existing theatrical equipment could properly illuminate the area. The stage, four hundred and fifty feet broad and four hundred deep, would swallow up all the illumination whole batteries of ordinary theatre spotlights could generate. Special projectors would have to be devised to throw a beam narrow enough and bright enough to produce the qualities of definition and color which G.P.B. desired for his nightly audience of ten thousand.

Nevertheless, the thing was done. Long before the bleacher seats were in place, two rectangular towers began to rise forty-five feet above the top of Cole's Hill. Like up-ended chocolate boxes, towers "A" and "B" soon carried ingenious fifteen-hundred-watt lights of Pevear's invention. Each of these projected an arc of light no greater than seven degrees. This meant a proper spot of light, no broader than twenty feet, at the front of the stage. It meant that from the towers a hundred pencil beams could converge upon any area of the stage to cut a ship's cabin, or a room, or a city street from the darkness. It meant an instantaneous curtain, and zero time for scene shifting. It meant color.

Pevear's "Pilgrim Projectors" thus ensured the brilliance and style of Rollo Peters' costumes and enlivened the rapid succession of scenes. They made possible new effects of light and the motions and masses of the dance, of light and the sounds of music, even of light alone. Soon G.P.B.'s scenario received another jotting: "The Pestilence, wholly music and lighting — 1 minute." For this Pevear prepared a color filter of pestilential green and Henry Gilbert wrote the greenness into music. Thus the seventh scene of the first episode of *The Pilgrim Spirit* came to read: "As the lights close on the Hunt tableau, there is darkness for 15 seconds. Then for 45 seconds the lights come on slowly, to reveal, where there have been activity and plenty in the preceding scenes, an absolutely empty scene."

This flood of sickness, filling the air and oozing its deathly green upon the dead waste of the sandy stage, simple and evocative in its symbolism, became one of the most effective things in the pageant. Thus a broad sweep of symbolism became G.P.B.'s distinguishing effect.

But before the pageant could be realized, there were difficulties not of the script or of the techniques of production. There were the simple human problems which arise when the extravagance of art impinges upon the native frugality and inertia of a New England town. There was something unusual about the dictatorship of the communiqués from the "Master of the Pageant" to the cast. Directions for the storage of costumes in specially provided bags, rules for behavior in the "rest tents," and G.P.B.'s thoughtful request for "coffee, a piece of cheese, an apple, and two sandwiches" for each person at rehearsals pleased some and irritated others. All were not used to G.P.B.'s sense of values, the speed with which he created and cut away, the absolute devotion he demanded. And then there were wind, tide, rain squalls that blew from the Cape.

Rain, indeed, was almost the pageant's undoing. The scheduled opening night, July 13, was more than unlucky; for a veritable cloudburst washed out some of the stage and postponed the opening for a week. On the evening of July 20, as G.P.B. looked out his observation window in tower "A," checking by telephone with Chalmers Clifton at the orchestra and chorus, with the entrance dispatchers who marshaled the cast for its cues, he could see the rain coming again. This time, there was not enough as dusk fell to claim the rain insurance, but more than enough to dampen all ardor. Thus it was a genuine triumph for G.P.B. when, having signaled that the show was to go on, he saw his players take their positions like troupers and the audience settle cheerfully upon newspapers to watch the show.

As lightning played in the sky, there was a fanfare of trumpets which passed to a hymn-like chord. Then, while the symphony played softly, from the canopied rock came a voice, loud and clear. This was G.P.B.'s prologue and his theme:

I, the rock of Plymouth, speak to you, Americans.

Here I rested in the ooze
From the ages primordial.
Men came and went: Norsemen,
Seamen of England, voyagers of France, Dutch adventurers;
Over and round me
The Indians worked, played, lived.
I was a rock of millions along the shore,
Waiting, — for what?
Came pestilence, sweeping the Indians from the land.
Not one remaining here at Patuxet, Accomack,
Cap St. Louis, New England, as the Indian, the French,
Prince Charles of England called this spot.
Around me the cleared fields waiting,

The bay swarming with fish,
The woods full of game, all waiting.
I, too, waiting, for what?
In England, growing, the spirit of man,
Freed by his Bible, read in his home,
Studied with passion.
Out of the Church of England — a Puritan.
Out of the Puritan, Separatists — of London,
Of Scrooby, of Sturton, of England,
Seeking freedom of thought, of living by truth.
Out of the Separatists, driven from England,
The Pilgrim.
England, stern mother, refuses him.
Holland, the foster mother, he leaves, still searching his freedom,
Sails westward, and comes to me, —
By chance, by choice, who knows?
To me the Pilgrims come, on me they stand,
As one by one they land.
Here they will work out their salvation.
For this I have been waiting, waiting.
Of me, the rock in the ooze, they have made a cornerstone of the
  Republic.

Since the action moved slowly on the soggy stage, G.P.B. began
to cut. Swiftly and with an expertness that left the audience unaware, he cut his account of the predecessors of the Pilgrims and
concluded his first episode with the pestilence scene. The next
two episodes were compressed to emphasize Hermann Hagedorn's
words and Edgar Stillman Kelley's music for "The Harrying
Chorus" without impairing his account of the growth of the Pilgrim conscience and the exodus to Holland. Edwin Arlington
Robinson's words and Leo Sowerby's music for "The Pilgrim's
Chorus" got similar emphasis, as did Josephine Preston Peabody's
"The Song of the Pilgrim Women" and Hagedorn's lyrics for
MacDowell's "1620." After quick commands over his ten tele-
phones in tower "A," G.P.B. cut the scene of the Pilgrim land-
ing at Plymouth to a single finger of light which reached out into
the bay to touch the Mayflower at anchor as the orchestra played
Chalmers Clifton's "Voyage to the New World."

So the two hours' traffic of his puddled stage brought as great
a testimony to G.P.B.'s leadership as he would ever have. While
the Pilgrims entered for the last time, convoying a corps of young

women who bore the flags of the forty-eight states, a concealed choir sang Robert Frost's "The Return of the Pilgrims." Down the center, toward the *Mayflower,* caught now and then by beams of light, the flags went. At the choir's final strains, the lights came full upon the *Mayflower,* and the stage and all the arbor blazed as searchlights swept the sky. Then the darkness dropped until only the *Mayflower* rode in the light. Solemnly, came the last words of the pageant, the voice from the rock: "With malice toward none and charity for all it is for us to resolve that this nation under God shall have a new birth of Freedom." Slowly the light faded on the *Mayflower* and there was a long pause before the applause came.

Reactions were mixed, and judgments upon the many parts of the pageant were various. Of course, local critics were generous; and some who came from a distance apparently expected more than they received. Yet all who thought about what they had seen agreed (however much G.P.B.'s reach had exceeded his grasp) that here had been a vision of great beauty and moments of magnificence.

Olin Downes, writing of the opening night for the *Boston Post,* found the high points in the pageant's music. The editors of *Theatre Magazine* pronounced the lighting arrangements "a new departure in pageantry." A reviewer for the *New Republic* went even further and said that Pevear's lighting had "extended the potential boundaries of the pageant, of the entire open-air drama and even, by implication, of the indoor theatre." The *Nation's* reviewer — finding the structure of the pageant "skilful and intelligent," the verse interludes "cold," and the dialogue "jejune" — thought that what had remained of the pageant's "unquestionable beauty of significant color and motion" was the "visibly symbolical."

When President Harding saw a later performance he spoke for all those who caught the dramatic impact of the pageant. "What impressed me most of all," he said to the reporters, "apart from the sheer beauty of the spectacle and the artistry with which it was presented, was the fine manner in which the spiritual significance of the tercentenary was brought out." There were others, perhaps, from whom G.P.B. might have preferred the accolade; but the President spoke well for his countrymen.

In the middle of August, but a few weeks before the playwrights of English 47 would again assemble in Massachusetts Hall, the great tower lights dimmed upon the *Mayflower* for the last time. As G.P.B. gathered his belongings from his control center, he prepared to leave an enterprise whose expenditures and income would amount to half a million dollars. For lighting alone he had spent ten thousand, and the mere rental of the *Mayflower* exceeded his Workshop budget for two years. Regardless of the limited success of some of his pageant ideas — such as his dependence upon the actual words of the Pilgrim fathers for dialogue — his efforts and those of his team had brought good will, mutual satisfaction, and a general public acclaim seldom accorded college professors outside the realm of politics.

At the close of the last performance, there were loud and continuing calls for the pageant's author. The townspeople of Plymouth, Duxbury, and Marshfield who had made the pageant possible gathered in the bleachers to honor G.P.B. and his team — Virginia Tanner, James Seymour, Chalmers Clifton, Stanislao Gallo, George Dunham, Mr. and Mrs. Michael Carr, Munroe Pevear, and Rollo Peters. Those of the cast remained in costume, for G.P.B. had directed that they keep their pageant dress as memento of their partnership. Through the cheering crowd came two who brought a silver loving cup, inscribed with affection and admiration for the "Master of the Pageant."

After a little while, G.P.B. came down from his tower and made his way through the throng to the center of the great stage. Crews were already hammering to dismantle the bleachers as the searchlights centered upon him. Inaudible to many were G.P.B.'s words of grateful acceptance, nor could they see the tired eyes through the reflections from his pince-nez. For a brief moment he stood upon his stage, a weary man in a rumpled suit, waving and smiling. Then, as if he had never really been among them, he was gone.

THE EXPERIENCE OF THOMAS WOLFE WITH PROFESSOR
Baker during three years of association with him in English 47
and the Workshop is, of course, individual and peculiar to the
genius that was Wolfe's. But there is a certain representativeness
about Wolfe's history in these days. For one thing, like many of
G.P.B.'s students in English 47, Wolfe came seeking fame and
found failure. His story suggests that perhaps G.P.B.'s greatest
work was not with the successful playwrights, but with those who
came to be playwrights and went away to be something else. Undoubtedly some of G.P.B.'s most effective teaching was achieved
with such "cures" of the itch to write plays as he administered
to John Mason Brown, Heywood Broun, and Thomas Wolfe.

Furthermore, G.P.B.'s enthusiastic belief in the obvious talent
of Wolfe until the Workshop laboratory and the crucible of experience proved that this gift was not for the stage was also typical
of the encouragement he gave to all who might be the writers of
the coming American drama. In the care, the inspiration, and
simple friendship which Wolfe received both as an artist and a
human being, there is also something representative of what was
available to all at the round table. Fortunately for G.P.B.'s own
history, Wolfe has recorded his failure as a playwright as well as
an aspect of G.P.B.'s character which is difficult to project — his
sense of humor.

On the second of October 1920, Thomas Wolfe wrote a letter
to his mother in which he told of his first meeting with G.P.B.
and his admission to English 47.*

George Pierce Baker is the great dramatic teacher up here. Koch is
a former student of his. When I tried to register up for his English 47
known all over the country as "The 47 Workshop" I was told I could
not by any means get in since the course is restricted to 12 people and
mature writers all over the country submit plays a year ahead of time
(one of his requirements) to get in. I went around and saw Mr. Baker

* This and the subsequent excerpts from letters of Thomas Wolfe to his mother,
reprinted from *Thomas Wolfe's Letters to His Mother*, copyright, 1943, by Charles
Scribner's Sons and used by permission of the publisher.

who just got home from England where he went to gather material for the pageant he is writing for the coming Pilgrim Tercentenary. He thawed out immediately when I told him I was under Koch at Chapel Hill for two years and he commented enthusiastically on the work Koch was doing saying he was one of his "pets." He asked me if Koch had produced any of my plays and I told him two. He then asked their names and altho he had not read them he was familiar with their titles, as he has kept up with their work. So he's letting me into the sacred circle of the "47 Workshop" and even suggested that we might put on a couple of Chapel Hill plays, one of mine included, "To show these people here what you're doing down there."

Then Wolfe phrased the motive and inspiration which warmed every young heart that sought to be one of the chosen twelve:

Nearly every year a play is taken by Baker from his class and put on Broadway, some of the most famous successes of recent years have been written here. "Stop Thief," "The Nigger," and many others. Of course I do not hope for any success like this in competition with seasoned and mature writers, but he told me, "When you come into my course it is with the intention of eventually being a playwright. If you have the ability I'll make one out of you." It is a great prospect for me, but I know I must work.

Toward the end of January 1921, Wolfe wrote to tell of

a trial performance of my one-act play which was put on tonight at the "47 Workshop" before a private audience of Workshop people. It is a strong play, I am told. And it will be produced I understand in the Agas Theatre at Radcliffe in March and from there it may be taken with two or three other one acts to Cleveland, Buffalo, and New York.

This was a revision of a play, *The Mountains,* which he had begun under Koch. It is interesting that upon the basis of this play, which was a wretched failure before the regular Workshop audience the following October, G.P.B. immediately chose Wolfe as one of his promising writers. It is perhaps for G.P.B.'s early enthusiasm, upon which Wolfe built too many castles in the air, that Wolfe was critical of his teacher as much as for the ultimate honesty with which G.P.B. judged him temperamentally unsuited for work in the dramatic form when he told the young man, "Your gift is not selection, but profusion."

It may be that G.P.B. erred egregiously in giving such a temperament as Wolfe's so much of what Wolfe later referred to as "Alas the *generous* enthusiasm of Baker." Certainly if G.P.B. erred anywhere in his teaching it was probably on the side of his generous spirit. But what is one man's poison may be another's drink, and there are apparently others beside O'Neill who would have thirsted mightily without such generous enthusiasm.

Be that as it may, G.P.B. had his own relationship to the success of his students. For the Workshop had now achieved such a complexity of existence that the annual discovery of a fresh talent in playwriting was almost a prerequisite to further good work. G.P.B. was perfectly honest about this and knew that he could not expect an annual discovery; yet he had his own hopes, as had his students, and he was perhaps as humanly swayed by his as they were by theirs. The simple fact in this matter when Wolfe came along was that Raisbeck and Barry were not developing into the playwrights G.P.B. had anticipated.

His hopes for Barry had hung on the winning of the Oliver Morosco prize for 1920–21. On the twenty-third of February, G.P.B. sent his protégé the following from Lower Massachusetts Hall:

After exasperating delays, the Morosco Competition was settled Monday night. As it will be published to-morrow, I may say to you that T. P. Robinson wins the prize with his comedy of character, The Copy. From the comments of the judges on your play, I think the best thing for it is to give it an immediate production here. The general feeling seemed to be that it is clever but on accustomed lines. Believing that it is better than that, I want to put it on at once and give some of these people who have been interested, but don't quite see its real quality, a chance to judge it rightly.
. . . The play will go on two weeks from Friday and Saturday, with the best people I have in it, and they are very good this year. If it works out as well as I hope, we should probably take it as the long play on the proposed trip of the Workshop in the week of April 18th to 24th. I want to try out two plays, yours included, between this time and April.

So G.P.B. watched Wolfe carefully at the same time that he tested Barry. Wolfe was already at work making a long play out of *The Mountains* when G.P.B. sent Barry's *A Punch for Judy* on the road for the first Workshop tour. With it went three one-acts: Kenneth Raisbeck's *Torches*, Louise Bray's *Mis' Mercy*, and Norman Lindau's *Cooks and Cardinals*. For this journey through Worcester, New York, Utica, Buffalo, and Cleveland, the stage manager was Rollo Wayne, the business manager, Edward Goodnow, and the electrician, Howard C. Forbes, who was assisted by Stanley McCandless. The acting company included John Mason Brown, Dorothy Sands, Jim Seymour, Harding Scholle, and Doris Halman.

When the company returned to Cambridge, G.P.B. wrote Barry on the twenty-eighth of April 1922:

I do not know how much Kenneth may have written you about the trip . . . I am enclosing a copy of H. T. Parker's criticism on Tuesday night's performance. You can see that we came off on the whole with flying colors.

Push the play all you can and let managers see it in the condition in which we acted it, for even thus it is quite as good as plays which have been successes on Broadway. You can improve it, but that improving can be done when the contract is in sight or signed. We have proved that this is a play that really delights an audience, and a mixed audience. The stage hands in New York followed it with closest attention. So have the young and the old, and the cultivated as well as the uncultivated, so our faith is justified.

I do not see much chance for a rest at present, but I hope to get up to my farm at the end of another week. At any time that you feel like coming on, you know where there is a room for you.

A fortnight later, Wolfe wrote his mother: "I am continuing with the Eng. 47 (the playwriting course on which I am putting most of my time) and with Eng. 14 a course in the Elizabethan drama." In these, Wolfe reported, his grades had been a B plus and an A minus respectively, which the secretary of the graduate school told him was extraordinary. For, although G.P.B. had reputedly given the recently defeated Democratic candidate for the vice-presidency, Franklin Roosevelt, his only B at Harvard, G.P.B. was known as a hard marker. Thus when G.P.B. read the prologue to the expanded version of *The Mountains* and pronounced it the best ever written at Harvard, Wolfe was convinced that his destiny was clear.

As Wolfe's second year with Professor Baker passed, Barry's

star had yet to rise. In the spring of 1922, Barry sent G.P.B. a play about a father who, trying to guide his son's artistic talents, reveals his own thwarted ambitions. Thinking that too much attention had been given to the comedy of callow youth, G.P.B. urged Barry to make more of the father's character. To this Barry replied that nobody was interested in people over thirty and thereby provoked a chuckle which had its revenge when G.P.B. made Barry postpone his marriage until the play was successfully revised.

Before this had been done, G.P.B. wrote to his former student, Theresa Helburn, Executive Director of the Theatre Guild:

> Lower Massachusetts Hall
> Cambridge, Mass.
> March 26, 1922
>
> Dear Miss Helburn: —
> I am asking Mr. Philip Barry to send you his last play, *The Jilts,* an American comedy which seems to me of unusual quality. I have no question in my mind that if Barry can get a public hearing or two, he will be on his feet as a dramatist. I should very much like to have the Theatre Guild start him.
> Will you do me the favor of giving the play as speedy a reading and decision as possible?
> My congratulations on your production of *He Who Gets Slapped.* I have not yet seen *Back to Methuselah.* It is one of the pleasures I have ahead of me, I hope.
>
> Sincerely yours,
> Geo. P. Baker

A month later, the Theatre Guild had rejected Barry's play. Now all the tensions and wearing cares which G.P.B. had escaped through the speed of his nervous drive began to gather weight as he slowed his pace once more. Troubled in his mind by his inability to fulfill his editorial commitments, G.P.B. wrote to Will Howe, April 20, 1922:

> I have been having a tempestuous time of it, for I have been trying to decide whether or not to accept an offer to leave Harvard which would give me everything I have not here and also I have not been as well as usual. These are the reasons I have stalled in my work for you. Now I have decided, bad as the conditions are here, to stay on and fight a bit longer.

What the offer was, where he might go — these things are not clear now. It might have been to Northwestern, to Carnegie, to Columbia, to Yale — such rumors were already moving among those who knew G.P.B.'s situation. However, it was not only to some other university that he might then have moved; for there were people in the theatre who were interested in cultivating the talents then to be seen in the university. Such a one was Henry W. Savage, Harvard '80, whose theatre holdings were extensive and whose ideas were progressive. In October 1922 he inquired of G.P.B. for someone to do a New York production along the lines of what the Workshop was doing. This may very well have been a veiled invitation to G.P.B. himself. If so, it was not the first of this nature, and G.P.B.'s reply to Savage interpreted the request as relevant to his students. On the thirtieth of October, G.P.B. wrote:

There are several persons who are entirely competent, so far as knowledge of the subject is concerned, to put on plays with the newer methods. Sam Hume's work, you, of course, know. Irving Pichel, who has recently been working with him, you also probably know about. I have heard that he is just now free and might be glad to find an opening in New York. Another very good person is Alexander Dean, who, until this autumn has been in charge of College Dramatics in the University of Montana, Missoula, Montana, but he has just gone to the Dallas Experimental Theatre, and could not, I suppose, break free before next summer. A man deeply interested in all this newer producing is Prof. S. A. Eliot at Smith College.

. . . When next I am in New York or when next you are in Boston, perhaps you will let me talk to you about your interest in the newer producing . . . I wish I could suggest a longer list of available men, but I simply cannot supply the increasing demand of good people for College Dramatics, Experimental Theatres and similar openings.

There were other possible links between the university and the professional theatre for which G.P.B. would have been an excellent connection. A few days after his letter to Savage, G.P.B. received the following from Franklin Sargent, written on the ninth of November:

Augustus Thomas, who is now, you know, the head of the Managers Association and in a position of real authority, has several plans.

One of them has been to interest the managers in relation to the Community and Little Theatres through the country. One of the problems has been to have these Theatres undertake the right sort of play in the right sort of way . . .

While Mr. Thomas is working at that end, he and I have conferred considerably, and I am now trying to work at the other end, from the educational side to see what can be done to interest Universities in the dramatic side of education . . . Thomas thinks that there can be a real relation established between the University educational work, at first more on the University Extension plan, and these Community and Little Theatre organizations. I don't know.

Certainly, as Mr. Eaton has stated in his article in the last number of Scribner's on "The Real Revolt in the Theatre," the new movement originated with you in your Work Shop, so you are responsible now, and liable to be responsible a great deal more in the future, for a possibly great Renaissance movement theatrically.

With no inkling of this state of affairs in G.P.B.'s own career, Tom Wolfe spent Thanksgiving at the Baker home. In the evening, G.P.B. took him to see *The Beggar's Opera,* after which they went backstage and met the company of rosy faced English girls. Not long afterward, Tom received a typewriter from Miss Monroe, G.P.B.'s secretary, to hasten along the play which the Workshop awaited.

However, Tom Wolfe was but one of the young people in whose welfare G.P.B. interested himself. At this time the leading lady of the Workshop company, Dorothy Sands, wished to become a professional actress, yet felt uncertain of her readiness for such a career. In the interest of preparing her for her professional debut, G.P.B. wrote to Franklin Sargent, February 27, 1923:

I want to find some American actress, preferably I should think retired, who might be willing to give a very able young woman, who has been acting with me, advice and instruction. I think this person really beyond class work, but I should like to have her watched, guided, and trained, particularly this summer, by someone who knows what the best traditions of the stage are, and how faults of technique might be corrected. If Ellen Terry were living in this country, she would be the ideal person. What I should like, would be someone who has played both Shakespeare and modern plays: someone who understands both the romantic and the modern manners. Is there any such? Genevieve Ward did just this sort of thing in England, but who is there at all like her on this side of the Atlantic?

A month later, Wolfe wrote his mother concerning his play, *Welcome to Our City:*

It's the most ambitious thing — in size, at any rate — the Workshop has ever attempted: there are ten scenes, over thirty people, and seven changes of setting.

Mama: get down and pray for me. Prof Baker is having Richard Herndon, the New York producer, up here to see the play when it goes on.

Herndon, the current sponsor of the Harvard Prize, was indeed looking for more of the success he now had at his Belmont Theatre. For weeks he had seen Philip Barry's *The Jilts,* renamed *You and I,* grow to the stature of a Broadway hit. The possibilities for Wolfe were exciting:

Herndon told Baker in New York last week that the [Barry] play ought to run through hot weather: that is to September or later. This means over 30 weeks for Philip Barry . . . and his royalties are at present about $700 a week. The contract reads that the movie rights are split equally between producer and author: they average around $15,000 — so young Barry — he is three or four years older than I am — stands to make a tidy little fortune.

In May, as the Workshop brought Wolfe's play along toward its opening night, G.P.B. told the author that it had "a much better chance of success than 'The Adding Machine,' " which was then closing after a three-month run in New York. But G.P.B. was perfectly clear in his basic criticism that *Welcome to Our City* needed serious pruning if it were to achieve such a success as Elmer Rice's play. Nevertheless, according to his usual procedure, G.P.B. left the details of such excision to be worked out by the playwright in the light of the experience of the Workshop.

Fully confident that Wolfe, "pig-headed" as he was, would make the necessary revisions, G.P.B. took the promise of this new play to Theresa Helburn. Wolfe wrote his mother: "Prof Baker is in New York to-day. He is going to see the Theatre Guild in my behalf. He is a wonderful friend and he believes in me. I know this now: I am inevitable. I sincerely believe the only thing that can stop me now is insanity, disease, or death." Tragically, it was none of these that stopped the giant from Catawba. It was

235

his own inability to select from his play the elements of success that were there.

Barry had already demonstrated his willingness and ability to revise his work to meet the practical requirements of successful production. As *You and I* played to standing room only, Wolfe steadfastly refused to do what the audience criticism at the Workshop indicated he must do. There was no question of what G.P.B. called "truckling to one's audience," of sacrificing the integrity of the play for a cheap and easy success. The fact, which G.P.B. had not readily understood, was that Wolfe was incapable of the technical discipline which the drama demanded. Thus the failures which taught Barry, only enraged Wolfe, and in his bitterness he blamed not himself but his teacher and the whole premise of training upon which G.P.B. had built the Workshop.

It is this bitterness, directed at G.P.B. and Kenneth Raisbeck and others who truly befriended him, which brewed the bite of satire in his picture of the Workshop and its people in *Of Time and the River*. For the point of his caricature of Professor James Graves Hatcher and of the "artists" who with Francis Starwick, Hatcher's assistant, make up the "celebrated course for dramatists" is that the course could not make Wolfe a dramatist. In view of the unmistakable identity of the persons satirized, and the simple debts of friendship which he owed those persons, to say nothing of their genuine belief in him, the sentence with which Wolfe concludes the twelfth chapter of his book and passes judgment upon G.P.B.'s work betrays the essential immaturity of a little boy who grew too big too fast.

Nevertheless, any biographer of George Pierce Baker must acknowledge a peculiar debt to Thomas Wolfe. For in the first view which he presents of James Graves Hatcher, Wolfe not only provides an accurate picture of G.P.B. in the 1920's, with touches which the photographs of this time only faintly suggest, but Wolfe asserts the essential humor which all intimates of G.P.B. recall even if they are incapable of reproducing any of its manifestations. Like his father, Dr. Baker, whose humor was famous with a few, and who could prescribe for palpitation of the heart the application of another palpitating heart, G.P.B. had a ready wit for the members of his family who were disposed to be responsive, for a few friends, and for the charmed circle at his round table. A daughter-in-law recalls his "delicious wit," a devoted member of the Workshop thinks warmly of his "grand sense of humor," but the evidence escapes them like a butterfly on a summer's day. There seem to be no humorous anecdotes, no personalia, no idiosyncrasies to prove that G.P.B. was a humorous man. Far too many knew only the serious dignity of his lecture platform manner; far too few ever heard him chuckle. It is this chuckle and the man behind the chuckle that Wolfe has nobly preserved.*

His appearance was imposing: a well-set-up figure of a man of fifty-five, somewhat above the middle height, strongly built and verging toward stockiness, with an air of vital driving energy that was always filled with authority and a sense of sure purpose, and that never degenerated into the cheap exuberance of the professional hustler. His voice, like his manner, was quiet, distinguished, and controlled, but always touched with suggestions of great latent power, with reserves of passion, eloquence, and resonant sonority.

His head was really splendid: he had a strong but kindly-looking face touched keenly, quietly by humor; his eyes, beneath his glasses, were also keen, observant, sharply humorous, his mouth was wide and humorous but somewhat too tight, thin and spinsterly for a man's, his nose was large and strong, his forehead shapely and able-looking, and he had neat wings of hair cut short and sparse and lying flat against the skull.

He wore eye-glasses of the pince-nez variety, and they dangled in a fashionable manner from a black silk cord: it was better than going to a show to see him put them on, his manner was so urbane, casual and distinguished when he did so. His humor, although suave, was also quick and rich and gave an engaging warmth and humanity to a personality that sometimes needed them. Even in his display of humor, however, he never lost his urbane distinguished manner — for example, when some one told him that one of his women students had referred to another woman in the course, an immensely tall angular creature who dressed in rusty brown right up to the ears, as "the queen of the angleworms," Professor Hatcher shook all over with sudden laughter, removed his glasses with a distinguished movement, and then in a rich but controlled voice, remarked:

"Ah, she has a very pretty wit. A very pretty wit, indeed!"

* This and the following description of the "Hatcherian chuckle," reprinted from Thomas Wolfe, *Of Time and the River*, copyright, 1935, by Charles Scribner's Sons and used by permission of the publisher.

To Wolfe, mountain of flesh that he was and mighty laugher when he laughed, G.P.B. was "one of those rare people who really 'chuckle' " and whose eyes "really 'twinkle.' " The physical translation in G.P.B. of the spirit of wit and humor into the fleshly attributes of a chuckle impressed Wolfe:

The Hatcherian chuckle was just exactly what the word connotes: a movement of spontaneous mirth that shook his stocky shoulders and strong well-set torso with a sudden hearty tremor. And although he could utter rich and sonorous throat-sounds indicative of hearty mirth while this chuckling process was going on, an even more characteristic form was completely soundless, the tight lips firmly compressed, the edges turned up with the convulsive inclination to strong laughter, the fine distinguished head thrown back, while all the rest of him, throat, shoulders, torso, belly, arms — the whole man — shook in the silent tremors of the chuckle.

The bitterly sarcastic pages in which Wolfe displayed what appears as an ambivalent response to Professor Baker's friendship and assistance were published but a few weeks after Baker's death. This circumstance, of course, made it impossible for those who admired and loved G.P.B. to discern the genuine warmth and affection which mingled with Wolfe's wrath. For them the bitterness was all. Yet had they seen the more than half a million words of manuscript which Maxwell Perkins pruned to make *Of Time and the River,* they would perhaps have gained a warmer and more generous picture.

One who read an early form of the "Professor Hatcher" material at Wolfe's request believes that the editing of the manuscript heightened the satiric materials at the expense of an initial warmth of affection. In support of this view, one thinks of Wolfe's fondness for the *Dialogues of Plato* and of the words of Alcibiades in the *Symposium* (Jowett's translation): "And now, my boys, I shall praise Socrates in a figure which will appear to him to be a caricature, and yet I shall speak not to make fun of him, but only for the truth's sake." It is to be remembered that the title page of *Of Time and the River* carries a quotation from the *Crito.*

And if those who were thus offended could have read some of Wolfe's letters to G.P.B. after both men had weathered the storms of mutual disappointment at Wolfe's failure to gain a welcome on Broadway, they might have sensed what is missing from the novel. For, although G.P.B. no longer expected greatness from his student as a playwright, he never doubted the magnitude of his talent for other forms of writing. Thus it is doubtful that the figure of "Professor Hatcher" was ever intended to gainsay the tribute which Wolfe sent to G.P.B. from the *Lancastria* as he embarked for Paris and the desperate venture of writing which finally brought success: "I think you know how I really feel toward you. You are just about the best friend I ever had."

XLIII   "YALE: 47; HARVARD: 0"

DURING THE AUTUMN MONTHS OF 1921, G.P.B. COM-pleted a third volume of *Plays of the Workshop* and assembled another collection of contemporary American plays for his friend Will Howe. This work went slowly, however, for he was troubled by the malaise which he had felt the year before in London. Moreover, he was annoyed and increasingly disturbed that his genuine successes with the pageant and with the Workshop tour had not brought any official favor to his hopes for a Harvard theatre. As his fifty-sixth birthday approached, he knew with gnawing certainly that such favor would have to come soon. The apparent impasse must be broken.

Since 1914, when Harvard had first published a pamphlet for the guidance of those who wished to study the history and technique of the drama, G.P.B. had proceeded in good faith to develop what appeared to be a new and legitimate field of university instruction. With each succeeding annual pamphlet, a part of the *Official Register,* G.P.B. had developed an integration of all of the Harvard curriculum which would contribute to the development of trained leadership in the American theatre. This little catalogue had been at least instrumental in bringing such people as Thomas Wolfe and Philip Barry to Harvard for graduate work. In 1916 he had begun to give summer school courses in play production and stage management — matters which, though never a part of the regular Harvard curriculum, had at least *quasi* recognition through their advertisement in the annual bulletin on courses in the drama.

So the pattern of hope and frustration wove through the years, separating G.P.B. from the regular objectives of the curriculum and setting his personal fortunes upon a bias almost incompatible with academic routine. In a lecture which he delivered at Sanders Theatre in March 1922, he told the assembled Radcliffe and Harvard alumni:

What we need, and need very badly, is a teaching of the Fine Arts in our colleges and universities with a view to creation; a far closer correlation of the different departments of the Fine Arts, so that a worker in any one of them shall not feel himself isolated and independent, but shall understand and depend on the sister arts. Above all, there should be competent instruction for people who wish to prepare themselves to become masters in the several arts of the theatre — its lighting, its scenery, its producing, and its plays.

He concluded with a plea that was almost painful: "For such a center we are ready at Harvard, could we only have the funds necessary for a proper equipment by which to develop what has gone as far as it can under cramped and unreal conditions."

Now the sponsorship of the Harvard Prize Play passed from Oliver Morosco to Richard Herndon, manager of the Belmont and Klaw theatres. Herndon — who regarded G.P.B. as a director in every way superior to Stanislavsky, Danchenko, or any of the foreign masters — suggested that G.P.B. direct a Prize Play production for him. However, this flattering opportunity presented an unorthodox extension of academic propriety that might have confused the whole educational process. His ambition blocked repeatedly, the line of cleavage now began to grow along which spread G.P.B.'s split with Harvard.

At the beginning of the 1923–24 season, G.P.B. made the last of his financial reports to the Workshop. In a printed brochure which included a subscription blank, he appealed for those annual pledges which alone supported the productions in Agassiz House. With more than an edge to his remarks on the niggling economy he had been forced to pursue, his summary for the preceding year began:

A year ago, The 47 Workshop sent its audience a statement as to its exact financial condition. It asked for $4,500, stating that between $3,000 and $3,500 was necessary for even very economical production of plays during the year, and that $1,000 was needed for office expenses. The total subscriptions from the audience amounted to a little over $3,200. It proved that the estimate for last year was almost exactly right: the productions cost approximately $3,000, ranging from $250 to $770 a performance; the office expenses were $786, and general expenses were $350 — making a total expenditure of $4,136. Consequently it became necessary, keeping the office expenses below what they should have been, to make up the difference between $3,200 and $4,200 by public performances. By dint of painful economy, The 47 Workshop at the end of the year had a balance of $60.

Reviewing the five productions which this money had made possible, he told them that three had been accepted by New York managers. Then he asked for the sum which would provide for what proved to be the Workshop's last year: "May not The 47 Workshop this year, in order to carry on this work, feel free from financial anxiety? That is what $4,500 will mean."

During his work on the Plymouth pageant, in as sharp a change of course as his abandonment of the teaching of argumentation had once marked, G.P.B. had permanently relinquished English 14 to John Tucker Murray. No longer was he the scholar of the history of dramatic literature who had edited texts and interpreted the theatre's past. Indeed, there was something of nostalgia in his gift to one of his graduating seniors of a copy of *The Development of Shakespeare as a Dramatist*. When John Mason Brown asked him to autograph the flyleaf, G.P.B. mused not without some wistfulness, "My goodness, did I write that? Did I really write that? It has all escaped me now."

Thus G.P.B. withdrew from the academic company whose highest calling was the preparation of candidates for the doctor's degree. Although he did not have the degree himself, G.P.B. always had entertained great respect for the training given such of his own doctoral candidates as Ernest Bernbaum and Stuart Pratt Sherman. Now, however, his heart and his intelligence were devoted to the living American theatre. When Professor Glenn N. Merry, of the State University of Iowa, inquired about the granting of the Ph.D. in such work as Tom Wolfe had pursued in English 47 for the M.A., G.P.B.'s reply clearly defined his relationship to the academic community. He wrote, November 10, 1922:

241

I don't believe that the authorities would allow the taking of a Doctor's degree in connection with my work in the technique of the drama. On the other hand, the work in the history course in the drama has long been counted to that degree. For myself, I do not quite see how the technical work has any relation to that high degree for research. I regard my courses, 47, 47-A and the 47 Workshop as schools for professional dramatists, professional scenic designers and professional and amateur producers. I do not think that any of that work should be counted toward a Ph.D. degree.

Nevertheless, he could not escape the impulses which made him a teacher. In January 1923, while he and Philip Barry readied *You and I* for its Broadway opening, G.P.B. was asked to speak at a Vassar memorial service for another teacher of playwriting. As so many college and university teachers were now doing, Gertrude Buck, of the 1915 Radcliffe class in English 47, had introduced a frank imitation of The 47 Workshop to Vassar, "The Vassar Workshop." Now, before her own work had made more than a brilliant beginning, she was dead. G.P.B.'s eulogy for her reflects his own sense of dedication:

As I look back over the thirty or thirty-five years in which I have been working in the theatre or on its edges, I am encouraged. There is enough that is discouraging, but I am encouraged because, in the first place, in the changed conditions that I can observe today, it is the universities and colleges that have done the work. We may allow a little for a certain betterment, a certain change of view and attitude which have come to us because we as a people have been more and more in contact with continental people, but I think that it is an almost negligible influence. It is just because, all over the country, increasingly since 1890, courses have been given which have treated the drama as one of the great fine arts, as something not necessarily a great cultural force, but something which has been a great cultural force, and may be today if properly respected.

It was precisely as a manipulator of this cultural force that G.P.B. viewed his relationship with the professional theatre. To the inhabitants of the Yard, he might seem some secret envoy from the footlights; but to the denizens of Broadway he was obviously a professor incognito.

For G.P.B., the day was now past when important work was to be done in the colleges merely by teaching the drama of literature, or by teaching playwriting, or even by the experimental production of plays. The professional qualities which he had attained with the Workshop productions pointed to something beyond the unfinished studio pieces which had once been his primary consideration. What he now saw as his task was the finished production of dramatic works. "Europe," he said, addressing the 1922 Recreation Conference at Atlantic City, "considers the drama as a fine art which consists not only in writing plays, but in producing them."

Something of this purpose is to be seen in his work with Barry's *You and I*. Not only did this very successful play receive the full Workshop treatment, but many details of the Broadway production were executed and tested in Cambridge. Some of the settings were designed by members of The 47 Workshop, and the Broadway product had as much of G.P.B.'s touch as any man can give a play of which he is not the producer. Further, he made Barry's play the first of a projected series, *Long Plays of the 47 Workshop*. For this volume G.P.B. wrote the following introduction which he addressed to the author:

It is not because thousands of people have been amused by *You and I* that I take pride in it. Rather it is because here you have written not a comedy of situation bordering on farce, but really a comedy of character. It is pleasant to go from your play with a renewed sense of the wholesome, fine-spirited people, who yet are keenly amusing, to be found all around us. Delicately, tenderly, and with no sentimentality, you suggest the affection and understanding of father, mother, and son. Most of all, I like *You and I* for the light, sure touch with which you reveal Matey's tragedy, the conflict of his business success with his artistic longings. When he first reveals his desires, there came from the audience in which I sat at the Belmont Theatre an odd, low murmur of male voices, — understanding, sympathetic, self-incriminating. That is the best testimony to the truth and artistry of your play you could desire. Humorously, yet gently, you have revealed to your generation one of the little tragedies of us, your elders . . .

A year after its opening, the play was still running; but G.P.B. was no nearer his theatre at Harvard. Now, although he preserved his urbane manner in the Yard, there was a distinct bitterness about his relationship with President Lowell. Walking past the president's office with Stanley McCandless one day, G.P.B. blurted angrily, "I get no support. I'm always ready to be thrown out of Massachusetts Hall." Among the intimates of the Workshop, there were sometimes outbursts of angry frustration. For not only was G.P.B. denied the theatre which he believed many stood ready to secure for him, but he was checked in the opportunities which Herndon repeatedly offered.

Some kind of crisis arrived in the fall of 1923, when Richard Herndon invited G.P.B. to direct Louis Wolheim and Ann Morris in Roscoe Brink's *Catskill Dutch*. Prior to its New York opening, the Workshop gave the play a production which Herndon and Jacques Copeau, the great French director, came up to Cambridge to observe. From the rise of the curtain Copeau had been thrilled by what he saw on the cramped stage at Agassiz House and had joined Herndon in urging G.P.B. to direct the New York production. Understandable as G.P.B.'s excitement was, the official position at University Hall was equally understandable: one could not be a member of the Harvard faculty and a director of Broadway plays at the same time. The Tercentenary Pageant at Plymouth had been quite another matter.

When G.P.B. took this answer to Herndon, he felt that his ambition was being curbed at all points and so expressed himself bitterly to his friend. Though he had no settled prospect elsewhere, he confided that he had at last decided to leave Harvard. It was then that Herndon suggested the formation of an independent producing organization to give G.P.B. the opportunities he desired. Herndon's idea was that the Workshop should come to Broadway — the Belmont Theatre should be its home.

That the Workshop could not be transplanted no one knew better than G.P.B., yet it was entirely feasible that certain key personnel might be included in a professional association similar to Miss Horniman's Gaiety Theatre company. Before long there was gold embossed stationery emblazoned with "The Cercle Plays and Players" which also declared that Professor George Pierce Baker was chairman of the group's advisory board, of which Walter Prichard Eaton, Louis Anspacher, James D. Barton, Augustin Duncan, and B. Iden Payne were members. Subsequent events postponed the plan, and it ever remained a dream of G.P.B.'s secret heart. Had his health permitted, following his retirement at Yale, he might thus have achieved his great ambition to direct in the professional theatre; but "The Cercle Plays and Players" were never more than the gilding of a hope.

Some reassurance from this scheme must have steadied G.P.B. during his remaining months at Harvard; for, in the spring of 1924, a fire in Massachusetts Hall brought a decision from President Lowell's office which changed the history of the Workshop. The nature of this change became public when G.P.B. sent to his faithful followers the last such announcement he was to make at Harvard:

To the Members of The 47 Workshop Audience:

I send you this message because, this coming College year, I shall not stand by the piano and talk to you of plans for The 47 Workshop and the doings of its members. Since we completed ten years of our work together, — some of us writing and producing, you stimulating and shaping by your attendance and comments, — I have felt the need of rest and a gathering of new impetus. However, until now I have not seen the time when I believed that I could rightly allow the activities of The 47 Workshop to cease for a year. Last Spring, a fire in the attic of Massachusetts Hall seriously burned the roof — admittedly for this The 47 Workshop was in no way responsible. The Harvard Corporation, however, decided that, instead of making temporary repairs, they would carry out a long-considered plan to restore Massachusetts Hall to its original use as a dormitory. At the moment, there is no space available in which The 47 Workshop can be carried on under feasible conditions. This seems, consequently, the right moment at which to take my desired sabbatical year.

All important memorabilia, — pictures, stage models, and so forth, have been temporarily placed in the Theatre Collection at the Widener Library. The records are in the hands of last year's secretary, Miss Elizabeth W. Munroe . . .

With pleasant anticipation of renewed work together, I am,

Gratefully yours,
George P. Baker
Director of The 47 Workshop

September 22, 1924

Meanwhile, discussions between G.P.B. and Edward Harkness concerning the establishment of a school of drama at New Haven had been in progress. Early in the year, Samuel H. Fisher, an associate of Mr. Harkness, had heard through Philip Barry of G.P.B.'s dissatisfaction at Harvard and had traveled with Harkness to Cambridge for conversations with G.P.B. Plans for establishing work in the drama as a department of the Yale School of Fine Arts had been under consideration since the inauguration in 1922 of Everett V. Meeks as dean of that school. Mr. Harkness, a principal benefactor of the Harvard Business School and of President Lowell's house plan, had agreed to finance a drama school at Yale if Dean Meeks could get an outstanding man to head the school.

After it had been established that Harvard anticipated no such employment of G.P.B. and that it would be proper to invite him to join the Yale faculty, Dean Meeks went to Boston. The first matter upon which he sought G.P.B.'s opinion was the cost of building and endowing a Workshop theatre and a school of theatre art. To this request G.P.B. suggested a million dollars — three hundred and fifty thousand for a theatre and school combined, the rest for its endowment. This he had calculated as often as one ever computed the cost of a dream.

Then Dean Meeks put a question, "If we get such a gift, would you come to Yale and take charge?"

At this G.P.B. laughed. Recovering his poise, he remarked that his visitor went pretty directly to the point. Then he said, "Naturally, I cannot give you an answer at the moment." There was a pause. Then, with a finesse and restraint that distilled years of frustration into a gracious gesture, he concluded, "But I will take it under consideration."

This decision occupied G.P.B. during the summer and fall of 1924 — from California, where teaching in the University Summer School he helped organize The Berkeley Playshop, to New York City, where he and Christina took for a while the apartment of an academic friend also on sabbatical leave. The difficulty lay not only in the fact that, but a few years from retirement at Harvard, he would have to make a completely fresh start at New Haven. Of course, he had friends there. But more difficult than such a change was the terrible challenge of a youthful dream come true.

In mid-November, G.P.B. had reached his decision. Since it was one which affected the hopes of others, he sent some communication to all whom he knew would care. To Edward Goodnow, one of the oldest of the Workshop friends G.P.B. would leave behind, went a brief note:

> 77 Park Avenue
> New York
> Nov. 24

Dear Edward, —
    Watch the Wednesday papers for an important announcement affecting yours truly. It's been mighty hard to make the decision, but when I explain it to you, I think you will see its rightness. Meantime, if anything brings you to N. Y. the latch string is out here, or whereever we be.

> Affectionately,
> G.P.B.

On Wednesday, November 26, the official announcement came from the office of President Lowell. G.P.B. had resigned. With the announcement, the press received copies of the president's letter to G.P.B.:

> Nov. 25, 1924

Dear Mr. Baker —
    The Corporation had no alternative but to accept your resignation with regret — a regret that will be felt by everyone connected with the University. We owe you a large debt of gratitude for all you have done for the University during your long service. In your early period you did more than anyone else has done for debating, and in the later years you have been the great teacher of dramatic writing in the United States. But the gift to Yale of one million dollars supplies an endowment which does not exist elsewhere. Sorry as I am to have you leave I must congratulate you on this endowment, and Yale upon securing you for the position.

> Very sincerely yours,
> A. Lawrence Lowell

At the same time, Yale announced that the endowment by Edward S. Harkness would provide for a department of drama and a theatre, both of which were to be directed by Professor George Pierce Baker. Amid the ensuing furor, which soon became a *cause célèbre,* Heywood Broun neatly summarized it all as "Yale: 47; Harvard: o."

G.P.B.'s own declarations upon the event were straightforward and quite characteristic. To the press he said:

247

There has been a disposition to indicate that my relations at Harvard were unpleasant. This is utterly untrue. They were of the most pleasant and congenial sort. However, the University authorities could not see their way clear to extend the work. Yale offered the opportunity and I accepted it.

He told Perceval Renier quite simply: "I could not go on any longer without a theatre."

XLIV CONTINUITY IN THE YALE
UNIVERSITY THEATER

TO A SURPRISING VARIETY OF PEOPLE THE GIFT OF Edward S. Harkness meant the end of something at Harvard and the beginning of something else at Yale. As George M. Cohan put it, a million dollars is a lot of change. Even Fred Koch seemed to think so as he congratulated G.P.B. on having "a million dollars for just the kind of Theatre Building you want and plenty of money for assistance in building up a real School of Drama." Many intimately acquainted with the event saw a complete break.

Perhaps this was most keenly expressed at the farewell which the Workshop gave G.P.B. as he was about to leave for Europe. For all who had gathered in Agassiz House for what the souvenir programme called "The Last Act," Gluyas Williams' Pierrots bid a sad "God Speed!" Amid many good wishes, including eleven hundred dollars for technical books G.P.B. might see in his travels, there was a fear that the magic of the Workshop was now at an end. This is evident in Doris Halman's programme verses for the occasion:

> There was a Hindu Dervish,
> A mighty magic man:
> Of nought he made more wonders
> Than other people can.
> Upon the desert drift he blew,
> And lo! a rose-tree sprang, and grew.
>
> The Dervish got a garden
> With water, seeds, and shears;

248

> And there his reddest rose-trees
> Were planted down the years.
> But, O, the magic's at the first, —
> When once he made a tree from Thirst!

Yet the old gentleman who symbolized Harvard University saw the inevitable continuity in G.P.B.'s work, and the eminent desirability of completing that work at Harvard. Charles W. Eliot wrote, November 26, 1924, to G.P.B.:

Your action is perfectly natural considering President Lowell's habitual indifference to you and your work; but I hope you will not commit yourself to spending the rest of your working life at Yale, no matter what she may do for your Department either now or during the next four years. It is quite sure that Harvard graduates in large number will protest against the treatment you have received and will gradually put up money enough to bring you back to Harvard. If you keep yourself free, you will be able to leave Yale for Harvard as soon as your Department is in full working order there.

The symbol of this continuity is the theatre which Mr. Harkness built at Yale. But for deference to Mr. Harkness in the matter of exterior decoration, and except for the exigencies of local ordinances and of technical problems beyond G.P.B.'s knowledge, this building is nothing less than the material expression of G.P.B.'s experience in the theatre. He could not have had a more personal and satisfactory monument.

There are various points in G.P.B.'s life where the monument takes form. His first thought of building a theatre may have come as early as his acting days at Brattle Hall; but his first public statements about a theatre appeared in 1902, when he returned from abroad with ideas for an endowed theatre in Boston. At this time he seems not to have been affected by the contemporary renaissance in European theatre design, for his plans for a Boston repertory group imply a conventional house for it not unlike the Castle Square Theatre.

By the beginning of 1910, perhaps because of Winthrop Ames, G.P.B. was ready to translate his own experience and need into a university theatre. The abortive endowment proposals of H. B. Harris at this time were the immediate stimulus for G.P.B. to consult Professor Langford Warren of the Harvard School of Architecture. Warren's modification of the Prinz-Regenten Theater in Munich was the result.

Around this stage and auditorium Warren grouped carpenter shop, paint shop, electrician's shop, sewing room, library, classrooms, and storage space for all the aids to imagination in the theatre. To the imitation of Littmann's seating plan, G.P.B. queried: "Is so steep and expensive a rise necessary?" Under the pressure of economy, Warren had preserved most of the German auditorium but had reduced the size of the stage.

Significantly, G.P.B.'s marginal comments upon Warren's drawings concentrate on areas behind the curtain. "What height is the stage part?" he asks. "I suspect it is much too low." To this he adds "Stage at least 70 ft. high." Upon Warren's thirty-foot square proscenium opening, he comments, "Wider and lower." Apparently, G.P.B. thought first of the space for his stage.

In subsequent Workshop years, there were at least two other plans for a Harvard Theatre in which the Yale edifice took form. Both were prepared by the firm of Blackall, Clapp and Whittemore, perhaps the leading American theatre architects of the time. The first of C. H. Blackall's designs, drawn in 1914 and prepared for an unspecified site, was an obvious attempt to realize the ideas G.P.B. had picked up in Germany in 1912 — some undoubtedly from the great Max Littmann himself. Blackall's plan shows a one-third reduction in the size of Warren's auditorium and a striking expansion of the area behind the curtain to provide for sliding and revolving stages. Moreover, at the same time that the seating capacity was reduced to 743, a balcony was added. Except for these shifts, the provision of ample scene storage area immediately behind the stage, and a large rehearsal room in the basement, Blackall's plan is clearly related to Warren's and repeats much of the previous distribution of work areas.

The second of Blackall's designs, which G.P.B. labeled "plans for making over Dane Hall," expresses G.P.B.'s thinking contemporary with his *Century* article on the Workshop. Because of the triangular shape of the Dane Hall site, the effective space available to stage and auditorium is comparable with that of the conventional American theatre. The result was a compact stage and auditorium in which the balcony and most of the preceding arrangements were followed, except that shop and storage areas now shifted to one side of the stage in order to fill the base of the triangle. The important development here is the abandonment of extravagant foreign ideas and a practical conformity to American theatre conditions.

In the course of a dozen years, G.P.B. learned much from Warren, more from Blackall, and had talked with the designers of the principal European theatres. His marginal notations upon the plans prepared for him show his growing certainty that the university theatre must reflect living tradition at the same time it provides a stage with maximum flexibility for the playwright's imagination. Accompanying this was his conviction that the auditorium must concentrate attention not upon the audience but upon the play. For to G.P.B., both in the auditorium and behind the curtain, the play was the thing.

Tangents of his thinking show in his remarks upon Blackall's second plan. G.P.B. asks for a "Model room for Director off stage" and a large rehearsal room above the auditorium, which had preempted most of the limited basement excavation. Requesting a machine shop and electrician's shop on the stage level, he also wished electric outlets provided in the footlight trough. Some of these ideas revert to his toy theatre; some are the reflection of Gordon Craig ideas seen at the Abbey Theatre and on Max Reinhardt's stages. Others derive from his Workshop association with two architects, both geniuses in stage lighting — Munroe Pevear and Stanley McCandless.

As a consequence of this history, G.P.B. had a clear picture in mind when he told Dean Meeks, President Angell, and Mr. Harkness the cost of a Workshop theatre. And when he accepted the invitation of these gentlemen to head the Yale Drama Department, it was mutually agreed that a theatre architect should execute the plans and that the exterior should be subject to the architects for the new Yale campus. It was also recognized that to harmonize the structure with the Gothic motifs already employed in other Harkness buildings was a procedure that waited upon

G.P.B.'s theatre objectives. Upon G.P.B.'s recommendation, the firm of Blackall, Clapp and Whittemore was thus engaged to design the Yale University Theater.

In organizing the Yale Department of Drama, G.P.B. also relied upon procedures and personalities already developed in connection with the 47 Workshop. Aside from his own courses, he could draw upon the work in the theory and practice of stage design, organized by Professor Arthur Pope at G.P.B.'s request in 1921 for the new theatre and drama school which G.P.B. hoped to see where Dane Hall stood. By 1924, this instruction in design was ready for further development under Pope's assistant, Donald Oenslager. Furthermore, the informal talks by theatre personalities to the Baker's Dozen, such as Clyde Fitch gave, had now developed into lectures on special problems which the Workshop heard from authorities like Lee Simonson. In an irregular fashion, there had already functioned at Harvard what G.P.B. during the winter of 1924 expanded into a curriculum for the new department at Yale.

This well-publicized project of a university theatre also brought ideas from friends and former students. From Chicago, where he was building the Goodman Memorial Theatre, Thomas Wood Stevens wrote: "I know something of what your preliminary work will have to be, after going through the job of equipping the theatre at Carnegie." From the New York office of the Theatre Guild, Maurice Wertheim sent G.P.B. a letter of introduction to the architects of their new theatre and suggested he observe operations as a member of the Theatre Guild Building Committee. Brander Matthews, Franklin Sargent, Fred Koch, E. C. Mabie, Hallie Flanagan, Alexander Dean — all knew aspects of the problems involved in organizing a university theatre school.

Before leaving for Europe, G.P.B. published some of his ideas in an article for the February 1925 issue of *Theatre Arts Magazine*. In "The Theatre and the University," G.P.B. described his general objectives:

Standards — informative, steadying standards — are what our young workers in the theatre need. They face audiences which, in spite of a growing understanding of the theatre are still preponderantly made up of people who blindly follow their emotional responses along the lines of least resistance. This means liking what is tritely theatrical rather than humanly right, liking what is easiest to feel, and consequently to understand. It is easier as an auditor to respond to signals, symbols, for mirth or pity than it is, through sympathetic understanding of a character or of the author's point of view, to feel amusement or pain to which most people are ordinarily insensitive. The dramatist must study the public early and late, not to truckle to its desire for signals and symbols but in order to learn how he may induce it to feel what he wants it to feel and feeling understand. For all this a theatre is necessary.

This body of standards, G.P.B. believed, would grow from the work of the university theatres about to burgeon across the land.

Such a theatre must be both conservative and flexible. Most of its students will later, in one way or another, live and work in the regular theatre world. Therefore it is important that they be trained under theatre conditions not more exacting than those ordinarily found in the commercial theatre. At the same time, they must not be trained so steadily with special devices for settings, lightings, etc., that they will find themselves at a loss when they become partners in productions touring the country. Here lies the danger in the training given by some experimental theatres. Students should be taught so that they can give the best production possible under the physical conditions of the stage on which they may work. On the other hand, the theatre in which they work should be sufficiently flexible to permit all kinds of experimentation.

On February 4, G.P.B. received from C. H. Blackall the first of five drafts of plans for the Yale University Theater. Drawn for a York Street plot which G.P.B. considered ideal, an area 125 feet wide and 175 feet long, these preliminary sketches apparently led him to hope that the theatre would be completed in a year. For at this time, with characteristic enthusiasm, he wrote in the new Yale catalogue, "It is expected that the theater and school building for the Department of Drama will be ready for use at the beginning of the second term, in February, 1926."

Not only did Blackall present a stage and auditorium basically unchanged from what he had designed for the triangular site at Harvard, his disposition of shops and function rooms was simply a shift from one side of the stage tower to various levels behind it. This produced a scene dock, paint frame, and carpenter shop directly behind the stage wall; subsequent revisions of this arrangement — suggested by Granville-Barker, Sir Johnston Forbes-Roberston, and Winthrop Ames — nearly doubled the stage depth by greatly enlarging the doors in this wall. Later changes also established the height of the stage at a few feet more than the seventy which G.P.B. had requested of Langford Warren in 1911.

The rehearsal room, above the auditorium in Cambridge, was pushed by New Haven regulations into the basement, where it had been in Blackall's first plan. Here it became a small experimental theatre with a cafeteria and second rehearsal room nearby. On the main stage above, small doors beyond the curtain on either side of the proscenium made possible the simulation of Greek and Elizabethan theatres. Other refinements not provided in the Dane Hall plans, many in stage lighting, now appeared. However, the simple fact of continuity from Cambridge to New Haven was everywhere apparent.

In the spring, while the Bakers journeyed leisurely from Vienna to Paris, the preliminary announcement of the organization of the Department of Drama appeared as a supplement to the Yale catalogue. Though the personnel was not named, four instructors were listed to assist in the work which fell outside G.P.B.'s immediate concern as Professor of the History and the Technique of the Drama; for he was also the Director of the University Theater, and Chairman of the Department of Drama. That is, there would be someone responsible for stage lighting in the University Theater productions and for teaching the history and theory of those practices in the classroom. In the same manner, someone would be in charge of scenic design, another would handle costume design and manufacture, and someone else who acted as stage manager and assistant director would assist G.P.B in teaching the techniques of production.

This staff was to assist in the teaching of twelve courses offered for the first semester of 1925–26. Five of these ("Forms of the Drama," "Playwriting," "Producing," "Advanced Producing," and "The Technique of the Drama") repeated courses G.P.B. had taught at Harvard. Only three courses in stage lighting had no parallel in the Harvard catalogue; the remainder in costume and scene design were essentially extensions of Professor Pope's Fine Arts 28. Here the continuity was evident in verbal repetitions from one university catalogue to another, but the Yale bulletin contained one small though important change. In token of the professional standards and traditions which G.P.B. wished to foster within an academic environment, G.P.B. now chose to be designated not by his official title but simply as "Mr. Baker."

By September, G.P.B. and Christina were back in New Haven. On the twenty-fourth, excavation for the new building began. On October 2, in the pages of the *Yale Alumni Weekly,* G.P.B. announced his staff for the coming year: assistant in directing, Hubert Osborne (MacDowell Fellow, 1917–18); instructor in costume, Evelyn Cohen; instructor in lighting, Stanley R. McCandless; and instructor in scenic design, Donald Oenslager. Only Miss Cohen, who had been with Osborne for some years in the Department of Drama at Carnegie Institute, had not been in the 47 Workshop.

This announcement followed a meeting between G.P.B. and Edgar Montillion Woolley, later famous for his portrayal of the irascible Sheridan Whiteside in *The Man Who Came to Dinner* but then the popular coach of the Yale Dramatic Association. Considered by many sons of Eli to be the rightful occupant of G.P.B.'s new chair, for he had since 1916 identified himself with the Yale hope for a theatre, Woolley was obviously not a candidate for any subordinate position. Thus when, in a tactical maneuver, G.P.B. offered Woolley an instructorship on his staff, the lines were drawn for a hostility which must at times have made opposition at Harvard seem mild.

To the Yale alumni G.P.B. explained the various purposes which would be united in the new building as those of "a repertory theater, plus the needs of a school, plus a clubhouse for the Yale Dramatic Association." Until the completion of the building, a solution to the problems raised by Mr. Woolley could remain in abeyance. Meanwhile, G.P.B. wrote in his account of "The New University Theater," the new department would have to proceed independently of the Yale Dramat:

While the theater is building, the Department of the Drama will have its temporary quarters at 52 Hillhouse Avenue. This commodious house has therefore been so adapted as to provide rooms for necessary carpentry, painting and storage, offices, two lecture rooms, dressing rooms for actors and actresses, and a small stage for trying out plays, and for the general use of students in stage technique. Though the producing conditions must be badly cramped till the theater building is ready, even this small stage can be made to provide at least elementary instruction in lighting, stage design, and play producing.

So the Hindu Dervish once more began to make a tree from Thirst. To do this, he had excellent materials among the fifty men and twenty-five women who enrolled as students. Among these was a loyal corps of former 47 Workshop people: Boyd Smith (successor to Allardyce Nicoll, of the University of London, as Chairman of the Yale Drama Department), Philip and Ruth Barber, Leslie Hotson, and Maurine Watkins (whose *Chicago*, a Broadway hit in 1926, was written in the first class of Drama 47). Among those students of the first year who were soon personalities in the American theatre, motion pictures, and radio G.P.B. could call upon Maurice Gnesin, Herbert Biberman, Lemist Esler, Raymond Knight, Harry Burnett, Raymond Crossett, Owen Davis, Jr., Rupel Jones, Sara Pryor, George Haight, and John S. Young.

These people had an immediate opportunity to show their talents, for G.P.B. scheduled the first Drama Department production scarcely a month after the beginning of classes. With two short plays from the last Radcliffe class in English 47, Helen Gaskill's *Celeste* and Hallie Flanagan's *Incense*, the Yale Drama Department made its bow to New Haven. Under conditions that made their success a brilliant accomplishment, G.P.B., Osborne, Miss Cohen, "Mac," "Don," and the students established the excellence of the new department. Shortly thereafter, by a most happy coincidence, G.P.B. was elected to the American Academy of Arts and Letters.

While the steam shovels gave way to concrete mixers on York Street, the people at Hillhouse Avenue settled into their developing routine. For their second production and only long play of the year, the staff chose *The Patriarch*, which Boyd Smith had brought from English 47 to Drama 47 for further development. While the students completed their projects for the new play, G.P.B. worked swiftly to shape the old coöperative habits of the 47 Workshop into the successful operations of classroom competition. Hurrying about the old mansion, often late into the night, he hummed softly what was sometimes audible as the first words of the old hymn, "Bless this House."

In December, Mme. Maria Ouspenskaya visited G.P.B.'s stage on Hillhouse Avenue with a group of her pupils from the American Laboratory Theatre. They came to give a demonstration of the methods of acting and direction, made famous by the Moscow Art Theatre, which she and Richard Boleslavsky had but recently brought to America. At this time, G.P.B. announced:

It is important that students of the drama meet and hear the leaders of the various movements in the theatre to supplement their work. We have recently been fortunate in hearing Mrs. Charlotte Chorpenning, a former member of the Forty-seven Workshop at Harvard, and the author of "The Sheepman," which was recently produced in Stamford, New Haven and Hartford. We have also had Channing Pollock, and next week Winthrop Ames will talk to the department on "Play Producing."

Within the week, G.P.B. took his students to New York for an evening at the Republic Theatre, where *Abie's Irish Rose* was in its second year of a phenomenal popularity. Thus G.P.B. fostered a catholic view of the theatre in his new school.

February 1926 came and the massive stage tower of the new building rose brick by brick as students assembled the scenery for Boyd Smith's play on the tiny Hillhouse stage. In March, McCandless and his students provided striking effects for two more one-acts from English 47: Frederick Day's adaptation of *The Fall of the House of Usher* and Raymond Knight's *When Shall We Three Meet Again?* In April and May came the first fruits of Drama 47: three one-acts — Howard L. Phillips' *The Way Things Happen,* Maude Humphrey's *Immersion,* and Harry McGuire's *Yella.*

So the year went successfully, though New Haven did not develop quite the intense personal devotion to G.P.B. and his work that had been remarkable in Cambridge. Perhaps this was because the Yale Workshop was financially secure; no longer compelled to appeal to the purse of his audience, G.P.B. may have missed touching its heart. Most of this new audience came to be amused rather than to support a cause, and many were not sure of their relation to what they saw. Nevertheless, there were new loyalties; and certainly no one in Cambridge was ever more faithful than President Angell, whose critique of each performance was always the first upon G.P.B.'s desk the following morning.

As the year drew into May, it appeared that the University Theater would be ready for its dedication sometime late in the fall semester. Unfortunately, nothing written in Drama 11 or Drama 47 was quite suitable for the occasion, unless Boyd Smith should bring his long play into shape. Of course, there were good plays from these classes, but considerations of subject matter, such as the controversial character of Maurine Watkins' play about a red-headed Chicago murderess, or problems of production ruled them out.

So G.P.B. scheduled Edward Massey's *Plots and Playwrights* for the first production of the second year. Originally produced by the Workshop in 1915, and included in G.P.B.'s 1920 collection of *Modern American Plays,* it was really too old — almost dated. Yet it might have to do. In this predicament, G.P.B. thought of Eugene O'Neill, whom he had proposed for an honorary degree at the June commencement in New Haven. At a time in their lives when each needed the other's assurance, O'Neill's honorary degree now meant very much to G.P.B.

On the fifth of May, G.P.B. wrote to his old student:

let nothing stand in the way of being here to receive the degree. When it is given to you next June it means to me, not only the honor to you but the establishment of this fact: hereafter a man writing on the subject of his choice as his mind urges him to write, will still meet with misunderstanding and doubt but there will be the precedent established that institutions of learning in this country should recognize him if his honesty of purpose results in genuinely significant accomplishment.

Tentatively, he suggested that O'Neill might like one of his plays to open the Yale University Theater.

To this O'Neill replied on the twenty-first:

My feeling about this award is only deep gratification. Coming from Yale, I appreciate that this is a *true* honor (in a century so bepestered with false and shoddy varieties!) and that this recognition of my work really should have a genuine significance for all those who are trying, as I am, to do original, imaginative work for the theatre. In addition I feel that, although Yale may have had the matter under consideration before you came there, still it should now, in all justice, be part of their interest to honor you through one of your students, and I would be as ungrateful for the fine encouragement and helpful criticisms received during my year in 47 as some of the malicious darned fools who write articles make me out to be, if this aspect of the honor did not also please me exceedingly.

His nomination for the opening was his new and unproduced play, *Lazarus Laughed.*

The staff had not really considered the matter, for each was busy with his share of furnishing the new quarters, yet it seemed assured that *Lazarus Laughed* would inaugurate G.P.B.'s Gothic theatre. Resting at Boulder Farm for a holiday, G.P.B. sent a note to the newest addition to his faculty which shows the chain of command and the mutual responsibilities in the completion of the theatre. The note went to Philip Barber, technical director:

N. H., July 3, '26

Dear Phil, —
          I have approved your white plan for the Carpentry Shop if the architects agree that you are not losing too much light by shutting off the two window partitions.

But what about desks or shelves or something to work on in the office? Should not these be included? If so, get into communication at once with Mac, as to this, for he is to report on as many of these plans as possible on Wednesday the 7th at 2 P.M. He is, as you probably know, now at 52 Hillhouse.

Hastily,
G. P. Baker

The controlling idea of all this planning is summarized in a report which "Mac" wrote for the *American Architect:*

The inevitable compromise between the fixed structural features which we specify today, and what we shall want tomorrow, can only be justified by the broad application of the principle of flexibility. Unencumbered space of ample proportions into which temporary structural features can be built, and portable equipment that can easily be replaced by later developments, are the elements of flexibility that are required in the theatre today. A university theatre is essentially a laboratory which is built to last for some time, and as

259

such, it must be built for the future much more than the professional theatre, where experimentation and perpetuity are, of necessity, somewhat limited.

Later, the difficulties of producing *Lazarus* became clear to G.P.B. and he turned his attention to Boyd Smith's play, now carefully revised. When it was evident that *The Patriarch* would make the most satisfactory production for the dedication of the new building, G.P.B. wrote O'Neill of the departmental decision that a play by a student of Drama 47 was perhaps more appropriate than one by a student of English 47.

As the opening night approached, G.P.B. found that his new cyclorama was not ready. Soon he had dispatched calls to the Theatre Guild, Morris Gest, David Belasco, and Winthrop Ames. Just a week before the opening, Ames telegraphed that he could find nothing large enough, that cycloramas so big as G.P.B. required were not used commercially. It was Belasco who came to the rescue, but on the day the original contractor met his deadline. So what might have been another interesting act of assistance from Broadway was declined with heartiest thanks.

Since mid-November, G.P.B. had sent letters of invitation to all his old friends in the theatre. To H. T. Parker went the following on November 23:

The invitations for the series of opening performances here in the University Theatre will go out this week, and of course, you will receive one for Friday, December 10th, the first of the series. I hope I may see you here personally and show you the building.

In printing anything in the *Transcript* about the forth-coming performances, I shall be greatly obliged if you will stress the idea that Saturday night's performance, December 11th, is particularly for the past and present audiences of the Workshop. I have done my best to reach with an invitation all persons who were members of the Workshop audience in Cambridge the last year of its existence there, 1924. It is quite possible, however, that with all the resulting confusion of papers from moving, I may have overlooked someone. I should be glad, therefore, if there could be some phrasing which would show that I have endeavored to reach all the individuals in that audience.

On the same day he wrote to Professor Vilem Mathesius, at the University of Prague:

I wonder if you, as a representative of your University and the students of your English seminar who have been so deeply interested in Eugene O'Neill, might care to send a word of greeting to us on this opening of the first University Theatre in the history of Universities.

And he was careful to advise the editors of *Billboard, Variety, Theatre, Theatre Arts* and other interested publications, as he did Arthur Hornblower on the twenty-ninth:

If you send some one of your staff to one of the opening performances of the University Theatre, will you kindly see that it is not reported in the amateur section? As we shall be producing in a Theatre and on a stage which provides professional conditions, we should like to be judged at least as semi-professionals. When we are trying to establish professional standards among our students, it may be distinctly harmful to the work if, when one of our productions is noticed, it is treated in the amateur section.

So the tenth of December 1926 arrived. With it came heartfelt good wishes from Lady Gregory, heartiest congratulations from Sir Johnston Forbes-Robertson, and a simple wish from an old 47 Workshop friend: "I hope that you yourself, just walking through it, sitting at rehearsals, writing in your office, touching with incredulous fingers the walls of the new stage, will know an amazing happiness and peace of mind."

From Paris, Granville-Barker cabled on the ninth: "Good luck. Thanks largely to you American Drama now takes rightful place among arts."

From London came a warm letter:

115A Harley Street
7th December, 1926

My dear Mr. Baker,
       I rejoice to know that by the time this reaches you the University Theatre at Yale will have opened its doors. My best wishes go out to the fortunate students. It would be difficult to conceive more favourable conditions than those under which they will henceforth pursue their work, and I predict that the result will be permanently ennobling to the American stage.

With cordial greetings to yourself, I am
Always yours most truly,
Arthur Pinero

Perhaps David Belasco's telegram spoke for New York, and Broadway, and every place in all America where there were those who loved the theatre. Regretful that his production of E. H. Sothern's new play made it impossible to attend the opening, Belasco telegraphed on the tenth:

Congratulations on the realization of your long cherished dream. It is a symbol of great progress in the American Theatre towards which you have labored so assiduously and with so much success. My profound appreciation for your splendid achievement and my heartfelt good wishes for a glorious future.

From Bermuda, Eugene O'Neill had already sent his regrets:

First, let me say that although it was a bit of a disappointment about "Lazarus," I sincerely admired the stand your faculty took regarding your theatre standing on its own efforts, especially on its opening bill. It is most emphatically what it ought to do. And I certainly hope the grand opening night will prove the big success you deserve, and I'm very sorry I can't be there to see it.

It was a gala evening. Afterward, G.P.B. spoke briefly from the stage, looking out into the faces of Winthrop Ames, Edward Knoblock, Chalmers Clifton, Richard Aldrich, Sidney Howard, Philip Barry, and others who smiled under the soft lighting at the obvious delight of their old teacher. As they listened to the tactful, earnest words of thanks he gave to Mr. Harkness, he seemed little changed from those evenings when he stood beside the piano at the opening of another season and thanked everyone for what their decisions had brought about. Standing before the luxurious, almost black, plum velvet curtain which hung in ample folds, the prim figure in evening dress spoke proudly and graciously — and with an unmistakable touch of old magic in the flowing black ribbon of his flashing glasses.

The following morning there was a note at G.P.B.'s office as well as President Angell's commendation and critique:

Sat. A.M.

My dear Baker:

Let me cheer over a most auspicious beginning last night. It was elating.

And the theatre is so exceptionally good — just what it should be it seemed to me.

Altogether — hurrah!

Winthrop Ames

Later, there were many others.

"To me," wrote one early student, "remembering the first Workshop performance at Cambridge, it all seemed too good to be true." And from another actor came admiration conditioned by a similar point of view: "Such a beautiful building and such perfect equipment. Shades of Agassiz . . . And what a feather in your cap to have Golden take the play."

At his desk in the new office a few days later, G.P.B. wrote to John Golden for an appointment to discuss the New York production of *The Patriarch*. Then he sent letters to Edward Sheldon, who was seriously ill, and those others who could not come. To Ed Goodnow went the following:

December 15, 1926

Dear Edward:

You will hear, of course, varying reports of last Saturday night. I think a good many of the Workshop group were a bit homesick for the old conditions, and that their judgment may be a little colored thereby. It was, however, a great evening in that so many of the old guard so loyally turned up to observe and comment. The keenest part of my pleasure was when anyone like yourself of the original group appeared — and there was a goodly number.

Altogether, I think I feel well pleased with the opening. I think it has established us here with the Faculty and students. Now I think we can move on more quietly, and, consequently, more satisfactorily.

Affectionately,
G.P.B.

Having underscored his repetitions of the phrase, "I think," he added the postscript: "Briggs would have suggested in English 5: Brain fag!!"

XLV   SEARCH FOR ANOTHER O'NEILL

AT THE CLOSE OF THE FIRST SEMESTER OF DRAMA 47, G.P.B. wrote to M. A. DeWolfe Howe on February 10, 1926: "I have always hoped that at some time there would be a renaissance of the literary spirit that marked Harvard undergraduate life between 1885 and 1910." Thus Drama 47 and the activities of the Yale Drama School continued G.P.B.'s search for a latter-day Moody, MacKaye, or Sheldon — a second O'Neill, or yet another Barry. His editions of *Yale Plays,* beginning with Boyd Smith's *The Patriarch,* were more than scripts for little theatre groups. The goal continued to be a worthy American drama.

Thus the significance of G.P.B.'s closing years rests not upon the great augmentation of means and equipment for his new theatre, nor upon the "professional" productions thereby achieved. During a general theatrical prosperity that elevated the arts of scenic designer and lighting specialists, G.P.B. steadfastly assumed that the first artist in his theatre was the playwright. In 1918, in his introduction to the initial volume of Workshop plays, he gave his basic credo: "The fundamental principle of The 47 Workshop — and to this it has held steadily throughout its history — has been that everyone from director to stage hands must coöperate in putting the play upon the stage as the author sees it." This was still true in the spring of 1933, when G.P.B. retired.

Worthy plays, he believed, were most likely to appear when the dramatist expressed what he really cared about. Each of his students who wrote from the heart was much in G.P.B.'s mind throughout the remaining Yale years, but it was probably the image of Eugene O'Neill that dominated his quest. To another old student, Norman Hapgood, G.P.B. expressed the artistic dedication for which he watched: "Eugene O'Neill was a joy in that way. No outside considerations affected him. Something took possession of him and he put it out. Then he worked at it ruthlessly until it was right as he saw it. In the real sense he was as one possessed. He was possessed by his vision."

In the lush prosperity which the theatre enjoyed during the late twenties, the young author's chief temptation was to serve the current craze for entertainment. Many good writers were lost in pursuit of what would please a nervous, foot-tapping audience that cried "Boop-boop-a-doo" while the stock market rocketed higher. Of these playwrights, G.P.B. told his students, "Ideas and form such workers copy well, but the individualizing something which turns a play into a work of art is lacking."

By 1927, Broadway was producing more shows than ever

before; but hard times had already begun for the serious play-wright. To be sure, Pulitzer Prizes had recently gone to Sidney Howard's *They Knew What They Wanted,* to George Kelly's *Craig's Wife,* and Paul Green's *In Abraham's Bosom.* Max Rein-hardt brought Shakespeare to Broadway; and Eva Le Gallienne gave it Ibsen and Chekhov. Yet the real taste of the time was served at the new Ziegfeld Theatre, which opened that year with *Rio Rita* and concluded the season with the prototype of *South Pacific, Show Boat,* by Jerome Kern and Oscar Hammerstein II.

The success which was increasingly withheld from such work as O'Neill's *The Great God Brown* went more readily to the work of tunesmiths and scenic designers. In a day which fostered the artistic vitality of Robert Edmond Jones at the Greenwich Village Playhouse, of Lee Simonson at the Guild Theatre, and Joseph Urban at the Ziegfeld, G.P.B. saw his Drama 47 students drift away from vigorous original dramatic composition. By the time of his retirement, only one in four of his students were primarily playwrights; the majority wished for careers as directors and designers.

Thus G.P.B.'s faith in the playwright was already a practical necessity in the theatre, though he was not disposed to proclaim any crisis. In the spring of 1927, upon his receipt of a gold medal from the National Institute of Social Sciences, he told the members of the Institute:

Lately I have heard much about the danger to the drama from the motion picture, the radio, and, last of all, the vitaphone and tele-vision. They are rivals, all of them, and threatening rivals, but do not, if you love the drama, lose courage . . . You cannot kill it. A part of every human soul, there is a world-wide response to this imita-tive action which interprets life. It will last, I suspect, as long as man himself lasts.

He never lost faith in the ultimate value of a good play, and whenever it was suggested that the theatre was going to the dogs, he was likely to chuckle, "I've heard their barking for a good many years."

However, he was seriously disturbed when the theatre failed to gain the vision of some young writer, or when an older one faltered in his career. Increasingly, as Eugene O'Neill began his own withdrawal, G.P.B. directed his students to what now became an ideal:

Always there has been a relentless facing of the facts of life as O'Neill sees them, with no sentimentality, no shaping of his material with box-office, or supposed feelings of the public in mind. There has been so constant a sense in the dramatist of life's ironies, great and little, that his plays must be tragedies or, at least, sternly ironic comedies. There has been, too, a steadily increasing sense on his part of the mystery of human life, of human relations.

While the Yale Drama School grew, and as the number of students and faculty increased, G.P.B. saw his main mission was still to provide the encouragement he had once given O'Neill. "It is not the absence of faults," he would say to the people in Drama 47, "but the abundance of powers that makes greatness." For his great ones he wrote:

The finer the spirit of the young artist the more unsure and secretly timid he is in trusting his instincts for expression. Basically he has a deep reverence for the best accomplishments of the past, even if he feels he cannot be satisfied to express himself in the same terms. In the great rhythm of emotional life he is too liable to mistake what is commonplace for something highly individual, merely because of its momentary intensity for him. What is really finely individual in his feeling and thinking about life, as he has read of it or experienced it, he too often passes over as of no consequence. He exults when he can sweep down the broad currents companioned by the multitude, oblivious that he may be lost in the crowd.

G.P.B.'s concern lest his finer spirits be so lost shows in his solicitude for the work of Maurine Watkins. Following her two years of English 47 at Radcliffe, Miss Watkins had spent some time reporting for the *Chicago Tribune* before enrolling for the first year of Drama 47 in order to complete a play about the American press. Though perhaps lacking the poetic gift of Josephine Preston Peabody, or the gentle sensitivity of Rachel Lyman Field, she had not only what G.P.B. considered a genius for satire but something to say about America.

At the time G.P.B. was rehearsing *The Patriarch* for the opening of the University Theater, Miss Watkins was in New York trying to sell her play, *Chicago*. At the Greenwich Village Theatre, she found that Macgowan, O'Neill, and Jones wanted plays like *What Price Glory* or Maxwell Anderson's slice of hobo life, *Outside Looking In*. The thesis play, she was told, was out of date. The word now was "vitality." What she should write was life in the dirt with a cuss.

After Sam Harris opened Miss Watkins' play in New Haven, G.P.B. wrote the author, January 3, 1927:

Now don't let an immediate success or any prospect of it carry you off your feet. You wrote a play with commendable purpose. It was well characterized and actable. Don't let any willingness on the part of anybody to turn it into a play to force as many laughs as possible change you from your original purpose. You wrote something that might have an effect on the conditions you ridicule. It may well be turned into something which will have no such effect.

A few days earlier, on the thirty-first of December, he had also written to Maurice Wertheim and the Theatre Guild:

It is a comedy, intensely satirical, treating the sentimentalization of the criminal in this country by the public, newspapers, lawyers, and even courts . . . Whatever happens to the play, I know it was written with honest intent and with knowledge of facts existing for Chicago, though not perhaps for other cities to the same extent.

Meanwhile, the University Theater had been dedicated with Boyd Smith's play which H.T.P. described to his Boston readers as one after G.P.B.'s heart:

The scene is the Blue Ridge mountains — America homely and regional. The six personages are native to the soil, firm-set in their solitudes, isolate from all men with their God of the Law. The speech keeps savor with the folk, without the obscurities of blurred or florid dialect. Butternut and high boots are the only men's wear.

Something of the sort had first come into the Workshop with Tom Wolfe's *The Mountains,* but G.P.B. had heretofore preferred the Phil Barry type of comedy to what was already associated with Fred Koch and the Carolina Playmakers. Continuing this interest in the serious regional play, G.P.B. toured the Southwest in the summer of 1927 in order to prepare for his second production in the new theatre, Covington Littleton's *Pueblo.*

Before his departure, G.P.B. wrote to one of his first students at Yale, then directing dramatics at a midwestern college:

267

Have you heard that Lemist Esler's *Machiavelli* is sold to Wm. Brady for Lionel Atwill, an autumn production. You know, of course, that Paul Osborn has sold, as the year closed, a play of his to Brock Pemberton . . . Adolphe Appia has also agreed to let Biberman translate his French book on lighting — or is it in German? I've for the moment forgotten.

That fall, as rehearsals began for *Pueblo,* G.P.B. wrote to Maurine Watkins on the ninth of November:

When are you going to cease to be a refugee in Canada and give us a new play? I am disturbed because I believe, as I have told you more than once, that you have a special gift in writing for the Theatre in your ability to see serious things comically. This, I believe, you should capitalize to the utmost, particularly now that your recent success is still in the mind of the public, especially the theatrical world of New York. I can understand that you may not have had a wholly happy experience in spite of your success in the theatre world, but you cannot afford not to have something worthy of you on the New York stage within a year. Otherwise, you will have to begin again. Therefore, forgive this letter if I am saying just what you do not want to hear, and charge it to an old teacher who believes heartily in your powers if properly guided by you, and who wants to see you going on increasing the reputation for really significant work which you have already won.

Knowing full well how Broadway might affect his playwrights, he knew also that those good plays which should some day be literature would never be so outside "the Theatre."

For his third major production, G.P.B. chose a romantic piece about medieval England, *Overlords,* by Talbot Jennings. Since 1928 was the centennial of Ibsen's birth, G.P.B. also undertook an uncut production of *Brand,* which "Don" and "Mac" set and lighted after the manner of Craig and Appia. When one of the characters appeared with a key to the church door, and the lines indicated a door which Oenslager's set did not provide, G.P.B. stopped the rehearsal with the question, "Where is the door?" Oenslager's explanation that the detail was not important, that the man should walk in the general direction of a door, brought G.P.B.'s characteristic, "Try it." At a later rehearsal, when Boyd Smith complained that he could not see something, G.P.B. rejoined, "Boyd, this is *new art* and you don't have to see."

Though said in jest, this reply betrayed G.P.B.'s irritation that in the scarcity of good play material he was falling back upon the decorative arts. So he was careful now, more than ever, lest the techniques and expertness of his scenic artists dominate the playwright. "Scenery as scenery," he would say, "is bad." Of course, part of this view could be attributed to his own limited visual imagination. The next year, when Oenslager's model of the *Winter's Tale* set had been on G.P.B.'s desk for a month, G.P.B. complained: "I wish they would hurry and get this thing done so I could see how it is going to look." He knew perfectly well how Shakespeare's own production might have looked, but this one involved the use of two revolving stages.

When designers buried a character in arguments over old-fashioned sets and new-fashioned sets, he reminded them that no technical matter was always right. If an actor, losing sight of the play, inquired what G.P.B thought of his technique in rendering a piece of business, he might have for an answer an icy, "Oh, are *you* in the play?" Of all those things which coöperate to realize the author's intention, G.P.B. would say, "Each has its place." For what he sought was an integration of the arts of the theatre, not the aggrandizement of any at the expense of the play.

His own productions illustrated his definition of a good production, for they were a smoothly working unity of many complimentary forces under a wise and skilled hand. To his students of production, he cautioned: "Even a slight over-emphasis in scenery, lighting, or acting, of movement or gesture over speech, of atmosphere over characterization, may send a play scuttling down to its doom." To his playwrights he suggested that the ideal was to write each play so that it could be played only one way. To himself he said of each play that came to his hand for production, "There is a way to direct this show, a unique way."

So he produced his student plays without changes of his own. Though he still read his student plays aloud in Drama 47, he seldom made more than a very brief comment upon them there. As he had done at his round table in Dane Hall, Fay House, and Massachusetts Hall, he let criticism come from around the table. Though he might strongly recommend something in private conference with the author, he never required changes. "I want you to see your mistakes on the stage," he would say quietly. One day, as he watched a first rehearsal of a scene written without due regard for what the characters would have to do upon the stage, an actor fell over a chair which the author had required in his script. Calmly, but with an unforgettable finality, G.P.B. said to the author sitting beside him, "You see what *you* did."

For his 1929–30 schedule, G.P.B. returned to regional drama with Talbot Jennings' *No More Frontier*. Here Jennings abandoned his romantic interest in medieval England (though he later wrote an unsuccessful play about Shakespeare and renaissance England for Leslie Howard) to tell the saga of Flint Bailey and his search for a new American frontier after the Civil War. In 1875, Flint leaves his father's home and general store in Indiana and journeys westward, settling with his sweetheart in the Alturas Valley of Idaho. Flint's children and grandchildren grow up as that frontier vanishes and the old man lives on into the age of air travel. When Flint finds that there is no more frontier in his native land, he knows, however, that his grandchildren are exploring the remote vastness under the sea and the new worlds in the sky. It was a play that excited G.P.B.'s thoughts of the future.

On this production he worked with new people, leaving Oenslager and McCandless to design and light the productions of Alexander Dean, who had joined the faculty the year before. Among these new assistants, G.P.B.'s principal help came from Frank Poole Bevan, a former design student added to the faculty that September as Instructor in Costume Design. A valuable student assistant that year was Edward C. Cole, later Technical Director of the Yale Theater. At the same time, Miss Constance Welch, from the faculty of Northwestern University whence Alexander Dean had come, began her work as Instructor in Diction. Previously, G.P.B. had initiated instruction in diction for his students with the assistance of Mrs. Margaret Carrington, who was John Barrymore's teacher in those matters when he prepared his first important Shakesperean role as Gloucester in *Richard III*.

This growing emphasis upon standards of diction for both writer and actor was but another aspect of the technical excellence G.P.B. sought for his theatre. However, it seems also to have had a personal basis in his growing distrust of his own voice and ear; for those extraordinary instruments now began to fail in their excellence.

One evening, on returning from a rehearsal of *No More Frontier,* he stepped to the fireplace to light a fire for Christina. Suddenly he stopped, stood still for several moments, then returned to his living-room chair. Some minutes later he said with a quiet laugh, "All of a sudden, I couldn't speak." More than once as he worked on the Jennings play he told Constance Welch, "I don't trust my ear any more." After 1930, though he seldom faced this reality, he was never again the vigorous teacher and lecturer he had been in the twenties. Throughout his last year of teaching, he was a seriously ill man.

Deploring the careless, staccato diction of his students when they came upon his stage, he saw in these matters a retrograde product of our machine culture. Thus his attention to the techniques of effective and beautiful speech was not only corrective but directed toward the excellence of dialogue which had distinguished the great dramatists of the past. Although he looked first to his playwrights, he also desired a comparable mastery of technique from his other theatre artists. His objective for these people was essentially what he wrote about stage electricians:

When we speak of the electrician in the theatre, we still think too much in terms of candles and gas, just as in the moving picture we are still too much under the spell of the regular theatre. The university theatre should not only train young electricians to lighting as real, as delicate, as suggestive as possible, but should abet them in all desired technical and imaginative experiments. Many an electrician thinks technically in watts and amperes, but not in terms of the imagination. Others riot in imagination, but are not properly based technically. Here, as elsewhere in the theatre, the leap inspired by imagination should be taken from a sure footing in technique.

With characteristic catholicity, he was identified after 1929 with the annual awards by the American Academy of Arts and Letters of gold medals for good diction over the radio and on the stage.

Between *No More Frontier* and his spring production, as he had done for so many years during the brief midyear vacation, G.P.B. filled speaking engagements about the country. In what was his last appearance before some audiences, he delivered a series of four lectures. Their titles catch the spirit of retrospect

271

and glance at the future which mingled in G.P.B.'s closing years: "Finding the Way — Jones, Pinero"; "What is True — Shaw"; "Readjustment — O'Neill"; and "The Present and the Outlook." There was yet no successor to O'Neill.

The spring of 1930 saw G.P.B. turning to a new and not entirely compatible mode for his second major production of the year, *The Searcher,* an expressionistic antiwar play by Velona Pilcher, an American playwright associated with London's experimental Gate Theatre. With an international gesture that was but a part of the National Theatre Conference he was then organizing, G.P.B. undertook to familiarize himself with the cinema-like techniques which O'Neill had employed increasingly since *The Emperor Jones* and *The Hairy Ape.*

Unsympathetic as G.P.B. was with the explosive angularity and harsh expressionistic effects of this bitter but poetic play, he put aside his own love of a romantic glow in the theatre and addressed himself with an open mind to what seemed both the present and the outlook. Though his instinct was for something settled at the end of a play, and though he preferred clear stage relationships — Juliet so, bier in the center, tall candles so, Romeo breaking through an obvious door — he forsook Jones and Pinero and tried to see with the eyes of the young men about him. One day as "Don" and "Mac" went rowing, they met G.P.B. with an armload of books and sketches for *The Searcher* and its quicksilver scenes on varying levels. With a cheerful nod at his burden, G.P.B. allowed, "Maybe I'll learn something about the use of a ramp."

In short order he knew the one way to direct the show. Equipping his production staff with headphones borrowed from the Yale R.O.T.C., he had telephone wires strung from his movie-projection booth high over the roof of the theatre to prop room, stage manager's desk, and through the floor to the rehearsal room. With a script, a cue sheet, and his telephone, G.P.B. coördinated the continuous movie-like action of the play. Numerical cues for the airplane, ambulance train, hospital ward, camp, and battlefield brought double-quick action which flowed smoothly throughout an hour and a quarter. Capturing a grace beyond reality in a production which should have made him at least slightly anachronistic, G.P.B. seemed even to his youngest assistant as young as himself. It was also characteristic that only one headset was equipped to permit reply.

Concurrent with his work on *The Searcher,* G.P.B. was engaged in writing and arranging for production at the Stevens Institute of Technology his last pageant, a piece which he planned to do in this new manner to celebrate the fiftieth anniversary of the American Society of Mechanical Engineers. Entitled "Control," this unusual pageant must accomplish within little more than an hour its expressionistic history of man's struggle to control his environment and himself. For the May 1930 issue of *Mechanical Engineering* G.P.B. explained:

Obviously, much of the material which should be shown in illustration of the remarkable development of mechanical engineering in the past fifty years, and the growing sense in such work that beauty may and must be combined with utility and power, have demanded the use of the motion picture instead of tableaux. It has also made necessary symbolic figures to bind the parts together. Inasmuch as the pageant celebrates the increasing triumphs of the mechanical engineer, it has seemed wiser to do without a band or orchestra, and to substitute electrical reproduction . . . As far as possible the dialogue repeats, or approximates words of the speakers as reported in letters, anecdotes, etc.

For G.P.B.'s unique pageant, Frank Bevan, Edward Cole, and Harold Burris-Meyer of the Stevens Institute integrated moving pictures, amplified sound, symbolic figures, and realistic scenes. Thus G.P.B. illustrated what he taught his playwrights: "Form is not rigid, is not a fashion, a moral or an artistic obligation, but something an artist chooses after much selective thought as the best medium for the expression to which he finds himself impelled."

This spring also brought a striking new play from Drama 47, a play excitingly reminiscent of O'Neill. In *Steel,* Harold Igo told of the search of "Hunky" for a new God in the molten steel of Youngstown. Not only was Hunky like Yank in *The Hairy Ape,* but the play made dramatic use of the interior of a steel mill much as O'Neill had exploited a dynamo in his newest play. Moreover, Igo, a somewhat older chap than G.P.B.'s usual student playwright, had, like O'Neill, done a little of everything — soldier, sailor, ranch hand, circus roustabout, Bible salesman. Now, in early May, G.P.B. read the first draft of *Steel* with growing elation. It was, he noted, a "very curious play; quite superbly written."

With Igo and O'Neill in mind, G.P.B. had but recently characterized the playwright for whom he sought:

In thought our college-trained young dramatist is usually too young to have his own slant on life, to have done much careful, independent thinking. He is consciously or unconsciously the immature product of his teachers or of the men he has read. That is why I want to deal, preferably, much preferably, with graduate students. I am coming to feel that I should like to work only with people between twenty-eight to thirty and forty-five. Before twenty-eight, young people rarely have "found themselves"; after forty-five, I have found that people write plays strongly influenced by the plays the writer saw in the impressionable years between seventeen and twenty-seven. My students have made, particularly the more mature, much effort to find forms adequate to their needs — three, four, five acts, scenes for acts, prologues, epilogues, etc. They have responded keenly to the experiments in method of O'Neill.

One of G.P.B.'s first activities in the fall of 1930, after his return from Europe, was to gather his faculty "family," as he often called them, for a rare occasion. For their comments he read to them the play which he obviously hoped to be able to produce that fall. A few days later he wrote Harold Igo on the tenth of October:

I am still thinking over the manuscript of "Steel" and I have talked it over with practically all the people who heard it the other night. There was a general appreciation of the fact that you have something here really notable and that you have done well with it, but there is also a feeling in enough of the hearers to give me pause that parts of the play still need further touching up . . . What mainly delays my decision is that we all feel it quite impossible to give you what your text demands in molten steel by any other means than light.

They conferred several times with "Mac," and G.P.B. wrote again on the thirteenth: "I don't feel that you and I are really

274

at odds on your play. The difficulty is that you are talking more about the scenery and I am talking more about the actors and dramatic action of the play apart from the scenery."

Although the technical difficulties were overcome to provide an astonishingly real furnace, Bessemer converter, and other terrifying machinery of a steel mill upon the Yale University Theater stage, some of the staff had serious doubts about the play as it went into rehearsal. Nevertheless, all supported it loyally because it was something about which G.P.B. cared very much. Each in his turn received the confidence that the play was as good as the early O'Neill. Unconsciously, perhaps, each brought to the December production some flavor of *Dynamo,* some hint of *The Hairy Ape.* Yet there was a more than slight touch throughout of the melodrama of Dion Boucicault, for some of the steel-mill horror seemed but a sophisticated variant of sawmill villainy and railway-track suspense.

Harold Igo completed the 1930–31 academic year, the first in which G.P.B.'s department conferred the degree of Master of Fine Arts, but did not take the degree. As the year passed, he worked at a trilogy of which *Steel* was the first part. Unfortunately, though he had several more good plays coming along, his great promise was no more productive at first than had been O'Neill's. Of course, G.P.B. believed in those plays, just as he had believed in O'Neill.

At the spring productions, which included *The Winter's Tale,* the audience received a little printed broadside which explained some of the recent policy of production. This, like the communications once issued to audiences at Agassiz Theatre, appeared over G.P.B.'s signature. It said in part:

Fortunately or unfortunately, the plays of those studying playwriting are by a large majority realistic, permitting a relatively small amount of imagination in the designing of scenery and costume. For this reason, three years ago, the policy of giving once each year some play which makes special demand upon the students most interested in design or in stage lighting was begun. The Faculty of the School decided that the play chosen each year should be something which the special audience for Drama School performances had not seen and would not be likely to see in this country.

Thus the Drama School had presented Ibsen's *Brand*, never before given in its entirety in America; Swinburne's *Chastelard*, never before produced; and the first production of Miss Pilcher's expressionistic play, *The Searcher*. These plays, unlike the usual run of plays written for commercial production to satisfy an established national taste for realism, offered special opportunities for imaginative settings designed on different levels, ramps, and steplike constructions. They even afforded experimentation, G.P.B. explained, in the use of light as a means of expressing the emotional tones of dramatic action.

For such reasons, ostensibly, the 1931–32 schedule opened with an O'Neill program: *Bound East for Cardiff*, written for English 47 at Harvard, which Alexander Dean and Constance Welch directed; and *The Emperor Jones*, which G.P.B. directed. A more compelling reason appears to have been the scarcity of producible student plays. Aside from four one-acts suitable for the small experimental theatre, there was that year upon the main stage but one long play from current playwriting classes — *Merry-Go-Round*, by George Sklar and Albert Maltz. To complete his program, G.P.B. turned once more to a play by Talbot Jennings, *American Wing*.

An obvious explanation for this state of affairs could be seen in February 1932, when G.P.B. attended a meeting of the National Theatre Conference at the State University of Iowa. Here, presiding as the first president of the conference, G.P.B. talked with representatives from colleges and universities across the land which now had their own departments of drama and active theatres, many staffed by his old students. It was no longer necessary for a young playwright to leave his native state or region in order to get what once could be had only from G.P.B. Moreover, amid all this multiplication of students of the arts of the theatre, there were not so many playwrights as there should be. G.P.B. was now certain of the diminution of the supply during the past decade, and he found people at the conference like Barrett Clark and Lee Simonson who were also acutely aware of this social phenomenon.

In October 1932, as G.P.B. prepared his last production, he recommended Harold Igo for a Guggenheim Fellowship. After that, G.P.B. saw another potential American playwright disappear in teaching and directing. It was what G.P.B. had experienced himself, and what he had so vehemently warned Tom Wolfe would happen to his creative powers if he entered the critical ways of teaching. However, for this fall he had a new playwright, and a strong play about Benedict Arnold. This was *The King's Coat,* by Fred Kleibacker, Jr., a young fellow who would bear watching.

But it was G.P.B. who was watched, and with growing anxiety by his production staff as he moved more and more unsteadily upon his stage. On the day before the dress rehearsal, word came that Mr. Baker had gone home ill. The "family" took over and the show went on. Later, when it was apparent to G.P.B. that his directing days were nearly at an end, he planned a farewell production. Calling Frank Bevan, G.P.B. talked of the play with which he desired to leave his theatre. It was *Iris* he wished to do now — that play by Pinero which he had seen open in London thirty years before. When Bevan demurred, G.P.B. suggested Pinero's *The Princess and the Butterfly,* a delightful comedy about vanishing youth. But for each suggestion, Bevan advanced some reasonable objection. After a few more conferences, G.P.B. apparently realized that his old magic had already made its farewell; for he said no more of the idea.

Shortly following the new year, he wrote to George Haight, whose new play, written in collaboration with Allan Scott, was at the Masque Theatre in New York. Said G.P.B. on January 16, 1933:

> I do want to see "Goodbye Again" as soon as possible, but I cannot state at the moment just when that will be. I am hoping to be in New York at the end of this week, but everything depends upon my improving condition. I have been hampered this past month and a half by a peculiar condition of the inner ear which affects my balance and keeps me staggering about like a non-observer of the Volstead law. However, if I see any chance to get down for your play at the end of the week I will telegraph you. I am delighted with your success, may it long continue.

That month, G.P.B. faced the bitter fact that he could no longer teach. Yet as he submitted his resignation from active work in the Department of Drama his concern was not for himself. On the tenth of March, upon departmental stationery, he wrote:

Dear Igo:

Will you please get to me as soon as possible your new play? We are in somewhat of a quandary as to our next production and there is a slight chance that yours might be chosen, if it is suitable. We must settle this by Tuesday next, the 14th, so if you could get me your play at once that I might read it over the week-end, it would be a great convenience.

Sincerely yours,
G.P.B.

XLVI   THE UNIVERSITY AND A THEATRE
FOR AMERICANS

THE HALF DOZEN YEARS WHICH FOLLOWED THE OPEN-ing of the Yale University Theater were days of fulfillment for G.P.B., a time of looking before and after as well as upon the achievement of a dream. Having exhibited his treasure to colleagues, friends, old students, and members of the profession, he now considered the future of which his theatre was but a part. At the new year he sent greetings to some three thousand individuals and organizations, inviting their attendance on February 11 and 12, 1927, as members of a national conference for the development of the American theatre.

Opening this conference, President James Rowland Angell welcomed three hundred and fifty representatives of nearly every national interest in the theatre. Though the majority were teachers of the drama and directors of amateur theatres, not all represented academic or civic organizations. Barrett Clark, for instance, came as a publisher of dramatic materials; Mrs. Edith Isaacs, editor of *Theatre Arts Monthly,* brought a fraternity of amateur and professional interests; and Louis Hartman, from the Belasco Theatre, spoke at one of the sessions on Belasco's techniques of lighting. In a time of fabulous show business, when Broadway saw nearly three hundred productions annually while the little theatres saw several thousands, the conferees were seriously concerned with the real prosperity of their native theatre.

Presiding, G.P.B. was not free to speak his personal views; however, it was evident that his purpose was to foster a working union of the forces present. Many professions of faith and views of alarm enlivened the meetings, expressions that spanned the land from Texas and California to New England. Yet it was a voice from Broadway and the Guild Theatre which expressed the common hope of the delegates. Objecting to the false division between amateur and professional, Lee Simonson told them:

It is my first belief that the future of the theatre in America depends very largely upon the little groups and community theatres . . . Only the smaller cities can give America an indigenous theatrical design. Above all, you have leisure, freedom to experiment, freedom from the rush of four-day week rehearsals and the race for Broadway openings. The heady concentration of drama in New York cannot continue indefinitely.

As G.P.B. adjourned the conference, which for various practical reasons had failed to federate its strength, he looked ahead to other opportunities for concluding his purpose.

A year later, the *New York Times* carried the following editorial comment on "Non-Metropolitan Drama" in its issue for April 6:

Teachers of the theory and practice of the theatre from Northern colleges, with Professor Baker at their head, and professional Broadway reviewers have met with representatives of university and community theatres of four Southern states, including Mississippi . . . All through the South, Mr. Atkinson reports to *The Times,* organizations are arising to develop a local drama "in place of what they are losing or never had."

Applauding the conference leadership of Paul Green, a student of Professor Fred Koch and a recent winner of a Pulitzer Prize, the editor hailed the meeting as a light on a darkening horizon. It was now clear that the movies and the increasing reluctance of Broadway producers to take their shows on the road had produced a rural scarcity of professional drama in a time of metropolitan plenty. In spite of a current supply of theatre craftsmen many times that of 1900, proportionately fewer people had an opportunity to attend the spoken drama than did so at the turn of the century.

Because this conference had been called by Fred Koch, G.P.B. was able to speak as a strong partisan for a national organization of the thousand or so nonprofessional theatres which were the only theatre for millions of Americans. He told the sixty delegates from little theatres in the South that only through union could they share the technical information and assistance they needed. "American drama in general," he said, with a polite reference to the Carolina Playmakers and Paul Green, "is to be likened to the pre-Shakespearian period, with its seeds of commanding growth." If American academic and civic playhouses would achieve something comparable to the European repertory theatres, and they could do so by uniting, the result might well be a theatre and a drama unsurpassed in history.

Meanwhile, the Yale Drama School had grown so rapidly as to strain what was all too soon becoming an inadequate provision for new functions. During the year after this second conference, Mr. Harkness appeared ready to provide for the necessary expansion of facilities. Though G.P.B. was not so sanguine as Alexander Dean, who talked in terms of an enormous accretion of endowment, he hoped now to build for a future far beyond his own remaining years. For his thoughts were now on the personal finalities that had haunted him in his youth.

On at least one occasion he revisited the old Providence Opera House, long since a movie house, and corresponded concerning its preservation. Now, when Edward Goodnow or some friend from the remote or recent past called upon him, G.P.B. asked easily and with the warmth of affection, "Tell me about the good old days." More frequent were the events which prompted him to write on February 26, 1929, to Herbert L. Clark, the secretary of his Harvard class: "I am very sorry to hear of the death of J. B. T. Tuthill, and I should like to write his widow. Tuthill is one of my earliest college recollections. Do you remember his famous palladium of American liberty speech?"

Within a few weeks of this note, G.P.B.'s flowers were at the grave of Henry Arthur Jones. Retrospect gave his remarks upon the drama the perspective of more than half a century.

Yet his thoughts grappled vigorously with the future as he sent a brief request in the autumn of 1929 to each of his faculty:

"Please give me your plans for the development of your department during the next twenty years." The following spring, Stanley McCandless drew plans for six stories behind the stage tower which would provide additional lecture rooms, a speech laboratory, storage for hundreds of costumes, a dining room and kitchen, museum exhibition space, and a much needed library with stacks for the several thousand books the school had acquired. To scout new ideas, G.P.B. again toured European theatres through the summer of 1930 while Frank Bevan studied the latest in German theatrical design.

When Bevan met G.P.B. and Christina in Munich, shortly before their return to New Haven, G.P.B. immediately brought the conversation around to his exciting plans for the Yale Drama School. He had not yet discovered that what had been happening in Wall Street while he was abroad would indefinitely postpone the generous wishes of Mr. Harkness. However, there was never a depression of his aim to make his school a future source of knowledge and freedom for the American theatre.

For several years he had been progressively disturbed at the Broadway failure of plays he thought deserved success. Through the twenties, in his public lecture, "Our Drama Today," he had repeatedly called for what he now believed only the university theatres could supply: "What is the basis of the whole trouble? What we need, and what we need very much, in this country, all over the country, is a theatre which gives good drama, well acted, at moderate rates, before a receptive public of eclectic and catholic tastes."

In our colleges and universities were sources of private and civil subsidy already habituated to the traditions of academic freedom; there, too, were audiences likely to cultivate eclectic and catholic tastes. This could develop a favorable soil for the seedlings he had seen flourish at New Haven only to wither in New York. The history of Boyd Smith's *The Patriarch*, Talbot Jennings' *No More Frontier*, J. H. Powell's *Brief Candle*, and Katherine Clugston's *Finished* he knew intimately, and angrily. Unless such plays could live and keep their authors writing, many fine talents would perish of inanition. Too many were already lost to Hollywood. Thus grew the theme of G.P.B.'s last great idea: to create an environment of freedom in which the university trained playwright could live and grow.

Speaking to theatre groups about the country, he reminded them of the freedoms which had been won in his own lifetime. The battle during his youth had been for freedom to put reality upon the stage: "All the drama in which I was brought up, was based on this: 'The stage is fixed mechanically. You cannot really put life on the stage; you must adapt life to the stage.'"

Later, he told them, there had been the struggle for beauty. Now the fight was to create a national theatre free to produce plays simply because they were good plays, or would lead to better ones. In the long view, this was a fight for the free evolution of new elements within a changing concept of the theatre itself.

Thus, he pointed out, the one-act play, practically extinct on the professional stage around 1900, had acquired new life and a higher form in the subsequent development of small experimental theatres. Now, a further extension of the idea of the theatre promised a further adaptation of this old form. "We see," he observed, "authors of the one-act trying experiments which bring it into relation with the motion picture and which fit it for use on the radio."

He liked to illustrate this evolution in the work of Eugene O'Neill, who — like Lady Gregory, Yeats, Synge, and Stanley Houghton — had written one-act plays as a distinct and new art form:

> What proves that O'Neill's experimentation with forms is not for its own sake but for definite artistic ends, what proves his indifference to supposed public response to given subjects or treatments, is that "Diff'rent" and "All God's Chillun" are in two acts . . . He would not spoil the handling of the material as he saw it, either by overcrowding it into one act, or by thinning it into three acts. "There is nothing predetermined about form," he seems to say again and again.

This concern with the art of O'Neill, whom G.P.B. now saw as America's greatest dramatist, was not only to encourage O'Neill but to secure for future American playwrights the free opportunity which he believed O'Neill had enjoyed. By way of illustration, G.P.B. liked to remind his conference listeners that the original production of *The Emperor Jones* had cost less than a thousand dollars. If a similar freedom were achieved for the unknown playwright today, the theatre would continue to evolve in a living response to vital experiment by artists yet unborn:

So experimenting, they will change our stage, arranged usually for types of scenery which held good thirty years ago, so that it shall be plastic. Within our memory, electricity has made over stage lighting, and even yet we have by no means fathomed its full possibilities in the theatre. The growing exactions of our dramatists are working the same revolution in everything else about the older and relatively rigid stage.

The impact of this line of thought upon his students can be seen in the following note which G.P.B. received from a Drama 47 playwright in the autumn of 1930: "I would like to know more about lighting for I can see that it has *body* as well as spirit and must be reckoned with as *material* the same as any other plot substance."

Another substantial element to which he directed his writers was the relation between the cadences and the rhythms of what he called "the curious, almost brutish staccato of our hurried speech of today." In his last published essay, he told the young dramatist that "his dialogue can never be perfect until he absolutely mirrors the emotions of the characters presented, and this mirroring is impossible till the national or local or individual rhythms of speech have been fathomed." An information center for the dissemination of technical knowledge about lighting and speech rhythms was already a necessity for the university playwright.

On the twenty-first of June 1931, G.P.B. wrote to J. Wong-Quincey, a former Drama 47 student who was now a professor at Tsing-Hua College in Peking:

I now expect to retire not later than three years from this June, and I may retire at almost any time before that date. Much depends on whether we get needed additions and improvements, for which we have recently asked. The whole matter is at present under consideration. In almost every direction we have outgrown our space, and we find teaching our work very difficult under existing conditions. When we built five years ago, I had no idea the work would grow so rapidly.

283

Within a few days he had sailed to observe British summer schools of the drama and to choose his successor.

At the Malvern Festival, whither he had gone with G. C. D. Odell, historian of the New York stage, G.P.B. met his man. This was Allardyce Nicoll, who had founded the College Theatre at Queen Mary College in the University of London at the time G.P.B. commenced his own work at Yale. In choosing Nicoll, leading theatre historian and authority on the nineteenth-century drama, G.P.B. thus indicated the balance of historical, technical, and creative abilities which he hoped would characterize future university leadership in the American theatre.

In these latter days, when asked how an inherently conservative leadership could keep abreast of revolutionary developments in the theatre, G.P.B. replied:

This is really very simple. First of all, any study of dramatic technique shows that a few fundamental principles in the relation of dramatist to public have held good from Aeschylus to the most mechanistic modern Russian. Cling to these in instruction. Let all that is of a period or of a man go. Secondly, don't stress rules, precepts; help the would-be dramatist to find self-expression. Don't bother him with rules while he is working. After all, the teacher here is more the midwife than the diagnostician. That is, don't worry the student with type, method, rules; help him to bring forth that which is creating in his mind and heart.

Between semesters, in February 1932, G.P.B. journeyed to Iowa City and the State University of Iowa, where some of the theatre people he had called together in 1927 were gathering. With support which Kenneth Macgowan and others had gained from the Carnegie Foundation, twenty-eight theatre organizations and many individuals now united to serve the interests of the American theatre. In short order they elected G.P.B. the first president of the National Theatre Conference. Phrasing many of their objectives and illustrating his argument with a history of the unhappy vicissitudes of a recent play in various Broadway managerial offices, he urged the necessity of organizing a dozen or twenty producing centres outside of New York, of supplying the theatres in these areas with good plays, and of providing through a central bureau of information the various technical assistance requisite to good productions for such plays.

A year later he was meeting his last playwriting classes, gathering his texts on the table at which he sat, neatly arranging them as he made his closing remarks. "I am not just sure," he said, pursing his lips and glancing down at his hands folded upon the books, "what the future of the theatre will bring." For a few phrases he talked of O'Neill, saying he believed O'Neill would soon leave his present manner of writing. Smiling quietly, he paused, then straightened briskly to continue, "I do believe, however, that extreme realism has about run its course, and I shouldn't be too surprised if the future drama turned out to be a romantic-realistic mixture." Rising, he picked up his books and steadied himself as he added, "I'm not asking you to believe me." Crossing quickly to the door, he turned, and his voice fell to a whisper, "I'm not even sure I believe myself." Then he was gone.

When Sidney Howard learned of this retirement, he wrote a valedictory to "G.P.B. of Harvard and Yale" which he sent to the *New York Times*. His concluding words were:

Whether, as some think and others boast, the screen has swallowed the theatre up forever, whether the theatre is dying of its own hardened arteries, no one can say. It seems probable that both stage and screen will presently emerge into a new and different energy. There are so few young playwrights coming along, that Baker's day, our day, seems sadly but truly like a termination.

On the opposite page of the issue in which this was published appeared a communication from Berlin, entitled: "The Pre-Hitlerite Theatre." This ended: "The present Berlin season is scrubby going . . . sooner or later the integrity and the enthusiasm of the provinces will surge back over Berlin." From Berlin to Broadway, there were many who shared G.P.B.'s hope that a new energy would awaken the theatre.

On March 4, 1933, G.P.B. was packing the personal effects — presentation copies, signed sketches, and photographs — which crowded his office, when he paused to write to Robert Hillyer:

I think we are not likely to return to Cambridge. We have a wandering desire and we are likely to divide our time between the New Hampshire Farm and wandering over the face of the earth. It seems unbelievable that I shall have a wealth of time at my disposal and it will be much appreciated.

Part of this wandering was already committed to National Theatre Conference business, for his presidential report to the June
meeting in Evanston would involve the current year of accomplishment in an energetic program for the future. The Conference
was now soundly organized on a decentralized regional basis, and
all member theatres were receiving information of good new
plays and how to produce them. Furthermore, useful handbooks
by such technical authorities as Richard Boleslavsky, Stanley
McCandless, Henning Nelms, and Rosamond Gilder had been
published by the conference during its first year.

As he prepared to vacate his office, G.P.B. looked at the new
portrait of himself which would soon hang in the Green Room.
It was a tired old man, not the rapier-quick dynamic young
teacher, that confronted him as he wrote to Dean Meeks, May
17, 1933:

I enclose a copy of some lines from the *Harvard Graduates'
Magazine* for March 1925 which may possibly be of some use to you in
formulating what you want to say in acknowledging the portrait. Do
not feel in any way bound to use it, but I give it to you for what it is
worth. It shows that I left Harvard with a certain amount of appreciation in certain quarters.

The departure of G.P.B. from Yale was widely noted, but
nowhere with more appreciation than the editors of *Theatre Arts
Monthly* showed when they devoted their Tributary Theatre issue of July 1933 to the enormous influence he had wielded. In
dedicating this issue they wrote:

His going marks the end of an era which stands a fair chance,
when it takes its place in history, of being considered the seedling
period of a national drama and of a national theatre that finds
expression, not through a single crowded row of playhouses in New
York but through a thousand theatres along the highways of the
whole country.

The following New Year G.P.B. and Christina were in Santa
Barbara, California. On the twenty-ninth of the month, G.P.B.
asked Edward Sheldon if he would write a recommendation for
a young woman who wished to act in a motion picture:

She much wants to play the lead in the picturizing of Miss McFadden's *Double Door*. I think she could play it and well. I saw the play in passing Westward . . .

We stay here till about Feb. 17 when we go to Tucson and Mexico for three weeks. Back in N. Y. late in April, when I hope to come in to see you, and then on to Boulder Farm till November.

Early in November he was once more in New Haven to call the third annual meeting of the National Theatre Conference to its February session in the Yale Theater. On the eighth, he was signing letters which his secretary had prepared when he turned suddenly and said, "Mrs. Hastings, I can sign no more." On the day before Christmas, the New York papers reported his presence at the Neurological Institute. On January 6, his tired heart stopped.

Perhaps the *New York Times* editorial on the day following the announcement of his death spoke for the nation. Venturing that it was impossible to determine exactly the extent of Professor Baker's personal contribution to the professional theatre, the editor said: "But this much is certain; the meagerly equipped course at Harvard raised the prestige of the theatre enormously. In addition to the many students it sent directly into the theatre, it has, in one way or another, graduated a host of educated theatregoers."

From the creators of the twentieth-century drama who had come to his round table, there was one who deserved to speak for all with his estimate of that contribution. In a letter to this editor and the nation, Eugene O'Neill wrote:

Only those of us who had the privilege of membership in the drama class of George Pierce Baker back in the dark age when the American theatre was still, for playwrights, the closed shop, star system, amusement racket, can know what a profound influence Professor Baker, who died last Sunday, exerted toward the encouragement and birth of modern American drama.

It is difficult in these days, when the native playwright can function in comparative freedom, to realize that in that benighted period a play of any imagination, originality or integrity by an American was almost automatically barred from a hearing in our theatre. To write plays of life as one saw and felt it, instead of concocting the conventional theatrical drivel of the time, seemed utterly hopeless.

287

In the face of this blank wall, the biggest need of the young playwright was for intelligent encouragement, to be helped to believe in the dawn of a new era in our theatre where he would have a chance, at least, to be heard. And of the rare few who had the unselfish faith and vision and love of the theatre to devote their life to this encouragement, Professor Baker's work stands pre-eminent. It is that encouragement which I — and I am sure all of the playwrights who knew and studied under him — will always remember with the deepest appreciation.

Not that the technical points, the analysis of the practice of play-making taught in his class, were not of inestimable value to us in learning our trade. But the most vital thing for us, as possible future artists and creators, to learn at that time (Good God! For any one to learn anywhere at any time!) was to believe in our work and to keep on believing. And to hope. He helped us to hope — and for that we owe him all the finest we have in memory of gratitude and friendship.

Later, he said that what he meant to emphasize in his letter to the *Times* was the greatest gift one human being can give another — the courage to believe in one's work and go on. He said he would always remember not the teacher but the man, the charm of his personality, his ability just by being himself to convey faith, and understanding, and sympathy, and friendship. Many men, he said, can teach, but only a fine, rare few can be in themselves an education in faith for others.

EPILOGUE

TO THE FAMILY SERVICE AT THE SWAN POINT CEMEtery came an old man, a cousin who remembered singing and going to the theatre with George. Where George had often driven his horse to visit his mother's grave, the trees were bare and there was yet no sign of spring. Days with George Baker in a world of Gilbert and Sullivan at the Sans Souci Gardens were now very far away.

On February 23, 1935, the third National Theatre Conference gathered in New Haven to consider "The New World of the Theatre." Gilmor Brown, Lee Simonson, Walter Prichard Eaton, Mrs. Edith Isaacs, John Mason Brown, and Sidney Howard, among many others, filled the Yale University Theater to pay tribute to G.P.B. and recall a world of pleasant memory. Sidney Howard spoke first.

In a rambling way, he tried to tell the things he remembered as they came to him. He said that every age of the theatre has its disciplinarians, those who direct its aspirations. For a past generation, he thought Augustin Daly and David Belasco had done this. For his own day, he said, the two had been Arthur Hopkins and G.P.B. On the playwrights of the post-Chekhov and post-Strindberg years, G.P.B. had left his mark of professional excellence — a stern Yankee standard of perfection. He had taught truths more valid than technique. "Write what you know to be true about your characters," he told his students, "and write nothing that you do not know to be true." He had taught that plays are important and their art an obligation.

Howard recalled his own year in 1915–16 as a graduate student in English 47 with Perc Reniers, Sam Behrman, and Kenneth Andrews. He told of his own efforts to write plays in blank verse and G.P.B.'s gentle chaffing. Of his days as a journalist after the war, still writing verse plays, and how he finally got *Swords* on the stage in 1921, just before Barry's success. He recalled G.P.B.'s presence at its opening and how they sat together through what was painfully and obviously a failure. How, after the final curtain, G.P.B. looked into Howard's tear-brimming eyes and began to chuckle, and the tears turned to laughter and they both laughed until they cried. And Howard never wrote again in verse.

He remembered collaborating with Ned Sheldon, and the wonderful feeling of friendliness and helpfulness he had found in the theatre from those who had studied with Professor Baker. In the lecture courses, he recalled, you could always tell when Workshop rehearsals were going badly because then G.P.B. read favorite scenes through the entire hour with all the dramatic fervor he was trying to instill in his cast. Howard said he read as well as any man he had ever heard, in a fine and clearly colored voice with sharp diction — frowning with intensity, his lips pursed at the corners, reading by preference the wild nobilities of Marlowe and Shakespeare. But he never called Marlowe "Kit," or Shakespeare "Will."

Howard talked of the house on Brattle Street, of evenings there in the study with the "Dozen," of Christina's gracious hospitality, and of the boys — whom he usually saw in fleeting glimpses through the study door. He remembered the dog, Bruno, and outside, when you left, the comfortably battered old Dodge.

He spoke of G.P.B.'s contribution to the American theatre through his playwrights. How he first of all developed an artistic conscience in them, without preachments, without pressure, usually without a definitely spoken word. How he made you aware of the shoddy, of the cheaply theatric as unworthy of serious consideration.

Howard said that he was not at all surprised to find that it was two of G.P.B.'s last students, George Sklar and Albert Maltz, who were the instigators of the newest and most flourishing theatre on Broadway. He told how he and Sam Behrman — the only Baker alumni present — attended a dinner with a number of playwrights who talked about G.P.B. as if he were their own teacher. Anderson and Sherwood and the lot spoke as if he had been a real force to them. "I wonder," said Howard as he concluded, "if we can know how much he dominated this whole generation of American dramatists."

John Mason Brown then rose to address the assembly. Obviously moved by Howard's remarks, he began by saying that in Mr. Baker's death he had lost an idolized friend, though he had not dared show him how he had admired him or how blindly he would have followed. He went back to Howard's "artistic conscience" and talked of Mr. Baker's nice distinction between the theatric which had integrity and that which had not — that he did not scorn plays like *Abie's Irish Rose* if they were true to character and plot and worked out their situations with honest craftsmanship.

He took up G.P.B. as an actor and director — his beautiful reading of plays — his amazing facility with dialects. He recalled the face that could be Sir Foppling Flutter, or an Indian, or a prostitute. How the most blasphemous scenes never disturbed him as he ripped out the oaths in the script before him, only occasionally hastening on with pinked cheeks. How he came on stage to show an actor some movement — hands clenched into fists and rammed down into his coat pockets, short quick steps like a tightrope walker. Then, as he turned toward stage front, how the hands came out of his pockets — and by the time he faced the imaginary audience, he was the character.

Brown stressed the youthfulness of G.P.B.'s spirit, of his continually renewing point of view which always made him an intellectual contemporary of his student. Though he had made a name for himself in the heyday of Pinero and Jones, he was of the present and of the future — from Sheldon to Sklar and Maltz. Thus his students were fitted for stage, screen, radio, and whatever might be the theatre to come.

Then Brown drew a picture of G.P.B.'s hail and farewell to the Yale Drama School, the valedictory of one gloriously in love for a lifetime. It was a life that had kept faith with the future, and a love that should guide toward the best. With the closing remarks of his tribute, he pointed to the great challenge which G.P.B.'s life must always remain to those who loved the theatre.

In this spirit, the Drama School faculty announced its "George Pierce Baker Cup" for the best production of a one-act play in a drama tournament to be held that spring in the University Theater. The cup was won by a company which produced an unusual short play about a taxicab strike. Written by Clifford Odets, one of the young founders of the Group Theatre, *Waiting for Lefty* subsequently played in New York as a prize-winning play and skyrocketed both the Group and Odets to fame.

Throughout the Group Theatre's experimentation with the play, a member of the organization and a leading actor in the cast was one of G.P.B.'s last students, Elia Kazan. During the long silence of Eugene O'Neill after *Mourning Becomes Electra,* and after Odets had turned to writing for Hollywood, Kazan's productions of the plays of Tennessee Williams brought to the American and English stages one of its most promising playwrights.

From the mid-century viewpoint, it may seem that the renaissance which marked the twenties was decorative rather than literary, more productive of stagecraft than of great plays. Thus the students of G.P.B.'s closing years appear to have become designers, directors, producers — such as Stewart Chaney, Maurice Gnesin, Elia Kazan. Many — such as George Haight, John S. Young, Alistair Cooke — have made their fame not in the theatre but in motion pictures, radio, and television. Indeed, much of the argument for teaching playwriting in the universities seems currently belied by the work of such self-taught dramatists as T. S. Eliot and William Inge. Even as one regards the Tennessee Williams free form of *Camino Real,* or the very popular extension of readings in evening clothes of parts of Shaw's plays to similar evenings with Dickens and Shakespeare, or the endless appeal of the Rogers and Hammerstein musical play, doubts may becloud the vision of a great American drama.

It is in such hours that those who love the theatre will hear a wise chuckle, "Of course, the form will change — the chief strength of the drama lies in its flexibility." In darkest times, there will always gleam G.P.B.'s pince-nez glance with its great hope and finer dream: "You may have unfortunate experiments, but eventually there is in sight an American drama that shall put us side by side with the Continental nations, expressing us as their drama has so perfectly expressed them."

APPENDICES AND NOTES

APPENDIX I

A LIST OF THE WRITINGS
OF GEORGE PIERCE BAKER

BOOKS

Systematic Expositions

The Principles of Argumentation. Boston: Ginn & Co., 1895; 2d edition (with Henry Barrett Huntington), 1905; 3d edition (with Henry Barrett Huntington), 1925.

The Development of Shakespeare as a Dramatist. New York: The Macmillan Company, 1907.

Dramatic Technique. Boston: Houghton Mifflin Co., 1919.

Dramatic Works

The Revolving Wedge: A Football Romance in One Act. (With Thornton M. Ware.) Boston: W. H. Baker & Co., 1896.

Peterborough Memorial Pageant. Peterborough, N.H.: MacDowell Memorial Association, 1910.

A Pageant of Hollis Hall, 1763–1913. Cambridge, Mass.: University Press, 1913.

The Centenary Pageant of Allegheny College; 1815–1915. Meadville, Pa.: Allegheny College, 1915.

The Pilgrim Spirit: A Pageant in Celebration of the Tercentenary of the Landing of the Pilgrims at Plymouth, Massachusetts, December 21, 1620. Boston: Marshall Jones Co., 1921.

Control: A Pageant of Engineering Progress. New York: American Society of Mechanical Engineers, 1930.

Editions and Compilations

Specimen Briefs Drawn by Students of Harvard College. Cambridge, Mass.: n.p., 1892; 2d edition, 1893.

Specimens of Argumentation: Modern. New York: Henry Holt & Co., 1893; 2d edition, 1897.

Endymion: The Man in the Moon, by John Lyly, M.A. New York: Henry Holt & Co., 1894.

Shakspere's A Midsummer Night's Dream. "Longmans' English Classics," edited by George R. Carpenter; New York: Longmans, Green & Co., 1896.

The Belles-Lettres Series. Section III: The English Drama from its Beginning to the Present Day. Boston: D. C. Heath & Co., 1902–1935.

The Good Natur'd Man and She Stoops to Conquer, by Oliver Goldsmith; the Introduction and Biographical and Critical Material by Austin Dobson, LL.D. (Edinburgh); the Text Collated by George P. Baker, A.B. "Belles-Lettres Series"; Boston: D. C. Heath & Co., 1903.

The Forms of Public Address. New York: Henry Holt & Co., 1904.

Some Unpublished Correspondence of David Garrick. Boston: Houghton Mifflin & Co., 1907.

As You Like It. "Renaissance Edition," *The Complete Works of William Shakespeare,* edited by Sidney Lee, Vol. X; Cambridge, Mass.: University Press, 1907. Also in, "Harper Edition," *The Complete Works of William Shakespeare,* edited by Sidney Lee, Vol. V; New York: Harper & Bros., 1907.

Charles Dickens and Maria Beadnell: Private Correspondence. Boston: Bibliophile Society, 1908.

Select Plays by Francis Beaumont and John Fletcher. "Everyman's Library," edited by Ernest Rhys; New York: E. P. Dutton & Co., 1911.

Hamlet, Prince of Denmark. "Tudor Shakespeare," edited by William A. Neilson and A. H. Thorndike; New York: The Macmillan Company, 1913.

Plays of the 47 Workshop. [*First Series.*] "Harvard Plays," Vol. I; New York: Brentano's, 1918.

Plays of the Harvard Dramatic Club. [*First Series.*] "Harvard Plays," Vol. II; New York: Brentano's, 1918.

Plays of the Harvard Dramatic Club. [*Second Series.*] "Harvard Plays," Vol. III; New York: Brentano's, 1919.

Plays of the 47 Workshop: Second Series. "Harvard Plays," Vol. IV; New York: Brentano's, 1920.

Modern American Plays. New York: Harcourt, Brace & Howe, 1920.

Plays of the 47 Workshop: Third Series. "Harvard Plays," Vol. V; New York: Brentano's, 1922.

Philip Barry. *You and I: A Comedy in Three Acts.* "Long Plays of the 47 Workshop" [Vol. I]; New York: Brentano's, 1923.

Plays of the 47 Workshop: Fourth Series. "Harvard Plays," Vol. VI; New York: Brentano's, 1925.

Frederick L. Day. *Makers of Light: A Play in Three Acts.* "Long Plays of the 47 Workshop" [Vol. II]; New York: Brentano's, 1925.

Representative Modern Plays. New York: Charles Scribner's Sons, 1926.

Yale One-Act Plays. Vol. I; New York: Samuel French, 1930.

Spring o' the Year: A Comedy in Three Acts, by W. H. Robertson. "Yale Plays"; Samuel French, 1931.

No More Frontier: A Play in Prologue and Three Acts, by Talbot Jennings. "Yale Plays"; New York: Samuel French, 1931.

PAMPHLETS

Harvard Debating: Subjects and Suggestions for Courses in Oral Discussion. (With Albert B. Hart.) Harvard University, 1896.

Some Bibliographical Puzzles in Elizabethan Quartos. Cedar Rapids, Ia.: Torch Press, 1910. Reprinted from *Bibliographical Society of America, Papers,* IV (1910), 9–20.

PARTS OF BOOKS

"Class Ode." *Harvard College: Class of 1887; Baccalaureate Sermon, Class Day Oration, Class Poem, Ivy Oration, Ode, Class Song.* Cambridge: W. H. Wheeler, 1887. P. 32.

"Preface." *Endymion: The Man in the Moon, by John Lyly, M.A.* New York: Henry Holt & Co., 1894. Pp. i–ii.

"John Lyly." *Ibid.* Pp. iii–clxxxix.

"Bibliography." *Ibid.* Pp. cxci–cxcvi.

"Introduction." *Shakspere's A Midsummer Night's Dream.* "Longmans' English Classics," edited by George R. Carpenter; New York: Longmans, Green & Co., 1896. Pp. ix–xxxiii.

"Mrs. Vincent." *Famous American Actors of To-Day.* Edited by Frederick E. McKay and C. E. L. Wingate. New York: Thomas Y. Crowell & Co., 1896. Pp. 194–203.

"John Lyly: *Alexander and Campaspe.*" Edited with Critical Essay and Notes. *Representative English Comedies,* edited by Charles M. Gayley, Vol. I, *From the Beginnings to Shakespeare;* New York: Macmillan, 1903. Pp. 263–332.

"The Text." *The Good Natur'd Man and She Stoops to Conquer.* "Belles-Lettres Series"; Boston: D. C. Heath & Co., 1903. P. 2.

"Preface." *The Forms of Public Address.* New York: Henry Holt & Co., 1904. P. iii.

"Introduction (An Open Letter to Teachers)." *Ibid.* Pp. ix–xxiii.

"The 'Prentices' Song." From *The Prodigal Son 1598,* performed Dec. 22, 1898. *Bear With Us; a Collection of Tavern Club Verses.* Boston: Tavern Club, 1905. Pp. 18–19.

"Preface." *Some Unpublished Correspondence of David Garrick.* Boston: Houghton Mifflin Co., 1907. Pp. vii–viii.

"Introduction." *As You Like It.* "Renaissance Edition," *The Complete Works of William Shakespeare,* edited by Sidney Lee, Vol. V; Cambridge, Mass.: University Press, 1907. Pp. ix–xxvi.

"Introduction." *As You Like It.* "Harper Edition," *The Complete Works of William Shakespeare,* edited by Sidney Lee, Vol. V; New York: Harper & Bros., 1907. Pp. ix–xxvi.

"The Plays of the University Wits." *The Cambridge History of English Literature,* edited by Adolphus W. Ward and A. R. Waller, Vol. V, *The Drama to 1642;* Cambridge: University Press, 1910. Pp. 121–141.

"Introduction." *Select Plays of Beaumont and Fletcher.* "Everyman's Library," edited by Ernest Rhys; New York: E. P. Dutton & Co., 1911. Pp. vii–xviii.

"The Educative Value for Children in Acting Shakespeare's Plays." Alice Minnie Herts. *The Children's Educational Theatre.* New York: Harper & Bros., 1911.

"General Introduction." *Lectures on the Five-Foot Shelf of Books,* edited by William A. Neilson, Vol. X; New York: Collier's Lecture Service Bureau, 1913. Pp. 3–15.

"Introduction." *Hamlet, Prince of Denmark.* "Tudor Shakespeare," edited by William A. Neilson and A. H. Thorndike; New York: The Macmillan Company, 1913. Pp. vii–xx.

"Dramatic Technique in Marlowe." *Essays and Studies of the English Association*, edited by Charles H. Herford, Vol. IV; Oxford: Clarendon Press, 1913. Pp. 172–182.

"Drama: General Introduction." *Lectures on the Harvard Classics*, edited by William A. Neilson; New York: P. F. Collier & Son, 1914. Pp. 369–386.

"Preface." *The Centenary Pageant of Allegheny College; 1815–1915*. Readville, Pa.: Allegheny College, 1915. Pp. i–ii.

"Introduction." Paul Hyacinthe Loyson. *The Apostle: A Modern Tragedy in Three Acts*. Translated by Barrett H. Clark. "The Drama League Series of Plays," Vol. XV; New York: Doubleday, Page & Co., 1916. Pp. vii–xix.

"Introduction." *Plays of the 47 Workshop*. [*First Series*.] "Harvard Plays," Vol. I; New York: Brentano's, 1918. Pp. vii–xxiii.

"Preface." *Plays of the Harvard Dramatic Club*. [*First Series*.] "Harvard Plays," Vol. II; New York: Brentano's, 1918. Pp. vii–xii.

"Introduction." *Plays of the Harvard Dramatic Club*. [*Second Series*.] "Harvard Plays," Vol. III; New York: Brentano's, 1919. Pp. vii–viii.

"Preface." *Plays of the 47 Workshop: Second Series*. "Harvard Plays," Vol. IV; New York: Brentano's, 1920. Pp. vii–ix.

"Introduction." *Modern American Plays*. New York: Harcourt, Brace & Howe, 1920. Pp. v–x.

"Preface." *Plays of the 47 Workshop: Third Series*. "Harvard Plays," Vol. V; New York: Brentano's, 1922. Pp. vii–ix.

"The Essentials of Drama." Herbert S. Mallory. *Backgrounds of Book Reviewing*. Ann Arbor, Mich.: George Wahr, 1923. Pp. 268–290.

"Foreword." Philip Barry. *You and I: A Comedy in Three Acts*. "Long Plays of the 47 Workshop"; New York: Brentano's, 1923. Pp. 1–5.

"Introduction." Edward Knoblock. *The Lullaby and Other Plays*. New York: G. P. Putnam's Sons, 1924. Pp. iii–vii.

"Foreword." Rachel Lyman Field. *Six Plays*. New York: Charles Scribner's Sons, 1924. Pp. vii–ix.

"The One-Act Play." Leroy Phillips and Theodore Johnson. *Types of Modern Dramatic Composition*. Boston: Ginn & Co., 1927. Pp. vii–xiv.

"Foreword." *The Collected Plays of Josephine Preston Peabody*. Boston: Houghton Mifflin Co., 1927. Pp. vii–xxv.

"Introduction." Frank Alanson Lombard. *An Outline History of the Japanese Drama*. London: Allen & Unwin, 1928. Pp. 13–14.

"Preface." Donald F. Robinson. *The Harvard Dramatic Club Miracle Plays*. New York: Samuel French, 1928. Pp. vii–x.

"Foreword to Presentation." *Control; A Pageant of Engineering Progress*. New York: American Society of Mechanical Engineers, 1930. Pp. v–vi.

"Foreword." *Yale One-Act Plays*. New York: Samuel French, 1930. P. ix.

"Foreword." *Spring o' the Year: A Comedy in Three Acts, by W. H. Robertson*. "Yale Plays"; New York: Samuel French, 1931. P. i.

"Foreword." *No More Frontier: A Play in Prologue and Three Acts, by Talbot Jennings*. "Yale Plays"; New York: Samuel French, 1931. P. i.

"Drama as a Career." *My Vocation, by Eminent Americans; or What Eminent Americans Think of Their Callings*, selected and arranged by Earl G. Lockhart; New York: H. W. Wilson Co., 1938. Pp. 115–122.

Published Letters

Letters to the Editor, a series of perhaps six on G.P.B.'s experiences in New Mexico and in his European travels, Spring and Summer, 1888, *Providence Daily Journal*. The dates of publication have not been discovered. Only those concerning the New Mexico scene survive in one of G.P.B.'s scrapbooks; these are not distinguished for anything more than his sympathetic interest in the Indians and their culture.

Letter to the Editor, published as "The Castle Square Theatre Stock Company," *Boston Evening Transcript*, May 10, 1905, p. 22.

Letter to Henry B. Harris, Cambridge, Mass., Dec. 22, 1909; published in various newspaper accounts of the Harris offer to assist in endowing a chair of playwriting, it appears in "To Found Chair of Dramatic Art," *Boston Herald*, Dec. 30, 1909, p. 5.

Letter to Louis Evan Shipman. Undated. Louis Evan Shipman. *The True Adventures of a Play*. New York: Kennerley Co., 1914. Pp. 9–12.

Letter to Philip Barry. Published as "Foreword." Philip Barry. *You and I: A Comedy in Three Acts*. "Long Plays of the 47 Workshop"; New York: Brentano's, 1923. Pp. 1–5.

Letter to Edward Knoblock. Cambridge, Mass., March 10, 1924. Published as "Introduction." Edward Knoblock. *The Lullaby and Other Plays*. New York: G. P. Putnam's Sons, 1924. Pp. iii–vii.

Portion of a letter to Barrett H. Clark, January 1926, first published in Clark's *Eugene O'Neill* (New York: R. M. McBride & Co., 1926), p. 18.

PERIODICALS AND SERIALS

Prose Narrative

"Deserted Houses." *Hypophet,* I (Providence High School, Oct. 18, 1882), 1.

"Block Island Wrecks." *Register,* I (Providence High School, April 16, 1883), 78.

"Professor Dunse's Researches." *Ibid.* (March 19, 1883), 59–60.

"Voyage of the Aana." *Ibid.,* II (Oct. 22, Nov. 5, 1883), 27–28, 36–37.

"A New England Legend." *Harvard Advocate,* XL (Nov. 27, 1885), 72–74.

"The Bargain of May 31st, 1793." *Harvard Monthly,* I (Feb. 1886), 206–213.

"Brother Filippo; a Story." *New England Magazine,* I, n.s. (Feb. 1890), 630–639; II (March 1890), 73–85.

"To Lift the Sadness." *Harvard Monthly,* XIX (Oct. 1894), 1–15.

Verse

"The Bust's Dilemma." *Register,* I (Providence High School, Nov. 27, 1882), 5.

"Erudition." *Ibid.* (Jan. 22, 1883), 26.

"Omnimanes." *Ibid.* (June 25, 1883), 118.

"A Reminiscence." *Ibid.* (March 19, 1883), 61.

"An Autumnal Wail." *Ibid.,* II (Oct. 8, 1883), 20.

"Beside the Stream." *Ibid.* (Feb. 25, 1884), 91.

"I Wonder How?" *Life,* IV (Nov. 20, 1884), 283.

"Now Winter Comes." *Harvard Advocate,* XXXVIII (Jan. 16, 1885), 197.

"The Hermit Thrush." *Harvard Monthly*, III (Oct. 1886), 7.
"The Coming of the Fog." *Harvard Monthly*, III (Jan. 1887), 156.
"On the Quay at Porta Portese." *Harvard Monthly*, IV (April 1887), 64.
"Class Ode." *Harvard Advocate*, XLIII (June 24, 1887), 145.
"Verses for the First Triennial Dinner, 1887." *Harvard College: Class of 1887, Secretary's Report No. 2 (1890)*. Melrose: Journal Job Print, 1890. Pp. 91–96.
"The Song of the Red Cloak." *Youth's Companion*, LXIV (Oct. 8, 1891), 536.

Addresses

"Intercollegiate Debating." An Address Delivered Before the Association of Colleges and Preparatory Schools of the Middle States and Maryland, at Philadelphia, Pa., December 1, 1901. *Educational Review*, XXI (March 1901), 244–257.
"The Teaching of Argumentative Discourse in High Schools." National Education Association. *Journal of Proceedings and Addresses of the Forty-Second Annual Meeting Held at Boston, Massachusetts, July 6–10, 1903.* Winona, Minn.: National Education Association, 1903. Pp. 460–466.
"The Mind of the Undergraduate." An Address Given before the Schoolmaster's Association of New York, *Eleventh Annual Report of the Schoolmaster's Association of New York and Vicinity, 1903–1904.* Pp. 91–101.
"Some Bibliographical Puzzles in Elizabethan Quartos." A Paper Read before the Bibliographical Society of America, at Bretton Woods, N.H., July 3, 1909. *Bibliographical Society of America, Papers*, IV (1910), 9–20.
"The Theatre, An Enterprise or an Institution?" *Proceedings of the Conference of Cities, Held in Connection with the Pageant and Masque of St. Louis, May 29–31, 1914.* Edited by Arthur E. Bostwick. St. Louis, Mo.: St. Louis Pageant Drama Association, 1914, Pp. 10–13.
"Address to the Graduating Class, Radcliffe Commencement, June, 1918." *Radcliffe Quarterly*, II (Aug. 1918), 99–104.
"Our Drama Today." An Address Given March 20, 1922, at Sanders Theatre for the Benefit of the Endowment Fund of Radcliffe College. *Harvard Alumni Bulletin*, XXIV (May 4, 1922), 734–744.
"Address." On the Occasion of the Memorial Meeting for Gertrude Buck. *Vassar Miscellany Monthly* (Feb. 1923), pp. 10–15.
"Problems and Standards." *Proceedings of the Conference on the Drama in American Universities and Little Theatres, Nov. 27, 28, 1925.* Pittsburgh: Carnegie Institute of Technology, 1925. Pp. 69–76.
"Forty Years of the Drama — A Retrospect." An Address before the National Institute of the Social Sciences, May 4, 1927. *National Institute of the Social Sciences, Journal*, XII (1927), 13–19.
"Address." In Connection with the Award by the American Academy of Arts and Letters of a Gold Medal for Radio Announcers for Good Diction over the Radio. *American Academy of Arts and Letters; Proceedings of Dec. 16, 1928, and April 23, 1929. Academy Publication* LXX (1929), 21–24.
"Speech in the Drama." An Address Broadcast from the Library of the American Academy of Arts and Letters, April 24, 1929. *American Academy of Arts and Letters; Proceedings in Commemoration of the Twenty-fifth Anni-*

versary of the Founding of the American Academy of Arts and Letters.
Academy Publication LXXII (1930), 170–213.
"Presentation Address." On the Occasion of the Presentation of the American
Academy of Arts and Letters Medal for Good Diction on the Stage. *Ameri-*
can Academy of Arts and Letters; Proceedings of its Literary Exercises,
November 10, 1932. Academy Publication LXXIX (1933), 34–38.

Periodical Articles

Review of L. C. Wyman's *Poverty Grass,* in *Harvard Monthly,* III (Oct. 1886),
42.
"George Farquhar." *Ibid.* (Nov. 1886), 53–63.
Review of *Through the Year with the Poets,* edited by Oscar F. Adams, in
ibid. (Dec. 1886), 126.
Review of Sarah O. Jewett's *A White Heron and Other Stories,* in *ibid.,* p.
125.
Review of J. T. Wheelwright's *The Child of the Century,* in *ibid.,* IV (May
1887), 124–125.
Review of *New Verses from the Harvard Advocate,* edited by Kilbourne
Tompkins, in *ibid.* (June 1887), 167–168.
"George Meredith." *Ibid.* (July 1887), 138–146.
Review of *The Works of John Marston,* 3 vols., edited by A. H. Bullen, in
ibid., pp. 209–210.
"Albert Schirmer." *Notes and Queries,* 7th series, I (Oct. 13, 1888), 288.
Review of Bliss Carman's *Low Tide on Grand Pre: A Book of Lyrics,* in
Harvard Monthly, XVIII (April 1894), 80–84.
"The Revival of Ben Jonson's *Epicoene; or, the Silent Women,* March 20,
1895." *Harvard Graduates' Magazine,* III (June 1895), 493–501.
"The Revival of Ben Jonson's *Epicoene, or The Silent Woman* at Harvard
University." *American University Magazine,* II (June 1895), 168–173.
"Debating at Harvard." *Harvard Graduates' Magazine,* VII (March 1899),
363–372.
"The Children of Paule's." *Harvard Monthly,* XII (May 1891), 85–98.
"Intercollegiate Debating." *Educational Review,* XXI (March 1901), 244–257.
" 'Tittus and Vespacia' and 'Titus and Ondronicus' in Henslowe's Diary."
Publications of the Modern Language Association, XVI (1901), 66–76.
"The Plays of Eugene Brieux." *Atlantic Monthly,* XC (July 1902), 79–86.
"The University. The Opening of the Year." *Harvard Graduates' Magazine,*
XI (Dec. 1902), 231–236.
"A New Source of the Changeling," *Journal of Comparative Literature,* I
(Jan.–March 1903), 87–88.
"Cecil Rhodes Scholarships in the United States." *Cornhill Magazine,* XIV,
n.s. (Feb. 1903), 238–244.
"The University. The Winter Quarter." *Harvard Graduates' Magazine,* XI
(March 1903), 393–399.
"The University. The Spring Term." *Ibid.* (June 1903), 539–545.
"The University. The Summer Quarter." *Ibid.,* XII (Sept. 1903), 48–53.
"The Dramatist and His Public." Review of Brander Matthews' *The Devel-*
opment of the Drama, in the *Lamp,* XXVII (Nov. 1903), 329–332.

"Some Recent Books on the Elizabethan Drama." Review of *The Elizabethan Shakespeare*, vol. I, edited by Mark H. Liddell; *Representative English Comedies*, vol. I, *From the Beginnings to Shakespeare*, edited by C. M. Gayley; and *The Complete Works of John Lyly*, 3 vols., edited by R. W. Bond, in the *Atlantic Monthly*, XCII (Nov. 1903), 706–711.

"The University. The Opening of the Year." *Harvard Graduates' Magazine*, XII (Dec. 1903), 229–234.

Review of Ben Jonson's *The Alchemist*, edited by C. M. Hathaway, in *Journal of English and Germanic Philology*, V (1903–1905), 381–384.

"The University. The Winter Quarter." *Harvard Graduates' Magazine*, XII (March 1904), 401–409.

"The University. The Spring Quarter." *Ibid.* (June 1904), 583–590.

"The University. The Summer Quarter." *Ibid.*, XIII (Sept. 1904), 64–69.

"The University. The Opening of the Year." *Ibid.* (Dec. 1904), 249–256.

"*Hamlet* on an Elizabethan Stage." *Shakespeare Jahrbuch*, XLI (1905), 296–301.

"Typical Commencement Events at Harvard." *Reader*, VI (Aug. 1905), 295–298.

"The Mind of the Undergraduate." *Educational Review*, XXX (Sept. 1905), 189–200.

"Some Unpublished Correspondence of David Garrick." *Atlantic Monthly*, XCVIII (Nov.–Dec. 1906), 598–617, 812–832.

"Travelers' English." *Education*, XXVII (April 1907), 448–457.

"Narrative in the Drama." *Reader*, IX (Jan. 1907), 211–217.

"A Group of Harvard Dramatists." *Harvard Graduates' Magazine*, XVII (June 1909), 599–607.

"George Rice Carpenter." *Harvard Monthly*, XLIX (Oct. 1909), 1–4.

"The Peterborough Pageant: As the Producer Saw It," *New Boston*, I (Oct. 1910), 256–261.

"Pageantry," *New Boston*, I (Nov. 1910), 295–296.

"William Vaughn Moody." *Harvard Graduates' Magazine*, XIX (Dec. 1910), 258–261.

"Practical Academic Drama." *New York Dramatic Mirror*, LXV (June 28, 1911), 5–6.

"Play-Making." Review of William Archer's *Play-Making*, in *Drama*, II (Nov. 1912), 163–171.

"What Parents Can Do for the Theatre." *Ladies' Home Journal*, XXIX (Nov. 1912), 24.

"Pageantry." *Art and Progress*, IV (Jan. 1913), 831–835.

"The Hollis Hall Pageant." *Harvard Graduates' Magazine*, XXII (Sept. 1913), 214–217.

"What the Theatre Can Do for the School." *Ladies' Home Journal*, XXX (Jan. 1913), 47.

"What the Pageant Can Do for the Town." *Ladies' Home Journal*, XXXI (April 1914), 44.

"Proposed Building for the Drama." *Harvard Alumni Bulletin*, XVI (May 1914), 512–515.

"The Pageant and Masque of St. Louis." *World's Work*, XXVIII (Aug. 1914), 389–399.

"The 47 Workshop." *Quarterly Journal of Speech Education,* V (May 1919), 185–195. Republished from "Introduction," *Plays of the 47 Workshop: First Series,* "Harvard Plays," vol. I; New York: Brentano's, 1918, vii–xxiii.

"The 47 Workshop." *Century,* CI (Feb. 1921), 417–425.

"Barrett Wendell. (1855–1921)." *Harvard Graduates' Magazine,* XXIX (June 1921), 571–576.

Review of Kenneth Macgowan and Robert E. Jones's *Continental Stagecraft,* in the *Atlantic Monthly,* CXXXI (April 1923), 12–14.

"The Theatre and the University." *Theatre Arts Monthly,* IX (Feb. 1925), 98–108.

"The New University Theatre." *Yale Alumni Review,* XXV (Oct. 1925), 75–77.

"O'Neill's First Decade." *Yale Review,* XV, n.s. (July 1926), 789–792.

"Forty Years of the Drama — a Retrospect." *National Institute of the Social Sciences, Journal,* XII (1927), 13–19.

"Rhythm in Recent Dramatic Dialogue." *Yale Review,* XIX (Sept. 1929), 116–133.

"Allied Arts in the American Theatre," *Yale Review,* XX (Spring, 1931), 607–608. Review of *Upstage,* by John Mason Brown.

"The Stage: Its Arts and Annals." Review of Theodore Komisarjevsky's *The Costume of the Theatre;* Lee Simonson's *The Stage Is Set;* Thomas W. Stevens', *The Theatre from Athens to Broadway;* Joseph S. Kennard's *The Italian Theatre,* 2 vols.; Anna I. Miller's *The Independent Theatre in Europe;* George C. D. Odell's, *Annals of the New York Stage,* vol. VII; and Reese D. James's *Old Drury of Philadelphia,* in the *Yale Review,* XXII (Spring, 1933), 638–641.

"From a Harvard Diary; Notes made in the Eighties." *Theatre Arts Monthly,* XVII (July 1933), 515–518.

Newspaper Articles

"Iris": Pinero's New Play. A Review and a Criticism." *Boston Evening Transcript,* Oct. 12, 1901, p. 18.

"The Play in London. Striking Productions of the Present Season. The Public, However, Has No Enthusiasm for the New or the Really Fine Dramas — A Criticism of 'The Sentimentalist' — The Idle Rich the Mistaken Theme of Most Playwrights." *Boston Evening Transcript,* Jan. 4, 1902, p. 16.

"The Young French Dramatist. His Public as Contrasted with the American." *Boston Evening Transcript,* April 9, 1902.

"The American Public and the Theatre. An Attempt to Analyze Public Taste." *Boston Evening Transcript,* June 7, 1902, p. 19.

"A Subsidized Theatre. Professor Baker Renews an Urgent Plea. Why Should our Public be Denied the Beauties of Foreign and Old English Drama Simply Because They Will Not Pay? — The Volkstheatre of Vienna as an example for Boston — Arguments and Objections Examined." *Boston Evening Transcript,* Sept. 10, 1902, p. 16.

"The Lowe Library, John Drew's Valuable Gift to Harvard." *Boston Evening Transcript,* Dec. 3, 1902, p. 24.

"The Drama." *New York Daily Tribune,* April 12, 1902, Part II, p. 2.

"The American Stage." *Boston Evening Transcript,* Oct. 7, 1907, p. 13.
"Reinhardt's Unique Shakespeare: His Production of Henry IV." *Boston Evening Transcript,* Nov. 30, 1912, III, 6.
"The Pilgrim Spirit in Pageantry." *New York Times,* July 17, 1921, Part III, p. 6.
"The National Conference on Drama." *New York Times,* Dec. 24, 1926, p. 6.
"The Shakespeare Memorial Theatre." *New York Times,* Nov. 18, 1927, p. 22.

UNPUBLISHED WRITINGS

Books

"A Plot Book of Some Elizabethan Plays." [Portions of this were printed in proof by Ginn & Company, *ca.,* 1897–1899. This title was listed in: (1) "Title Index," *U. S. Catalog, Books in Print,* 1899. (2) Oscar F. Adams, *A Dictionary of American Authors,* Boston: Houghton Mifflin & Co., 1897. The 2d, 3d, and 4th editions of this (1898, 1899, and 1901) repeat this listing.]

Dramatic Works

"Not Sentimental." [A Play in Four Parts, 1884.]
"The Mills of God: A Play in One Act." (With Thornton M. Ware.) [Copyrighted by Thornton M. Ware and George P. Baker, 1894.]
"The Deed's Creature: A Play in Four Acts." [*ca.* 1895.]
"The Masque of the Prodigal Son." [Produced December 22, 1898, at the Tavern Club, Boston.*]
"The Farce of the Party and the Tart." (With Thomas R. Sullivan and Clayton Johns.) [Produced December 22, 1898 at the Tavern Club, Boston.]
"Mistress Beatrice Cope: A Play in Four Acts." [Copyrighted by George P. Baker, 1901.]
"Office Hours from 1 to 3: A Farce in One Act, Adapted from the French." (With Thornton M. Ware.) [Copyrighted by Thornton M. Ware and George P. Baker, 1901.]
"A Page from History." [Produced December 21, 1909, at the Tavern Club, Boston.]
"The Troth." [A Reading Given by George P. Baker, February 17, 1912 at the Tavern Club, Boston.]

* This and subsequent references to Tavern Club Dramatic Performances are from "Chronology of Tavern Club Events," M. A. DeWolfe Howe, *A Partial (and Not Impartial) Semi-Centennial History of the Tavern Club, 1884–1934,* Boston: Tavern Club, 1934, pp. 255–273.

APPENDIX II

PUBLISHED PLAYS, WRITTEN BY G.P.B.'S STUDENTS AT HARVARD AND RADCLIFFE

Plays of the 47 Workshop. First Series. "Harvard Plays," vol. I; New York: Brentano's, 1918. Contains: Rachel Lyman Field, "Three Pills in a Bottle"; Hubert Osborne, "The Good Men Do"; Eugene Pillot, "Two Crooks and a Lady"; William L. Prosser, "Free Speech."

Plays of the Harvard Dramatic Club. First Series. "Harvard Plays," vol. II; New York: Brentano's, 1918. Contains: Winifred Hawkridge, "The Florist Shop"; Howard Brock, "The Bank Account"; Rita Creighton Smith, "The Rescue"; Kenneth Andrews, "America Passes By."

Plays of the Harvard Dramatic Club. Second Series. "Harvard Plays," vol. III; New York: Brentano's, 1919. Contains: Esther W. Bates, "Garafelia's Husband"; Cleves Kinkead, "The Four-Flushers"; Louise W. Bray, "The Harbor of Lost Sheep"; Farnham Bishop, "Scales and the Sword."

Plays of the 47 Workshop: Second Series. "Harvard Plays," vol. IV; New York: Brentano's, 1920. Contains: Doris Halman, "The Playroom"; Eleanor Hinckley, "The Flitch of Bacon"; Norman Lindau, "Cooks and Cardinals"; Kenneth Raisbeck, "Torches."

Plays of the 47 Workshop: Third Series. "Harvard Plays," vol. V; New York: Brentano's, 1922. Contains: William F. Manley, "The Crow's Nest"; M. A. Kister, Jr., "The Hard Heart"; Louise W. Bray, "Mis' Mercy"; Arthur Ketchum, "The Other One."

Plays of the 47 Workshop: Fourth Series. "Harvard Plays," vol. VI; New York: Brentano's, 1925. Contains: Elizabeth H. Sullivan, "The Strongest Man"; Frederick L. Day, "The Slump"; James Mahoney, "The Mourner"; William H. Wells, "Brotherhood."

Elizabeth McFadden, *The Product of the Mill.* New York: Samuel French, 1912.

——— *Why the Chimes Rang.* New York: Samuel French, 1915.

Cleves Kinkead, *Common Clay.* New York: Samuel French, 1914.

Eugene O'Neill, "Bound East for Cardiff" In *Provincetown Plays. First Series.* New York: Frank Shay, 1916).

Edward Massey, *Plots and Playwrights.* Boston: Little, Brown & Co., 1917.

Doris Halman, "Will o' the Wisp" (In *Representative One-Act Plays by American Authors*. Boston: Little, Brown & Co., 1919).

Philip Barry, *You and I: A Comedy in Three Acts*. "Long Plays of the 47 Workshop"; New York: Brentano's, 1923.

———— *The Youngest*. New York: Samuel French, 1925.

Frederick L. Day, *Makers of Light*. "Long Plays of the 47 Workshop"; New York: Brentano's, 1925.

APPENDIX III

PUBLISHED PLAYS, WRITTEN BY G.P.B.'S STUDENTS AT YALE

Yale One-Act Plays. New York: Samuel French, 1930. Contains: Harry McGuire, "Yella"; Grace D. Ruthenburg, "Hans Bulow's Last Puppet"; E. P. Conkle, "Minnie Field"; Maurice Gnesin, "The Mistress"; Maude Humphrey, "Immersion"; Leopold Atlas, "L."

Boyd Smith, *The Patriarch.* "Yale Plays"; New York: Samuel French, 1931.

W. H. Robertson, *Spring o' the Year.* "Yale Plays"; New York: Samuel French, 1931.

Talbot Jennings, *No More Frontier.* "Yale Plays"; New York: Samuel French, 1931.

Katherine Clugston, *Finished.* "Yale Plays"; New York: Samuel French, 1931.

Lemist Esler, *The Grey Fox.* New York: Samuel French, 1928.

APPENDIX IV

YALE PRODUCTIONS PERSONALLY DIRECTED BY G.P.B.

(Prompt scripts, stage manager's scripts, light plots, and other production records for these plays are on file in the George Pierce Baker Dramatic Library, Department of Drama, Yale University)

Feb. 10, 11, 1926. Boyd Smith, *The Patriarch*

March 3, 4, 1926. Frederick L. Day, *The Fall of the House of Usher,* one-act adaptation

May 24–28, 1926. Claire Williams, *The Best Cellar*

Feb. 10–12, 1927. Boyd Smith, *The Patriarch,* Revised Version. Opening Production, Yale University Theater

June 1–3, 1927. J. Wong-Quincey, *Peking Politics*

Dec. 13, 14, 1927; Feb. 22, 1928. Covington Littleton, *Pueblo*

May 1928. Henrik Ibsen, *Brand*

Nov. 21, 22, 1928. Talbot Jennings, *Overlords*

March 15, 16, 1929. Robert J. H. Powel, *Brief Candle*

May 28, 29, 1929. A. C. Swinburne, *Chastelard,* Adapted by Talbot Jennings

Dec. 17, 18, 1929. Talbot Jennings, *No More Frontier*

March 20–22, 1930. Velona Pilcher, *The Searcher*

Dec. 16, 17, 1930. Harold Igo, *Steel*

March 30, 31; April 13, 14, 1931. William Shakespeare, *The Winters' Tale*

Nov. 14, 16, 17, 1931. Eugene O'Neill, *The Emperor Jones*

March 23, 24, 1932. Talbot Jennings, *American Wing*

Dec. 16, 17, 1932. Fred R. Kleibacker, Jr., *The King's Coat*

APPENDIX V

THE HARVARD
PRIZE PLAYS

JOHN CRAIG PRIZE PLAYS

Florence Lincoln's *The End of the Bridge.*
    Opened at the Castle Square Theatre, March 6, 1911, for a 9-week run.
Elizabeth McFadden's *The Product of the Mill.*
    Opened at the Castle Square Theatre, January 29, 1912, for a 5-week run.
Frederick W. Ballard's *Believe Me, Xantippe!*
    Opened at the Castle Square Theatre, January 20, 1913, for an 11-week run.
Cleves Kinkead's *Common Clay.*
    Opened at the Castle Square Theatre, January 7, 1915, for an 18-week run.
Charlotte Chorpenning's *Between the Lines.*
    Opened at the Castle Square Theatre, February 7, 1916, for a 5-week run.
Kenneth Andrews' *The Year of the Tiger.*
    Opened at the Castle Square Theatre, April 23, 1917, for a 2-week run.

OLIVER MOROSCO PRIZE PLAYS

Rachel Barton Butler's *Mama's Affair.*
    Opened January 20, 1920, at Winthrop Ames's Little Theatre.
T. P. Robinson's *The Copy.*
    Not produced.

RICHARD HERNDON PRIZE PLAYS

Philip Barry's *You and I.*
    Opened at the Belmont Theatre, February 19, 1923, for a year's run, followed by a year on tour.
Henry Fisk Carlton's *Up the Line.*
    Opened at the Morosco Theatre, November 22, 1926.
Dorothy Heyward's *Nancy Ann.*
    Opened March 31, 1924, at the Forty-Ninth Street Theatre.
Roscoe Brink's *Catskill Dutch.*
    Opened at the Belmont Theatre, May 6, 1924.
T. P. Robinson and Esther Willard Bates's *Be Your Age.*
    Opened at the Belmont Theatre, February 4, 1929.

APPENDIX VI

BIOGRAPHICAL MATERIALS
NOT CITED IN "NOTES"

BOOKS

Adams, Oscar Fay. *A Dictionary of American Authors*. Boston: Houghton Mifflin Co., 1901.

Bailey, David W., ed. *Harvard Alumni Directory*. Cambridge: Harvard University Press, 1934.

Baker, Blanch M. *Dramatic Bibliography: An Annotated List of Books on the History and Criticism of the Drama and Stage and on the Allied Arts of the Theatre*. New York: H. W. Wilson Co., 1933.

Baker, Christina Hopkinson. *The Diary and Letters of Josephine Preston Peabody*. Boston: Houghton Mifflin Co., 1925.

"George Pierce Baker," *Encyclopedia Americana*, III, 60. New York: Encyclopedia Americana Corp., 1949.

"George Pierce Baker," *Encyclopaedia Britannica*, II, 944. Chicago: University of Chicago, 1948.

"George Pierce Baker," *The New International Encyclopedia*, II, 544. 2d ed.; New York: Dodd, Mead & Co., 1923.

Brown, Rollo Walter. *Harvard Yard in the Golden Age*. New York: Current Books, Inc., 1948.

Eaton, Walter Prichard. "George Pierce Baker," *Dictionary of American Biography*, XXI, 45–46. Ed. Harris E. Starr. New York: Charles Scribner's Sons, 1944.

Davis, Mary W., *et al. Dramatic Compositions Copyrighted in the United States 1870–1916*. 2 vols.; Washington, D. C.; Government Printing Office, 1918.

Clark, Barrett, John Mason Brown, *et al. George Pierce Baker: A Memorial*. New York: Dramatists Play Service, 1939.

Grover, Edwin Osgood, ed. *Annals of an Era: Percy MacKaye and the MacKaye Family 1826–1932*. Washington, D. C.: The Pioneer Press, 1932.

Hart, James D. *The Oxford Companion to American Literature*. New York: Oxford University Press, 1948.

Hartnoll, Phyllis, ed. *The Oxford Companion to the Theatre*. London: Oxford University Press, 1951.

Harvard College. Class of 1887. Secretary's Reports, Nos. 1–8 (1887–1933).

Harvard University Catalogue, 1883–1924.

Harvard University. Quinquennial Catalogue of the Officers and Graduates 1636–1925. Cambridge: Harvard University, 1925.

Historical Register of Harvard University 1636–1936. Cambridge: Harvard University Press, 1937.

Howe, M. A. DeWolfe. *A Venture in Remembrance.* Boston: Little, Brown & Co., 1941.

Jones, Doris Arthur. *Taking the Curtain Call: The Life and Letters of Henry Arthur Jones.* New York: The Macmillan Company, 1930.

Morison, Samuel Eliot, ed. *The Development of Harvard University Since the Inauguration of President Eliot 1869–1929.* Cambridge: Harvard University Press, 1930.

New York Times Index, 1913–1935. New York: New York Times Co., 1913–1935.

Perry, Clarence Arthur. *The Work of the Little Theatres.* New York: Russell Sage Foundation, 1933.

Phelps, William Lyon. "George Pierce Baker," *Commemorative Tributes of the American Academy of Arts and Letters,* pp. 320–323. New York: American Academy of Arts and Letters, 1942.

Quinn, Arthur Hobson. *A History of the American Drama from the Civil War to the Present Day.* 2 vols.; New York: Harper & Bros., 1927.

Santayana, George. *Persons and Places: The Background of My Life.* New York: Charles Scribner's Sons, 1944.

Simonson, Lee. *The Stage is Set.* New York: Harcourt, Brace & Co., 1932.

Sumner, John Osborne. "George Pierce Baker," *Harvard College. Class of 1887. Fiftieth Anniversary Report,* pp. 26–32. Cambridge: Harvard University Press, 1937.

Thomas, Augustus. *The Print of My Remembrance.* New York: Charles Scribner's Sons, 1922.

Vizetelly, Frank H., ed. "George Pierce Baker," *The New International Year Book . . . 1935,* pp. 67–68. New York: Funk & Wagnalls, 1936.

Who's Who in America, I–XVIII (1899–1935). Chicago: A. N. Marquis Co., 1899–1934.

Zeitlin, Jacob, and Homer Woodbridge. *Life and Letters of Stuart P. Sherman.* 2 vols.; New York: Farrar & Rinehart, 1929.

SERIALS

"George Pierce Baker," *Transactions of the Rhode Island Medical Society,* IV (1889–1893), 332–337.

Brown, John Mason. "The Four Georges: G. P. Baker at Work," *Theatre Arts Monthly,* XVII (July 1933), 537–551.

Clark, Barrett H. "Letters from Sidney Howard," *Theatre Arts Monthly,* XXV (April 1941), 276–286.

Eaton, Walter Prichard. "Baker's Method of Making Playwrights," *Bookman,* XLIX (June 1919), 478–480.

McCandless, Stanley. "A Map of these United States Showing the Influence of the Work of George Pierce Baker (1890–1924)," *Theatre Arts Monthly,* IX (Feb. 1925), 106–108.

MacKaye, Percy. "Professor of Dramatic Literature at Harvard," *American Magazine,* LXXIII (Dec. 1911), 180–182.

McLaws, Lafayette. "A Master of Playwrights," *North American Review,* CC (1914), 459–467.
Moses, Montrose J. "American Professors of Dramatic Literature," *Independent,* LXXI (Oct. 12, 1911), 813–816.
Morton, D. M. "Yale University Department of Drama," *Theatre Arts Monthly,* X (April 1926), 254–261.
Smith, Boyd. "The University Theatre as It Was Built, Stone on Stone," *Theatre Arts Monthly,* XVII (July 1933), 521–534.
Wendell, Barrett. "English at Harvard," *Dial,* XVI (March 1, 1894), 131–133.
Wernaer, R. M. "Work of the Drama League of Boston," *Nation,* XCIX (Sept. 10, 1914), 310–311.

Newspapers

Brown, John Mason, "Two on the Aisle: Professor George Pierce Baker as a Teacher of Playwriting, an Historian, a Director and a Man," *New York Evening Post,* Jan. 9, 1935.
Eaton, Walter Prichard. "Harvard Drama from Another Angle: Broadway Influences Versus the Larger Aim and Outcome," *Boston Evening Transcript,* Feb. 11, 1915, p. 14.
Kinkead, Cleves. "Prof. George P. Baker's Method of Playwriting Explained," *New York Times,* Sept. 5, 1915, VI, 3.
Macgowan, Kenneth. "Professor Baker's Laboratory Theatre," *Boston Evening Transcript,* April 6, 1913, III, 2.

UNPUBLISHED

Ames, Winthrop. "Notes Made during a Tour of the Theatres of England, France, and Germany, from Nov. 22, 1907, to Jan. 6, 1908," in the Theatre Collection of the New York City Library.
Baker, George Pierce. Correspondence with Archibald Cary Coolidge, Harvard Archives.
——— Correspondence with William C. Lane, Harvard Archives.
——— Correspondence with Edward P. Goodnow, in the possession of Mr. Goodnow, Boston, Mass.
Blanchard, Arthur F. " 'Baker's Dozen' at Harvard," an undated manuscript in the Harvard Archives.
"The 47 Workshop: Its History and Influence," a scrapbook collection of letters, programmes, and general memorabilia, in three volumes, in the Harvard Theatre Collection.
Harvard Dramatic Club. Records, constituting the archives of the Harvard Dramatic Club, in the Harvard Theatre Collection.
Kinne, Wisner P. Correspondence, 1949–1953, with family, students, and friends of George Pierce Baker.
Phelps, William Lyon. "The English Drama, Studied with Mr. Baker, 1890–91," a notebook in the Yale University Library.
"Quinquennial Folder for George Pierce Baker," biographical clippings in the Harvard Archives.
Santayana, George. Letter to G.P.B., London, May 17, 1887, in the Yale University Library.

Turrentine, Percy Winfield. "Lecture Notes, 1916–1917, English 14," in the possession of Professor Turrentine, Arkadelphia, Arkansas.

Tryon, Virginia Vaughn. "The 47 Workshop: Its History and Significance," an unpublished M.A. thesis, pp. 142, presented to the School of Speech, University of Southern California, 1933.

Whitley, Alvin. "Pinero, Jones and the Social Play," an unpublished M.A. thesis at Columbia University.

Withington, Robert. "Lecture Notes, 1910–1911: in . . . Comparative Literature 19 lhf, Professor George P. Baker; and English 47, full course, Professor George P. Baker," in the Smith College Library.

Notes

I: ANTECEDENTS — TOY THEATRE —
THE SPIRIT OF 1876

G.P.B.'s disclaimer of an enthusiasm for genealogy appears in a letter he wrote to C. E. Baker, May 6, 1926. Though perhaps not an enthusiast in such matters, he was a member of the Sons of the American Revolution and appears to have been familiar with the following histories of his ancestors: Orrin P. Allen, *Descendants of Nicholas Cady of Watertown, Mass., 1645–1910* (Palmer, Mass.: Published by the Author, 1910); George H. Tilton, *A History of Rehoboth, Massachusetts* (Boston: Published by the Author, 1918); and a MS Baker Genealogy compiled by Susan E. Slade in 1907, now in the library of the Rhode Island Historical Society, Providence.

Dr. Baker's journal is in the library of the Harvard Medical School.

The accounts of G.P.B.'s childhood and his toy theatre are from an interview of Mrs. Sarah Potter Sumner with W. P. Kinne, Providence, R. I., Feb. 15, 1950. The Potter family lived but a few doors away from the Baker home.

For an account of Stevenson's toy theatre, see "A Penny Plain and Two Pence Colored," in Stevenson's *Memories and Portraits* (New York: Charles Scribner's Sons, 1892), pp. 223–224. An account of its American counterpart may be seen in George Speaight, *Juvenile Drama* (London: MacDonald & Co., 1946), pp. 231–232. For an example of what children did in their home theatres see M. T. Caldor, *Social Charades, and Parlor Games* (Boston: Lee & Shepard, 1873).

II: PROVIDENCE AND
THE AMERICAN THEATRE

The first history of an American city stage to be published outside of Boston and New York was Charles Blake's *An Historical Account of the Providence Stage* (Providence: George H. Whitney, 1868). This was continued by George O. Willard, whose *History of the Providence Stage, 1762–1891* (Providence: Rhode Island News Company, 1891) is a detailed source for the theatrical events of G.P.B.'s childhood and youth. For a contemporary account of the national theatre, see T. Alston Brown's *History of the American*

Stage (New York: Dick & Fitzgerald, 1870) and his *History of the New York Stage* (2 volumes; New York: Dodd, Mead & Co., 1903).

Mrs. Sarah Potter Sumner, in an interview with W. P. Kinne, Providence, March 25, 1950, continued her recollections of G.P.B.'s childhood.

G.P.B.'s first memory of the stage occurs in his "Forty Years of the Drama — a Retrospect," *The National Institute of Social Sciences Journal*, XII (Nov. 1, 1927), 14.

The whole text of the dedicatory prologue may be found in Laurence Hutton and William Cary, eds., *Occasional Addresses* (New York: The Dunlap Society, 1890), pp. 94–97.

For an account of these elements of dramatic taste, see Montrose J. Moses, "The Drama, 1860–1918," *Cambridge History of American Literature*, ed. W. P. Trent *et al.* (New York: Macmillan, 1933), III, 269–271; Ralph H. Ware, *American Adaptations of French Plays on the New York and Philadelphia Stages from 1834 to the Civil War* (Philadelphia: University of Pennsylvania, 1930), pp. 14–67; and Brander Matthews, "The American on the Stage," *Scribner's Monthly*, XVIII (1879), 321–333. These matters are also excellently treated in Richard Ludwig's "The Life and Work of William Winter," an unpublished Harvard doctoral thesis of 1950.

G.P.B.'s *Dramatic Technique*, still the authoritative book of its kind and recently reprinted, was first published in Boston by Houghton Mifflin in 1919.

III: STANDARDS IN READING,
ELOCUTION, AND JOURNALISM

The literary elements of G.P.B.'s grammar school education are set forth in William A. Mowry, *Recollections of a New England Educator, 1838–1908* (New York: Silver, Burdett & Co., 1908), pp. 117–157. The official records of G.P.B.'s attendance at the Mowry and Goff school are in the John Hay Memorial Library at Brown University. An account of G.P.B.'s high school training can be derived from the *Twentieth Annual and Second Decennial Catalogue of the English and Classical School . . . 1883* (Providence: Rhode Island Printing Co., 1883), and the records of the old school which are now in the office of James F. O'Neil, Principal of the Providence Classical High School. The records of the Providence High School Debating Society during G.P.B.'s presidency of the society are in the library of the Rhode Island Historical Society, Providence.

Granville-Barker stated his high regard for G. P. B.'s reading to Arnold Whitridge, who related it to Mrs. George Pierce Baker.

For a brilliant account of this development in acting style, see Edward W. Mammen, *The Old Stock Company School of Acting* (Boston: Trustees of the Public Library, 1945), pp. 32, 61–62. A similar development in the teaching of reading can be discerned in Henry W. Simon, *The Reading of Shakespeare in American Schools and Colleges* (New York: Simon and Schuster, 1932), pp. 26–37.

Perhaps as ubiquitous as today's "how-to-do-it" manuals of the newsstands were the little books on home theatricals, of which a good representative was

E. E. Burton's *Burton's Amateur Actor, a Complete Guide to Private Theatricals* (New York: Dick & Fitzgerald, 1876). G.P.B. may have received a copy of this on his tenth birthday.

The pronouncement of the young editor upon standards of reading may be seen in "Editorial," *Register,* I (April 30, 1883), 84.

IV: DRAMA AND REALITY

The social background of this mania for the theatre can be seen in Arthur M. Schlesinger, *The Rise of the City, 1878–1898* (New York: The Macmillan Company, 1933), pp. 290–302; the U. S. Census Office, *Population of the United States in 1860,* p. 657; and *Statistics of the Population of the United States,* 1880, pp. 744–745. For evidence of the strong popular interest in journalism concerning the theatre, see Frank L. Mott, *A History of American Magazines, 1865–1885,* III (Cambridge: Harvard University Press, 1938), 198–205; 417–421; 457–480; and 548–551.

This early use of the term "naturalism" occurs in Octavius Brooks Frothingham, "The Theatres," *Nation,* II (April 5, 1866), 428–429.

"Fans" of that day were supplied with such biographical material as A. S. Seer's *Ernesto Rossi: A Biographical and Critical Sketch* (New York: Published by the Author, 1881). An account of Salvini's New York debut occurs in G. C. D. Odell, *Annals of the New York Stage,* IX (1870–1875), 12 vols. (New York: Columbia University Press, 1927–1940), 455–456.

The two clippings which G.P.B. put in his scrapbook were: "Rossi's Debut," *Boston Daily Globe,* Oct. 4, 1881, p. 19; and "Rossi in Othello," *Providence Journal,* Oct. 18, 1881, p. 8.

For the Providence reviewer's source, see George Henry Lewes, *On Actors and the Art of Acting* (New York: Henry Holt & Co., 1878), pp. 112, 194. The Providence Athenaeum purchased this book on March 18, 1878.

The item from the *New York Herald* of Nov. 1, 1881 is quoted by Odell, XI (1879–1882), 451.

V: HARVARD FRESHMAN AND
THE BOSTON STAGE

Unless otherwise specified, G.P.B.'s letters written in Cambridge during his first year are from his 10 Frisbie Place address; those of his subsequent student days are from 7 Holworthy Hall.

G.P.B.'s description of Matthew Arnold at Sanders Theatre occurs in a letter to Dr. Baker, Nov. 14, 1883.

G.P.B.'s undergraduate library loans are listed in the annual charge books of the Harvard College Library, now in the Harvard University Archives.

VI: ENTER WENDELL AND IRVING

G.P.B.'s 1907 evaluation of Irving appeared in "Music and Drama: Professor Baker Talks of the American Stage," *Boston Evening Transcript,* April 7, 1907, p. 13. For evidence of Irving's impression upon Wendell, see M. A. DeWolfe Howe, *Barrett Wendell and His Letters* (Boston: Atlantic Monthly Press, 1924), p. 53.

In an interview with W. P. Kinne, Northampton, Mass., May 28, 1950, Professor Samuel A. Eliot, Jr., recalled family theatricals at the home of his grandfather, President Eliot. He remembers that in some of these G.P.B. took part.

VII: HARVARD AND THE THEATRE

An account of a well-known Harvard undergraduate dramatic club may be found in Lloyd McKim Garrison, *An Illustrated History of the Hasty Pudding Club Theatricals* (Cambridge: Hasty Pudding Club, 1897). The story of the dedicatory performance at Sanders Theatre is told in Henry Norman, *An Account of the Harvard Greek Play* (Boston: James R. Osgood & Co., 1882).

For a contemporary account of George Riddle, see "Harvard's Actor," *Boston Sunday Herald,* May 22, 1881, p. 7. A similar review of his successor's history occurs in "Mr. Dixon Jones's Debut," *Boston Evening Transcript,* Sept. 1, 1886, p. 4. E. F. Edgett, an editor of the *Boston Transcript* who was once David Belasco's publicity man, has written the biographical account of Riddle in the *Dictionary of American Biography,* ed. Dumas Malone, XV (New York: Charles Scribner's Sons, 1935), 591–592.

The *Springfield Republican* editorial is quoted in "Note and Comment. Henry Irving at Harvard," *Daily Crimson,* April 8, 1885, p. 4.

The context of President Eliot's view of the subsidiary value of rhetorical and oratorical work is to be found in his "The Changes Needed in American Secondary Education," reprinted in *A Late Harvest* (Boston: Atlantic Monthly Press, 1924), p. 107.

VIII: SOMETHING TO WRITE ABOUT— *HARVARD MONTHLY*

The text of Howard's lecture is included in his *The Autobiography of a Play* (New York: Columbia University Dramatic Museum, 1914).

The Oxonian orientation of these young men can be seen in "Editorials," *Harvard Monthly,* I (Oct. 1885), 36.

M. A. DeWolfe Howe, who was fourth in the succession of editors-in-chief of the *Harvard Monthly,* most generously discussed the early history of this publication on two occasions with W. P. Kinne during 1952.

IX: FARQUHAR, MEREDITH, AND
A LITERARY PHILOSOPHY

G.P.B.'s essays on Farquhar and Meredith appeared as: "George Farquhar," *Harvard Monthly*, III (Nov. 1886), and "George Meredith," *Harvard Monthly*, IV (June 1887).

For the climate of critical opinion in which G.P.B. wrote his essay on Meredith, see René Galland, *George Meredith and British Criticism 1851–1909* (Paris: Les Presses Françaises, 1923), pp. 47–70; and Elmer J. Bailey, "George Meredith in America," *Studies in Language and Literature in Celebration of the Seventieth Birthday of James Morgan Hart* (New York: Henry Holt & Co., 1910), pp. 46–47. The statistics relative to publications concerning Meredith are from Maurice Buxton Forman, *Meredithiana; Being a Supplement to the Bibliography of Meredith* (Edinburgh: Bibliographical Society, 1924), pp. 105 ff.; and Bailey's bibliography in his "George Meredith in America," p. 56.

Meredith's letter to G.P.B., July 22, 1887, has been published in *Letters of George Meredith; Collected and Edited by his Son*, 2 vols. (New York: Charles Scribner's Sons, 1912), II, 398–399.

X: GRADUATION — FRUSTRATION AND
WANDERJAHR — ENTER CLYDE FITCH

The details of G.P.B.'s plans for editorial work in New York are contained in his letters to his father, March 4, 1887, and a week later. Here, also, he discusses the appointment at a "Western University."

For the text of G.P.B.'s commencement ode, see *Harvard College. Class of 1887. Baccalaureate Sermon, Class Day Oration, Class Poem, Ivy Oration, Ode, Class Song* (Cambridge: W. H. Wheeler, 1887), p. 32.

The "sketch à la Maupassant" is in G.P.B.'s "Western Notebook, 1887." Since all of his notebooks were apparently kept as sources for future writing, it is perhaps significant that his last were those which he kept during his 1912 tour of the European theatres.

For an account of the activity of some of these Bostonians in Paris that summer, see Virginia Harlow, *Thomas Sergeant Perry: A Biography* (Durham, N. C.: Duke University Press, 1950).

Clyde Fitch's novel about the Mosher girls was *A Wave of Life*, first published serially in *Lippincott's Magazine*, beginning Feb. 1891. See Montrose J. Moses and Virgina Gerson, eds., *Clyde Fitch and His Letters* (Boston: Little, Brown & Co., 1924), pp. 36–46.

XI: HARVARD INSTRUCTOR

The list of topics and speakers at the Mermaid Club is from printed programs which formerly belonged to George Santayana and to M. A. DeWolfe Howe, now in the Harvard Archives.

XII: ENGLISH 14

The quotations from G.P.B.'s lectures are derived sequentially from the following dated notations in the William Lyon Phelps notebook, "The English Drama, Studied with Mr. Baker, 1890–91," now in the Yale University Library: Nov. 5, 1890; Feb. 11, 1891; Nov. 26, 1890; Oct. 2 and 9, 1890; Oct. 29, 1890; Oct. 22, 1890; Dec. 19, 1890; and March 11, 1891.

XIII: WENDELL POINTS THE WAY

G.P.B.'s only published short story was "Brother Filippo," *New England Magazine,* I (Feb. 1890).

These words of Santayana are to be found in his letter to William Lyon Phelps, Rome, March 16, 1936. This letter is in the Yale University Library.

For this element of isolation in Wendell's character, see Howe, *Barrett Wendell and His Letters,* pp. 108–113.

The favorable review of "Brother Filippo" appeared in the New York *Independent,* March 13, 1890.

Scudder's comment upon G.P.B.'s writing appears in a letter to G.P.B., Nov. 5, 1891.

For the context of these statements about "argumentation," see G.P.B.'s *Principles of Argumentation,* pp. iv, 14.

President Eliot's advice appears in his letter to G.P.B., July 25, 1898.

XIV: ACTOR AND PLAYWRIGHT —
ENTER WINTHROP AMES

The greeting and advice from Clyde Fitch are in his letter to G.P.B., The Albany, Piccadilly, July 15, 1891.

The praise of G.P.B.'s acting is from Mrs. C. H. Toy's letter to G.P.B., Feb. 5, 1893. For the background of this acting, see Pauline Jones, *Cambridge Social and Dramatic Club, 1890–1910* (Cambridge, 1910). For further evidence of G.P.B.'s proficiency as an actor, see "Records of the Cambridge Social Dramatic Club, Vol. I, Jan., 1890 to Jan., 1897," Harvard Theatre Collection.

The review of G.P.B.'s farce, "The Pleasures of Travel," is from an undated clipping from the *Boston Budget,* in G.P.B.'s scrapbook, "Programmes."

"Marlowe," produced by the Radcliffe Idlers Club, was presented June 19, 20, 1905, and reviewed by most of the Boston papers on June 20. Abbie Farewell Brown, reviewing the play for the *New York Times,* June 24, 1905, attributed much of the quality of the production to G.P.B.'s initiative.

For an account of Ware, see "Thornton Marshall Ware," *Harvard College. Class of 1903. Decennial Report. June, 1913.* (Cambridge: Harvard University Press, 1913). Ware died in 1912.

The closing quotation is from "George Pierce Baker," *Harvard College. Class of 1887. Fiftieth Anniversary Report* (Cambridge: Harvard University Press, 1937), pp. 26–32.

XV: A DRAMATIC LIBRARY FOR AMERICA

Lowell's interest in the old drama appears in his *Conversations*, in his articles in the *North American Review* and *Atlantic Monthly*, and in his 1887 Lowell Institute lectures, published as *The Old English Dramatists*, the final volume of *Lowell's Prose Works* (Boston: Houghton Mifflin Co., 1893). For information on Lowell's edition of the old plays, see Horace E. Scudder, *James Russell Lowell*, 2 vols. (Boston: Houghton Mifflin Co., 1901), II, 78.

The congratulations of George Lyman Kittredge may be found in his letter to G.P.B., Dec. 2, 1894.

Undoubtedly, there are earlier American treatises upon the subject; but G.P.B.'s *Principles of Argumentation* appears to have been the first major exposition of its kind. Certainly this book helped establish what is now called "Speech" in the place once occupied by rhetoric and oratory in the American college curriculum.

Felix Schelling's high appraisal of G.P.B.'s editorial ideals occurs in his letter to G.P.B., Jan. 14, 1905.

XVI: ELIZABETHAN EXPERIMENT

For some of the history of this archaeological interest in the theatre, see *The Playhouse of the Sixteenth Century* (Edinburgh: The River-Side Press, 1904), pp. 24–26; and William Poel, *Monthly Letters* (London: T. Werner Laurie, Ltd., 1929), p. 82.

G.P.B.'s account of the work of the committee appears in his "The Revival of Ben Jonson's *Epicoene; Or, the Silent Woman*, March 20, 1895," *Harvard Graduates' Magazine*, III (June 1895), 493–501.

G.P.B.'s relation to the Delta Upsilon revivals was discussed by Professor Ernest Bernbaum (from 1898 to 1916 a Harvard student, faculty member, one of the "Baker's Dozen," and member of Delta Upsilon) in an interview with W. P. Kinne, Cambridge, Oct. 9, 1951. For a representative contemporary account of a part of this relationship, see "Professor Baker Lectures on the Play to be Performed by the Delta Upsilon Society," *Boston Evening Transcript*, March 17, 1899, p. 9.

G.P.B.'s account of the 1904 revival with Forbes-Robertson appeared in his "'Hamlet' on an Elizabethan Stage," *Shakespeare Jahrbuch*, XLI (1905), 296–301.

XVII: PUBLIC LECTURES — "IS NOT THIS THE BEGINNING OF AN EPOCH?"

The quotations in this chapter are, unless otherwise indicated, from G.P.B.'s notes for the following lectures. Though some of these were prepared in relation to his academic teaching, all were delivered in the years indicated to public audiences.

1895: "Talk on Dramatic Technique"; "The Development of the Drama in the Nineteenth Century"; "The American Drama To-Day"; and "Lecture III, Harvard, English 14, 1895."

1898: "The Drama of the Century."

1899: "The Drama of To-Day," parts of which are reproduced in the *Boston Evening Transcript*, July 20, p. 7.

1900: "Tom Robertson and the Beginnings of the Renascence of the English Drama," and "The Drama of the Next Decade," both developed for his new Radcliffe course in the contemporary drama; and "The Theatre as a Social Force."

1901: "Irish Players and their Plays," public lecture, Boston, Jan. 20, 1901.

XVIII: HARVARD THEATRE COLLECTION

Louis Evan Shipman, whose communications of this period are frequently written upon stationery of The Players, 16 Gramercy Park, New York, wrote to G.P.B. concerning John Drew's gift on Nov. 5, 12, and Dec. 7, 1902. Shipman's successful adaptation this winter of the *Crisis,* by Winston Churchill, the American, made Shipman one of the earliest of G.P.B.'s students to become known in the theatrical world and undoubtedly did much to publicize G.P.B.'s relation to that world.

The Coolidge-Baker correspondence, from which the details of the acquisition of the Shaw Collection were developed, is in the Harvard Archives among the Archibald Cary Coolidge papers.

XIX: EDUCATING THE AMERICAN AUDIENCE

G.P.B.'s articles were: " 'Iris': Pinero's New Play. A Review and a Criticism," *Boston Evening Transcript,* Oct. 12, 1901, p. 18; "The Play in London. Striking Productions of the Present Season. The Public, However, Has No Enthusiasm for the New or the Really Fine Dramas — A Criticism of 'The Sentimentalist' — The Idle Rich the Mistaken Theme of Most Playwrights," *B.E.T.,* Jan. 4, 1902, p. 16; "The Young French Dramatist. His Public as Contrasted with the American," *B.F.T.,* April 9, 1902, p. 16; "The American Public and the Theatre. An Attempt to Analyze Public Taste," *B.E.T.,* June 7, 1902, p. 19; "A Subsidized Theatre. Professor Baker Renews an Urgent Plea. Why Should Our Public be Denied the Beauties of Foreign and Old English Drama Simply Because They Will Not Pay? — The Volks-theatre of

Vienna as an Example for Boston — Arguments and Objections Examined," *B.E.T.*, Sept. 10, 1902, p. 16.

XX: A DRAMATIC WORKSHOP
AT RADCLIFFE

The opening quotation is from Howard's "Autobiography of a Play," *In Memoriam Bronson Howard, 1842–1908* (New York: American Dramatic Club, 1910), p. 88. Howard's letter to the editor, dated April 30, 1888, appeared in the *New York Tribune*, May 8, 1888.

Edward Knoblock's recollection is in his *Round the Room: An Autobiography* (London: Chapman & Hall, Ltd., 1939), pp. 42–43.

For an unpublished account of the origins of the course and the source of the quotations concerning G.P.B.'s suggestions to his Radcliffe class, see Agnes Morgan, "Notes on English 47 at Radcliffe, June 20, 1951," Radcliffe College Archives.

For a contemporary account of the importance of "theatre" at Radcliffe, see Katherine Searle, "College Plays," *Radcliffe Magazine*, VII (Dec. 1904), 16–28.

G.P.B.'s desire to overthrow Aristotle is expressed in his own lecture notes, Radcliffe College, English 46, 1904.

Ernest Bernbaum expressed his summary of G.P.B.'s teaching in an interview with W. P. Kinne, Cambridge, Oct. 9, 1951.

XXI: COMEDY AND THE
COMING AMERICAN DRAMA

These two lectures, "Low Comedy and Farce" and "The Nature of High Comedy," delivered at Fay House, April 2 and 7, 1904, exist among G.P.B.'s lecture notes in typescript which was obviously prepared from some stenographic or phonetic reproduction of his discourse. Both lectures have been edited in G.P.B.'s hand, as if for some purpose such as his other notes subsequently served in the preparation of his book, *Dramatic Technique*. These are the only lecture notes relative to English 47 which survive among the Baker papers.

XXII: "THE MIND OF THE UNDER-
GRADUATE" AND PLAYWRITING

G.P.B.'s dissatisfaction with the undistinguished undergraduate mind is apparent in his "The Mind of the Undergraduate," *Educational Review*, XXX (Sept. 1905), 189–200; and "Introduction (An Open Letter to Teachers)," *The Forms of Public Address* (New York: Henry Holt & Co., 1904), p. xi.

XXIII: ENGLISH 47

The recollections of G.P.B.'s early work in English 47 are, in sequence, those of J. J. Hayes, Maurice Ferber, Paul Davis, Henry K. Dick, and E. Bradlee Watson. The concluding summary of G.P.B.'s procedure is derived from the recollection of Paul Davis, Mark Reed, and others who, like those just quoted, very kindly took time to send the author an extended account of their memories of the course.

G.P.B.'s remarks on "illustrative action" are from notes taken by Robert Withington in 1910 on the lectures in Comparative Literature 19, The Forms of the Drama, Harvard College.

XXIV: IDEAS FOR A NEW THEATRE

G.P.B.'s letter in support of the Philadelphia project appeared in "Opinions of Many Men Concerning the Benefits to the Drama to be Expected from an Endowed Theatre: Professor G. P. Baker Builds High Hopes on the Plan," *New York Daily Tribune*, April 2, 1903, II, 2.

For an account of Lorin Deland's relations with Major Higginson and Winthrop Ames in the operation of the Castle Square Theatre, see Margaret Deland, *Golden Yesterdays* (New York: Harper & Bros., 1940), pp. 306–314.

The National Theatre Blue Book which Archer mentions in his letter of Nov. 8, 1904 apparently refers to an early form of *Scheme and Estimates for a National Theatre* (1907), published in America in 1908, and revised by Granville-Barker as *National Theatre* (1930).

G.P.B.'s letter endorsing the value of what Ames and Deland were doing appeared as "The Castle Square Theatre Stock Company," *Boston Evening Transcript* (May 10, 1905), p. 22.

G.P.B.'s remarks on the ideal size of a theatre occur in "Music and Drama. Professor Baker Talks of the American Stage," *Boston Evening Transcript,* Oct. 7, 1907. Although this story is not initialed, it is probably the account of a chat which G.P.B. would very naturally have had with H. T. Parker, the editor of this section of the *Transcript,* who had recently returned from London and Paris.

XXV: SHAKESPEARE'S SUPREMELY PLASTIC STAGE

The sequence of quotations from *The Development of Shakespeare* (New York: The Macmillan Company, 1907) is: pp. 2–3, 18–19, 33, 98–99.

XXVI: "AMATEUR DE TOUT CE QUI TOUCHE AU THÉÂTRE"

The first letter from Christina Baker to Mrs. Wheaton, although marked as written from 6 rue de l'Abbaye, is not dated. The second is likewise a part of an undated series from this same address.

The account of the first Harvard Dramatic Club production appears in James C. Savery, "The Harvard Dramatic Club and its Play," *The Burr McIntosh Monthly,* XVIII (Feb. 1909), 16–18.

XXVII: THE NEW THEATRE AND HOPES FOR A HARVARD THEATRE

For an account of the New Theatre negotiations which involved Archer and Granville-Barker, see Charles Archer, *William Archer: Life, Work, and Friendships* (New Haven: Yale University Press, 1931), p. 291; and "New Theatre Founders Meet," *New York Daily Tribune,* April 3, 1908. The writer is indebted to William M. Milton, author of an unpublished Harvard doctoral dissertation on Granville-Barker, for information concerning some of the New Theatre background.

The Walkley review, which G.P.B. clipped, appeared in "Mr. Walkley's Opening," *Boston Evening Transcript,* Dec. 18, 1909, II, 6.

XXVIII: IDEAS FOR A CIVIC THEATRE

The report of the royal commission was published as *The Drama in Adult Education* (London: H.M. Stationery Office, 1926), and the testimony concerning G.P.B. occurs on p. 111. For a view of G.P.B.'s work against the background of the Little Theatre Movement, see Kenneth Macgowan, *Footlights Across America* (New York: Harcourt, Brace & Co., 1929).

XXIX: PAGEANTS AND THEATRES FOR AMERICA

G.P.B.'s account of the writing of his first pageant appears in his "The Peterborough Pageant: As the Producer Saw It," *New Boston,* I (Oct. 1910), 256–258. Since this project brought G.P.B. into the MacDowell Colony, and since he was thus able to influence Edward Arlington Robinson's entry into the colony the next year, where he did some of his most important writing, an interesting view of this relationship is presented in Hermann Hagedorn's *Edward Arlington Robinson: A Biography* (New York: The Macmillan Company, 1938), pp. 261–271. G.P.B. said to Hagedorn: "Robinson ought to go to Peterborough. It will be good for Robinson and good for the Colony." Robinson went.

The programme note quoted appears in *Peterborough Memorial Pageant* (Peterborough, N. H.: MacDowell Memorial Assn., 1910), p. 4.

The magazine, *New Boston,* was one of the instruments of reform employed by "Boston–1915," a committee organized in 1909 by Louis D. Brandeis, Edward A. Filene, James J. Storrow, and other civic leaders. In this apparatus to secure the moral, political, and cultural improvement of Boston, G.P.B. was an "Executive Director for Fine and Industrial Arts."

XXX: PRIZE PLAYS

For the remarkable demand in which Harvard dramatists seemed to stand that year, see "Dramatic Notes," *Harvard Crimson,* Sept. 30, 1911, p. 4.

George Abbott's recollection of the magic of G.P.B.'s name occurs in his letter to W. P. Kinne, June 12, 1950.

XXXI: "THE THEATRE OF BEAUTY"

The quotation from *Dramatic Technique* occurs on pp. v–vi.

Yeats's address to the H.D.C. appeared in part in "The Theatre of Beauty," *Harvard Crimson,* Oct. 6, 1911, pp. 1, 5. The entire text of this address was published under the same title in *Harper's Weekly,* LV (Nov. 4, 1911), 11.

For an account of the Amy Lowell affair and the Toy Theatre, see S. Foster Damon, *Amy Lowell: A Chronicle* (Boston: Houghton Mifflin Co., 1935), pp. 162–165.

XXXII: FEMININE INFLUENCE

For an account of the graduate work in playwriting which Tom Wolfe did with G.P.B., see Richard S. Kennedy, "Thomas Wolfe at Harvard, 1920–1923," *Harvard Library Bulletin,* IV, No. 2 (Spring, 1950), 172–190 and IV, No. 3 (Autumn, 1950), 304–319.

The quotation from *Dramatic Technique* occurs on p. 5.

G.P.B.'s remarks in Pittsburgh are from an unidentified clipping in one of his scrapbooks. Since the Little Theatre did not open until March 12, 1912, and G.P.B. sailed for Liverpool at the end of July, the address was made during the interim.

XXXIII: ENGLISH AND IRISH EXPERIMENT

Mark Reed's remembrance of G.P.B.'s reaction to Houghton's death appears in Reed's letter to W. P. Kinne, June 21, 1950.

The Gordon Craig letter to G.P.B., though headed "7 John St., Adelphi," is not dated.

The Bijou contest to which G.P.B. refers in his letter to Miss McFadden was B. F. Keith's "Bijou Play Contest," of which Walter Hampden and G.P.B.

were judges. The first prize which these judges awarded went to a one-act play by George Abbott. In 1912, Winthrop Ames offered a prize of $10,000 in order to get good American plays for his new Booth Theatre. This prize went the next year to a play now nearly forgotten: Alice Brown's *Children of Earth*.

XXXIV: GORDON CRAIG — REINHARDT — PLANS FOR A HARVARD THEATRE

The quotation of the *Times* review is from a clipping in G.P.B.'s journals for the 1912 tour of the European theatres. These journals were working notes, without character as literary records, arranged in chronological and geographical order. Unless otherwise indicated, the quotations in this chapter are from the 1912 journals.

XXXV: "THE NEW MOVEMENT" AND THE WORKSHOP

The principal sources for this chapter have been the author's correspondence with Samuel J. Hume and Irving Pichel and his conversations with Munroe Pevear, Professor Arthur Pope, Donald Oenslager, and Stanley McCandless, as well as a scrapbook, "The 47 Workshop: Its History and Influence, Vol. I," which G.P.B. caused to be kept as the "archives" for the organization.

The description of the sets for *Why the Chimes Rang* is in Constance D'Arcy Mackay, *The Little Theatre in the United States* (New York: Henry Holt & Co., 1917), pp. 189–190.

The reference to the little theatre group in Pittsfield is in a letter from Alice Harrington Parke, wife of the director, to G.P.B., May 1, 1913.

The statement concerning the need for "plasticity" on the American stage occurs in "German Stage Devices," *New York Tribune,* June 8, 1913, IV, 5.

G.P.B.'s first published plan for a Harvard theatre appeared in "Proposed Building for the Drama," *Harvard Alumni Bulletin,* XVI (May 13, 1914), 512–515.

XXXVI: "PROPOSED DRAMATIC EXHIBIT"

In 1876, before the organization of the Philadelphia Exhibition was completed, provision had been made by the Centennial Commission for the inclusion of international dramatic exhibits in Class 313 (Music and Drama) of Department III (Education and Science). See *United States Centennial Commission. International Exhibition. 1876. Official Catalogue* (Rev. ed.; Philadelphia: John R. Nagle & Co., 1876).

XXXVII: BEAUTY VS. BROADWAY —
ENTER EUGENE O'NEILL

The first quotation is from Frederick L. Day, "The Anvil Theatre," *Theatre Arts Monthly*, XXIX (Jan. 1945), 56.

O'Neill's two evaluations of his work for English 47 appear respectively in Barrett H. Clark, *Eugene O'Neill: The Man and His Plays* (New York: Dover Publications, Inc., 1947), p. 28; and in a letter from O'Neill to Richard Dana Skinner, n.d., quoted in Skinner's *Eugene O'Neill: A Poet's Quest* (New York: Longmans, Green & Co., 1935), pp. vii–x. See also the sections in Clark's book which are entitled, "He Goes to Harvard," pp. 25–29, and "Experiment," pp. 53–55.

Lee Simonson's remarks are from his *Part of a Lifetime* (New York: Duell, Sloan and Pearce, 1943), pp. 8–9.

The classmate was Mark Reed, whose reflections are from his letter to W. P. Kinne, June 21, 1950.

Lottie Chase Ham's question appeared in the *Boston Evening Transcript*, Feb. 6, 1915, Part III, pp. 6, 14.

XXXVIII: WAR AND TRANSITION

Gordon Craig's note to G.P.B., from the Arena Goldoni, Florence, is undated, except for the year, 1915.

G.P.B.'s statements about the needs of the playwright and the country's need for trained directors occurs in his preface to *Plays of the 47 Workshop* (New York: Brentano's, 1921), pp. xx–xxii.

XXXIX: SEARCH FOR AMERICAN DRAMATIC
MATERIALS — ENTER PHILIP BARRY

The words from G.P.B.'s introduction to *Modern American Plays* (New York: Harcourt, Brace & Co., 1921) appear on p. x.

G.P.B.'s letter to the Governor's Commission, addressed to William Carroll Hill, was written Feb. 7, 1920.

The letter from G.P.B. to Arthur Lord, Leyden, Holland, is not dated.

XL: WORKSHOP CRISIS

The commendation of the Workshop appeared in "Eyvind of the Hills Staged in Boston," *Christian Science Monitor*, March 17, 1917, p. 6.

Donald Oenslager's recollection occurs in his *Scenery Then and Now* (New York: W. W. Norton Co., 1936), pp. 246–247.

The subsequent quotations concerning the Workshop are from G.P.B.'s "The 47 Workshop," *Century*, CI (Feb. 1921), 417–425.

XLI: PLYMOUTH PAGEANT

The typescript notes for G.P.B.'s Lowell Lecture, "The Pilgrim Spirit," are included with Plymouth Pageant materials, Harvard Theatre Collection.

The Plymouth Pageant scenario, manuscript and typescript, in the Harvard Theatre Collection, is catalogued as Thr 1211. 101. 03 F*. These are the only catalogued Baker papers in the Harvard Library.

The pestilence scene in *The Pilgrim Spirit* (Boston: Marshall Jones Co., 1921), occurs on pp. 14–15. The prologue appears on pp. 5–6.

The following reviewers are referred to in their order of quotation:

Olin Downes, "Dramatic in Extreme," *Boston Post,* July 21, 1921, p. 4.

"The Pilgrims at Plymouth," *Theatre Magazine* (Nov. 1921), p. 356.

Oliver M. Sayler, "The Return of the Pilgrim," *New Republic,* XXVII (Aug. 10, 1921), 302–303.

Ludwig Lewisohn, "The Plymouth Pageant," *Nation,* CXIII (Aug. 24, 1921), 210–211.

The statement of President Harding appears in Frederick W. Bittinger, *The Story of the Pilgrim Tercentenary Celebration* (Plymouth, Mass.: The Memorial Press, 1923), p. 85.

XLII: ENTER TOM WOLFE

For an excellent history of Tom Wolfe's experience under Professor Baker, see Richard S. Kennedy, "Thomas Wolfe at Harvard, 1920–1923," previously cited. The author is also indebted to Mr. Kennedy for the opportunity to read and discuss with him portions of his unpublished Harvard doctoral thesis on Thomas Wolfe.

With the exception of the last Wolfe letter quoted, all of Tom Wolfe's letters are from *Thomas Wolfe's Letters to His Mother,* ed., John Skally Terry (New York: Charles Scribner's Sons, 1943); these are, in the order of their appearance, from pp. 10–11, 20, 25, 45, 48, and 49.

The description of Professor Hatcher and of the "Hatcherian chuckle" are from Wolfe's *Of Time and the River* (New York: Charles Scribner's Sons, 1935), pp. 130–131.

Wolfe's regret at the generosity of G.P.B.'s enthusiasm appears in Kennedy, p. 186. The closing Wolfe letter to G.P.B. occurs in Kennedy, p. 317. Both of these quotations from the *Harvard Library Bulletin,* IV (1950), are made with the permission of Mr. Edward C. Aswell, Administrator of the Estate of Thomas Wolfe.

XLIII: "YALE: 47; HARVARD: 0"

G.P.B.'s eulogy for his old student was published as: "Address, On the Occasion of the Memorial Meeting for Gertrude Buck," *Vassar Miscellany Monthly* (Feb. 1923), pp. 13–14.

His address to the Ninth Recreation Conference, Haddon Hall, Atlantic City, Oct. 11, 1922, was reported in the *New York Times* for that date.

G.P.B.'s letter of May 15, 1923, to Philip Barry was published as "Foreword," in *You and I: A Comedy in Three Acts,* the first of the series of "Long Plays of the 47 Workshop" (New York: Brentano's, 1923) which G.P.B. hoped would be an important collection of contemporary drama.

The football score summary, widely repeated without attribution, appears to have been coined by Heywood Broun. See Broun's "Professor George Pierce Baker," in *Collected Edition of Heywood Broun* (New York: Harcourt, Brace & Co., 1941), pp. 115–118.

G.P.B.'s disclaimer of unpleasant relations at Harvard appeared in the *New York Morning Telegraph,* Nov. 27, 1924.

The statement to Reniers appears in Percival Reniers, "Behind the Scenes of the 47 Workshop," *New York Times Magazine,* Dec. 7, 1924, p. 14.

XLIV: CONTINUITY IN THE YALE UNIVERSITY THEATER

Fred Koch's compliment is from his letter of Dec. 3, 1924, written at Chapel Hill, N. C., where he directed his Carolina Playmakers at the University of North Carolina.

Thomas Wood Stevens expressed his sympathy in a letter of Jan. 10, 1925, to G.P.B., from the Art Institute of Chicago, Office of the School.

The quotations from G.P.B.'s "The Theatre and the University," *Theatre Arts Magazine,* X (Feb. 1925), appeared on pp. 101 and 104.

G.P.B.'s "The New University Theater" appeared in the *Yale Alumni Weekly,* XXXV (Oct. 2, 1925), 75–77.

The announcement of visiting lecturers appeared in "Mme. Ouspenskaya at Yale," *New York Times,* Dec. 12, 1925, p. 4.

G.P.B.'s letter of May 5, 1926 to Eugene O'Neill is quoted in *George Pierce Baker: A Memorial* (New York: Dramatist's Play Service, 1939), p. 22.

The report of Stanley R. McCandless on the new theatre appeared in his "Electrical Layout of the Yale Theatre," *American Architect,* CXXI (March 20, 1927), 365–368.

Eugene O'Neill sent his regrets in a letter to G.P.B., from Hamilton, Bermuda, Dec. 7, 1926. The originals of this and his May 21 letter to G.P.B. are in the Baker correspondence at the Yale Drama School, in the office of Boyd Smith, Chairman of the Yale Department of Drama, New Haven.

XLV: SEARCH FOR ANOTHER O'NEILL

G.P.B.'s statement about O'Neill as a student occurs in Norman Hapgood, "A Professor with a New Idea," *Hearst's International Cosmopolitan,* May 1925, p. 76.

G.P.B.'s reminiscent speech was published as "Forty Years of the Drama — a Retrospect," *National Institute of Social Sciences, Journal,* XII (1927), 18.

This sense of G.P.B. that O'Neill fulfilled his old "not sentimental" ideal occurs in his "O'Neill's First Decade," *Yale Review,* XV (July 1926), 790.

G.P.B.'s statement concerning the young playwright's confusion of the commonplace and the original appears in his "The Theatre and the University," *Theatre Arts Monthly,* IX (Feb. 1925), 101.

H. T. Parker's review of the opening of the Yale Theater was published as "University Theater," *Boston Evening Transcript,* Dec. 11, 1926, p. 14.

G.P.B.'s remarks about electricians, technique, and the imagination appear in "The Theatre and the University," p. 104.

G.P.B. defined the mature playwright whom he hoped to teach in his article, "Training the Playwright of the Machine Age," pp. 175–179 in Oliver M. Sayler's *Revolt in the Arts* (New York: Brentano's, 1930).

XLVI: THE UNIVERSITY AND A THEATRE FOR AMERICANS

On November 27–28, 1925, there convened at the Carnegie Institute of Technology a "Conference on the Drama in American Universities and Little Theatres." This appears to have been the inception of the National Theatre Conference. Professor Baker's meeting on February 11–12, 1927, was thus the second of a series of conferences held at Pittsburgh, New Haven, Evanston, and Iowa City before the National Theatre Conference was officially organized, early in 1932. Many men were active in this growth, but major importance must be attached to the continued work of Kenneth Macgowan during these years under two grants from the Carnegie Foundation. Macgowan's book, *Footlights Across America* (1929), and his article, "A Dozen Rubicons," *Theatre Arts Monthly,* XIII (July 1929), reported his observations that the national theatre must unite.

Lee Simonson's address is quoted in "Pollution of Stage Denounced at Yale," *New York Times,* Feb. 12, 1927, p. 12.

G.P.B.'s lecture, "Our Drama Today," published in the *Harvard Alumni Bulletin,* XXIV (May 4, 1922), 734–744, represents the thinking upon which was based his work a decade later to effect a decentralization of the American theatre.

G.P.B.'s observation on the relation of one-act plays to movies and the radio appears in his "The One-Act Play," in LeRoy Phillips and Theodore Johnson, *Types of Modern Dramatic Composition* (Boston: Ginn & Co., 1927), pp. vii–xiv.

G.P.B.'s remarks on dialogue appear in his last essay, "Rhythm in Recent Dramatic Dialogue," *Yale Review,* XX (Sept. 1929), 116–133.

His admonition to cling, in the teaching of drama, to the fundamental principles is from his "Training the Playwright of the Machine Age," pp. 175–179 in Oliver M. Sayler's *Revolt in the Arts* (New York: Brentano's, 1930).

For an account of G.P.B.'s last lecture, see Elihu Winer, "Baker's Last Drama Lecture: From Aeschylus to Behrman," *New York Herald Tribune,* Jan. 13, 1935, V, 4.

Sidney Howard's remarks on "G.P.B. of Harvard and Yale," appeared in the *New York Times,* Feb. 5, 1933, IX, 3.

The dedication of the special issue appeared in "The World and the Theatre: Dedication to G.P.," *Theatre Arts Monthly*, XVII (July 1933), 483.

The *New York Times* editorial, "G.P.," appeared on Jan. 8, 1935.

O'Neill's letter to the editor was published as "Professor G. P. Baker," *New York Times*, Jan. 13, 1935, IX, 1.

Eugene O'Neill's letter to Christina Baker, Sea Island, Ga., Jan. 20, 1935, from which the final paragraph of the chapter is derived, is among the Baker papers at the Yale Drama School.

EPILOGUE

This is based upon the accounts of the meeting which appeared in the New York, New Haven, and Yale University newspapers; upon the recollections of various people now at the Yale Drama School who were present at the occasion; and upon an undated letter from Mrs. Boyd Smith to Mrs. George Pierce Baker.

As he brought his manuscript to completion, it was the good fortune of the author to be able to consult Mrs. Virginia Tryon Brown's unpublished master's thesis, "The 47 Workshop: Its History and Significance," presented in 1933 to the School of Speech, University of Southern California. Mrs. Brown, a member of Professor Baker's second class at Yale, did this thesis with the assistance of Professor Baker, whose annotations on her manuscript and correspondence with its author have corroborated the present author's own research.

ACKNOWLEDGMENTS

MY FIRST THANKS GO TO MRS. GEORGE PIERCE BAKER and her sons, and to William Van Lennep, Curator of the Harvard Theatre Collection, without whose steady encouragement there would have been no book. With them I wish to thank Howard Mumford Jones, without whose warm insight the idea for the book would not have developed.

Special gratitude is due the librarians of the public libraries of Providence, Boston, New York, New Haven, and Cambridge; of the private libraries of the Boston Athenaeum, the Providence Athenaeum, and the Rhode Island Historical Society; and of the university libraries at Brown, Columbia, Yale, and Harvard. Particular assistance has been received from Mr. Kimball C. Elkins and his assistants in the Harvard Archives; Miss Ruth Davenport and Mrs. Elizabeth Borden and their assistants at Radcliffe College; Dr. Henry Wells, Curator of the Brander Matthews Dramatic Museum; Mr. George Freedley, Curator of the Theatre Collection of the New York City Public Library; Miss Caroline Jakeman and her assistants in the Houghton Library; and Mr. John Shea, in the Widener Library. For their invaluable help I wish especially to thank Miss Mary Reardon, of the Harvard Theatre Collection, and Miss Mary Grahn, librarian at the Yale Department of Drama.

Professor Boyd Smith and the faculty of the Yale Department of Drama I remember warmly for their hospitality and ready assistance. Mr. Rollo Walter Brown will recall my thanks for his suggestions about biographical writing. Mr. John Mason Brown knows how much I am indebted to him. The host of friends and students of Professor Baker who graciously took time to write or talk to me I cannot sufficiently thank.

All citations and quotations of unpublished materials which appear herein refer, unless otherwise specified, to materials in the uncatalogued George Pierce Baker Collection in the Harvard Theatre Collection. My gratitude to the publishers and proprietors of other materials used in the book is implicit in the notes which acknowledge my specific indebtedness.

The unpublished materials referred to in the notes have been used with the kind permission of the following proprietors: Mr. George Abbott; Mr. Michael Albery, trustee of the will of the late Henry Arthur Jones, and Mrs. John Maxse, granddaughter of the illustrious playwright; Mrs. Winthrop Ames; Mr. Frank Archer, executor of the late William Archer; Mr. James T. Babb, Librarian of the Yale University Library, proprietor of the Phelps notebook; Mrs. George Pierce Baker; Professor Ernest Bernbaum; Mrs. Sylvia C. Bowditch, daughter of the late Horace Scudder; Mr. W. N. Caw, executor of the late Stanley Houghton; Mr. Daniel M. Cory, literary executor of the estate of the late Professor George Santayana; Mr. Gordon Craig; Mr. Paul Davis; Miss Martha E. Dick, executrix of the estate of the late Professor Henry K. Dick; Mrs. Harry E. Donley, sole heir of the next of kin of the late Henry Taylor Parker; the literary executors of the late President A. Lawrence Lowell, Miss Nora A. Dwyer and Professor Henry A. Yeomans, the biographer of President Lowell; Professor Samuel A. Eliot, Jr., grandson of the late President Charles W. Eliot; Mr. Maurice Ferber; Mrs. Henry D. Gasson, granddaughter of the late Professor William J. Rolfe; Miss Doris Halman; Professor J. J. Hayes; Mr. Cyril W. Hogg, Managing Director of Samuel French, Ltd., London, literary proprietors of the estate of the late Sir Arthur Wing Pinero; Professor Henry C. Kittredge, son of the late Professor George Lyman Kittredge; Mr. Ernest M. Lofgren, executor of the estate of the late Mr. Richard W. Fitch, literary executor of the late Clyde Fitch; Mrs. Edward MacDowell; Mr. Kenneth Macgowan; Mr. Percy MacKaye; Miss Elizabeth McFadden; Mr. C. D. Medley, administrator of the estate of the late Harley Granville-Barker; Mr. Keyes D. Metcalf, Librarian of the Harvard College Library, repository of the Archibald Cary Coolidge papers; and the family of the late Professor Coolidge; Mrs. Carlotta Monterey O'Neill; Miss Agnes Morgan; Mr. Mark Reed; Dr. Calvert R. Toy and Mrs. Jane Toy Coolidge, executrix of the estate of the late Nancy Toy; Mrs. Florence Lewis Speare; Mrs. Sarah Potter Sumner; Mr. E. Bradlee Watson; Dr. Henry M. Wells, Curator of the Brander Matthews Dramatic Museum, Columbia University; Mr. Barrett Wendell and Mr. William G. Wendell; Professor Robert Withington; Mr. Philip Wittenberg, trustee of the estate of Franklin Haven Sargent; Miss Mary Young (Mrs. John Craig).

The photographs presenting the life and work of Professor Baker before his departure to Yale University are from the Harvard Theatre Collection, with the exceptions of the Koenig sketch and the picture of The 47 Workshop in costume; these are used with the kind permission, respectively, of Professor Boyd Smith and Miss Eleanor H. Hinkley. The photographs by Mr. Morris Shapiro and other materials illustrative of Professor Baker's Yale University Theater productions, from the files of the Yale Department of Drama and of the Commercial Photo Service, New Haven, were most courteously supplied by Mr. Frank Poole Bevan, Mr. Edward C. Cole, and Miss Mary Grahn. Mr. Shapiro's production photographs of *Brand, the King's Coat,* and *The Emperor Jones,* are reproduced with the kind permission of *Theatre Arts.* Photographs of the O'Neill and Barry inscriptions were made by Mr. F. G. Ludwig, of the Yale University Library. The picture of Professor Baker with Lupe Velez and Ramon Novarro is reproduced through the courtesy of Mr. Floyd Fitzsimmons of Metro-Goldwyn-Mayer.

My happiest gratitude I save for the last. Though I have no words adequate, I know that its communication will be understood by my wise and cheerful wife.

W. P. K.

Cohasset, Massachusetts
March 1954

INDEX

347